MICHAEL COLLINS

DR JAMES MACKAY has had a lifelong interest in Michael Collins. At Glasgow University he majored in Irish history and wrote his Master's thesis on his boyhood hero. This new biography realises a longstanding ambition to do justice to one of the great figures of the century. Widely regarded as the world's greatest authority on the life and works of Robert Burns, Mackay's definitive biography, *Burns,* won the 1994 Saltire Society Book of the Year award. He is also the author of *Vagabond of Verse: A Biography of Robert Service, Brave Heart: William Wallace, Allan Pinkerton: The Eye Who Never Slept* and *Sounds Out of Silence: A Life of Alexander Graham Bell.* He is currently working on biographies of Andrew Carnegie and Sir Thomas Lipton.

MICHAEL COLLINS
A Life

JAMES MACKAY

MAINSTREAM
PUBLISHING
EDINBURGH AND LONDON

For Claire

Copyright © James Mackay, 1996
All rights reserved
The moral right of the author has been asserted

This edition 1997

First published in Great Britain in 1996 by
MAINSTREAM PUBLISHING COMPANY
(EDINBURGH) LTD
7 Albany Street
Edinburgh EHI 3UG

ISBN I 85158 949 X

A CIP catalogue record for this book is available from the British Library

Subsidised by THE SCOTTISH ARTS COUNCIL

Typeset in Centaur
Printed and bound in Great Britain by Butler & Tanner Ltd

Contents

Introduction

IT IS WITH SOME TREPIDATION THAT I, A SCOTSMAN — AND A Presbyterian at that — have ventured to write this book; but, quite simply, it is something which I have always wanted to do.

When I was a small boy we had an Irish maid. To Kitty Murray, who hailed from County Monaghan, I owe a debt of half a century not only for teaching me to write the monastic uncials and showing me some of the differences between Irish and Scottish Gaelic, but also for kindling my interest in the Laughing Boy. She herself had no first-hand knowledge of Michael Collins, having been born after his death, but her father had personally known both the Big Fellow and General O'Duffy, and the fund of anecdotes concerning them were passed down in the best oral tradition from father to daughter and thence to this impressionable little boy. I have no doubt that many of Kitty's tales presented a highly romanticised view of her idol, but they stuck with me. I read everything I could find about him, and this drew me inexorably into the study of Irish history. At Glasgow University I took twentieth-century Irish history as my special subject, and wrote my thesis on Michael Collins and the Treaty period.

This is actually my sixth book on an Irish topic. The others dealt with aspects of Irish philately and postal history — harmless enough, one might suppose, but politics are very closely intermingled even in these matters, and I have to admit that, although I approached these projects without bias and wrote in as objective and even-handed a manner as I could, I nevertheless attracted a certain measure of controversy.

In *The Story of Eire and her Stamps* (1968), for example, I referred to an unusual essay or trial for the series of stamps issued by the Free State in December 1922. This was a design, by an unidentified artist, for a threepenny stamp, featuring a profile of a moustached Michael Collins wearing a trilby hat, based on a Hogan press photograph of November 1921, at the time when he and Arthur Griffith were negotiating the Treaty in London. This design was rejected of course, but I added a comment that it was a matter for regret that no Irish stamp had ever commemorated the Big Fellow. I added the pious hope that the fiftieth anniversary of his death (in 1972) would not be allowed to pass unmarked. This book was widely reviewed in the Irish press, but the oddest review was that published in *The Cork Examiner* which, ignoring the rest of the text, commented at length on the author's percipience in recognising the true worth of Michael Collins, and launched an attack on the Irish government for having treated the memory of the great national hero so shabbily. It was not until 1990 and the centenary of Michael's birth that this wrong was finally righted, and a 32p stamp bearing the portrait of General Michael Collins was released. Even today, more than three-quarters of a century after his untimely death, Michael Collins is regarded in many parts of Ireland and beyond as 'a hot pratie', as a government official put it to me in Dublin recently. One need only study the correspondence columns of Irish newspapers on both sides of the Irish Sea in recent years (since the notion of making a biographical film was first mooted in 1987, for example) to realise the heat and passion, both for and against, which the name of Michael Collins still engenders.

Although this has been, for me, very much a labour of love, I have tried to let the facts speak for themselves. In the pantheon of great heroes of all time Michael Collins must stand high; he is arguably one of the truly great figures of this century, and certainly no other Irish leader, North or South, comes anywhere close. His violent death two months before his thirty-second birthday robbed Ireland of the one man who might have brought the civil war to a speedy conclusion and might even have nipped partition in the bud and spared the generations then unborn from the suffering and anguish of more recent times.

In writing this book I have had the help of many people, not only in Ireland itself, but also in Britain and, farther afield, in Canada, the United States and Australia. Some of them, like the former Black and Tan whom I met in Lanarkshire many years ago and who was haunted for the rest of his life by the memories of terrible deeds in Ireland, prefer to remain anonymous. Others, such as the crofter in the Isle of Barra who many years ago gave me a grim account of the dark doings of Major Percival and hoped that one day I would expose him, I would name if I could but I regret that at this remove in time I cannot recall their names. For this I give my profound and humble apology. I am, however, indebted to the following individuals: Freddy Anderson, John Barrington, Mrs C.M. Bayliss, Clive Brookes, Pat Carolan, Denis Cromie, Felix M. Cronin, the late Fred Dixon, Carmel Gunning, the late H.G. Leslie

Fletcher, Philomena Hartford, John Holman, Tommy Killoran, John Lahiffe, Robson Lowe, Hugh Macdonald, Joe McPeak, Vera Neary and her sons Liam and Kevin, Frank O'Hara, Pat O'Hara, Liam O'Rinn, Maurice O'Shea, Maurice Shepperton, Michael Sheridan, Susan Smith, Alun Southwood, Hugh Taylor and Kenneth Tierney.

For unstinted assistance with my researches over many years as well as for permission to reproduce illustrations and copyright material I am also grateful to the staff of the Mitchell Library, Glasgow, and the Library of the University of Glasgow; Shepherds Bush Library, London; the British Library, London; the Scottish National Library, Edinburgh; Trinity College Library and the National Library of Ireland, Dublin; the Public Record Office of Ireland; the National Museum of Ireland; the Hugh Lane Municipal Gallery, Dublin; the Kilmainham Restoration Committee, Dublin; the Office of Public Works, Dublin; Post Office Archives, Mount Pleasant; An Post, Dublin; and the Hammersmith and Fulham Borough Archives, West London.

James Mackay,
Glasgow,
February 1996

Prologue

Know, that I would accounted be
True brother of a company
That sang, to sweeten Ireland's wrong.
WILLIAM BUTLER YEATS, *To Ireland in the Coming Times*

THERE WAS A SHARP FROST THAT THURSDAY MORNING, 16 JANUARY 1916. The sea was calm, and as dawn broke, the night mists cleared to an exceptionally bright day. The passengers who had dozed fitfully in the main cabin were stirring; some were already out on the foredeck for their first glimpse of land. Among them was a man in his mid-twenties, his keen grey eyes shaded by the brim of his new peaked cap. Although clad in a belted tweed overcoat, he shivered slightly as a sough of wind swept across the bows.

Above average height – five foot eleven, in fact – he was powerfully built and somehow gave the impression of being much taller than he really was. He had a broad face, a jovial peasant's face, framed by tousled dark brown hair and divided by a long, finely chiselled nose above a generous mouth. His most distinctive feature was his eyes, deep-set and wide apart. Even in repose, there was a genial, good-natured twinkle in them. When he laughed, which was often, they gave his face a crinkly effect; when he was angry, they flashed with fire and struck terror in the beholder, but within seconds they would dance and twinkle good-humouredly again. He had a frank expression and a steady, penetrating gaze which those who had something to hide would find extremely disconcerting; but most people who ever met him would fall immediately under his spell. The extremely mobile features betrayed exceptional nervous energy. Animated was a word often applied to him, yet it failed to do justice to the deep emotional, intellectual and spiritual feelings that gave him his zest for life, his restless energy for action.

An immediate impression of Michael up to this time was of someone younger than his years; boyish charm is an attribute that recurs frequently in contemporary descriptions of him. Yet there was something else, hinted at by the set of his lower jaw. It bespoke the quiet thoroughness, the passion for neatness and order, the astonishing attention to detail in all his work, the mastery of all aspects of any problem he ever tackled. In the years to come this resoluteness would give way to ruthlessness; his features would fill out, his jowls become heavier, and the eyes acquire a diamantine glitter. But the broad smile, the boyish grin, the infectious laugh would never leave him.

Ten years living and working in London had subtly refined his brogue, but in passion or anger or boisterous good spirits the thin veneer of the metropolis would vanish and he would revert to the thick sounds of West Cork. This burly, barrel-chested young man possessed a deep voice, described variously as gruff or gravelly, a bear-growl of a voice; yet it could become soft and husky when occasion demanded. It was a voice that readily betrayed the fire, the passion or the emotion of the speaker. He had the true Celtic temperament, a man who was easily moved to tears, but with the inner strength not to mind showing his feelings.

For all his height and bulk, he moved with the grace of a ballet dancer. He held himself erect and strode purposefully, with a jaunty, slightly swaggering air. He had one mannerism, a toss of the head to shake back the mop of hair that fell across his brow.

What set him apart from the majority of the other steerage passengers, grimy-faced and crumpled of clothing after a night carousing on deck or huddled on the hard wooden benches, was his appearance: not just the cap, overcoat and grey suit which still possessed the smell of brand-newness, but the pink cheeks and closely shaven chin above the starched collar and the clean white shirt. Even in the cramped conditions of this ship, his fastidiousness ensured that he had performed his ablutions with accustomed care.

Anyone who gave him a second glance that morning would have taken him for what he was – a good-looking young Irishman, a shop assistant or an office worker perhaps. Bystanders might reflect wryly that he was one of those well set-up young fellows who, faced with conscription into the British armed forces, had suddenly rediscovered their Irishness and were bolting back to the Emerald Isle to avoid the draft.

It had, in fact, been ten years since this young man had left his birthplace in the far south-west of Ireland. A strapping teenager, insouciant, precocious and with the worldly wisdom of someone who had never been farther than Clonakilty before, he had boarded the Dublin train, apprehensive yet eagerly looking forward to this great adventure. Wearing his new serge suit, the unaccustomed roughness of his first long trousers chafing his calves, and carrying a small, cheap suitcase containing a change of linen and his favourite books, he had taken the mail-steamer to Holyhead and the train to London, a world away from West Cork. Amid the jumble of unfamiliar sounds and sights that crowded in on him during his first twenty-four hours away from home, he would remember the kindliness of fellow passengers, the agricultural labourers and the navvies, often boys not much older than himself, forced by sheer necessity to uproot themselves and seek work in a foreign land. He himself might possess a diploma setting out his scholastic attainments as well as the precious certificate of fitness issued by the Civil Service Commission and the all-important letter that assured him of a relatively well-paid job, but he did not feel superior to these others. They were drawn together by the common denominator of harsh reality. Ireland could not support them, and so they must leave the land they loved and make their living elsewhere.

Now, he could not help contrasting the fellow travellers who had befriended him on that fateful journey ten years ago with the motley crowd today. The predominant colour was khaki; the deck was thronged with soldiers going home on furlough, laden down with webbing equipment, rifles and bayonets, with the mud of Flanders still staining their tunics. A few of them had been pacing up and down the deck all night, peering constantly into the murk for the tell-tale signs of enemy submarines, to the irritation or amusement of their comrades. Such fears were by no means groundless; two years later a U-boat would torpedo the mail-steamer *Leinster*, with the loss of more than 450 passengers and crew. But most of the soldiers who sprawled in the gangways and huddled on the benches were dead to the world and past caring. Most of them were only going on leave, a brief respite before the next Big Push; but a few lucky ones were bound for a posting in Ireland, a cushy billet if ever there was one. Far from the appalling carnage of the Western Front, remote even from the Zeppelin air-raids on England, Ireland was a haven of tranquillity.

Occasionally one of the soldiers would eye the fine-looking youth with scarcely veiled hostility, as if to say 'Why are you not in uniform?', but others regarded him more tolerantly: 'Ah well, ye're well out of it!' In the wee small hours, he had even broached the bottle of Jameson's in his coat pocket and passed it round a couple of the Tommies from an English county regiment. 'Drink up, me lads,' he thought grimly. 'Soon I may be fighting you.'

Now, as the first long rays of the wintry sun eased the morning chill, the ship entered Dublin Bay and approached the line of quays stretching along the North Wall. The young man gazed intently at the panorama spread before him. Beyond the forest of masts lay the wharves — how tawdry and seedy it all looked — and the grey-blue haze from a thousand chimneys through which he discerned the steeples of the many churches and the two cathedrals. Near at hand he made out the distinctive shape of the Customs House, and beyond, in the city centre, the Four Courts, the Bank of Ireland, the Mansion House and the Palladian outline of Trinity College. And there, crouched on a ridge above the Liffey, was the menacing bulk of the Castle, the hated symbol of seven centuries of English domination.

The generous mouth tightened dourly at this sight.

CHAPTER I

Boyhood, 1890–1906

A great host with whom it is not fortunate to contend, the
battle-trooped host of the O Coileain.
OLD IRISH SAYING

THE COLLINSES IN THE WEST OF COUNTY CORK ARE DESCENDED
from the O Coileain, lords of Ui Conaill Gabhra from time immemorial. Long
before William the Conqueror set foot on the sister island, the O Coileain were
famed for their ferocious warrior skills. The Conqueror's great-grandson,
Henry II, received the grant of Ireland from Pope Adrian IV on condition that
he brought law and order to the Irish Church and State. The genuineness of the
Papal Bull Laudabiliter setting forth this shady deal is open to question; but the
Irish, a devout race, swallowed the mandate from His Holiness and meekly
submitted. The immediate occasion for the Anglo-Norman invasion, in 1170,
was ostensibly the restoration of Dermot McMurrough, King of Leinster, who
had been ejected four years previously. When Dermot conveniently died and
was replaced by the Norman magnate FitzGilbert, the Irish rose in revolt under
Rory O'Connor, King of Connacht. King Henry himself then crossed over to
Ireland on 17 October 1171, a date that would later be engraved on the mind
of every Irishman. The conquest of Ireland was sudden and all-embracing; the
petty kings were replaced by Norman barons and the rigours of feudalism
imposed. In one of the many uprisings of that fateful decade the O Coileain
were expelled from their lands in County Limerick (today Upper and Lower
Connelloe). A small remnant managed to cling on to Claoghlas in the far
south-west of the county till the late-eighteenth century when they were
dispossessed by the Fitzgeralds. Meanwhile, the main body of the clan
migrated southwards, almost as far as they could possibly go, to West Cork,
one of the remotest and poorest areas in the far south-west of Ireland.

Not far from Galley Head, the promontory that separates the bays of
Clonakilty and Rosscarbery, lies the straggle of cottages and farmhouses at the
crossroads known as Sam's Cross (after a notorious highwayman, Sam

Wallace). Near this hamlet, nestling in the hills midway between the two market towns, is the tiny farm of Woodfield, ninety acres in extent, which had been tenanted by the Collins family for generations. At the crossroads itself stands the Four Alls tavern which, for many years, was kept by Jeremiah Collins (and is today run by his grandson, Maurice) and still has its curious signboard inscribed 'I Rule All, I Fight for All, I Pray for All, but I Pay for All', captions to pictures of a king, a pikeman, a priest and a farmer respectively. In a cottage across the road was born Mary Anne O' Brien in 1855. She was scarcely out of her teens when she married one of the Collins brothers who tenanted Woodfield.

Woodfield was not untypical of the farms in this part of Ireland, with its small, stony fields on the long slope of a windswept hillside. Subdivision over the centuries had reduced it by the early-nineteenth century to a few scattered acres providing little more than subsistence farming. It was occupied by four brothers, Maurice, Thomas, Patrick and Michael John Collins.[1] They could not afford to marry, and for years they struggled, four ageing bachelors, to make a go of the farm. Somehow they weathered the Great Hunger of the 1840s and the upheavals of the Young Ireland rebellion in 1848, and were swept up in the temperance crusade of Father Mathew the following year, unreservedly accepting the supposition that strong drink was a weapon of the English squirearchy to keep the Irish docile.

In 1850 Pat and Tom, now in their fifties, had a brush with a couple of squireens who were trampling through their crops in pursuit of a fox. The Collins brothers were extremely fortunate not to be ejected from their tenancy, but for manhandling the huntsmen and driving them off their fields, Pat and Tom spent a year in Cork Gaol. Once a month Michael mounted his garron and made the fatiguing journey, through Timoleague and Bandon, to the county town twenty miles away to the north-east, bringing pathetic comfort to his gentle elder brothers whose uncharacteristic eruption had cost them so dear.

These monthly journeys to and from Cork turned Michael's soul to iron. In the very year that Pat and Tom were convicted, an association demanding the Three Fs — Fair rent, Free sale and Fixity of tenure — was formed with the avowed intention of extinguishing landlordism altogether. Out of this association would evolve the Land League in 1879 which would eventually achieve these aims, but along the way there would be constant heartache and numerous setbacks as the Land Leaguers battled against the vested interests of the landowning classes. In the end, it would take a worldwide depression in agriculture combined with three wretched harvests in a row (1877–79) before the Westminster parliament passed the great Land Act of 1881. The youngest of the Collins brothers chafed at the seeming lack of progress towards justice for the tenantry and sought other solutions.

Michael Collins was a fervent admirer of a Rosscarbery man, Jeremiah O'Donovan Rossa, who tried to give fresh impetus to Irish nationalism by founding the Phoenix National and Literary Society. The authorities viewed this as yet another subversive organisation and, in the wake of the 1848 uprising, it was suppressed. The Phoenix was reborn, however, a decade later. On St Patrick's Day 1858, James Stephens and Thomas Clarke Luby founded a secret society known as the Irish Republican Brotherhood, recruiting former Phoenix members with the help of money raised in America from survivors of the 1848 rising. In America the movement came to be known as the Fenians (after the heroic Fianna of Irish mythology) but in Ireland itself it was usually known by its initials. Despite being condemned by the Catholic Church as a secret society whose members were bound by oath, the IRB grew steadily, though its achievements were quixotic rather than real – an abortive invasion of Canada (1867), the rescue of political prisoners from a convict settlement in Western Australia (1876) and the invention of the submarine (1881), designed by John Holland to bring down the mighty Royal Navy.

What role, if any, Michael John Collins played in this secret brotherhood is unknown. By 1875, at the age of sixty, the youngest of the four brothers took a bride forty years his junior. Mary Anne seems to have provided a much-needed woman's touch to the spartan bachelor farmhouse. Michael now had a warm house and a woman to love. Early in 1877 their first child, Margaret, was born, to be followed at more or less eighteen-month intervals by John (Johnny), Johanna (Hannie), Mary, Helena, Patrick and Kathleen (Katie). The children's names were chosen according to the strict formula of the period: Margaret was named in honour of Michael John's mother; Johanna after Mary Anne's mother, and the third daughter after Mary Anne herself. Similarly, John was named after Michael's father, Patrick after his uncle, and the third son, the last of the eight children, would be named Michael, after his father.[2]

Raising a family in old age must have left Michael John little time for politics. The 1880s were a decade in which the Invincibles of the IRB turned to more extreme action: the murder of Lord Frederick Cavendish, Chief Secretary for Ireland, and his assistant Thomas Burke in Dublin's Phoenix Park on 6 May 1882, was the prelude to a bombing campaign in the heart of the enemy's capital which began the following year and climaxed on 24 January 1885 with the simultaneous dynamiting of the House of Commons, the Tower of London and Westminster Hall. The explosions had little effect, however, and the IRB soon sank back into lethargy. The limited attainment of political objectives, mainly through the Land League founded by Michael Davitt in 1879, and the Home Rule party led by Charles Stuart Parnell, seemed to promise independence gradually by constitutional means, although it tended to polarise Ireland along sectarian lines. By 1890 the collaboration between the

Liberal party led by Gladstone and the Home Rule party seemed about to bear fruit, when it was destroyed by a divorce. When Captain O' Shea, an Irish MP, divorced his wife Kitty and cited Parnell as co-respondent, the Catholic hierarchy called for the latter's resignation. Parnell refused and his party was violently split down the middle.

The O' Shea–Parnell scandal was coming to a head when Mary Anne was far advanced in her eighth and last pregnancy, complicated by a bad fall in which she saved the baby she was carrying but broke her ankle. The fracture was inexpertly set, leaving her with a bad limp for the rest of her days, but she struggled on with her chores. One autumn evening she milked her cows as usual, then did a large baking and attended to other household duties before retiring to her bed where, early on the morning of Thursday, 16 October, she gave birth to her third son. Later that day, Father Peter Hill having been summoned from Rosscarbery, the newborn infant was solemnly baptised. The parish register shows that he was christened Michael, although he went through a phase in childhood where he assumed a middle name, James (after his mother's father), and sometimes signed his name 'M.J. Collins', but he dropped this affectation as he got older.

Mary Anne was only thirty-five, but three years had elapsed since Katie had been born. The baby's father was now seventy-five, but his powers, both physical and intellectual, were undiminished by the passing of the years, and he would retain the appearance and vigour of a man half his age right up until his death in March 1897. The baby who bore his name became the favourite child of Michael's last years. Young Michael, in turn, was very close to his elderly father and when he was very young would accompany him everywhere and in his own childish way try to help about the farm.

Life at Woodfield in the 1890s must have been idyllic. Mary Anne doted on her youngest, and the boy's sisters adored him unreservedly; 'We thought he had been invented for our special edification,' commented Hannie Collins many years later.[3] Little Michael grew up in a close, loving environment. It would not have been surprising had all this love and attention turned his head, but he seems to have gained the positive benefit of self-assurance without the negative quality of becoming self-centred. His earliest memories were of his parents and his sisters, of cuddling up to his mother as she milked the cows and softly crooned the Irish ballads which she had learned from her grandmother. It was Michael's earliest exposure to the Irish language; years later he would regret that he had not had the opportunity to speak it as a native.

Old Michael John appears to have been a rather austere, forbidding figure, awkward and reserved with his older children; but young Michael's perception of him was quite different. In extreme old age Michael opened out to his last-born, whom he regaled with the myths and legends of old, as well as exciting deeds and tragic tales from Ireland's history. Running like a golden thread through this oral education was the rank injustice of the antiquated system of landholding. Some day this must be put right, and the land restored to the people who actually tilled the soil. In fact, the Land Purchase Act of 1885 made it practicable for tenants to buy their farms. The landlord would receive eighteen times the annual rental from the government, and the tenant would repay this sum over forty-nine years. Later legislation would accelerate the process by providing generous bonuses (up to an eighth of the purchase price). Taking advantage of this concession Johnny Collins would eventually undertake the purchase of Woodfield in 1903. By 1921, two-thirds of the land in Ireland had passed from the old landowning class to the tenantry under voluntary transactions of this kind, and one of the first acts of the Free State administration was to complete the process.

Although the worst excesses and injustice of the old land system had been mitigated by the time Michael was a little boy, the collective folk memory was sharply etched with bitter memories. As late as 1886, when Johnny was nine, he had been the terror-stricken witness of an eviction, watching the local stalwarts of the Royal Irish Constabulary manhandling the tall gallows contraption used to batter down the mud walls of a cotter's cabin before the thatch was torched, as the evicted family huddled shivering on a frozen November afternoon and watched their house go up in flames. Johnny never forgot the look of sullen, impotent rage on the face of the cotter. Shortly before Michael was born, an old man was forcibly evicted as he lay on his deathbed. On that occasion one of his sons was goaded into attacking the land-agent with a pitchfork, putting a tine through the man's eye. What became of the assailant is not recorded, but apparently there were no evictions in that area thereafter.

All this was before young Michael's time, but he himself had a memory of 'factor's snash' that would remain with him till the end of his life. On the very day he himself was killed he reminisced about an incident when he was no more than five. His father was ill at the time, and for some reason it fell to the boy to pay the rent of £4 6s 8d. On his way to the land-agent's office in Rosscarbery, Michael chanced to see, in a shop window, a football priced at a shilling. Oh, how he longed for that football, and he quickened his step in the hope that the agent would reward him for prompt payment by giving him a shilling discount, as was sometimes the case. But the man took the full amount, snapping nastily, 'Tell your father he's a fool to trust such a small lad with so much money.' Right there and then, Michael vowed that there would be no land-agents in Ireland if he ever had his way.

In March 1897 the old man died. Michael was with him at the end and often recalled his last words: 'I shall not see Ireland free, but in my children's time it will come, please God.'

In adulthood Michael's memory of his father's appearance became hazy, but he had an instant recall of the old man's precepts, and frequently peppered his speeches and his conversation with his sayings. Testimony as to the character of the father is abundant: unflinching honesty, a rather dour integrity and a rigid set of moral principles were tempered by the essential humanity of the man. Tender feelings for those worse off than himself extended to the beasts of the field; even the rooks who nested in the trees around the little farmhouse were left unmolested. A concern for others would be an outstanding characteristic of Michael Collins to the end of his life, and it is idle to speculate that some of the worst excesses of the civil war, perpetrated after his death, might have been avoided.

There are also many anecdotes that illustrate his total absence of fear, even as a very small child. These stories, however, probably reflect the attitudes of the raconteur rather than revealing the truth about Michael; for an absence of fear is a dangerous quality and this, indeed, may have been ultimately his undoing. Certainly the story told by his brother Johnny, of the toddler wandering off and subsequently being found asleep amid the straw on the floor of the stall housing a vicious stallion that only old Michael John could control, suggests foolhardiness born of ignorance. Astonishingly, little Michael was found curled up, fast asleep, between the animal's hooves. Another story tells how his sisters had taken him up to the loft above the living quarters, and how he fell through the trapdoor to the kitchen floor below, unscathed; but that smacks of the miraculous, rather than proving any point about Michael's bravery or fortitude.

More important was the influence of the old man on the development of the boy's intellect. Time and again, one sees examples of the tendency among the higher classes of society to decry the peasantry as little removed from the beasts of the field; yet there is abundant evidence in all peasant societies of the great store set upon education. This may not be an education in the formal sense of school, college or university, but it is education in its purest form, the education that springs from within. Old Michael John, born in the year of Waterloo, had grown up in an era when the Catholic peasantry was subject to harsh penal laws and social restrictions which extended to education among other things. It was left to the peasantry to redress the balance as best it could, through the system of hedge-schools, often conducted (as the name implies) in the open air.

Despite pitifully limited resources, the itinerant hedge-schoolmasters imparted an enthusiasm for learning which encouraged men and women, young and old, to carry on the process on their own. Literacy was the key to this self-education and the system, despite its primitive nature, produced an incredible number of fine scholars. Michael John had received what little formal education he possessed from Diarmuid O Suilleabhain, a cousin on his mother's side, who inculcated a love of languages. As a result, Michael had a good grounding in English and French as well as classical Irish, and then went on to acquire a deep knowledge of Latin and Greek, besides the more abstruse aspects of pure mathematics. In addition to the many skills required of the small peasant farmer, who must needs turn his hand to ploughing and thatching and all aspects of animal husbandry, Michael John was adept at carpentry and cabinetmaking, fashioning his own furniture and constructing the doors and windows of his farmhouse or the mangers and stalls for the cattle and horses. An old man who had such a wealth of experience and an extraordinary range of skills and accomplishments, both practical and cerebral, must have been a source of wonderment to an impressionable boy. Many of Michael John's anecdotes concerning the epic struggles of Ninety-Eight (the year in which his elder brother Patrick had been born) had the ring of truth underscored by the fact that he had got them from the lips of Diarmuid O Suilleabhain himself, and he, it was well known locally, had been 'out' in that historic year and had fought shoulder to shoulder with Wolfe Tone himself. It is hardly surprising that young Michael should develop such a keen sense of history, and a consciousness of his people's role in it.

Michael developed into a sturdy lad, big for his age but also precocious beyond his years. From earliest childhood he had related easily to his much older brothers and sisters, to his mother and above all to his father who treated him as an equal and never spoke down to him. To this may be attributed his independent spirit; his father had taught him well, at an early age, to think for himself, to question everything. This extended into the field of religion. The Collinses were devout, but this did not necessarily mean that everything about their faith was accepted unquestioningly. There is abundant evidence to suggest that Michael, in the middle period of his life, took religious observance rather lightly, but in the last three years of his life he came back to his faith and in the stressful period of the Truce and the Treaty, as well as in the civil war that followed, he often found solace in the Mass and the Rosary.

Having learned to read and write at his father's knee, Michael was sent off to the neighbourhood school at the tender age of four and a half. The nearest establishment was the National School at Lisavaird, about two miles from the farm. Opened in 1887, it served this little community for many years but is now used as a shed for J.J. Hurley's farm machinery business. This was a one-teacher school, catering for pupils of all ages from five to twelve. What had been so ably begun by old Michael was continued by Denis Lyons, one of those truly exceptional schoolmasters whose influence on their students lasts a lifetime. Apart from his skills as a pedagogue, Lyons had a genius for motivating his youthful charges. Ironically, the National School system had been established by the government with the express purpose of eradicating any sense of Irish nationalism from the children, and undermining any subversive notions that they might have imbibed with their mothers' milk. Denis Lyons, however, was a seasoned veteran of the IRB who managed to conceal his Fenian sympathies from the authorities while promoting his belief in physical force, if need be, to achieve the aims of an independent Ireland. It is hard to believe that Lyons, who sailed so close to the political wind, was not detected by the board of education; but perhaps the authorities chose to turn a blind eye rather than lose a teacher of his outstanding calibre.

At any rate Michael benefited from both the fundamentals of a sound education and the subtle extracurricular activities. Many years later (in Frongoch detention camp) Michael shed some light on this. 'In Denis Lyons, especially his manner, although seemingly hiding what meant most to him, was this pride of Irishness which has always meant most to me.'[4]

Another powerful influence on the young boy was James Santry. With Lyons, he was Michael's first tutor:

> capable of – because of their personalities alone – infusing into me a pride
> of the Irish race. Other men may have helped me along the searching path
> to a political goal. I may have worked hard myself in the long search,
> nevertheless, Denis Lyons and James Santry remain to me as my first
> stalwarts.[5]

Santry was the village blacksmith. Symbolically, his smithy was close to the school, and it was the boy's father who brought him in contact with a man who had been his longtime comrade in the IRB. A born story-teller, Santry would often have the lad spellbound with his yarns, made all the more vivid because his father before him had forged on that very anvil the pikes which armed the insurgents in the uprisings of 1848 and 1867, while he could proudly claim that his grandfather had fought at Shannonvale in the rising of 1798.

Interestingly, Michael's respect for Lyons was reciprocated. There is yet extant a school report in the schoolmaster's neat handwriting, dating from 1901 when Michael was about eleven years of age:

> Exceptionally intelligent in observation and at figures. A certain restlessness
> in temperament. Character: Good. Able and willing to adjust himself to all
> circumstances. A good reader. Displays more than a normal interest in
> things appertaining to the welfare of his country. A youthful, but neverthe-
> less striking, interest in politics. Coupled with the above is a determination
> to become an engineer. A good sportsman, though often temperamental.[6]

The comments on politics and engineering were bracketed with a further shrewd observation, 'Either one of these could possibly become finalised at maturity.' It was an assessment that would secure Michael a coveted place at the higher-grade school in Clonakilty.

After old Michael's death, Mary Anne decided that the old farmhouse was too cramped for her large family now reaching adulthood. With remarkable singlemindedness and organisational ability – traits inherited in no small measure by her youngest son – she set about having a new house erected alongside the old, and superintended every detail down to the landscaping of a flower garden, regarded at the time as an unnecessary extravagance. The family moved in at Christmas 1900. In the new, more spacious scheme of things, Michael now had his own bedroom, with a fine window that looked north towards the hills and wooded glens of Knockfeen. The room was very sparsely furnished, from choice, the boy's only concession to ornament being a rather sombre poem entitled 'Moonlight in my Prison Cell' which he framed himself with passe-partout. His sole luxury was a little bookcase containing an amazingly catholic range of reading matter. To be sure, there were books about his great heroes, Wolfe Tone and Robert Emmett, martyrs of the risings of 1798 and 1803 respectively, the writings of Thomas Davis (read again and again and leaving an indelible mark on Michael's own political philosophy), the essays and poetry of the Sullivan brothers including 'God Save Ireland' which became the Fenian anthem, the patriotic novels of Banim and Kickham, O'Donovan Rossa's autobiographical *Prison Life*, and many others with a strong political theme. But alongside them were the novels of Scott, Dickens and Thackeray as well as Shakespeare's plays and the poems of Thomas Moore.

With Katie, the sister closest to him in years, Michael read *The Mill on the Floss* and once said to her, 'We're like Tom and Maggie Tulliver.' Katie riposted that he could never be cruel like Tom, but Michael blurted out, after a hesitant pause, 'I could be worse.' This seemingly casual remark remained sharply etched in his sister's mind. Years later, when the horrible deeds on both sides in the civil war were made known, she would ponder on Michael's words. Did he, perhaps, have some premonition of the ruthlessness which, though devoid of cruelty, circumstances would force on him? If so, she took some comfort from the fact that he died when he did, before the worst excesses were perpetrated and tarnished the reputation of his contemporaries.

At the turn of the century this very close-knit family began to drift apart. First to go was Hannie, who secured a clerical post in the Post Office Savings Bank in London in March 1899.[7] This was inevitable, for Woodfield could not provide work for everyone, and it was always assumed that some at least – the brighter, more energetic and more restless – would some day go forth into the world. Oddly enough, only one was drawn by that powerful magnet, America;

in 1902 Patrick departed for the New World, never to return. When Helena left home to become a novitiate in an English convent, her last sight of home was Michael running along the road after the horse and trap, waving frantically until he was swallowed up in the dusty haze. Johnny would remain to work the farm, and suffer grievously during the Troubles when the Black and Tans burned down the farmhouse as a reprisal against Woodfield's most notorious son. Until the late-1980s the house that Mary Anne erected with so much care was a grassy ruin, a stark reminder of these terrible times. As the centenary of the birth of Michael Collins approached, however, the ruins were tidied up and gardens laid out to form the Michael Collins Memorial Centre, inaugurated in October 1990.

Margaret married Patrick O'Driscoll, proprietor and chief reporter of the Clonakilty newspaper. In due course they would give Michael board and lodging while he continued his studies. During this period the boy got an excellent grounding in the art of concise writing. As part-time cub reporter, he was given plenty of journalistic assignments, covering weddings, social events, football matches and the like. Having to get across the story in a limited number of words would prove an excellent training. The terse, matter-of-factness of local journalism never left him, and would be the hallmark of the reports and directives issued during the years of conflict.

One thing appears to be lacking from Michael's early boyhood; he seems not to have had any close friends of his own age. After his father died, he preferred his own company, often going for long solitary walks through the beautiful, wild countryside. Sometimes he would carry a book with him, usually Davis, which he read and reread, ruminating over its precepts: education, knowledge, toleration, unity, self-reliance, all fused by love of country. This was the Davis recipe for a sovereign Ireland in which Nationalist and Unionist, Catholic and Protestant would sink their differences and work together for the common good. These were ideals which made a lasting impression on Arthur Griffith, twenty years Michael's senior and already making a name for himself. And, in turn, Griffith attracted the attention of the precocious schoolboy. In an essay written at the age of twelve, Michael extolled his new-found hero:

> In Arthur Griffith there is a mighty force afoot in Ireland. He has none of
> the wildness of some I could name. Instead there is an abundance of wisdom
> and an awareness of things which ARE Ireland.[8]

This is all the more remarkable because, at that time, Griffith's potential was recognised by very few politicians. The star of John Redmond, leader of the revitalised Irish Parliamentary Party, was then in the ascendant. By 1902, when Michael penned this essay, Griffith had been out of active politics for more than a decade, a victim of the scandal that destroyed the Parnellite faction.

After Parnell's death in 1891, Griffith turned instead to the cultural renascence of Ireland and threw himself wholeheartedly into the Young Ireland League, the Celtic Literary Society and the Gaelic League which strove to save the native language from extinction. At the turn of the century he founded Cumann na nGaedheal, a federation of patriotic youth clubs of various hues and aims whose common factor was their detestation of the Irish Parliamentary Party led by John Redmond. In the same essay Michael expressed himself trenchantly against the Redmondites as 'Slaves of England' and 'chains around Irish necks'.

There was no point in merely deploring the self-serving policies of the Irish Parliamentary Party; it was necessary to come up with a viable alternative. With such stalwarts as Maud Gonne and W.B. Yeats working for Cumann na nGaedheal, Griffith could call on some of the sharpest intellects of the period in developing his political ideas. Behind Cumann na nGaedheal, moreover, was the IRB which imparted the separatist complexion of the movement. These strands became entwined in 1905 when Griffith formed a new political party whose name in Irish literally meant 'We Ourselves', though it is often translated as 'Ourselves Alone'. The party was Sinn Fein.

While these political developments which would have such long-term repercussions on Ireland were in the making, Michael was attending classes at the National School in Clonakilty (now the West Cork Museum). At Lisavaird Michael had been head and shoulders above his peers; in Clonakilty he faced much stiffer competition, but by the end of his first term he had found his feet and was consistently at the top of his class. Mary Anne, now in her late forties and in poor health, feared for the future of her brilliant but erratic son. 'I am afraid he will get into mischief,' she confided in one of her daughters, perhaps with some premonition of the dangerous years ahead. Mary Anne was anxious that Michael should follow in Hannie's footsteps and pass the all-important Civil Service examination that would give him a job for life and a good pension at the end of his career.

The headteacher, John Crowley, concurred. At the age of fourteen Michael was weaned away from any residual notions he may have had about becoming an engineer and put into Crowley's special class which he coached relentlessly for the Civil Service examination. There were very few options. With a good pass in the school certificate examinations Michael could hope for little opportunity locally beyond recruitment into the Royal Irish Constabulary (a prospect which he found distasteful). So he gave way to his ailing mother's wishes and diligently studied for the Civil Service examination, sister Margaret keeping an eye on him. The only break from his studies came on Saturday mornings when he would set off along the winding country road, skirting the

Curragh Lough, and down to the gleaming cottages of Sam's Cross and the welcoming farmhouse beyond.

In 1904 he acquired his first bicycle. Little did he realise, as he cycled along the country lanes exploring the hauntingly beautiful countryside on the south coast, that the day was not far off when he would wage war on the mighty British Empire – from the saddle of a bicycle.

Apart from intellectual pursuits, Michael, who was even then above average height and broad of frame, excelled at all manner of individual sports but had little real aptitude for team games in which his fiery temper often led to a punch-up on the field. He was exceptionally strong and well built, energetic and enjoyed the rudest of health. Among his favourite sports were wrestling, running, jumping and horse-riding. Sean Deasey, a contemporary at Clonakilty, later recalled that his classmate was 'powerful in figure for his age, and a veritable terror at the sport of wrestling'.[9]

Katie was the nearest thing to a boon companion at this period, and they would often go for long bike rides together at weekends; but in his last year in school Michael formed a close friendship with Sean Hurley, whose family background was very similar. In the summer vacation they stayed turn about in each other's homes, wrestling, cycling and working in the fields together. What attracted them to each other was primarily kinship – they were second cousins – but they also had a very similar political outlook. Both boys dreamed passionately of an independent Ireland, but Sean was the more realistic, down-to-earth of the two, whereas Michael's optimism for the future was unbounded. Years later Sean would recall the day that they cycled past the house occupied by a landlord who had earned a reputation in bygone years for heartlessly turning out his tenants. Michael cried out vehemently, 'When I'm a man we'll have him and his kind out of Ireland!'[10]

Late in 1905 Michael passed the Civil Service examination with flying colours and in due course received notification that he had been appointed to a clerkship in the Second Division at an annual salary of £35.[11] He had the choice of several government departments but he opted for the Post Office Savings Bank, where his sister Hannie was already established. He completed the school term at Clonakilty and in July 1906 prepared to leave the little world of West Cork for the excitement and uncertainties of London. Before he left home, he tramped round the lanes and fields that he had known all his life. Now, on these beautiful summer days, he began to see the old familiar places through new eyes. He was leaving, perhaps for ever.

CHAPTER 2

London, 1906–16

You don't know you're Irish till you leave Ireland.
TRADITIONAL SAYING

MICHAEL COLLINS WOULD SPEND NINE AND A HALF YEARS, ALMOST a third of his life, living and working in London. Family tradition, followed by all previous biographers, states that throughout that entire period he lodged with Hannie in a furnished flat at 5 Netherwood Road in West Kensington. In fact, Michael and his sister resided at various addresses in West London, and only settled in Netherwood Road in 1914.

Hannie, eleven years older than Michael, had passed the Civil Service Open Competition in March 1899 and three weeks later had been appointed a Clerk Second Class in the Post Office. She went to work as a ledger clerk in the Post Office Savings Bank and retired on 15 April 1940, having given a life of faithful if undistinguished service in which her only promotion, to Higher Clerical Officer, had come in 1928.[1] At the turn of the century, on her salary of a pound a week, Hannie had taken a bedsitting-room not far from her place of work, at 6 Minford Gardens in Shepherds Bush. Her landlord, Albert Lawrence, was a master baker who let out rooms to Scots or Irish clerks and shopmen, but the quiet-spoken girl from West Cork was his favourite and he kept a fatherly eye on her. Hannie, touchingly, always addressed him as 'father', a habit which Michael easily acquired when he came to London as a Boy Clerk in July 1906. When she got word that her youngest brother was coming to work alongside her, she had asked Lawrence if he could find a room for him. The elderly baker took to the boy immediately, 'for he was always jolly and sincere'.[2]

In 1908 Lawrence moved to Coleherne Terrace, South Kensington, where he opened a bakery on the ground floor and let rooms above. Hannie and Michael moved with him: 'Don't think we're going to leave you, Father,' said Michael. Lawrence also recalled that 'There were some fine political arguments in my house. I had an Englishman and a Scotsman as well as other Irishmen living with me, and they would talk politics nineteen to the dozen.' This cosy arrangement continued until Lawrence retired and sold his business in 1913.

Hannie and Michael then moved to a flat at 28 Princes Road, Notting Hill. Eight years later, in Dublin, Michael met Sir William Darling, then on the staff of the British administration in Dublin Castle. They discussed books at great length and discovered a mutual interest in the novels of G.K. Chesterton. It transpired that Michael's favourite was *The Napoleon of Notting Hill*, Darling concluding that the young Irishman was 'almost fanatically attached to it', as he recorded in his memoirs, *So It Looks to Me*, published in 1952. Early in 1914, however, Michael and his sister returned to Shepherds Bush, renting a substantial flat – two bedrooms, a sitting-room, kitchen and bathroom – on the upper floor of 5 Netherwood Road. The landlords, Willison Brothers, had a dairy on the ground floor. Next door, Henry Brough ran a pharmacy and sub post office.[3]

For fifteen years in the 1970s and 1980s the London Irish community tried to persuade the Greater London Council to erect a plaque to Michael's memory. Michael O'Halloran, MP for Islington North, had first raised the matter in the 1970s, and latterly Ken Livingstone gave the campaign his backing, but it was not until 1986, when Labour gained control of Hammersmith Borough Council, that the dream became a reality. It was planned to get the newly appointed Irish ambassador to unveil the plaque in April 1987 but due to damage to the terracotta plaque in transit from a pottery in the north of England, it was not until 10 July that it was unveiled by Clive Soley. The plaque, mounted high on the wall, bears a facsimile of Michael's signature with his birth and death dates below. The original idea of including the inscription 'Irish Nationalist and Soldier' was dropped, and no indication is given on the plaque of who Michael Collins was, other than saying that he resided there in 1914–15. The ceremony was followed by an evening of Irish song and poetry in Shepherds Bush Public Library under the appropriate title of 'The Laughing Boy'.[4]

The flat latterly occupied by Hannie and Michael was in a typical yellow-brick terraced house; apart from some stucco ornament including mascarons on the window arches, it was no different from countless others thrown up at the end of the nineteenth century to accommodate the vast army of artisans, shop-workers and clerks employed in the metropolis, and nowadays divided into bedsits. The rooms at Minford Gardens and Coleherne Terrace would have been very similar. In his first year in the Savings Bank Michael's salary of fifteen shillings a week barely covered the rent and his living expenses, though in 1907 Hannie's salary was raised to £75 per annum. On the basis that two can live as cheaply as one, brother and sister pooled their meagre resources. Inevitably most of the domestic chores fell on Hannie but, devoted to her clever kid brother, she never complained.

Early each morning they would leave their lodgings and walk round the corner into Blythe Road, at the far end of which stood the vast red-brick pile of the Post Office Savings Bank. Shortly after Hannie had come to London, this department of the Post Office, which had grown a hundredfold since its inception in 1861, was moved from the City to a site in West Kensington adjoining Olympia. On the very spot where Michael and scores of other clerks laboured daily on the ten million accounts and deposits totalling £200,000,000, a few years previously Buffalo Bill and his cowboys had thrilled multitudes by their daily enactment of the rescue of the Deadwood stagecoach from marauding Indians. The Prince of Wales (later King Edward VII) had laid the foundation stone in June 1899 and the Savings Department completed the move by Easter Monday 1903.[5]

Edwardian London was a melting-pot. Thousands of young men and women flocked into the world's largest city of the time, not only from every part of the British Isles but, increasingly, from the Continent also and farther afield. Although the ethnic mix was not as exotic as it would become forty years later, it was nevertheless a cultural, linguistic and racial maelstrom. Many of the youngsters rapidly became deracinated and acquired the cosmopolitanism and easy tolerance of the typical Londoner of the period. Apart from the Jewish community, largely confined to the Aldgate district in the East End, the one immigrant group which tended to retain its cultural identity was the Irish. Even there, though, the bonds could weaken. Many a young Irishman, liberated from the claustrophobic constraints of his faith and family, cheerfully abandoned both and assimilated easily, marrying a girl who might herself have migrated from Scotland, Wales or the English provinces. If he did not wish to go to Mass on Sunday morning, there was no father (or mother) figure breathing down his neck. If he wanted to read what, at home, had been condemned as 'bad books', he was perfectly free to do so.

On the other hand, there were many young men and women, cast adrift in an alien environment, who clung together tenaciously and reinforced each other's Irishness. Things which had been taken for granted at home, or ignored altogether, now became important. If Michael had been tempted by the bright lights and the thousands of blandishments to stray and turn his back on his nationality, there was big sister Hannie at his elbow. He joined the Sinn Fein Club in Chancery Lane and it was in London that he even made his first attempt to learn Irish, attending Gaelic League classes for some time. This first essay into the mysteries of the native language seems not to have progressed very far beyond the ability to write his name *Miceál O Coileain* in Gaelic uncials and to make the happy discovery that so many of the words and phrases that peppered everyday conversation in West Cork were, in fact, Irish.

In April 1907, at the age of fifty-two, Mary Anne died of cancer after a long and painful illness. Her obituary in *The West Cork People* of 16 April, by 'one who knew her' – probably her son-in-law, Pat O' Driscoll – included a touching little ode extolling her simple, homely hospitality. She remains a rather shadowy figure compared with her husband, yet her influence on Michael was not inconsiderable. It has often been said that the qualities of kindliness and generosity in Michael came from her. Though not as devout as his mother by any stretch of the imagination, her son shared her easy-going, tolerant attitude to those of other faiths. It is highly significant that, on the night Mary Anne died, it was her Protestant neighbours who were at her bedside, and many others came to her funeral. Michael himself abhorred the sectarianism which, since the 1880s, had threatened to weaken the cause of Irish independence; in the all-too-brief period allotted to him as head of state he dealt very firmly with any manifestation of partiality or victimisation along sectarian lines.

Under Hannie's influence Michael did not kick over the traces, although she must have had some anxious moments. Far worse, in many respects, than the temptations of London life in general were the attitudes and outlook of a certain element in the London Irish community which had abandoned the church for the pub and accompanied heavy drinking with a strident anti-clericalism. P.S. O'Hegarty, who got to know him well in the London period, left a very perceptive pen-picture of the adolescent Michael:

> Everybody in Sinn Fein circles knew him, and everybody liked him, but he was not a leader. He had strong individuality, clearly-held opinions, and noticeable maturity even as a boy of seventeen when he made his appearance in Irish circles in London. But his place was rather as the raw material of a leader than as a leader. When he came to London as a mere boy, he fell into spasmodic association with a hard-drinking, hard-living crowd from his own place, and their influence on him was not good. During most of his years in London he was in the 'blast and bloody' stage of adolescent evolution, and was regarded as a wild youth with plenty of ability, who was spoiled by his wildness. Not that his wildness was any deeper than the surface. Behind it his mind grew and his ideas enlarged.[6]

Michael never lost his faith – that was too deeply ingrained in him – but he went through a phase as he approached manhood when he was decidedly hostile to the Catholic Church. On one occasion in 1909 he caused a furore at a Sinn Fein meeting when he delivered a tirade against the priesthood's role in Irish history, attacking the spineless attitude of the hierarchy and concluding violently, 'Exterminate them!'[7]

Despite the advantage of having an elder sister to comfort and guide him, Michael's immediate feelings on coming to London were homesickness compounded by an immense loneliness. London, with its hustle and bustle and its overwhelming size, was a terrifying prospect for a teenager whose world had hitherto been bounded by Rosscarbery and Clonakilty. 'Loneliness,' he once said to Patrick Hodges, 'can be of two sorts: the delighted loneliness of the traveller in the country; and the desperate loneliness of the stranger to a city.'[8] For many weeks he was thoroughly miserable. The news from Woodfield was far from good; after his departure, Mary Anne seemed to lose the will to live, though in truth her decline was due to a malignant tumour, and nine months later she was dead.

Gradually, Michael recovered his equilibrium and found the congenial companionship of Irish boys of his own age. Quite a number, perhaps slightly older, were also employed as clerks at the Savings Bank. In an organisation of this size, with many hundreds of employees, there was an active social life offering a wide range of sporting, intellectual and recreational facilities. Significantly, Michael did not become involved in any of these. Instead, he gravitated towards the distinctive social milieu of the London Irish. Interestingly, Hannie provided a powerful corrective to the more extreme Irish nationalist tendencies. Her Irishness manifested itself mainly through her regular attendance at Mass and Confession; but she worked alongside mainly English girls and in the years before Michael joined her she had made many close friendships with English families. Through her, Michael was drawn into Hannie's social circle and thus got to know many English people in a relaxed atmosphere. This social experience was to stand him in good stead years later when he was deeply involved in the critical stages of the negotiations with the British government. Then, Michael would lack the awkwardness and the stiffness, perhaps born of a sense of inferiority, that plagued Arthur Griffith. Above all, close contact with the English at work and at home gave Michael a profound understanding of the Ould Enemy.

Nevertheless, he was inexorably drawn into a specific section of the London Irish community. It began within months of his arrival when he came to the notice of a group of Irish businessmen in the capital who devoted their spare time and a great deal of their cash to the welfare of young Irish boys and girls working in the strange city. In particular, they organised the distinctively Irish sports under the banner of the Gaelic Athletic Association which had been formed in 1884. Michael, who had never been all that keen on team games, found himself recruited by the Geraldine Hurling Club, and, never having handled a *camánn* before, soon took to this Irish brand of shinty with all the zest of a convert. Michael usually played midfield or back. Ned Lynch, who played for a rival team, remembered Michael as 'an effective though not particularly polished player, a good sportsman as long as the game was fair, but liable to fly into a temper if he suspected foul play'.[9]

Ever the rugged individualist, Michael tended to dominate his team. Big for his age, tough as nails and loud with it, he polarised the club just as he would the nation. There were those who, even at seventeen, idolised him; just as equally there were those who heartily detested what they regarded as his bullying tactics. In 1908 he put himself forward as candidate for the vice-captaincy of the hurling team. Not surprisingly the election was fiercely contested but Michael won by the narrowest of margins. Once he was on the committee, however, he exhibited qualities of organisation and administration, as well as eloquence and persuasiveness in argument that others found hard to resist. A year later he was elected to the London County Board of the Gaelic Athletic Association, and a few months after that he secured the most powerful position in the Geraldines when he became secretary, a post which he retained until he left London six years later.

The secretaryship came to him at a crucial time in the club's fortunes, when the initial interest in Gaelic games was on the wane, and there was a move to introduce soccer, rugby and cricket. To Michael, this was rank heresy, and he denounced these 'garrison games' by which the British sought insidiously to promote 'the peaceful penetration of Ireland'. What, one wonders, would he have made of Ireland in the 1990s making a name for herself in world football – and with an Englishman, Jack Charlton, as the national team manager! The controversy split the Association, most of whose clubs seceded, leaving the demoralised Geraldines among the rump. In his first half-yearly report to the club Michael lashed out at the dissension in the ranks:

> An eventful half-year has followed a somewhat riotous general meeting. Great hopes instead of being fulfilled have been rudely shattered . . . Our internal troubles were saddening, but our efforts in football and hurling were perfectly heartbreaking. In no single contest have our colours been crowned with success . . . In conclusion I can only say that our record for the past half-year leaves no scope for self-congratulation. Signs of decay are unmistakable, and if members are not prepared in the future to act more harmoniously together and more self-sacrificingly generally – the club will soon have faded into an inglorious and well-deserved oblivion.[10]

The following July it was minuted that 'The Secretary read his report. It was not flattering to the members.' As Michael wrote this minute himself, it shows an uncompromising attitude when he believed himself to be right, even if everyone else was wrong. Significantly, this minute concluded on a triumphant, self-congratulatory note: 'The report was adopted after the exhibition of marked enthusiasm by a few members.' Already Michael was attracting a band of devotees who would follow him come what may. One of them was his cousin and old schoolfriend, Sean Hurley, who had now followed him to London.

This trait of wanting to have his own way and showing a marked impatience with those who took a contrary view was early evidence of strong will rather than self-will, for in sporting matters as later on in politics Michael sincerely believed that he was working solely for the common good. For this reason he was essentially a realist and a pragmatist, ready to change his mind if he felt that circumstances had altered. This characteristic would be central to his actions a decade later.

As Michael reached his majority, the complexity of his character was clearly evident. Those who knew him in the London years paint a picture of a restless young man, a go-getter, whose dynamism was matched by his personal magnetism. Others remembered him ruefully as ruthless, single-minded, domineering and forceful, a man who did not mince his words or suffer fools lightly. He was a driven man, impelled by some sense of destiny, perhaps – but it is easy to say that with the benefit of hindsight. What is clear, though, is that Michael had to excel in anything he undertook, whether it be his clerical work at the Savings Bank or in the promotion of the Geraldines. What made him a bad loser on the hurling field was that he hated to be beaten. In a team game, unfortunately, he had to rely on others, and there were often fierce recriminations when he felt that he had been let down badly. He much preferred sports in which he could compete as an individual. He took part in sports meetings where, in running and jumping, he could pit himself against other athletes.

At work and play, Michael approached everything with a manic thoroughness and wholeheartedness. 'He lived his life with such intensity and at such a power level that the pedestal which he himself had built with his own efforts must never be chipped or even tarnished in any way.'[11] Michael Collins, in effect, was a hard act for Michael Collins to live up to, but it explains the strange mixture of bluff geniality and coolness by turns, the extraordinary generosity one moment and the cold calculation the next. When things were going well, especially on the sports field, he would often exhibit a schoolboyish rumbustiousness and a very rough bonhomie which stopped short of hooliganism, but only just. And then his mood would change like lightning and he would be as controlled and self-contained as ever. It is small wonder, therefore, that one of his closest acquaintances from this period would later write:

> I can claim to have known Michael Collins as well as, if not better than, most people. Even so, I thought my personal knowledge of him to be no more than surface knowledge. He was a very difficult person to really know.[12]

The clerical work to which Michael was assigned at the Savings Bank was routine and dull, mainly concerned with the checking and issue of dividend warrants and the periodical auditing of passbooks which had to be sent to West Kensington every time withdrawals exceeded a certain limit. The work was relatively simple, and Michael had mastered it within weeks. It is incredible that he stuck it out for four years. At first, however, he had a clear set of goals. There were Civil Service examinations which were the necessary hurdles to promotion, and in particular he had set his sights on the newly unified Customs and Excise Service where the prospects were good and the pay excellent. This entailed qualifications in accountancy, taxation, commercial law and economics, so Michael enrolled at the King's College evening classes. His reading during this period ranged from Adam Smith to Addison and Locke, the one to give him a broad understanding of economics, the others to improve his style in writing essays. One of the papers he was required to write discussed the British Empire and its future. He wrote passionately about Ireland as England's oldest colony, acquired by military force and mismanaged for centuries. He concluded on a defiant note: 'Every country has a right to work out its own destiny in accordance with the laws of its being . . . The first law of nations is self-preservation, and let England be wise and not neglect it . . .'[13]

In London, Michael began keeping a little commonplace book in which he jotted down disparate facts and figures, just as he chanced upon them, covering a very wide range of topics. It was all part of the process of self-improvement and it seems to have been undertaken in that same voracious, indiscriminate manner in which he read books. Hannie tried to give some direction to his reading, recommending such contemporary writers as Arnold Bennett, G.K. Chesterton and H.G. Wells. Michael was also an avid theatre-goer, and he both read and saw the plays of Barrie and, above all, Shaw. Significantly, his favourite was *The Man of Destiny* and he copied out passages of it which he carried in his wallet. This led him to read everything he could by or about Napoleon. Did he subconsciously model himself on the young artillery officer who became a general of brigade at twenty-four and First Consul (effectively head of state) at thirty? 'Centuries will pass before the unique combination of events which led to my career recur in the case of another,' Napoleon told Las Cases at St Helena in 1821; but exactly one hundred years later history would repeat itself.

One other aspect of Michael that forcibly struck his compatriots in London was his extraordinary clannishness. Even perfect strangers found themselves warmly embraced if Michael detected the Cork accent. If, on the other hand, they hailed from Limerick or Tipperary (let alone points farther east) he would adopt an air of condescension mingled with sorrow. When Robinson's *Patriots* was staged in London, Michael went along to boo, because Robinson had dared to suggest that the people of Cork preferred the cinema to a revolutionary meeting. The farther he was from West Cork, in effect, the more intense became his feelings for the place and everything and everyone concerned with it. Often in his mind's eye he would see the little thatched and whitewashed cottages of Sam's Cross, or the trim farmhouse up the hill, or Jimmy Santry's forge. 'His reading regularly out-distanced his powers of reflection, and whenever we seek the source of action in him it is always in the world of his childhood that we find it.'[14]

Once he became an established civil servant, Michael was entitled to two weeks' annual leave. Invariably he returned home, never pausing to sample the delights of Dublin in passing but going straight from the quay to the railway station for the first train bound to the south-west. Family ties were strengthened when his brother John married Katty Hurley, Sean's sister. As the years passed, Michael became the favourite uncle for an ever-increasing tribe of young nephews and nieces. He adored these small children and romped with them like an overgrown schoolboy. It is a great tragedy that Michael never had a family of his own.

In an age when people made their own entertainment, ceilidhs were commonplace. Michael, on his own admission, was an indifferent singer, though he took part in the old come-all-ye's which went on interminably. His forte was the dramatic monologue, his favourite being 'Kelly and Burke and Shea' which he would recite with great gusto and appropriate gesture.

According to the contemporary press, relations between Ireland and Britain during this period were, on the surface, fairly satisfactory; but English complacency seemed blind to the realities of the situation. Successive Home Rule bills brought before Parliament by the Liberals had been defeated. On the last such occasion (1893) the bill had passed the Commons, only to be thrown out by the Lords by an overwhelming majority of 419 to 41. Another attempt to settle the Irish question was made by the Irish Council bill of 1907 which was intended to establish a purely Irish body to spend in Ireland the proceeds of Irish taxation. This bill, however, was unacceptable to the Irish people and was withdrawn. Herbert Asquith introduced his Home Rule bill in 1912; again, it comfortably passed the Commons (367 to 267) but was rejected by the Lords. In the interim, however, the Parliament Act of 1911 had ensured that the Lords could not veto bills indefinitely; the bill, if passed in three successive sessions in the same Parliament of the Commons, would automatically become law without the assent of their Lordships. Ireland was seething with discontent at the pusillanimity of Westminster, but there was a new spirit of hope in the air. It could only be a matter of time before Home Rule was secured.

Some Irishmen were questioning this never-ending round of going cap in hand to Westminster. Griffith, in the inaugural number of *The United Irishman*, put the matter in a nutshell: 'If the eyes of the Irish Nation are continually focused on England, they will inevitably acquire a squint.' Shortly before he founded Sinn Fein, Griffith also published a tract, *The Resurrection of Hungary*, in which he outlined the progress of that country to nationhood and suggested that there were useful lessons for Ireland to be learned from this.

In the first decade of this century Griffith saw the way ahead by constitutional means. Nationalists would have to gain control of the boroughs and counties through the local elections as a prelude to contesting seats at Westminster. The first opportunity arose in 1907 when Sinn Fein contested the by-election in North Leitrim; although the candidate lost, he polled a creditable third of the votes. In his commonplace book Michael noted that he intended to propose that five shillings be sent from the funds of his local branch of Sinn Fein, with the hope that a further five shillings might be raised at the meeting itself. After the meeting, at which he pleaded eloquently for the financial support of members, he noted triumphantly, 'Done. £2', indicating that four times as much had actually been raised.

It has not been ascertained when Michael enrolled as a member of Sinn Fein, though he was an enthusiastic attender of meetings from early in 1907 when he was still only sixteen. Of greater importance at the time, and of infinitely greater significance in the long term, however, was his enrolment in the Irish Republican Brotherhood. It will be remembered that Michael John Collins had been a member of the IRB, and it would have been natural for his firebrand youngest son to follow suit. In London, Michael had come to the attention of Dr Mark Ryan, a gentle, scholarly man who was instrumental in rousing the interests of many young London Irishmen in all aspects of Gaelic culture but also infecting them with fervent nationalism. Moreover, one of the older clerks in the Savings Bank was Sam Maguire who befriended Michael and became his mentor. It was Sam who proposed Michael for induction into the Brotherhood, at a secret meeting held in Barnsbury Hall in North London in November 1909. (Maguire, who died in obscurity, is remembered today in the trophy awarded in the All-Ireland Gaelic Football Championship, known as the Sam Maguire Cup.)

This event was a major landmark in Michael's life; henceforward the IRB would be his consuming interest. He had joined at a time when the Brotherhood was getting a new lease of life, thanks to Tom Clarke, one of the old-style Fenians who, having served fifteen years' penal servitude for his part in the dynamite campaign of the 1880s, had gone to America. In 1908 he had returned to Ireland and begun to revitalise the movement. Three years later a group of young bloods led by Sean MacDiarmada rallied behind the titular headship of Tom Clarke and gained control of the IRB's Supreme Council.

MacDiarmada gave the movement the impetus needed to place it in the forefront of the independence campaign.

Michael rapidly became one of MacDiarmada's apostles. Within months of joining the IRB, Michael was on the local committee and a year later he was promoted to Section Master; in 1914 he was appointed Treasurer of the London and South England district. Michael's meteoric rise in the movement is testimony to his tireless energy and drive, as well as to his formidable organisational skills. This was a valuable apprenticeship for the years ahead.

When Sinn Fein was reorganised in 1917 and subsequently embraced all shades of nationalist opinion, it seemed as if the power of the IRB was on the wane and, indeed, there were many who thought that the Brotherhood had gone out of existence. In fact, it continued as the secret society it had always been, wielding immense influence behind the scenes, and would provide Michael with his power base in the crucial years of the Troubles and the civil war. The distrust and even overt hostility towards the IRB was by no means confined to the Catholic hierarchy; the secrecy and intrigue of the IRB were deeply resented by non-members. Eventually the divergence between Sinn Fein and the IRB would become one of the factors leading to the civil war of 1922–23.

Probably in 1913 or 1914, Michael gave a paper at an IRB meeting which reveals the political development of his mind, as well as shedding light on the emphasis which, even then, he placed on organisation. Speaking about the various movements that had come and gone, even the early IRB which had declined, he continued:

> But, by comparison, this revitalised IRB is a vastly different proposition to former movements. In, for example, organisation. Organisation, a lack of it, was chiefly responsible for the failure of several risings of recent times. It is, therefore, of great significance – and of some urgency also – that, if and when the occasion should demand it, the IRB should be even better organised, and so better prepared to meet such an emergency. A great deal of the organisation will, of course, have to be theoretical – that is the danger. Whereas in practical organisation there is no danger for the element of luck and chance does not enter into it. A force organised on practical lines, and headed by realists, would be of great consequence. Whereas a force organised on theoretical lines, and headed by idealists, would, I think, be a very doubtful factor.[15]

Induction into the IRB was a watershed in Michael's life. Politics now left him little or no time to pursue his studies; and Albert Lawrence states that

Michael failed the Civil Service exams 'because he was giving so much time to those Irish meetings'. Besides, a career in Customs and Excise had lost its appeal. Henceforward Michael would devote himself wholeheartedly to the cause of Irish independence. Everything he did, every book he read, would be in furtherance of this objective. First the studies at King's College were abandoned, and then in April 1910 Michael resigned from the Post Office Savings Bank to take a more remunerative though hardly more interesting position with Horne & Company, stockbrokers at 23 Moorgate where he was placed in charge of the messengers. Shortly after the outbreak of the First World War in August 1914 he left this firm to become a clerk at the Board of Trade in Whitehall, on the greatly enhanced salary scale of £70–£150 per annum. In his application he wrote:

> The trade I know best is the financial trade, but from study and observation
> I have acquired a wider knowledge of social and economic conditions and
> have specially studied the building trade and unskilled labour.[16]

He also stated that he was proficient at typewriting and double-entry bookkeeping and making trial balances. Interestingly, he gave his date of birth as 16 October 1889 rather than 1890. 'Perhaps his youthful appearance demanded such redressing of the balance,' comments Margery Forester[17] but, in fact, the senior clerical position required a minimum age of twenty-four, and at this time Michael was short of the requisite by two months.

On 4 August 1914, the very day that war broke out, Michael was at Greenwich Park, Liverpool, playing for London against Scotland in the final of the Hurling Championship of Great Britain. On that fateful day he met one of the Liverpool Irish, Frank Thornton, who would some years later become one of Michael's most trusted lieutenants during the Black and Tan Troubles.

In London, in the years immediately before the war, other men encountered Michael and formed an indelible impression of him. The Shamrock Bar in Fetter Lane off Fleet Street was one of the favourite pubs of the London Irish and it was there that Michael was introduced by Sam Maguire to Peadar Kearney, composer of *The Soldier's Song* which is now the Irish national anthem. Kearney would later recall Michael as 'a tall, good-humoured boy, who gave no indication of the road before him'.[18]

Although Irish Home Rule had been a plank in the Liberal platform for many years, the result of the general election of January 1910 (fought on the issue of the People's Budget which inaugurated the Welfare State) meant that a minority Liberal government could only survive with the support of the Irish Nationalist MPs. A second election, in December 1910, made little change; the Liberals gained four seats, but this was hardly conclusive and left the Asquith administration as dependent on the Nationalists as ever. Politics entered a new and extremely stormy phase in which militancy was the keynote. Ironically, this was triggered off not so much by the Irish question as the burning issue of votes for women. With so much hostility in the air, so much social, intellectual and political restlessness, the nation hardly noticed at first the slippery slope down which it was rushing in Irish affairs.

The Home Rule bill, which Asquith had introduced in 1912, finally passed the House of Commons in May 1914. The bill, which would have conferred limited autonomy on Ireland, was modest in its purpose and fell far short of the outright independence which many Nationalists sought. Because it envisaged a united Ireland, however, it roused the ire of the Ulster Protestants, who reacted violently. Taking a leaf out of their Presbyterian history, they published a Covenant which attracted over 400,000 signatures. At the end of 1912 the Ulster Volunteer Force was founded by Sir Edward Carson and abetted by many prominent figures in both Ireland and Britain. 'Ulster will fight; Ulster will be right!' Lord Randolph Churchill had written as far back as May 1886. Now, almost thirty years later, Carson and his cohorts were reiterating this threat and laying plans for the establishment of a separate government in Belfast should the bill become law. When the bill passed the Commons in May 1914 the Lords (powerless to veto it any longer) tried to amend it by expressly excluding the six counties of North-East Ulster. In July King George himself interceded in a vain attempt to effect a compromise. The bill, in its original form, eventually passed both Houses of Parliament in September 1914, but effectively it was nullified by a simultaneous Act which provided that it should not come into force until after the First World War, the government promising to bring in a bill dealing with the Ulster situation. This bill never materialised.

If it was all right for Ulster Protestants to defy the government by taking up arms, then the IRB could do likewise. In November 1913 the Irish Volunteers were called into being by Professor Eoin MacNeill of University College, Dublin, blissfully unaware that his paramilitary force, designed purely for the defence of Home Rule, had been infiltrated by the IRB which had a more offensive role in mind. The government, likewise unaware of the separatist tendencies of the Irish Volunteers, allowed the movement to continue drilling; it could hardly suppress it so long as it turned a blind eye to the UVF. When the latter obtained 35,000 rifles, several hundred machine-guns and tons of ammunition through the activities of gun-runners operating in and out of Larne with the connivance of the authorities, the Irish Volunteers made their own frantic attempts to procure arms.

On 26 July 1914 a fanatically pro-Irish Englishman named Erskine Childers, a British civil servant who had fought as a trooper in the Boer War and had attained some celebrity from his yachting thriller *The Riddle of the Sands* (1904), sailed his own yacht *Asgard* into Howth Harbour and unloaded 900 obsolete Mauser rifles and thousands of rounds of cartridges. Coogan, while researching his own biography, stumbled across a tale that Michael himself had been present on that occasion, and lived in Howth 'with good-looking girls'.[19] Subsequent research revealed that a girlfriend was, indeed, lodging at 1 Island View, Howth, around that time, but no confirmation of Michael's involvement has ever been found.

The Irish Volunteers swiftly unloaded the precious cargo but on the way back to Dublin were intercepted by the Royal Irish Constabulary, backed by heavily armed troops of the King's Own Scottish Borderers. A few Mausers were lost in the ensuing scuffle, but the Volunteers managed to get the bulk of their arms safely to Dublin. Unfortunately, a hostile crowd tried to block the police and the military at Bachelors' Walk. Stones were thrown, and the forces of law and order responded by firing live ammunition at point-blank range into the densely packed crowd. Several people were killed and many more wounded in what would later be regarded as the first outrage in a war that lasted, in one form or another, for nine years.

Across the water, the London IRB also raised Volunteer companies. At the end of 1913, when he was still living at Princes Road, Notting Hill, Michael gathered a handful of like-minded young men about him and formed a Volunteer unit. As a latter-day Napoleon of Notting Hill, it was Michael's first essay in soldiering. Though proposed by Edward Lee for a captaincy on the strength of this little company which Michael had raised, nothing appears to have come of it, for on 25 April 1914 Michael transferred to Number One Company, London Brigade, being then inducted as a member by his kinsman, Sean Hurley. A close companion of this period was the Irish writer, Padraic O'Conaire; they would drill each week at the German gymnasium in King's Cross, using reconditioned Martini-Henry rifles and making a weekly contribution towards the cost of the weapons they would one day own personally.

This escalation of imminent conflict was accelerated by an incident, a month earlier, at the Curragh, the British Army's principal base in Ireland, when a number of senior officers declared their extreme reluctance to take action against the Ulster Volunteers. Inaccurately known to posterity as the Curragh Mutiny, the incident demonstrated forcibly that the government could no longer rely on its own armed forces should it become necessary to coerce Ulster into accepting Home Rule with government from Dublin. The mutineers were led by Brigadier (later General Sir) Hubert Gough who received the written assurance of the Director of Military Operations, General (later Field-Marshal) Sir Henry Wilson that the army would not be thus employed. Both men, incidentally, were Irishmen.

The situation was complicated by the existence of yet another paramilitary body in southern Ireland. Following the Dublin lock-out of 1913 (an industrial dispute marred by ugly riots brutally suppressed by the Royal Irish Constabulary), the workers' leader James Connolly led the Citizen Army, actually formed by a Protestant Nationalist, Captain Jack White whose father was none other than Field Marshal Sir George Stuart White VC – proving that Nationalism often crossed the sectarian divide.

On the outbreak of the First World War, Home Rule was put on the back burner for the duration. John Redmond pledged the Nationalists to support Britain in the coming struggle but in so doing he lost control of the Home Rule movement to men who would shortly demand much, much more. Thousands of Irishmen, both North and South, volunteered to fight on the British side for the rights of small nations against German domination. Redmond's brother would be killed on the Western Front, while Erskine Childers would earn the Distinguished Service Cross with the Royal Naval Air Service before resuming the fight for Ireland.

Meanwhile, Michael continued to work at the Board of Trade by day and drill with the Volunteers by night. The confrontation with the Ulstermen had been postponed, but some day there would be a showdown, and the Irish Volunteers would have to be prepared. For the British Expeditionary Force the government relied on volunteers at first, but after the retreat from Mons in 1914 and the bloody stalemate of Neuve Chapelle in the spring of 1915, new recruits were not so ready to come forward. It was then that conscription was first mooted. At a time when it seemed that this might apply to the British Isles as a whole, Michael's brother Pat wrote to him from Chicago urging him to emigrate to America. 'If you don't take a chance you will never get anywhere,' he wrote. 'A little nerve is all that's necessary.'[20] Pat also feared – rightly, as it turned out – that England's difficulty would be Ireland's opportunity. Just as Wolfe Tone's rebellion of 1798 had coincided with the French Directory's plans for the invasion of England, so there could well be a rebellion in Ireland while British garrisons there were depleted. Pat even went so far as to send Katie the money for Michael's passage to the United States, and he was nonplussed when Michael returned the cash saying that if there were any trouble he would be in the thick of it. This was the first inkling he had of Michael's clandestine activities.

Shortly afterwards, however, in May 1915, Michael resigned from the Board of Trade and took up employment with the Guaranty Trust Company of New York at its London office in Lombard Street. Previous biographers have implied that he took this step in the hope that, if the worst happened, he could get a transfer to the head office in New York, although Coogan has hinted that he may have been ordered by the IRB to seek this position with a view to gaining wider experience of high finance.[21] This seems to be arguing from the benefit of hindsight. All of Michael's work experience from 1906 onwards would, of course, fit him admirably for his cabinet post of Minister of Finance, but in 1915 it seems hardly likely that this was remotely considered.

In any case, the clerical job with the Guaranty Trust was not a particularly responsible or onerous one. After Michael's death his office manager, Robert Mackey, wrote that 'the staff, who were privileged to know him, will never believe that he could do an unworthy act'.[22] On the other hand, noted Mackey:

> Only on very rare occasions did his sunny smile disappear, and this was usually the result of one of his fellow clerks making some disparaging, and probably unthinking, remark about his beloved Ireland. Then he would look as though he might prove a dangerous enemy.

Until recently, biographers of Michael Collins did not present a fully rounded portrait of the man. There was never any reference to activity of an amatory nature. The reader would be left wondering whether there might have been more to those seemingly innocent references to boyish wrestling bouts with close friends, or the doglike devotion of Joe O'Reilly who was his constant companion throughout the last years of his life. It was possible that he was so consumed with politics that he never had time to think of sex. The only writer to touch briefly on the subject was Frank O'Connor, who ingenuously assured his readers that Michael was 'shrewd enough' to know about the evils of prostitution 'only at second hand through the novels of Tolstoy and Shaw'.[23] Those who were closest to Michael in the London years formed a very different view. His second cousin, Nancy O'Brien, who also worked in the Post Office Savings Bank, saw him frequently in the pre-war period: 'All the girls were mad about him. He'd turn up at the céilidhe with Padraic O'Conaire and would not give them a reck.' Nancy, who probably knew him as well as anyone, described him as the sort of man that women would either take to instinctively or subconsciously wish to put down. She considered that most of the girls of his own background found him arrogant or overbearing. The nickname of 'the Big Fellow' which began to be attached to him in this period was a reference to his swollen head rather than to his physical height. And Coogan has furnished a very shrewd analysis of Irish girls and their attitude towards such a man: 'In the battle of the sexes, the strong-minded Irish Catholic women have always displayed to a high degree the sexual combativeness of the peer group.'[24]

Coogan also deserves credit for discovering the love in Michael's life at this period. If Michael might be said to have had a steady girlfriend, it was Susan

Killeen from County Clare, who also worked in the Savings Department at West Kensington and shared lodgings with Nancy O'Brien in London and again later in Dublin. Michael probably saw her at the Savings Bank, but contact was developed through the Cumann na nGaedheal socials and dances. Following the outbreak of the First World War she returned to Ireland and worked in P.S. O'Hegarty's bookshop in Dawson Street, Dublin, and it was she who was lodging with Mrs Quick at Howth around the time of the *Asgard* incident. Susan and Michael were apparently very close while she was in London but after her return to Dublin the affair tapered off. She would upbraid him for not writing more frequently, and he, in turn, would profess: 'I really do hate letter-writing, and I'm not good at it and can't write down the things I want to say – however, don't think that because I don't write I forget.'[25] She would remain on friendly terms with him, although romantically as well as politically they were drifting apart.

In the same letter Michael admitted sombrely that 'London is a terrible place, worse than ever now – I'll never be happy until I'm out of it and then mightn't either'. This black mood was to some extent engendered by the usual squabbling that had broken out among the Irish community. Should the Irish Volunteers follow Captain Redmond's example and fight in Flanders? Many of them did, under the aegis of Redmond's renamed National Volunteers; but the rump remained true to their principles and held aloof. At a meeting in St George's Hall, Southwark, when a Redmond nominee was seeking election to office, he concluded his speech with the words describing John Redmond as 'a man I would go to hell and back with'. From the back of the hall came the voice of a heckler in the unmistakable accent of West Cork: 'I'd not trouble about the return portion of the ticket.'[26]

Although the principle of voluntary enlistment had not been abandoned, the Derby Scheme, launched in October 1915, aimed at calling up men as they were required, starting with single men. The response to this semi-voluntary scheme proved inadequate, so the government drafted remedial legislation. By the Military Service Act, due to take effect on 1 January 1916, full-blown conscription was introduced. Significantly, it was confined to men resident in Great Britain and did not apply in Ireland where the loyalty of so many young men was suspect. If Michael stayed in London he would be drafted into the British Army, which he saw as a betrayal of Ireland. Besides, he was beginning to hear rumours of renewed clandestine military activity in Ireland, and late in 1915 he went over to find out what was afoot. In Dublin he had a brief meeting with Sean MacDiarmada and Tom Clarke in the latter's tobacconist's shop in Great Britain Street near the Rotunda. The old dynamiter merely looked sharply at Michael over the top of his spectacles and told him to return to London and await further orders. Around Christmas he returned to England

and a few days after the Military Service Act came into force on New Year's Day he attended a Volunteer meeting which had been called to discuss the situation. Liam MacCarthy, a London county councillor, was in the chair and gave his audience the hint that it would be safer if they returned to their native hearth and home.

Michael's response was to give the Guaranty Trust Company a week's notice, saying that he would not wait for his call-up but intended to enlist right away. Touched by his obvious patriotism, Robert Mackey congratulated him and gave him an extra week's salary as a parting bonus, which Michael promptly donated to the IRB. On 14 January 1916 he terminated his employment, packed his bags, kissed Hannie goodbye and caught the train for Holyhead. The following day he set sail for Ireland.

CHAPTER 3

The Easter Rising, 1916

In ainm Dé, agus in ainm na nglún d'imigh romhainn . . .
(In the name of God and of the dead generations . . .)
OPENING LINE OF THE PROCLAMATION OF INDEPENDENCE

BACK IN DUBLIN, MICHAEL LOST NO TIME IN CONTACTING SEAN MacDiarmada again. Through him he obtained part-time employment, 'Working three days a week 10 to 4 as financial adviser to Count Plunkett for which I get lunch each day & £1 a week', as he wrote to Hannie at the end of January. In fact his job was more prosaic than he implied: when Countess Plunkett went to Europe her daughter Geraldine needed a reliable clerk to handle her mother's property accounts at Larkfield, the Plunkett residence at Kimmage, a penny tram-ride from the city centre. Miss Plunkett discovered that Michael, though new to the work, was a very quick learner, and she was impressed by his efficient, businesslike manner. What he might lack in the social graces he made up in his engaging boyishness. Her tubercular brother, Joseph, heavily embroiled in planning revolution, also recognised Michael's potential for espionage. Joe lent Michael a copy of Chesterton's novel, *The Man Who Was Thursday*, and particularly drew the budding revolutionary's attention to the precept of the President of the Central Council of European Anarchists that 'if you don't seem to be hiding nobody hunted you out'. It was a lesson Michael learned well, later raising unobtrusiveness to a high art.

In an adjoining field, George Noble, Count Plunkett, had thoughtfully provided tents where 'the refugees', young men who had fled from England to avoid conscription, camped out while waiting for the call to a duty more to their liking. Among them was Rory O'Connor, sensitive, cultured and a fine musician, a rather saturnine young man who had not come from London but had been working as a mining engineer in Canada and had returned to Ireland when he heard rumours of the imminent rising, and was employed at the Larkfield camp as chief instructor in bomb-making. During the Black and Tan War (1919–21) he would be Director of Engineering and a close colleague of

Michael; but close friendship would be cast aside in the civil war when O'Connor joined the anti-Treaty forces. In the early part of 1916, however, he was singularly impressed with Michael: 'There was no one at Kimmage to equal him.' Whenever Michael visited the camp at Larkfield, the refugees would josh him with cries of 'Who killed Mick Collins?'. Rising to the bait, he would sail into them, fists flailing, and there would be an almighty scrum as everyone piled on top of the Big Fellow. After the usual tussle they would be the best of friends again.

Michael did not share the rigours of an Irish winter under canvas, but lodged briefly with Sean Hurley at the farmhouse of a family friend named Belton in Inchicore before securing a room at 16 Rathdown Road. By February, when not advising Miss Plunkett, he was also working part-time for Craig Gardiner & Company, a firm of accountants in Dawson Street. Here he met two brothers and fellow clerks, Joe and George McGrath, with whom he struck up a friendship that endured to the end of his life – and even beyond, for Joe McGrath would become one of the staunchest and most generous upholders of his memory. To the McGrath brothers is due a characteristic anecdote of this period. One day, while engaged on an audit with a Loyalist Protestant firm, Michael had hot words with one of the clerks. The accountant in charge of the audit was alarmed when he looked out of his office and saw the young firebrand from Cork squaring up to fight. He called him over and remonstrated. An accountant should have no politics; he should do his job and avoid political discussions even when provocation was offered. Michael listened obediently, and then a smile broke over his face.

'As a matter of fact,' he said cheerfully, 'it wasn't about politics – only religion!'[1]

In his spare time he took up his studies of Irish once more, enrolling at classes in the Keating branch of the Gaelic League. Here he met several of the men who would later play a very big part in his life. There was Dick Mulcahy, nicknamed 'the tic-tac man' from his habit of making extravagant gestures with his fingers while speaking animatedly. A medical student at University College, he would abandon his vocation to become Chief of Staff of the Irish Republican Army, and would eventually follow Collins as Commander-in-Chief of the National Army. Then there was Gearoid (Gerald) O'Sullivan, Michael's cousin and a fellow Corkman who would become Adjutant General of the IRA. Charles Burgess, small, dapper and stiff as a ramrod, the son of a Yorkshireman and an Irish mother but born in County Carlow and preferring to be known by his Gaelic name of Cathal Brugha, was aptly described by Mulcahy as 'brave and brainless as a bull'. In the cabinet of the Provisional Government he would be Minister of Defence, and thus nominally Michael's boss in his role as Director of Intelligence; but Michael would also be Minister of Finance, a position which (in his eyes at least) was superior to Defence. Therein lay the key to the clash of personalities which grew into a mutual antipathy so ferocious that it was one of the factors leading to the civil war.

As April drew on and plans for the rising were finalised, Michael worked very closely with Sean MacDiarmada. Nancy O'Brien met them both during Easter Week. Over tea and buns in a Dublin café, the two men openly discussed details of the insurrection in front of her. That Saturday, Michael ran into Nancy again and they talked briefly in Sackville Street before taking a fond farewell on the bridge. She had originally planned to go home to Sam's Cross for Easter, but her transfer to the General Post Office in Dublin had come through and she was due to report there for duty on the following Tuesday. Michael quipped that she might have rather a long wait. This thought was uppermost in her mind the following week when she watched the progress of the insurrection from a safe vantage-point on Howth Head and felt anguish and despair as she saw the General Post Office go up in flames. Other friends and acquaintances who met Michael over that fateful weekend say that he was 'jocular and fooling about as usual'.[2]

His true state of mind must have been very different. Already key elements in the plan were going fatally wrong; the Rising was doomed to failure from the outset. A great deal depended on outside aid and to this end John Devoy, leader of the Fenian Brotherhood in New York, was asked to contact the German government and take them up on their promise (made early in 1915) to supply arms and men. As regards the latter, Sir Roger Casement, recently retired from the British Consular Service after a distinguished career in Africa and Latin America, was already in Germany where he had been trying to raise an Irish brigade from among the prisoners-of-war in German camps, but he gave up the attempt when only a handful of men volunteered. When the Germans refused to send a cadre of officers to train the Volunteers, a bitterly disillusioned Casement returned to Ireland with the intention of urging the military council to call the whole thing off. Ironically, he was arrested as he stepped ashore from a German submarine at Banna Strand, County Kerry, and would subsequently be tried and convicted of high treason in London. Not content with hanging him, the British government did their best to assassinate his character by circulating forged documents purporting to be part of his personal diaries.

To be sure, the Germans did despatch a substantial quantity of weapons – 20,000 rifles, ten machine-guns, a million rounds of ammunition and some explosives – on board an elderly freighter called the *Aud* which sailed from Lübeck, bound for the Kerry coast. Unfortunately, the military council changed the plans for the landing of the arms, putting back the rendezvous by twenty-four hours. Ironically, in view of Michael's elaborate but ill-fated plans to steal wireless equipment, the *Aud* was not equipped with radio, so the skipper kept the original appointment, and was promptly seized by the Royal Navy. Naval Intelligence had intercepted and decoded a signal from Devoy to Padraig Pearse, so the British were better informed than the *Aud*, which steamed straight into a trap. Escorted by British warships, she was heading for the naval base at Queenstown (Cobh) when her skipper succeeded in scuttling her in the approaches to the harbour.

On Good Friday Michael had met Colm O'Lochlainn and a squad of four men – Con Keating, Charlie Monaghan, Donal Sheehan and Denis Healy – on Aston's Quay, handed them train tickets to Kerry, and took Colm's bicycle (which ended up on one of the barricades on the Abbey Street corner a few days later). Unaware that the *Aud* had no wireless, Michael had devised a plan whereby Colm's sqaud were to steal radio equipment at Cahirciveen in order to contact the *Aud*. They had taken the train to Killarney, where they were met at 7.15 p.m. by Tom McInerney and Sam Windrum driving two cars. They got in and drove off, but in the dark on the twisting road they became separated. Not only did they fail to rendezvous with the ship, but McInerney's car with Keating, Sheehan and Monaghan on board, accidentally drove off the end of the pier at Ballykissane and the three Dubliners were drowned. Keating was the only man who knew how to operate radio equipment, and with his death the project to contact the *Aud* had to be aborted anyway.

Earlier that fateful day, Maurice 'Moss' Moriarty, car-hirer of Tralee, picked up Austin Stack, a solicitor's clerk who was also commandant of the Kerry Brigade, and drove him northwards. A little way out of the town, they were flagged down by two men whom Stack recognised. Together they drove on through Ardfert and Banna Strand to Ballyheige where they stooged around for some time, becoming increasingly agitated. Having failed to sight the *Aud* they drove back to Tralee, but on the way they were stopped by a police patrol. The two strangers then identified themselves as 'Michael Collins, Accountant, General Post Office, Dublin' and 'David Mulcahy of 44 Mountjoy Street, Dublin'. The man posing as Mulcahy was, in fact, Sir Roger Casement's co-conspirator Dan Bailey, a member of the Irish Brigade recruited from Irish prisoners-of-war in Germany, but the address he gave was of a house where Michael and other Sinn Fein leaders often stayed. The man who gave his name as Michael Collins was, in fact, Con Collins (no relation). Back in Tralee they went to the home of a Mrs Slattery in Rock Street before splitting up. All three, along with Roger Casement himself, were arrested shortly afterwards.[3]

Meanwhile, back in Dublin, the real Michael Collins booked a room at the Metropole Hotel in Sackville Street, across the roadway from the façade of the General Post Office, and spent a tense Sunday night with his tubercular friend

Joe Plunkett. In particular he brooded over the death of Con Keating, one of the London Irishmen whom he had known intimately for several years.

Easter was very late that year. Monday, 24 April 1916, was a mild sunny day in Dublin, which was virtually deserted, huge crowds (including most of the officers and men from the British garrison) making their way out of the city in the early morning to the Fairyhouse racecourse for the first big meeting of the season. Apart from a few bystanders, the only people who were to be seen in the city streets were members of the Irish Volunteers and the Citizen Army. Of late, men in the makeshift uniforms of these paramilitary organisations had begun drilling more openly, and such a spectacle was commonplace.

Dublin was quiet nonetheless on this Easter Monday morning. Although it was a public holiday, many civil servants were on duty. The General Post Office, a handsome building in the neo-classical style, was open for business as usual. Hamilton Norway, the Secretary of the Post Office, was at his desk in the spacious office which he occupied on the first floor.[4] At 11 a.m. he received a telephone call from Dublin Castle, the Viceroy's headquarters and seat of government, requesting his presence at an urgent meeting. He set off immediately and was soon in conference with Sir Matthew Nathan, the Permanent Under-Secretary, and Major Ivor Price, the Military Intelligence Officer. Price had got wind that something was afoot and suggested to Nathan that a pre-emptive round-up of known subversives would defuse the situation. Nathan (who, until recently, had been Secretary of the Post Office in London) appreciated better than most the importance of a clampdown on postal, telegraphic and telephonic communications as part of the action, and had summoned his erstwhile colleague Norway to the Castle to ensure the secrecy of the proposed operation. Apart from these three, and a few orderlies and unarmed constables, the Castle was deserted and virtually undefended. The men planning the wholesale deportation of Sinn Fein leaders were blissfully unaware that, at that very moment, the Castle was under attack, but a squad of Volunteers (consisting of nine men, two girls and a Fianna boy), who marched up to the gate, contented themselves with shooting Constable James O'Brien (the first casualty of the Rising) and disarming the sentry before swiftly withdrawing, little realising that, with a little audacity, the Castle could have been theirs for the taking.

This half-hearted, half-cock assault on the bastion of British Imperial might is oddly symbolic of the Easter Rising as a whole, an event in which high drama and noble deeds were mingled with indecision, pure farce and division.

Sir Matthew Nathan had every right to be apprehensive. In January the Supreme Council of the IRB had taken the momentous decision to stage an uprising on 23 April, Easter Sunday, and formed a military council to organise the logistics and strategy. Chief among the plotters were Patrick Henry (Padraig) Pearse, son of an English father and an Irish mother. Born in 1879, he was a notable Gaelic scholar and poet who dedicated himself to the ideal of an independent Irish-speaking nation; his speeches and writings played an important part in the revival of the national spirit. He founded St Enda's (boys) and St Ita's (girls) schools at Rathfarnham. In the insurrection he was designated as President of the Provisional Government of the Irish Republic and Commander-in-Chief. The visionary and the poet in him is evident in the wording of the Proclamation of Independence.[5]

The first signature on this historic document was that of Thomas J. Clarke, given pride of place as the elder statesman of the independence movement. Born in 1858, the very year in which the IRB itself was founded, he had been a member since the momentous year of 1867, the last attempt at insurrection in Ireland. Given a life sentence of penal servitude for his part in the terror campaign of the early 1880s, he was released from prison in 1898, emigrated to America and returned to Ireland in 1907. From his little tobacconist's shop on the corner of Great Britain Street at the top of Sackville (now O'Connell) Street, he and his 'young squirts' reorganised the IRB and put new life in the movement.

The next signatory was John MacDermott, better known to posterity by his Gaelic name of Sean MacDiarmada. Born in 1884, he was a barman-turned-journalist and professional revolutionary, actually employed full time by the IRB at a salary of thirty shillings a week to travel the country and organise the Uprising. Though stricken by polio in 1912 he made a good recovery but thereafter walked with a heavy limp. Thomas MacDonagh, born in 1878, was a poet, dramatist and critic, a co-founder (with his brother-in-law, Joseph Plunkett) of the Irish Theatre, a brilliant classical scholar and a lecturer in English literature at the National University. He was a close friend of Pearse, whom he assisted at St Enda's, and was Director of Training in the Volunteers. His wife was the sister of Grace Gifford, fiancée of Joseph Plunkett, the youngest signatory. Born in 1887, the son of a Papal count, Joseph too was a poet of distinction and editor of *The Irish Review*. He was a founder member of the Volunteers and the military plans for the Rising are believed to have been largely his work. Shortly before Easter Week he had had an operation for glandular tuberculosis, but he left his sick bed to take part in the fighting. Barely able to stand, he was literally supported for much of the time by Michael Collins.

Edward Kent, better known as Eamonn Ceannt, was born in 1881. His involvement with the Gaelic League, founded in 1893, brought him into close contact with Pearse. One of the earliest Volunteers, he worked closely with Plunkett on the military plans.

One signature that was conspicuous by its absence from the Proclamation was that of Professor Eoin MacNeill. Because the founder of the Volunteers saw the force as purely defensive, he was deliberately excluded from the planning. When he finally discovered that the manoeuvres scheduled for the Easter weekend were merely a cover for an all-out insurrection he did his best to countermand the orders, even going so far as to place an advertisement in *The Sunday Independent* which stated firmly: 'No parades, marches or other movements of Irish Volunteers are to take place'. This only caused confusion in the ranks; what had been carefully planned as a co-ordinated rising all over Ireland was reduced, in the end, to an outbreak in the heart of Dublin. Even this was not a coup in the classic sense, with a synchronised seizure of such key points as the railway, police and power stations, the Castle and the military barracks, but rather a revolt for revolt's sake, 'a blood sacrifice to the gods of Irish nationalism'.[6]

MacNeill was not the only senior figure from whom the plans were concealed. In contrast with the middle-class poets and visionaries (or dreamers) who dominated the Volunteers, James Connolly, leader of the Transport and General Workers Union and an avowed Marxist, was a potential threat. His Citizen Army, relatively well armed since the lock-out of 1913, had been threatening to take unilateral action, and the IRB were afraid that he might foil their own plans by premature action. Consequently, in January, Connolly was kidnapped and spirited away to a secret three-day meeting with Pearse, the result being that he was co-opted into the leadership of the rebellion. Connolly, born at Edinburgh in 1868, was second to Clarke in age but took one of the leading parts in the revolt.

Thus it was that, on St Patrick's Day, 17 March 1916, the troops of the Irish Volunteers and the Citizen Army paraded together for the first time. This was, in fact, a dress-rehearsal for the events of Easter Monday. Shortly before noon on 24 April, Connolly, Pearse and Plunkett emerged from Liberty Hall, the TGWU headquarters, and led off a body of about sixty irregulars of both formations (now welded together to form the Army of the Irish Republic). They were dressed, for the most part, in a motley assortment of military cast-offs which had been procured for them by Dr Thomas Dillon. This company, including the London Irish contingent from Kimmage, were lining up outside Liberty Hall when who should appear but their old chum Mick Collins, resplendent as a staff-captain in khaki service dress, gleaming Sam Browne belt and peaked cap, one of the few officers who really looked the part. 'The temptation was too great. They began to make fun of him. Collins went white and clenched his fists.'[7]

The ragged column passed down Sackville Street, trundling a hand-cart containing their rifles, shotguns and revolvers, and halted outside the General

Post Office. James Connolly, now designated as Commandant-General of the Irish Republican Army, gave the order to charge. The men picked up their weapons and clattered up the steps into the building, swiftly disarming the constable of the Dublin Metropolitan Police on duty, and summarily ejected the counter clerks and their customers. The windows on the ground floor were smashed and hastily barricaded, and sentries posted. At the rear of the building the Telegraph Instrument Room contained its normal complement of female telegraphists under the supervision of Miss Gordon, the Assistant Superintendent. A sergeant and three privates were also on duty; troops had been posted to guard the Instrument Room since the outbreak of the First World War, but only a few weeks before Easter 1916 their ammunition was suddenly withdrawn, so that on that fateful morning they were virtually unarmed. When they heard shots being fired at the front of the building they barricaded the door in the corridor connecting the public office with the Instrument Room, but by this time the insurgents had entered by the back door and sprung into the room. This party was led by The O'Rahilly, who shot the sergeant when he made to resist. The O'Rahilly was one of the more quixotic figures of the Rising; he had been despatched by a horrified MacNeill to stop the insurrection but at the last moment had decided to throw in his lot with the rebels.

Shortly after midday the seizure of the General Post Office was complete with scarcely any bloodshed. Much confusion exists as to the details, and the various versions published conflict with official reports (often themselves contradictory) and eye-witness accounts. Some say that the green, white and gold tricolour was flown from the pole on the roof of the Post Office; others say that a green flag, inscribed 'Irish Republic' in gold letters, and the Plough and Stars banner of the Citizen Army were flown instead. Consensus of opinion, backed by the most informative sources, now opts for the first version. The task of hoisting the tricolour from the flagpole was given to the youngest officer present, Michael's cousin, Gearoid O'Sullivan.

Some policemen were helpless bystanders, but a troop of lancers, escorting an ammunition waggon, came clattering down Sackville Street. The insurgents opened fire, killing one and wounding two others. The lancers withdrew in some confusion, but managed to drag the ammunition waggon away with them. By now quite a crowd had gathered at a safe distance to watch and wait for the arrival of the police and troops. A boy with a handful of broadsheets came out of the Post Office and distributed them to the crowd. Pearse himself came out on to the steps and read the Proclamation in a voice shaking with emotion.

'Irishmen and Irishwomen,' he began, 'in the name of God and of the dead generations from which she receives her old traditions of nationhood, Ireland, through us, summons her children to her flag and strikes for her freedom . . .'

Michael, his jaw thrust forward resolutely, stood immediately behind Pearse on the steps of the General Post Office and scanned the street carefully while his Commander-in Chief read the Proclamation to the end, a process which took several minutes. There was no reaction from the crowd, neither boos nor applause, while the document was read. At the conclusion, a party of Volunteers emerged from the building and began pasting up copies of the Proclamation on the walls and pillars. Joseph Plunkett read out the document beside Nelson's Pillar nearby and an attempt was then made to blow up this symbol of English domination. Three charges of explosive failed to budge it from its plinth, and it remained a prominent landmark in O'Connell Street for a further fifty years. Shortly before the jubilee of the Rising was to be celebrated, the monument was successfully demolished by 'person or persons unknown'.

The rest of Easter Monday was spent by the insurgents in reinforcing their garrison in the Post Office, bringing in lorry-loads of men, provisions, arms and ammunition. The windows and parapets were sandbagged, snipers were posted and coils of barbed wire were strung across the street outside. Michael himself carried out an intensive search of the building, checking provisions and stores that might prove useful during the expected siege. When he chanced upon two tierces of porter he had the alcohol tipped down the canteen drain. 'They said we were drunk in Ninety-Eight,' he commented. 'They won't be able to say it now.'[8] Then he helped to tie up a British officer, Lieutenant A.D. Chalmers of the 14th Royal Fusiliers, who had breezed into the main hall of the Post Office to buy a penny stamp for a letter home and now found himself a prisoner-of-war.

'Don't worry,' Michael reassured the terrified officer as he bundled him into a telephone kiosk. 'We don't shoot prisoners.' Chalmers remained in captivity until Friday when he was given the choice of being shot immediately or running the gauntlet of soldiers' fire to draw it off the escaping rebels. It was an offer he could not refuse.

The Metropole, where Michael and Joe Plunkett had spent the previous night, was commandeered and its food supply seized (on nominal payment of a ten-pound note). The rebel leaders were beginning to act in characteristic manner. While Connolly, brisk and businesslike as ever, bagged an office, installed a typist and coped with the logistical problems, old Tom Clarke, harassed and excited, berated everyone and anyone for the mistakes that were being made. Meanwhile, Pearse, the President of the Provisional Government, was overwhelmed by a deep depression which he could not shake off. Having spoken to the people, as he put it, he had nothing meaningful to contribute, so he slouched in a corner. The O'Rahilly, scion of an ancient Irish family and bearer of an anachronistic title, was regarded as a bit of a buffoon. Now he was to play the role of a grotesque court jester to his melancholic President.

Elsewhere in the city the insurgents had concentrated on points of logistical rather than strategic value – Boland's Bakery, the Guinness Brewery in Marrowbone Lane and Jacob's Biscuit Factory. St Stephen's Green was also occupied and trenches dug on its perimeter but, when the counter-attack came, it proved to be a death-trap, indefensible against gunfire from the surrounding high buildings, in particular the Shelbourne Hotel. The rebels failed to appreciate the military importance of Trinity College, which was built like a fortress, and made no attempt to seize it, although it was held by only a handful of cadets from the University Officers' Training Corps.

The seizure of the General Post Office and Telegraph Exchange, on the other hand, was a master stroke. The insurgents cut most of the cables and telephone lines leading into Dublin and all communications with the outside world were severed by 12.45 p.m. News of the rebellion reached Holyhead telegraph office at 2.30 p.m. and London shortly afterwards. The War Office and Admiralty were informed but were powerless on this public holiday to do much. The rebels failed to seize the main Parcels Office in Amiens Street near the terminus of the Belfast railway line, though, and this was to serve as the spearhead of the counter-attack. S.S. Guthrie, the Superintending Engineer of the Post Office, sent an expert telegraphist to Bray in an attempt to pick up the telephone wire to the Castle. His car was fired on several times and it took eight hours to complete the short journey out to Bray. Sporadic firing near the centre of Dublin broke out in the evening and gunfire continued till about 2.30 a.m. on Tuesday morning. At 1.15 a.m. Guthrie located the break in the cable and managed to repair the thirty-six wires which had been cut. By dawn Amiens Street was in telephone contact with the Castle and the naval base at Kingstown (Dún Laoghaire).

During the night the government forces were galvanised into action. Colonel Cowan, Acting Military Governor of Dublin, brought in 800 infantry from the Curragh and 150 troops from Belfast in the early hours of Tuesday morning; twenty-four hours after the Rising began he had some 3,500 troops and the Admiralty gunboat *Helga* poised for action against the 1,200 insurgents. On the postal side, services were, not surprisingly, disrupted completely. Hamilton Norway managed to get through the cordon of insurgents round the Castle in the evening of Easter Monday and reached his home about midnight. The following day Norway and his Chief Clerk, J.J. Coonan, set up temporary headquarters in the Royal Hibernian Hotel in Dawson Street. For the first time in recorded history the Irish Packet was suspended and no mails went in or out of Holyhead and Fishguard. When the service was resumed a week later, rigorous censorship was applied to all mail emanating from southern Ireland.

By Monday night the insurgents were entrenched in a few strongpoints: Commandant Michael Mallin and his second-in-command, the Countess Markievicz (née Constance Gore-Booth), at St Stephen's Green and the College of Surgeons; Tom Clarke and Sean MacDiarmada in the Moore Street area; Eamonn Ceannt and Thomas MacDonagh at the South Dublin Union and the Guinness buildings in Marrowbone Lane; and a young mathematics teacher named Eamon de Valera held Boland's Mill. Born in New York in 1882 of a Cuban father and an Irish mother, he was committed at the age of two to the care of his grandmother in Limerick. Educated at Blackrock and the Royal University, he became a fervent Nationalist.

At Connolly's instigation, the men in the General Post Office began tunnelling through the labyrinthine basement on Monday night in order to secure an escape route through the cellars into the adjoining buildings in Moore Street at the rear in case the Rising failed. Meanwhile, an enormous crowd had gathered in Sackville Street to watch the fun. The mood of the mob ranged from the derisive to the downright hostile. In particular, the insurgents came in for some very salty invective from the women in receipt of separation money (in respect of husbands and sons in the British forces) who felt that these 'bluidy pro-Germans' would, by their actions, lead to this income being cut off. Then somebody kicked in the window of a confectioner's shop and pilfering of sweets and chocolates rapidly escalated into wholesale destruction of premises and looting on a grand scale, Clery's department store being a particular target. The first conflagration in Sackville Street, late that night, came from one of the shops across the way from the Post Office, which looters put to the torch.

On Tuesday morning a squabble broke out in the GPO between the London Irish and Desmond Fitzgerald, in charge of the commissary, who was refusing them rations because they did not have the requisite documentation. Desmond (who would later become Michael's Director of Propaganda) recalled what happened:

> Michael Collins . . . strode in one morning with some of his men who were covered with dust and had been demolishing walls and building barricades, and announced that these men were to be fed if it took the last food in the place. I did not attempt to argue with him, and the men sat down openly rejoicing that I had been crushed . . . But while they were eating, those of our most regular and assiduous customers who appeared at the door of the room were told to disappear or they would be dealt with.[9]

Fitzgerald added that Michael was the most efficient officer in the whole building. He alone, it appears, had the good sense to compile a list of the names and addresses of the Volunteers under siege in the Post Office – in case it would be necessary, later on, to identify casualties.

As it turned out, this was a wise precaution. At 5 a.m. on Wednesday, the *Helga* nosed her way up the Liffey and began the counter-attack by bombarding Liberty Hall, which was reduced to rubble in four hours. This onslaught was the signal for a ferocious assault on all the rebel-held strongpoints. Machine-gunfire from the upper floors of buildings nearby raked St Stephen's Green continuously and it was here that the insurgents sustained their heaviest casualties. Terrible street fighting continued all through Wednesday, Thursday and Friday, but the position of the rebels rapidly deteriorated as more and more troops, together with artillery, were drafted in from England. Two brigades of infantry, assisted by batteries of eighteen-pounder field-guns, were landed on Thursday and speedily thrown into action. By Friday General Sir John Maxwell (hurriedly appointed Commander-in-Chief, Ireland, earlier in the week) had 30,000 troops in the inner Dublin area pitted against the 1,200 rebels. The ring of steel gradually grew tighter and tighter around the Post Office, the heart of the rebel position.

During this terrible week Michael frequently showed himself resourceful and resolute under fire. His courage was cold and calculating rather than reckless, but he had a calming effect on his comrades and an inner strength that communicated itself to them. His cheerful good humour never once deserted him and even when the carnage and destruction seemed appalling he could joke with a comrade, 'Don't worry, ye old cod, we'll rebuild it, and the whole city, in ten years – if necessary.' After one particularly ferocious fusillade he and Gearoid O'Sullivan went up to the melancholic Pearse and asked if he would mind them popping out for a bit. They had a date with a couple of girls and didn't want to stand them up! Whether that was true or not, it was a good story. A month later Michael himself left a more matter-of-fact account of this terrible time:

> Although I was never actually scared in the GPO I was – and others also – witless enough to do the most stupid things. As the flames and heat increased so apparently did the shelling. Machine-gunfire made escape more and more impossible. Not that we wished to escape. No man wished to budge. In that building, the defiance of our men, and the gallantry, reached unimaginable proportions.[10]

The British forces did not have it all their own way by any means. At Mount Street Bridge they ran into heavy fire from De Valera's men and sustained the heaviest casualties of the Rising. But in and around the Post Office the situation was looking desperate. Connolly had gone out to reconnoitre and took a bullet in his thigh. Pearse rallied himself, and made another of his rambling speeches, starting on a high note but rapidly descending into maudlin despondency. He clutched at the straw of a German landing and even sent men precariously out on to the roof to keep an ear out for the sound of German gunfire from the coast. Michael grimly noted the men wearing rosary beads and scapulars round their necks, but even this was a consolation he could not share. 'I'm the only man in the whole place that wasn't at Confession and Communion,' he later admitted. Pearse, overwhelmed with the enormity of the deeds he had unleashed, mooned about disconsolately. But there was an other-worldly, almost saintlike quality about him, too. He spent precious hours, when he should have been snatching sleep, comforting a young British soldier who had been grievously wounded.

From all sides shells rained down on the once-proud building and the end was inevitable. The Post Office, with its maze of basement corridors and stout walls, was well constructed to withstand bombardment and at one stage the military considered using poison gas to eliminate the rebel stronghold. Happily, this idea was rejected, but a combination of high-explosive and incendiary shells turned Sackville Street and Lower Abbey Street into a raging inferno in which it seemed that no one and nothing could survive. The rearguard, led heroically by The O'Rahilly, was mown down by machine-guns in the closing encounter, and this relic of an old Irish aristocracy was virtually cut in half by the murderous enfilade. Under cover of the blaze, the troops closed in, but it was not till Saturday morning that the final shelling and the capture of the General Post Office took place.

The majority of the defenders had, during Friday night, succeeded in tunnelling their way out of the burning building, through to the shops lining Henry Street. Here, a desperate charge was needed to cross the street under fire. The men crouched against the wall, petrified, while Connolly from his stretcher raved at them and urged them forward. Michael emerged, pistols in both hands. Returning the enemy's fire, he shouted encouragement to the others and, half-crouching, sprinted across the street with the others at his heels. Along with Pearse, Connolly and a few others, he escaped under the noses of the besiegers and took refuge in a nearby grocer's shop. Cold and wet, they spent a miserable night, mitigated only by a bottle of whiskey which Michael miraculously produced. He and his friends, Fionan Lynch and Jim Ryan, smoke-begrimed and in a very sombre mood, shared the bottle, sure that this would be their last. Desmond Ryan left a graphic picture of this desperate scene of which he was an eye-witness:

Michael Collins sat in a corner, a look of horror in his eyes, a pallor spreading over his face. Disjointed words told Harding that O'Rahilly's eviscerated corpse and the riddled civilians on the blood-clogged cobbles had come to life in one man's imagination, straining his control to breaking point. Moans escaped him and he huddled into his corner at every far-away sound. Macken went swiftly to Michael Collins and spoke to him in cheerful undertones . . . Collins looked up, and back, stoical and impassive, with the rest of the doomed Volunteers, waiting for the end.[11]

Michael's dejection was brought on by the knowledge that his beloved cousin, Sean Hurley, had been killed only minutes earlier in one of the last desperate hand-to-hand encounters as the remnant of the insurgents tried to break out. Just what this loss must have meant to Michael can be gauged by the feelings about Sean expressed in a letter to a friend some time previously:

He has the sharpness of wit to see my own particular mood. We think the same way in Irish matters. We have walked London's streets on many a night, silently, because our thinking was elsewhere . . . I appreciate him because his mind seems compact whereas mine fritters away hours in idle thought. At worst he is a boon companion, at best there is no one else I would have as a friend.[12]

At 3.30 p.m. on Saturday, Padraig Pearse surrendered his sword to Brigadier-General W.N.C. Lowe, who treated him with great courtesy. One by one the others emerged from their last refuge and laid down their weapons. Michael looked up with a toss of his head at the smoking shell of the Post Office and smiled crookedly. 'The flag is still flying, anyway.'

With Pearse's party were several Red Cross nurses and women of Cumann na mBan who had shared the rigours of the siege no less than the men. One of them, Elizabeth O'Farrell, had the dangerous mission of taking Pearse's surrender order to the commandants still holding out in other parts of the city. From the British viewpoint, the heroines of the Rising were the twenty female telephonists who were besieged in the Central Telephone Exchange in Crown Alley for five days and nights and endured great discomfort, not to mention danger, from rebel bullets, in order to keep essential telephone links going. The failure of the insurgents to seize this building cost them dear, for it provided the military with their one remaining link with the rest of the country and the outside world. When it was all over, a grateful government paid the girls fifteen shillings overtime – less the cost of their food and the hire of the mattresses on which they had slept in the Exchange.[13]

After the surrender of the Post Office came the clearing up. The intense heat in the final blaze reduced everything combustible to a fine white ash – records, stamp stocks, postal and money orders, stationery and cash – yet miraculously

£185 was found among the debris and one of the rebel prisoners had £149 10s which was promptly confiscated. Hamilton Norway commandeered an armoured car, made by Guinness Brewery out of a lorry chassis and an engine-boiler, to get about the city for even after the surrender occasional snipers continued to take pot-shots at the soldiery. His seventeen-year-old son Nevil, on holiday from his school in Shrewsbury, served with a Red Cross ambulance during that fateful week, and acted with distinction and great bravery under fire. As Nevil Shute he was later to acquire an even greater distinction as an aircraft designer and novelist.

Pearse's last act as head of the Provisional Government was to issue the order to the commandants of the various battalions around the city to cease fighting and lay down their arms. Surrender notes were also written by MacDonagh and Connolly. The Third Battalion, under de Valera, was the last to comply, a fact which was to enhance his reputation in the years to come. In Sackville Street, at the very centre of the fighting, the scene was nightmarish; horribly mutilated corpses littered the rubble-strewn street lit by the fires that raged unchecked. It was not until the following day that the Dublin fire brigade could get to grips with the holocaust. Those who surrendered were lined up and marched off between lines of steel-helmeted troops, bayonets fixed. Michael, his beautiful new uniform grimy and badly scorched by the flames, noted ruefully the slight, white-haired figure of old Tom Clarke, still defiant and holding himself erect as he passed his little shop where, only a week ago, he had been selling Woodbines to the soldiers who were now guarding him. MacDiarmada, limping badly from the polio, aggravated by lack of sleep, leaned heavily on a stick, as did Joe Plunkett, coughing ominously. At the top of Sackville Street, they were halted near the Rotunda Hospital. The courtesy shown by Brigadier-General Lowe was not emulated by his subordinates. Now that the insurgents had been disarmed they were at the mercy of their captors, drawn from one of the regiments drafted in from Belfast. One particular tormentor was Captain Lee Wilson of the Royal Irish Rifles who stood out because he was improperly dressed, sporting a brocade smoking-cap with a long silken tassel instead of the regulation peaked cap or steel helmet. Brutalised perhaps by service on the Western Front, he behaved in an abominable manner, cursing and mocking the prisoners, striking them with his swagger cane or kicking them unmercifully. Seeing some nurses at the windows of the hospital, this sadistic brute selected several prisoners, one at a time, whom he ordered his troops to strip naked. Sean MacDiarmada and Ned Daly (Tom Clarke's brother-in-law) were among those selected by Captain Wilson who then wreaked his own particular perversions on them, heedless of the icy rain now falling, crushing testicles with fiendish delight. One of the men chosen for the Wilson treatment was Tom

Clarke, probably on account of his age. The officer, now half-mad with rage, screamed at the old man and ripped the clothes off him himself. So violently was this undressing performed that an old wound from the Fenian days of more than thirty years previously was reopened. This was too much for Michael who dashed forward to protest at this torture, but Wilson paused only long enough to give the protester a savage kicking. Michael never minded that beating, vicious though it was, but what he could never forget was the sadistic treatment of Tom Clarke. Five years later, Wilson, by now a District Inspector in the Royal Irish Constabulary, was gunned down on Michael's express orders, his bullet-ridden corpse dumped by the roadside in a remote part of County Wexford.

It was a cold night, exacerbated by great cruelty. The prisoners were made to stand in the open, while a heartless rain drenched and chilled them to the bone. They were forced to relieve themselves where they stood. In vain they huddled together for warmth; the Tommies guarding them prodded them with their bayonets and forced them to stand apart. Those who collapsed from fatigue or their wounds were violently forced to their feet. Michael got a second kicking that night, from a burly sergeant this time, when he tried to pass a malted milk tablet to one of his stricken comrades. Conditions improved remarkably when the Royal Irish Rifles stood down and handed over their charges to an Australian regiment for the remainder of the night. Many of the Aussies were of Irish descent, perhaps even numbering among their ancestors some of the rebels of Ninety-Eight and later insurrections who had been transported. Now mugs of tea materialised, and cigarettes and bars of chocolate were surreptitiously passed to the bedraggled prisoners. At this manifestation of common decency many of the prisoners, who had taken their beatings and insults impassively, broke down and wept openly.

Demoralised by their night in the open air, the prisoners were eventually marched through the war-torn streets in the grey dawn light to Richmond Barracks in Inchicore, where the detectives of G (Political) Division of the Dublin Metropolitan Police were waiting to interrogate them. The prisoners were herded into one end of the barracks gymnasium and kept standing for hours while they were scrutinised, one by one, by the G men. Those whom they recognised as ringleaders were segregated from the common herd; they would be subject to a rudimentary court-martial before facing a firing-squad. Michael was one of those selected, although he was not on the wanted list. The reason for his selection may have been simply that he was too smartly dressed; the sight of him in his officer's tunic may have been like a red rag to a bull. On the other hand, the selection may have been carried out in a random, haphazard manner, for Michael himself rectified the situation by the simple expedient of merely sidling back to the other side of the gym when the guards were not looking. Frank Kelly, who was among the prisoners, later stated that someone on his side of the room called out Michael's name several times; and out of curiosity the Big Fellow casually strolled across to see who was calling him.[14] Whatever the circumstances, the carelessness of the police and military let slip the man who would become their most formidable enemy.

Other prisoners were not so fortunate. The converse happened to Sean MacDiarmada who, having evaded detection during this initial screening process, was about to board the ship taking the ordinary prisoners off to England, when he was spotted by an alert detective named Daniel Hoey and pulled out of the crowd to join the other ringleaders earmarked for special treatment. Michael was standing right beside him when this happened, and his heart missed a beat when he saw his IRB chief hauled away. With 238 other prisoners, Michael was marched to the docks on the afternoon of 30 April. As they stood in line, waiting to go up the gangplank, they were furtively approached by one of the detectives who asked them, under his breath, if there was anything he could do for them, any messages he could take for them. Not surprisingly, the prisoners were extremely suspicious, thinking it some sort of trick. Michael was unaware at this time of the terrible conflict of loyalties and the anguish of some of the police, torn between their oath to maintain law and order and pity for their unfortunate countrymen. The detective was Joe Kavanagh who, in years to come, would be one of Michael's most valuable moles within the police establishment.

The following morning the prisoners disembarked at Holyhead and immediately entrained for the military detention barracks at Stafford. They were joined by another 203 men a week later, and a further 58 on 13 May.[15] Michael was now 'Irish Prisoner 48F', an appellation that caused him wry amusement. 'Is one expected to lose one's identity, one's humanity, to become instead a numbered nonentity?' he asked rhetorically.[16] The detention barracks, where generations of defaulters, deserters and military criminals had been confined, was a dismal Victorian gaol, with cells, landings and wings like any other prison. The food was deplorable, the conditions rigorous and the monotony almost unbearable; but at least, while there was life, there was hope.

Officially the Rising ended on the afternoon of 29 April. Four days later the first executions took place in the high-walled stonebreakers' yard at Kilmainham Gaol, Pearse, Clarke and MacDonagh being the first to face the firing squad. Eamonn Ceannt was shot on 8 May and Connolly was executed on 12 May. His shattered leg had become gangrenous and he was taken on a stretcher to the execution yard and then roughly lifted into a chair to face the fusillade. Serious illness was no mitigating factor. Sean MacDiarmada, who had almost got away with the other prisoners, was one of the last to be executed, being shot on the same day as Connolly. The most bizarre incident concerned Joseph Plunkett. At 1.30 a.m. on the morning of 4 May he was married to his fiancée, Grace Gifford, in the chapel of Kilmainham Gaol and exactly ten minutes later he was led out to be executed. Several weeks after the Rising, Sir Roger Casement was brought to trial before the Lord Chief Justice in England on charges of high treason. He was sentenced to death on 29 June and executed by hanging at Pentonville on 3 August, the tragic end to a man who had spent a lifetime in the British Consular Service and been knighted in 1911. Before his execution he was stripped of his knighthood. For almost half a century his remains lay buried in Pentonville, despite the entreaties of successive Irish governments to have them brought back to Ireland. In 1965, on the eve of the fiftieth anniversary of the Rising, the British authorities relented and Casement was duly interred with full military honours in Glasnevin Cemetery, alongside many other heroes of those troubled years.

Sixty-two insurgents were killed during the Rising, and sixteen were executed in the aftermath. No fewer than 256 civilians were killed, including six men shot by Captain Bowen-Colthurst in a frenzy; one of the captain's victims was the pacifist Francis Sheehy-Skeffington, a harmless old buffer who just happened to be in the wrong place at the wrong time. The slaughter of Sheehy-Skeffington, Thomas Dickson and Patrick MacIntyre, among others, at the hands of this officer excited more horror than the general carnage of that terrible week. Similarly, the summary court-martial and execution of the ringleaders, the horrific circumstances in which Joe Plunkett was married and James Connolly shot, revolted the public on both sides of the Irish Sea, and severely damaged Britain's reputation for fair play all round the world. By contrast, Bowen-Colthurst was acquitted at his court-martial, his plea of temporary insanity being readily accepted. In particular, the execution of Padraig's brother, Willie Pearse, apparently for no other reason than that he was the brother of the celebrated rebel, caused such a wave of revulsion in England itself that the government was in danger of losing popular support at a crucial point in the European war. Ned Daly, Tom Clarke's brother-in-law, was also singled out for execution, as was Major John MacBride who had fought for the Boers in the South African War. Several other men who had been condemned to death subsequently had their sentences commuted to penal servitude for life. Among those was Eamon de Valera, reprieved on account of the fact that he had been born in New York of a Cuban father.

By that time the damage had been done. The first Irish Republic lasted 124 hours and seemed doomed to the double stigma of failure in accomplishment and futility in aim. But, as W.B. Yeats wrote later, 'All changed, changed utterly; a terrible beauty is born.'

CHAPTER 4

Republican University, 1916

Stone walls do not a prison make
Nor iron bars a cage.
RICHARD LOVELACE, *To Althea, from Prison*

AT STAFFORD MICHAEL PROVED TO BE A MODEL PRISONER. HE quickly knuckled down to the routine of the prison. Somehow he thrived on the harsh discipline of the place; he was a soldier and, by God, he would show the guards that he was as good a soldier as they were. Keeping a tidy cell and toeing the line, however, are negative qualities. Michael soon developed the subtle knack of getting on the right side of the guards, and then getting them on his side. It was during this period that his qualities of leadership truly developed. The Easter Rising had been an infinitely maturing experience, yet he never lost the devil-may-care boyishness that endeared him to so many, before and since. But now he developed a positive genius for breaking down barriers and instinctively establishing a rapport with his gaolers as well as his fellow prisoners. During his time at Stafford, and later at Frongoch, Michael had the Tommies eating out of his hand. Given the circumstances, and the attitude in England that the rebels had been treacherous murdering bastards, stabbing the mother country in the back in the middle of the Great War, Michael's ability to disarm his guards was all the more remarkable.

For three weeks the prisoners were kept segregated and confined to their cells. They were deprived of contact with each other and had only limited communication with their guards. Yet Michael seems to have understood his gaolers from the beginning, and knew when to banter and joke with them, and even bully them occasionally, to get his own way. Only when free association was permitted did the full horror of the executions and reprisals dawn on those who had survived. During this initial period, when communications were strictly forbidden, Michael even managed to get a letter smuggled out to Hannie. Dated 16 May, it vividly conveys the feelings of such a free spirit as Michael's at being incarcerated in such harsh circumstances:

Positively you have no idea of what it's like, the dreadful monotony, the heart-scalding eternal brooding on all sorts of things, thoughts of friends dead & living, especially those recently dead, but above all the time, the horror of the way in which it refuses to pass . . . it is only with the utmost effort that I can concentrate my thoughts or be at all rational – you see I seem to have lost acquaintance with myself and with the people I knew. Wilde's 'Reading Gaol' keeps coming up. You remember 'All that we know who be in gaol . . .'[1]

He concluded on a brighter, more positive note, asking his sister to procure for him 'a few good (& long) novels in cheap editions, and if still at the flat, Heath's *Practical French Grammar* or some such text book'.

Michael's spirits rose when the initial restrictions were gradually relaxed. Books and letters were permitted from about 24 May and free association a week later. Instinctively he realised that men who had been cooped up in tiny cells for several weeks needed hard physical exercise to take their minds off the dreadful news, so he quickly organised the sort of rough and tumble games at which he excelled. An improvised match of Gaelic football, using a ball made of rags bound with twine, was just the thing to release pent-up tensions. There was also a form of boisterous leap-frog called Weak Horses involving two teams. Somehow the biggest and heaviest men always seemed to be in the team opposing Michael who was targeted for some particularly rough treatment. Inevitably his hair-trigger temper would flare up (which was the object of the baiting, of course) and an almighty punch-up would result. Just as quickly, his temper would subside and they would all be the best of friends afterwards. In Stafford Michael had all the manic restlessness of the caged beast. He associated with a gang of 'wilders', always on the lookout for others to tease and manhandle, and often getting some hard knocks himself in return. One of his idiosyncrasies noted at this time (though it may have been a hangover from schooldays) was his habit of taking a bite out of his opponents' ears.

Many of the reminiscences from this period recall Michael as a tearaway, a roaring boy, a broth of a boy, above all the Laughing Boy, often regarded by the older prisoners as a pain in the butt, disturbing the even tenor of their dreary lives with his endless practical jokes and schoolboy japes. Cards was one of the few diversions that helped while away the time. Never a card-player previously, Michael now took up this pursuit with the same manic intensity he brought to bear on everything he did. So long as he had a good hand, all was well and good; but when dealt a poor hand he soon lost interest in the game. 'He looked into his neighbour's cards, reneged, upset the deck, or created a diversion by dragging the most likely-looking winner on to the floor,' wrote Frank O'Connor.[2] The same applied to beds and other possessions; so long as they were someone else's they were there for his amusement, but let no one dare to interfere with his! On a one-to-one basis he could usually get away with it, but he was frequently on the receiving end of concerted attacks.

Amid all this high-spirited larking about, which seems, in the main, to have been devoid of any malice or serious intent, there were a few prisoners who observed that there was more to Mick Collins than met the eye. Beneath all this rather childish horseplay and infectious laughter there was an essentially complex, serious individual who spent a good part of each day in his cell wrapped in study. As well as French, he resumed his studies of Gaelic and Irish history. Well might he state later on that the nine months in confinement were his 'Republican University'.

When letter-writing was officially permitted he began corresponding with Susan Killeen again, addressing her in the Irish form of Siobhain which he sometimes wrote phonetically as Sheevaun. Though addressed 'My dear Siobhain' and signed 'Love, Michael', these letters were remarkably free of endearments or even personal matters. Instead, they tended to be very brisk and businesslike, as Michael used Susan as a conduit to the wives, mothers and other relatives of prisoners. Typical was the letter of 1 June:

> Could you get in touch with some of the CmBan people and ask them to look up Mrs Kirwan of Maynooth whose husband is here. They have five or six children who are not I am afraid being attended to at all. Also Mrs Little, 32, The rear of Upper Clanbrassil St, more or less similarly placed. If you could get hold of a Miss Kearney she might be able to help . . .[3]

Although the number of men and women involved in the Easter Rising could not have exceeded 1,200, the authorities eventually rounded up more than twice that number and deported them to mainland Britain where they were dispersed to prisons all over the country. Of course, many of the prisoners were known members of Sinn Fein, the Irish Volunteers, the Citizen Army and other proscribed organisations, but not a few were lifted off the streets on the merest whim. In the course of the summer many of these unfortunate people were weeded out of the penal system and sent home. If they had not been Republican in their sympathies previously, a spell in one of His Majesty's prisons soon cured them of residual loyalty to Britain. For every prisoner detained rightly or wrongly, there were wives, parents, brothers, sisters, sons and daughters, friends and other relatives, to whom the brutality of the police, military and officialdom in general in the aftermath of the Rising would bring about a hardening of attitudes, on a scale unparalleled in any of the earlier insurrections. The executions, which added so substantially to the pantheon of Irish martyrdom, were the immediate catalyst; but the detention of the 2,519

— an unprecedented number — had a more lasting effect in changing the political climate, creating a hostility towards Britain in areas where little or none had existed before, as well as reinforcing traditional hatreds in the more staunchly Republican areas.

The prisoners were originally spread throughout the penal system in a dozen gaols from Perth and Glasgow in the north to Lewes and Reading in the south. After several weeks it was decided to remove them from association with ordinary convicts and concentrate them in a single camp. For this purpose the authorities selected Frongoch, four kilometres north-west of Bala, Gwynedd, in North Wales. The name, now more commonly spelled Fron-Goch, was modified by the detainees who renamed it Francach, in Irish literally a Frenchman, but a colloquialism for a rat. In this sense it was well named for the camp was overrun with rodents.

Before the war this sleepy hamlet, at the junction of the main road from Bala to Porthmadog and the mountain road to Corwen, set amid some of the most breathtakingly beautiful scenery in Britain, had been notable only on account of its distillery which provided the sole alternative employment to sheep-farming. The distillery, however, had closed down some years previously and the population of Frongoch was in decline when war broke out. In 1915 the disused distillery became the nucleus for a camp erected to house German prisoners-of-war. These were now dispersed to other prison camps so that Frongoch could be used exclusively as a concentration camp for the Irish. The concentration camp system had been invented by the British and used very effectively during the later stages of the Boer War; the term would acquire sinister connotations twenty years later, but in 1916 it betokened a relatively benign régime. Strictly speaking, the inmates were not prisoners but detainees, a subtle distinction perhaps, but one which was reflected in the more relaxed atmosphere of the camp. The advance party of Irish detainees arrived on 9 June and others came in batches over the ensuing month.

Michael wrote to Susan from Stafford on 27 June, mentioning that transfer notices had been served on about 130 of the prisoners there. He was not one of them, although he knew that his own move was imminent. One thing he was not happy about: at Frongoch detainees were permitted to send only one letter a week, whereas at Stafford no limit was set. Significantly, Susan was the recipient of the first letter Michael wrote from Frongoch, on the very day he arrived there. Unfortunately it is undated, but was presumably written early in July. While appreciating the rugged beauty of the scenery, Michael was taken aback by the poor sanitation and primitive conditions. The detainees were accommodated in huts sixty feet long and sixteen feet wide, thirty men in each — 'Not too much room to spare!' he added ruefully. The weather was bad at the time of his arrival; a prolonged spell of heavy rain had reduced the camp ground to a morass of slippery, shifting mud which remained a serious problem all summer. Typically, Michael wrote, 'Of course when we've made roads etc. the place will be much better,' and he concluded on a jocular note. Referring to the unpleasant cold weather, he quipped, 'I cheer them all up by asking them – what'll they do when the winter comes?'[4]

Once he had settled in and the weather improved, Michael revised his initial dismal view of the camp. The brick buildings of the old distillery had been converted into a cookhouse, hospital, artists' studio, barber's shop, tailor's and shoemaker's workshops, and a large workshop for carpentry and metalwork. There was also a detention block for recalcitrants and the administrative building which included the censor's office. How effective censorship was, however, is a matter for speculation. Many of the Frongoch letters now preserved by postal historians lack the PC (Passed Censor) marks and have the ordinary postmarks of Bala or Corwen, bearing out the testimony of a number of internees to the fact that some of the sympathetic guards would post letters on request. It also explains the discrepancy between the one letter a week which Michael was allowed to write, and his many letters that actually far exceeded that limit.

The distillery area comprised the South Camp, while the majority of the hutments formed the North Camp, the whole being enclosed by a high barbed-wire fence. Within the camp itself the men were quite free but, as Michael wrote to Sean Deasey:

> I'm here and that's the thing that matters. Prating about home, friends and so on doesn't alter the fact that this is Frongoch, an internment camp, and that I'm a member of the camp. There's only one thing to do while the situation is as it is – make what I can of it.[5]

In a later letter to Deasey, written on 12 September, Michael wrote mordantly:

> I grow more wondrous every day, for here at Frongoch by my own count at least a quarter of the men in the North Camp know very little about the Rising. One man, a former labourer of my acquaintance, said that he was just forced off the street in the round-up. His only crime appears to be that he was walking the streets.[6]

In another letter to Deasey, dated 29 September, Michael commented on the different attitudes of the prisoners: 'It is pitiable to see those who have given way to imprisonment now enforcing on themselves the extra burden of loneliness. Many of them are family men.' By now there was some friction between those who had been active in the Rising and those who had been caught up in the subsequent round-up – the latter, not unnaturally, blaming the former for the predicament they found themselves in.

Michael was originally in charge of hut number ten and later number thirty-two, under the overall command of the senior internee, M.W. O'Reilly, former Vice-Commandant of the Dublin Brigade. All officers of the rank of commandant and above had either been executed, or were serving life sentences in civilian gaols. O'Reilly fearlessly championed the rights of the detainees and was very quick to pounce on any attempt by the camp authorities to impose restrictions, or to treat them as if they were convicted felons. He constantly demanded that they should be treated as prisoners-of-war, protected by the Geneva Convention. The authorities ignored this and, tiring of O'Reilly's constant complaints, quietly transferred him to Reading Gaol.

Gradually, the number of detainees declined. Men were taken in batches to London for a lengthy screening process by a body known as the Advisory Committee on the Internment of Rebels, designed to rectify the injustice of the indiscriminate round-up. Michael himself was sent in one batch of detainees and held briefly in Pentonville while his case was considered. A letter to Susan, shortly after his return to Frongoch, described his horror at seeing from his cell window the ordinary convicts exercising in the yard: 'Each convict seems to have cultivated a ghastly expression to match the colour of his turf-ash-grey garb. Broad arrows everywhere.'[7]

By the end of August the numbers of internees at Frongoch had dropped from over two thousand to fewer than 650, and with the end of the brief Welsh summer imminent, the authorities decided to close the North Camp and move all the detainees into the more substantial buildings of the South Camp. This was a marked improvement and, accompanied by a regimen of route-marches under guard through the surrounding moorland, it was the period that Michael enjoyed best – if he may be said to have enjoyed any part of his confinement at all. He found those twenty-mile tramps along moorland tracks exhilarating, and noted smugly that he and his fellow internees were often in much better physical shape than their guards (generally older soldiers, no longer fit for the rigours of the Western Front).

Many of the jobs about the camp were performed by local tradesmen and contractors, and Michael was intrigued to hear them chatting together in Welsh. This impelled him to redouble his efforts to master Gaelic. His admiration of the Welsh, a brother Celtic race who had managed to retain their distinctive language and culture, even went so far as trying to learn Welsh himself. One of the local lads who worked in the camp was Robert Roberts. As old as the century, he was too young for military service, but worked as an assistant in the camp canteen. At an impressionable age, he seems to have come quickly under the spell of the burly leader of hut thirty-two, 'the noisiest in

Camp North with ceaseless activity'. He noted that Michael was always dressed in good clothing, though he rarely wore a collar and tie, and his army boots were never polished. Interestingly, Roberts noted that Michael 'had a great sense of humour but was a very stern disciplinarian'. This probably alluded to an incident in which some of the internees stole some cherrywood pipes from a box displayed on the canteen counter, when the boy's back was turned:

> I reported what was going on and we complained to the senior prisoner, who was Michael Collins. He arranged to assist us by locking the canteen door and searching each prisoner. If a prisoner had one pipe or box of matches he was given the benefit of the doubt. Otherwise stolen goods were returned.[8]

Michael persuaded Roberts to obtain a Welsh dictionary and grammar, as well as alphabet cards, some chalk and other visual aids, so that he could study Welsh and perhaps encourage some of the others to take an interest in their fellow Celts. Roberts was only too happy to oblige. In his memoir, he added, 'Collins must have told his mother about me, because she sent me a small present of a tie-pin in the pattern of a shamrock inlaid with green Connemara stone for my kindness to her son.' For Michael, who had lost his mother nine years previously, this harmless deception (probably involving Susan) was calculated to win the boy over by showing how much he thought of him. Over fifty years later Roberts would recall his best-known prisoner with affection:

> Michael Collins was very highly respected, especially by the civilian canteen staff. The manager used to remark that whenever we took a problem to him he always listened logically. He used to be one of the first to the morning Mass and one of the first at the breakfast table, the best meal of the day . . . He was a heavy smoker but would go without, proving that he was more self-willed [sic] than the rest . . . wonderfully fit, he could out-walk everyone on the route-marches into the Welsh hills and would arrive back in camp none the worse for wear while some of the guards fell by the wayside.[9]

Frongoch gave Michael ample time not only for his language studies and keeping fit, but also to ponder on his future course of action. From his letters to Susan and others it is clear that he had the opportunity to read newspapers and magazines. He was as well informed as anyone on the state of Ireland in the aftermath of the Rising and also had the chance to discuss the political situation with fellow detainees. During that fateful week, of course, he had been in a position to observe the architects of the rebellion at very close quarters. Later he would analyse the sequence of events and the characters of the leaders. On 6 October he wrote to Kevin O'Brien at great length. O'Brien, a close friend from his Savings Bank days, was born and bred in London and certainly did not share Michael's belief in physical force as a means of solving Ireland's problems; but contact was resumed (probably by O'Brien) when Michael was in Frongoch, and this encouraged the latter to air his views:

> It is so easy to fault the actions of others when their particular actions have resulted in defeat. I want to be quite fair about this – the Easter Rising – and say how much I admired the men in the ranks and the womenfolk thus engaged. But at the same time – as it must appear to others also – the actions of the leaders should not pass without comment. They have died nobly at the hands of the firing squads. So much I grant. But I do not think the Rising week was an appropriate time for the issue of memoranda couched in poetic phrases, nor of actions worked out in a similar fashion. Looking at it from the inside (I was in the GPO) it had the air of a Greek tragedy about it, the illusion of being more or less completed with the issue of the before-mentioned memoranda. Of Pearse and Connolly I admire the latter the most. Connolly was a realist, Pearse the direct opposite. There was an air of earthy directness about Connolly. It impressed me. I would have followed him through hell had such action been necessary. But I honestly doubt very much if I would have followed Pearse – not without some thought, anyway.
>
> I think chiefly of Tom Clarke and MacDiarmada. Both were built on the best foundations. Ireland will not see another Sean MacDiarmada.
>
> These are sharp reflections. On the whole I think the Rising was bungled terribly, costing many a good life. It seemed at first to be well organised, but afterwards became subjected to panic decisions and a great lack of very essential organisation and co-operation.[10]

Clearly what Michael had in mind was to rebuild on those 'best foundations', the Irish Republican Brotherhood, which alone could provide the 'very essential organisation and co-operation'. In the latter part of the Frongoch period Michael was not only the senior prisoner from the British viewpoint but also Head Centre of the IRB, and as autumn changed to winter he busied himself with building up his power-base within the camp. Also at this time he developed the concept of a system of insurance which would free Ireland from the financial thraldom of London. Out of this arose the New Ireland Assurance Company, one of the largest businesses of its kind in Ireland. In the 1920s its directors included M.W. O'Reilly and another Frongoch alumnus, Denis McCullough, both of whom worked closely with Michael in 1916 and later years.

At a more mundane, practical level, Michael gradually asserted his control not only over the prisoners but also over the way the authorities ran the camp. Sometimes the detainees were paid small sums for essential work, though the rates were pitiful. For example, they were offered work in the nearby slate quarries at fivepence an hour, but threepence an hour was deducted for 'upkeep' and the train fares to and from the quarries. Not surprisingly, Michael rejected this offer, which did little to endear him to the camp authorities who regarded him as a tiresome barrackroom lawyer.

The perennial problem of mud in the camp was solved by laying down footpaths of ashes and clinker from the boiler-house, and for hauling these cinders the inmates were paid threepence an hour. When the camp commandant, Colonel Heygate-Lambert, tried to get the detainees to empty the rubbish-bins around the soldiers' barrack block without payment, Michael put his foot down and flatly refused to co-operate. In retaliation, the authorities had the detainees removed, in groups of eight at a time, to the otherwise deserted North Camp to cool their heels. During these spells of detention in the cold, uncomfortable huts of the North Camp all privileges were suspended. Although forced to go without newspapers and cigarettes, the detainees maintained a stubborn solidarity and by October the commandant was forced to back down. In this confrontation with the authorities, Michael was the undisputed leader and the incident consolidated his power over the others. He was adept at finding ways of raising the morale of his fellow internees, especially when this entailed getting the better of the camp authorities. By autumn he had organised a highly sophisticated system of smuggling luxury items into the camp and uncensored letters out. Many of the guards, tempted by the prospect of some of the German gold which the leading insurgents (including Michael) were reputed to have salted away, seem to have been only too ready to co-operate. As the political situation in Ireland quietened down, the attitude of the guards relaxed. After all, these men were not *real* prisoners like the bloody Jerries . . .

Meanwhile, in Whitehall, there was some debate in government circles about what to do with the detainees. Only those sent for court-martial as a result of the screening process and convicted were subsequently transferred to civilian gaols to serve their sentences. Someone had the bright idea of drafting the remainder into the army where harsh discipline would soon knock the Shinner out of them and turn them into cannon fodder in no time. ('Shinner' was a term applied indiscriminately to all rebels and Republicans, whether members of Sinn Fein or not.) Rumours to this effect swept the camp, and Michael countered by ordering detainees to withhold their names. This caused considerable hardships and there must have been many an internee who silently cursed Mick Collins for his stiff-necked attitude towards authority. Anyone who dared to voice doubts as to the wisdom of the Collins philosophy of 'Sit down – refuse to budge – you have the British beaten. For a time they'll raise war – in the end they'll despair,' soon found himself on the end of a tirade of invective. A tongue-lashing from Michael Collins was a terrifying experience. It cowed many, but left others sullen and resentful. Magnified in scale as well as time, this abrasive quality would make for Michael many enemies. A more compromising, placatory attitude and a more diplomatic approach might have been just as effective in the long run, but that was never Michael's way, and in the end it would be his downfall.

Early in October the Frongoch Sports were held. Michael took part in shot-putting against fellow Corkman Sean Hales who was the Munster champion weight-thrower. These two sturdy giants were the only prisoners who could throw the 56-pound weight, though Sean could hurl it a few feet farther. The Sports were one of the topics raised in the House of Commons during a debate on the Irish detainees on 18 October. The Irish Nationalist MPs were sniping at the government front benches, when Major John Newman commented, 'Only a few days ago at Frongoch internment camp the interned prisoners had a course over which they did a 100-yard sprint, and they had hop, skip and jump, and other sports.' Ten days later the winner of the 100-yard sprint wrote indignantly to Hannie:

> Major Newman said he noticed we held sports here and that the 100 yards was won in 10¾ seconds (10⅘ was correct, by the way) which didn't seem to show any neglect in the way of feeding etc. Naturally he doesn't think of all the parcels one gets and what one spends in the canteen. Actually there isn't a solitary man here of no matter how slender an appetite who could live off the official ration. You know there are two or three committees supplying us with additional vegetables and sometimes apples & cocoa. Of course all the MPs are only on for trying to make capital out of us.

Long before Mahatma Gandhi developed his doctrine of passive resistance in India, Michael had shown the effectiveness of this when dealing with authority. Colonel Heygate-Lambert had no sooner given way over the vexed question of the soldiers' garbage-cans than he was confronted with the stubborn refusal of prisoners to answer to their names at the parade-ground roll-call. When the matter came to a head and the detainees were ordered to give their names, some two hundred followed Michael's lead and refused to comply with the order. For this they were moved back into the confinement of the North Camp with all privileges withdrawn. The effectiveness of this punishment was weakened as a result of the system of communications and smuggling which Michael had previously organised. Nevertheless, this was to be an extremely testing time for the 'unidentified internees', as they were classed. On 2 November this group retaliated by starting a hunger-strike. Heygate-Lambert riposted that he would have discipline in the camp even though it was filled with nothing but dead bodies.[11] Eamonn Tierney, terrified of conscription, went mad as a result, while four others suffered such a breakdown in health as a result of close confinement in fetid conditions that they were dead within the year, and many others suffered serious illnesses of various kinds. The two camp doctors, ordered by the commandant not to treat the unidentified internees, suffered the anguish of breaking their Hippocratic oath; one of them, Dr Peters, 'worried by statements concerning the treatment of prisoners', broke down and drowned himself in the River Tryweryn which ran past the camp.[12]

This desperate situation came to light when Michael succeeded in smuggling out a message to William O'Brien who published a devastating exposé in *The Cork Free Press* on 11 November. The story was picked up by several British newspapers, notably *The Manchester Guardian* and led to such a clamour of public opinion on both sides of the Atlantic that the government could no longer suppress the matter. Questions were asked in the Commons, and finally, on 21 December, Henry Duke, Chief Secretary for Ireland, was forced to announce an amnesty.

Michael himself never lost heart. Even when the tussle with authority was at its grimmest he remained optimistic that good sense would prevail in the end. In another letter to Hannie he described some of the more intellectual pursuits. There were twenty-nine men in his hut, 'a nice crowd, a few good readers & widely read too'. Between them they had put together quite a good library:

> A most weird collection though. To give you an idea – Service, Swinburne, Shaw, Kipling, Conrad, Chesterton, lots of Irish Broad-sheet stuff, etc. etc. We had Service last night and I was put through it for Dangerous Dan McGrew & some others. There is an interesting collection of American verse in a very large volume from the Quays. The variety in the way of raggedness, cheap binding & fairly good binding is unique. Would be very glad to receive *Punch* each week.

The choice of *Punch* seems singularly odd, given that satirical magazine's savage caricatures of the Irish in general and their Uprising in particular. To Sean Deasey, Michael wrote on 8 December:

> This state of affairs can't last much longer. While many of the men are looking forward dismally to the prospect of spending Christmas here, I would not be surprised to find myself at home for that event.[13]

This seems to have arisen from a Home Office enquiry into camp conditions. Michael was one of the four detainees interviewed early in December by Sir Charles Cameron. After listening to a seemingly endless list of inadequacies in the camp facilities and the prisoners' diet, Cameron wearily asked if there was *anything* of which they got enough. 'Yes,' said Michael shortly. 'Salt!'

Clearly this situation could not continue indefinitely. On 21 December the Chief Secretary for Ireland admitted that the risk of keeping untried prisoners any longer in detention appeared greater than the risk of releasing them. On the following evening the detainees were paraded as usual. Without any preamble, the camp adjutant, in a brief speech, told them that all of them would shortly be released. Prisoners from the north, south and west of Ireland would go that very night, the rest following the next day. He asked for the names, addresses and home railway stations of the two batches of men. Immediately the detainees suspected a ploy to trap them. Michael himself spoke out against this in no uncertain terms. There was an uneasy silence and the men on parade held their breath, wondering what would happen next in this glowering contest. Then the adjutant sighed wearily and explained slowly that no trap was intended. As a compromise, he suggested that the internees compile their own lists. Michael agreed to this, taking personal charge of the two lists.

That was the end of the matter. The first batch of men was taken by lorry to Holyhead that evening and put aboard the overnight packet steamer. The second group left Frongoch the following day, and as they changed trains at Chester and marched along the platform for the boat train they sang *Deutschland über Alles*. 'Most of us were anti-German, really,' one of the detainees commented later. 'The British are a patient people. They took no notice.'

Michael was among the last to leave, arriving back in Dublin early on the morning of Christmas Day itself. With Gearoid O'Sullivan, he called on Joe O'Reilly, a Corkman who had also been in Stafford and Frongoch but had been released some time previously. The exuberant pair burst into the room O'Reilly was sharing with a friend, and the unfortunate man found himself on the receiving end of a bear-hug and a 'Collins kiss' that left both ear-lobes bitten and bleeding. To make amends, Michael (who seems to have spent the night on the steamer carousing) poured the best part of a bottle of port down O'Reilly's throat and then rushed off, leaving him to explain, as best he could, to his startled room-mate that it was only the Big Fellow having a bit of fun. Michael continued in and out of pubs all day until the evening when 'he was lifted on to a sidecar, and oblivious of the world, was whirled off and bundled by his friends into the Cork train'.[14]

CHAPTER 5

Prelude to War, 1917–18

The whole world is in a state of chassis.
SEAN O'CASEY, *Juno and the Paycock*, I. i.

MICHAEL WAS NOT IN THE BEST OF MOODS WHEN HE ALIGHTED from the train at Clonakilty. He was hungover and, to his dismay, discovered that the Boxing Day shutdown of local transport meant that he had to walk all the way to Woodfield. He was chilled to the bone by the time he reached the farm, only to learn that his grandmother O'Brien had just died. Mercifully, this gentle old lady had never grasped the significance of the Easter Rising or of Michael's part in it, let alone his absence over the past year. Michael's sombre mood only deepened when he called on Sean Hurley's mother to pay his condolences. Afterwards he wrote to Hannie, saying, 'I think poor Sean Hurley's mother felt his loss more keenly when I came home than at any other time.' Brother John and his wife Katty were ill at this time, and Michael's despondency was compounded by the feeling that the people around Sam's Cross had little comprehension of what was going on outside their cosy little world, and even less sympathy with the cause for which Michael had so recently risked his life. To Susan he wrote, 'It seems that the spirit prevailing here anyway is very poor. The people are much too careful and I've sustained myself principally on rows since returning.'[1] After three weeks kicking his heels around the farm and 'drinking Clonakilty wrastler on a Frongoch stomach', he set off for Dublin, apparently leaving home just before RIC detectives called in connection with a fracas in Cork involving one Michael Collins. His family would maintain that this was nothing more than police harassment and that he had nothing to do with any brawl in Cork; the very idea was unthinkable! For the first time in his life, Michael gave the police the slip, but it would not be the last.

In Dublin he was reassured to find that attitudes towards the late insurgents were much more positive. Public opinion had now swung round in favour of the Shinners. This sea-change was largely brought about by the realisation that the British government, led by the wily Lloyd George (who had succeeded Asquith in December), had no intention of including the six counties of North-east Ulster in whatever form of autonomy was granted to the remaining twenty-six counties.

The Ireland of 1917 was a different place from the country Michael had left nine months earlier. Nominally Dublin Castle was still the seat of government but it had been emasculated and demoralised. Sir Augustine Birrell, the urbane Chief Secretary at the time of the Rising, had been made a scapegoat and in the aftermath of his dismissal many other heads had rolled. Many of the career civil servants had now adopted a policy of keeping a low profile and doing as little as possible. All really important decisions were taken from London anyway. The Castle also contained the nerve centres of both police administrations, the Metropolitan Police covering Dublin itself, and the Royal Irish Constabulary covering the country as a whole. Although the rank and file of both organisations had been carefully vetted (and contained a high proportion of Protestants), there was now a significant minority of policemen who were covertly sympathetic to the Nationalist cause. Joe Kavanagh, the G man who had been so moved by the pathetic sight of the defeated rebels mustered in Parnell Square the previous April, was by no means the only officer who would increasingly question the policy of his superiors as well as his own role.

Ireland had been placed under martial law since Easter, but a measure of how stable the situation was thought to have become was the recall of the unpopular General Maxwell in November and the lifting of martial law. The release of the Frongoch detainees the following month was perceived as a gesture that things were gradually getting back to normal. There was a certain amount of agitation for the release of the convicted prisoners, currently serving sentences of penal servitude in England, and in fact the British government conceded this point by releasing them all (including de Valera) on 18 June 1917. At first the Irish looked towards the new British prime minister with cautious optimism. After all, was he not a Celt, just like themselves? Perhaps the Welsh wizard would succeed where so many others before him had failed.

In fact, those who yearned for Home Rule – and that was the great majority of people in southern Ireland – were now disillusioned with the constitutional processes which had been so blatantly flouted by the Orangemen under Carson. Within a month of the Frongoch release, Sinn Fein was being reorganised as an umbrella for all manner of Republican and Nationalist viewpoints. On 20 January Count Plunkett, who had extended hospitality to the London Irish at Kimmage, was formally expelled from the Royal Dublin Society, belated recognition of the fact that one son (Joseph) had been executed for his part in the late rebellion, while two others (George and John) were currently serving long sentences of penal servitude for the same offence. The

Count bounced back immediately when he announced his intention of offering himself as a candidate in the forthcoming by-election in North Roscommon. Michael, who had resumed contact with the Plunkett family immediately following his return to Dublin, saw this as an opportunity to strike a blow against the Irish Parliamentary Party as well as gain some valuable publicity for the Republican movement. He went to Roscommon and over the ensuing week tramped through the snow and slush of the county, campaigning vigorously on behalf of his late commandant's father. The result was a resounding defeat for the Redmondite candidate, Plunkett polling 3,022 votes against 1,708 for the Irish Parliamentary Party and 687 for an Independent Nationalist. This spectacular result immediately posed the question: would Plunkett take his seat at Westminster or would he abstain? The consensus of Nationalist feeling was that abstention was the only way to protest against continuing government from London, and in the end this was the course adopted by Count Plunkett, though his decision 'was not received very enthusiastically by some of the most energetic of his supporters', as Michael himself recorded subsequently.

Back in Dublin, Michael desperately needed a job that would provide him with a steady income. Fortunately his record in the Rising and particularly at Frongoch had raised his standing immeasurably among the Nationalists in general and the IRB in particular. Shortly after the Rising, Kathleen Clarke, widow of the IRB leader, had formed the Volunteer Dependents' Fund, later amalgamated with the Irish National Aid Association to succour the widows, orphans and dependents of those killed or imprisoned as a result. The fund was generously supported not only in Ireland itself but overseas, particularly in the United States. At first Joe McGrath had worked as Secretary on a purely voluntary basis, but as the work escalated he decided to step down and make way for someone who would do the job full time on a salaried basis. The Association's governing committee assented, and apportioned the modest sum of fifty shillings a week for the Secretary's salary. This was somewhat less than Michael might have earned in a middle-ranking clerical position with Craig, Gardiner; but he realised the political implications of the post and jumped at the opportunity. Michael, who seems to have been extremely casual about the job interview, perching on the edge of the desk swinging his leg, to the annoyance of some of the committee, thought that he had been lucky to get the appointment. Unbeknown to him, however, senior colleagues in the IRB had done a great deal of canvassing and string-pulling to ensure his selection – not so much on Michael's own account but because they were determined to gain control of this important organisation. Besides, Kathleen Clarke, seeing in Michael something of Sean McDiarmada, took to him immediately. 'If he's another Sean, he'll be all right,' she said. Her hunch was soon proved correct. She entrusted him with a precious list of IRB members. 'I was never sorry for this,' she later recalled. 'I gave all that information to Mick. It gave him the leeway to get ahead and he had the ability and the force and the enthusiasm and drive that very few men had to work on that.'

Any reservations that the committee might have had about appointing young Mick Collins were soon dispelled, for he proved to be a tireless and energetic worker, a meticulous book-keeper and a genius at wheedling money out of the unlikeliest people. In his office at 10 Exchequer Street, in the very shadow of Dublin Castle itself, he worked diligently on the books, but much of the work was peripatetic. Even in the pub, if a friend bought a round of drinks, Michael would pocket the change for the National Aid Fund, punctiliously issuing a receipt for the cash he had purloined. His first task was to reorganise the office, installing a counter barrier to keep garrulous time-wasters at bay. While Michael won the admiration and respect of the committee for his brisk efficiency, there were others who disliked his brusque manner and objected to his pushy behaviour. But even those who were put off by his truculence had to admit that no one worked half as hard as he did. He would often be seen cycling home at midnight after completing his rounds. If someone appealed to him for help, it was never too far, or too late in the day, for him to get on his bike and take the cash in person. When there was a problem with cash-flow he thought nothing of taking the money out of the pittance he was paid. Many times it broke his heart to come across old comrades from the Rising or Frongoch who were now down on their luck. For such a highly emotional young man, the stress of dealing with these men, often broken in spirit, must have been tremendous. He may have been short with those who could afford to contribute but who refused or were niggardly, but he seems to have had an instinctive tenderness and compassion for those who were genuinely in distress. There are many anecdotes that testify to the essential humanity of the man during the time he operated the fund.

All the hard work for a pittance was compensated by the fact that the job gave Michael entrée to everyone who was anyone, right across the Nationalist spectrum at that time, and he was now in the very thick of the struggle. It was at this time that he first came into contact with Oliver St John Gogarty, the prominent Dublin surgeon, writer and Nationalist sympathiser who would later describe Michael as possessing 'the quickest intellect and nerve that Ireland bred'. For such a big man, he moved with the natural grace of a ballet dancer. Gogarty also noted that he had beautiful hands like those of a woman, and a smooth skin 'like undiscoloured ivory'.

The election of Count Plunkett had turned out to be something of an anti-climax, especially when he called a public meeting on 19 April at which he calmly announced that he intended forming his own political party and proposed that all existing political groupings should be scrapped. The Sinn

Fein leader, Arthur Griffith, back in Ireland after completing a term of imprisonment in Wandsworth and Reading, distrusted the Count; but the IRB were just as distrustful of Griffith whose views were then regarded as far too moderate. Griffith clung tenaciously to the notion that Ireland could achieve her ends by constitutional means. Collins and the physical-force men utterly repudiated such a policy. That spring of 1917 marked a watershed between moderates and extremists, with Griffith and Michael Collins in opposing camps. Henceforward Michael's secret organisation in the IRB would be waging a campaign against Griffith and the moderates that would be hardly less intense than his campaign against the representatives of British authority.

In the middle of the power struggle between Plunkett and Griffith for control of the moral high ground, there was a second by-election. With the practical experience gained at Roscommon behind him, Michael threw himself into this campaign, organising meetings, making speeches – and falling madly in love. The Sinn Fein candidate on this occasion was Joseph McGuinness, actually languishing in Lewes Gaol. This was a novel situation on which his supporters capitalised with posters showing a man in prison clothing with the slogan 'Put him in to get him out'. McGuinness (who was extremely reluctant to get involved) was elected by a hair's breadth. On the first count the seat was awarded to the IPP candidate, but then a bundle of ballot papers was discovered and on a recount McGuinness was declared the winner by a mere thirty-seven votes.

During the by-election campaign Michael, accompanied by Harry Boland and Gearoid O'Sullivan, stayed at the Greville Arms in Granard 'which was run by four beautiful sisters and their brother ... They were lovely, glamorous girls and had all the right ideas,' as Brighid Lyons Thornton, a relative of McGuinness, described them.[2] Christine (Chrys) Kiernan, aged twenty-seven, was the eldest and then there were Laurence (Larry) aged twenty-five, Catherine Brigid (Kitty) aged twenty-four, Helen Josephine, twenty-three, and Maud (Mops), twenty-one. Their parents had died when they were teenagers and they had learned self-reliance at an early age. In addition to the Greville Arms, 'a lovely hotel' in the main street, the Kiernans owned the store which combined a grocery, a hardware shop, an undertaking business and timber yard as well as a public bar, while round the corner, on the other side of Market Street, was their bakery which served the town and the surrounding district. The Kiernan girls were staunch Nationalists, educated at St Ita's, Padraig Pearse's school for young ladies. Larry had tremendous business flair, and during the First World War the various Kiernan enterprises boomed. Maud was the most hard-headed of the five, and kept the books, but the others mucked in and shared responsibilities for the hotel, bar, store and bakery.

According to Sean MacEoin,[3] Michael was originally attracted to Helen Kiernan 'who oozed charm', but she was already engaged to a local lawyer, Paul McGovern. Frank O'Connor claimed that 'on the night before her wedding [Michael] went to her hotel and pleaded with her not to go through with her marriage' and that during the wedding speeches he was so agitated that he shredded his handkerchief'. He then transferred his affections to a second sister, Kitty, with whom Harry Boland was also in love. Kitty had a very pleasing personality: clever, capable, articulate, well groomed, poised, always impeccably dressed, pretty rather than beautiful. She did not have a particularly good voice, but part of the liberal education at St Ita's had given her a keen musical appreciation, and her favourite song at this time was 'I know where I'm goin' but the dear knows who I'll marry'. At least five young men were paying court to her simultaneously, but Harry Boland and Michael Collins emerged as the front-runners. The correspondence between Kitty and her two suitors, published in 1983 under the title *In Great Haste*, traces the course of this triangular affair, with Michael gradually emerging triumphant. His affair with Susan Killeen never picked up after his return from Frongoch, although they remained on friendly terms. The youngest Kiernan sister, Maud, was courted by Thomas Ashe, soon to become another martyr for the cause.

Ironically, McGuinness's reluctance to stand in this election, despite the fact that he came from a popular and much-respected local family, may have stemmed from the advice which he was given by de Valera, who wrote to him from Dartmoor saying 'most of us here consider it unwise'. Exactly why de Valera was so hostile to Nationalist prisoners contesting by-elections is not clear, although it may be that it went against his hidebound principles to acknowledge the existence of the British parliament by getting involved in one of its elections. Michael, who masterminded the campaign, chose to ignore Dev's wishes, and thereby incurred the displeasure of the man who, even then, was widely regarded (and regarded himself) as the Republican leader.

The propaganda effect of the Longford by-election cannot be over-emphasised. Count Plunkett may have been blackballed by the Royal Dublin Society but he was almost an Establishment figure and his election had been a slap on the wrist for the Irish Parliamentary Party; but the election of a convicted felon struck at the very heart of the British government, at a critical time in its relationship with the United States which had just entered the war, not so much an ally of Britain as an enemy of Germany. Attempts to draw the Americans into the struggle, ever since the *Lusitania* was torpedoed off Ireland in 1915, had been bedevilled by the Irish question. In the end, it was only the interception of a German promise to Mexico (to detach California, Texas and other states stolen by the USA in the 1840s and hand them back to their rightful owner, in return for support), that goaded the Americans into declaring war.

The British government may have been extraordinarily deaf to the wishes of the majority in Ireland, but it was increasingly sensitive to American opinion; and it was this which finally impelled Lloyd George to have a go at tackling the Irish problem. His response was to call the Irish Convention, a body allegedly representing all shades of opinion in Ireland, to examine every aspect of the problem and come up with a solution. As a gesture of good intent, the prisoners from the Rising and its aftermath were amnestied on 15 June, and six weeks later the Convention came into being. It was to deliberate, off and on, for a year, but it was doomed from the outset. It was far from representing accurately the various political opinions in Ireland, North and South. The Ulster Protestants and Southern Unionists had a very substantial representation, compared with the 5 per cent allocated to Sinn Fein. Even this token representation was undermined by Griffith's insistence that delegates to the Convention should be elected by the Irish people. Meanwhile, the released prisoners returned to Ireland to a tumultuous welcome, shortly followed by a much-publicised meeting in Dublin at which the ex-cons signed a petition addressed to President Woodrow Wilson and the American Congress which had enormous impact on the other side of the Atlantic.

Thus the twin actions, the release of the prisoners and the summoning of the Convention, merely drove a deeper wedge between Britain and Ireland.

Major William Redmond, MP for East Clare and brother of the IPP leader, who had set such a shining example to the Irish Volunteers by joining up on the outbreak of war, was killed in action at the battle of Messines on 7 June 1917 and this precipitated a third by-election. There could hardly have been a more dramatic confrontation between the old and the new political forces in southern Ireland, and Michael might have been expected to hurl himself wholeheartedly into the campaign. On this occasion, however, he pleaded pressure of business in Dublin, preoccupied as he was with providing employment or cash and clothing for the 122 recently released prisoners; but as Michael fervently subscribed to the doctrine that if you wanted something done you gave it to a busy man to do, his excuse has a hollow ring to it. The fact that the candidate – surprise, surprise – was de Valera himself may have had some bearing on Michael's decision. Only two months previously de Valera had condemned Republican participation in by-elections for an alien parliament, but now here he was calmly standing his principles on their head. As it turned out, the election in East Clare was a personal triumph of such a magnitude for de Valera that he would continue to represent that constituency for four decades. He easily defeated P.J. Lynch, the IPP candidate, and launched himself upon the national political scene. For the first time since April 1916 the Volunteers, now smartly uniformed but armed with pick-helves rather than Mausers, appeared in public. They ensured that the ballot was conducted properly and their disciplined, soldierly appearance created a very favourable impression. Soon afterwards, William T. Cosgrave won a by-election in Kilkenny by 772 votes to 392 and set himself on the road to the premiership of the Irish Free State, a position he would hold for ten years until ousted by de Valera in 1932. Politically, this by-election was significant because the Kilkenny Nationalists could not agree on a local candidate and appealed to Sinn Fein headquarters in Dublin; Willie Cosgrave was the party's nominee and, in fact, the first official Sinn Fein candidate since the unsuccessful contest at North Leitrim a decade earlier. These by-election successes were crowned by the defection of Laurence Ginnell, one of the more independently minded IPP members of parliament, who alone had had the courage to speak out against the executions of May 1916. Now, in the aftermath of the victories in East Clare and Kilkenny, Ginnell announced that he, too, would boycott Westminster.

Michael's excuse for not electioneering in East Clare could have been justified, for, in addition to his full-time work for the National Aid Association he was working behind the scenes for the IRB. In July he moved his main office to 32 Bachelor's Walk and, remarkably, continued to work from there throughout the ensuing four years, even when he was the most wanted man in Ireland. In July 1917, however, he was chiefly preoccupied with drafting important changes to the Volunteer Constitution, foreseeing that, when the next round came, sound organisation would be the key to success.

In mid-1917, moreover, at a time when Sinn Fein was very much the dominant force in Nationalist politics, Michael was also concerned with reorganising the IRB. There were many people, including some members of the Brotherhood itself, who felt that it had outlived its usefulness and decided to throw in their lot with Sinn Fein. De Valera, who had briefly flirted with the movement before the Rising, now came out emphatically against it, on the somewhat specious grounds that it was a secret society and, as such, was condemned by the Catholic hierarchy. In this he was supported by Cathal Brugha, another ex-IRB stalwart, who now roundly dismissed it as a sheer waste of time. Michael, on the other hand, was now a member of the Supreme Council of the IRB, and was forced to speak out on its behalf:

> There are many things to be said in favour of Sinn Fein, many of whose ideals are but the re-weighed ideals of the IRB. But the things to be said in favour of Sinn Fein do not outweigh the uses of the IRB which is respected and acknowledged by many who will think twice about the prospects of Sinn Fein. This is a time when to be united is to have the strongest asset. Instead of which there is a growing undercurrent of unrest.[4]

This, and an emotional appeal for unity from another IRB man, Thomas Ashe, was in the nature of a rearguard action. De Valera, backed by Brugha, helped to give Sinn Fein predominance, and thereafter the IRB sank into the background. Its position was not as weak as many people supposed, as it merely reverted to its characteristic secrecy. It was still sufficiently a force to be reckoned with for the British to include it specifically in the Treaty negotiations in 1921 and it would continue to provide Michael with his power base till the day he died. Nevertheless, the emergence of the de Valera–Brugha clique at this time was to have tragic repercussions five years later. It must be said that most of the animosity in this instance was on Brugha's side. What began as a distrust of Michael's motives would one day blossom into outright hostility and then deadly enmity, and Cathal Brugha was not the man to have as an enemy. The archetypal hard man, during the Rising he had been severely wounded during the defence of the South Dublin Union and left for dead by his retreating comrades; but they rallied when they heard shots from his revolver and a defiant chorus of *God Save Ireland*. He was found, propped up against a wall, just like the legendary hero Cuchullain, and this epithet stuck to him ever afterwards. He sustained several bullet wounds, and was also punctured by shrapnel; although subsequently sentenced to death he was spared a firing squad because he was at death's door anyway. His sentence was commuted to life imprisonment, but he made a good recovery and created quite a furore when he turned up at a Volunteer meeting after his release, still hobbling on crutches. Oddly enough, in view of his firebrand reputation, he differed from Michael fundamentally on the role of the Volunteers in the coming conflict, regarding them (as Eoin MacNeill had done) as a purely defensive force, whereas Michael argued vociferously that the Volunteers would have to take the offensive, on their own terms, if they were to have any hope of defeating the British.

In this dispute de Valera and Brugha tried to detach two prominent IRB men from the Collins faction. Harry Boland, a tailor of Dublin, was a very close friend of Michael who later joined the de Valera camp; in this case one may suspect that this disenchantment with the Big Fellow arose primarily over Kitty Kiernan. The other ally who would later change sides was Austin Stack, the lawyer and All-Ireland footballer who had commanded the Kerry Volunteers. He had been implicated in the *Aud* and Casement incidents, for which he was sentenced to death but later reprieved. Only recently returned from prison in England, he was to fall victim to Lloyd George's carrot-and-stick policy in August that year. The reaction of the British to Sinn Fein's electoral success was to invoke the Defence of the Realm Act with a vengeance. This measure, known as DORA for short, had been called into being to deal with German spies and subversive elements on the outbreak of the war, but was also used as a cudgel to beat the Irish. Its provisions included deportation, courts-martial and unlimited detention, the catch-all criterion being any activity calculated to spread disaffection among the lieges.

Along with Stack, Thomas Ashe and Fionan Lynch were arrested. Michael was devastated at the news of the arrests: Ashe was a close colleague in organising public meetings and clandestine IRB activity while Lynch, with whom Michael had polished off the whiskey on the last night of the Rising, actually roomed with him at 44 Mountjoy Street. The three men were quickly brought to trial for sedition but refused to recognise the court and offered no defence. They were sentenced to one year, eighteen months and two years respectively. In the circumstances, the sentences were remarkably light; but there was a serious principle at stake. In Mountjoy Prison the men were treated like ordinary convicts while they insisted that they were political prisoners. There were already about forty DORA convicts in the prison, but the arrival of the Ashe trio impelled them to protest about their status. The most effective method open to them was the hunger-strike which was co-ordinated by Stack and began on 20 September. The prison authorities reacted by removing the hunger-strikers' beds, bedding and boots. After five days on the cold flagstones, the protesters were subjected to forced feeding. As one of the ringleaders, Ashe was apparently the first to get this barbaric treatment whereby nourishing fluid was administered by means of a thick rubber tube thrust roughly down the victim's throat and thence into the gullet. As a medical technique for nourishing patients unable to take food orally, it was well established, and when administered with care under proper circumstances it was quite acceptable, if rather uncomfortable. But undertaken by prison orderlies, with burly warders on hand to restrain those who tried to resist, this practice amounted to torture. There was, of course, also the danger that the fluid might get into the windpipe instead and thus enter the lungs.

Fionan Lynch saw Ashe being dragged off down the corridor and cried out, 'Stick it, Tom boy!' Ashe replied, 'I'll stick it, Fin.' But rough, inexpert handling caused the unfortunate Ashe to drown on the life-giving fluid. He was rushed to the Mater Misericordiae Hospital but never regained consciousness, and was officially pronounced dead a few hours later.

The revolting circumstances of Tom Ashe's death provoked an immediate and overwhelming response in Dublin, and Michael was determined to make the most of the occasion. The men executed in 1916 had been unceremoniously interred in prison yards, but now the people had a martyr whom they could mourn in style. Michael saw to it that the corpse was dressed in a Volunteer uniform, he himself providing the shirt. More than 30,000 people filed past the bier in the hospital to pay their last respects. At the public funeral, representatives of Nationalist organisations from right across the country and the political spectrum joined with vast crowds of Dubliners at Ashe's funeral, conducted with full military honours and the most spectacular demonstration for many years. The Metropolitan Police made themselves scarce, tacitly leaving it to the officers and men of the Dublin Brigade under the command of Dick McKee to marshal the throng. Volunteers from the Dublin Brigade provided the cortège and escort that marched with military precision through the streets for the first time since April 1916. At the graveside the Volunteers fired three volleys, then Michael, in commandant's uniform, stepped forward and spoke in Irish and English, his voice thick with emotion: 'Nothing remains to be said. That volley which we have just heard is the only speech which it is proper to make above the grave of a dead Fenian.' In this emotionally charged atmosphere the sight of the Big Fellow with tears streaming down his cheeks made as great an impact as the terseness of his words. The effect of Ashe's death on Michael was summed up in a letter to Sean Deasey shortly afterwards:

I grieve as perhaps no one else grieves. And yet our comradeship had not been of long duration. He was a man of no complexes. Doing whatever he did for Ireland and always in a quiet way.[5]

On I November, after three weeks of public hearing, the coroner's inquest concluded that Ashe had died unlawfully. The proceedings were extensively reported in the press and included the dramatic testimony of Stack and Lynch. The coroner, announcing his verdict, lashed out at this inhuman punishment and condemned forced feeding in forthright terms. For good measure, the prison authorities in particular and the Castle administration in general came in for a great deal of criticism. The authorities were forced to back down; the DORA prisoners were given special-category status and then, after they were transferred to Dundalk (which precipitated a renewal of the hunger-strike), the authorities caved in completely and released them all on 17 November. In Lewes Gaol the previous year, Ashe had written a poem entitled *Let Me Carry Your Cross for Ireland, Lord!*.

Let me carry your Cross for Ireland, Lord!
My cares in this world are few,
And few are the tears will fall for me
When I go on my way to you.

Let me carry your Cross for Ireland, Lord!
For Ireland weak with tears.
For the aged man of the clouded brow,

And the child of tender years.
For the empty homes of her golden plains,
For the hopes of her future, too!
Let me carry your Cross for Ireland, Lord!
For the cause of Roisin Dhu.

Now this was printed as a leaflet and countless thousands were distributed under the emotive heading of *The Last Poem of Thomas Ashe*. Its mixture of piety and patriotism struck a responsive chord in Catholic Ireland and was one of the most potent propaganda weapons as 1917 came to a sorry end.

While the protracted inquest proceedings were still going on, the annual Ard Fheis or Convention of Sinn Fein was held on 25 October. At this meeting de Valera was elected to the presidency of Sinn Fein. Arthur Griffith would probably have won the presidency if it had been forced to a vote, but he was aware that the IRB was backing de Valera and in the interests of solidarity he generously gave way, accepting the vice-presidency instead. Austin Stack (still in Mountjoy) and the moderate Darrell Figgis were appointed joint Honorary Treasurers, with William Cosgrave and Laurence Ginnell as Honorary Treasurers. Michael and his close friend Harry Boland were among the two dozen elected to the Executive Council. This Convention set the seal on the emergence of Sinn Fein as the potent force rallying all shades of Nationalist opinion, from the ultra-conservative Irish Nation League to socialists and Marxists, from the moderate constitutionalists to the 1916 revolutionary wing led by de Valera, Collins and Brugha. A considerable amount of wheeling and dealing had gone on behind the scenes before the Convention took place in order that the movement should make a good show of solidarity. The only thing that the disparate elements had in common was their opposition to the Irish Parliamentary Party. Hostility towards the British hardly came into the reckoning; Home Rule was regarded almost as a foregone conclusion, and it only remained to decide what particular form it would take.

The programme finally hammered out was a curious blend of the original Sinn Fein platform, enunciated by Griffith a decade earlier, of industrial and economic development influenced by the philosophy of the German economist, Friedrich List (who advocated protectionism and nationalisation), together with the policy of abstaining from the Westminster parliament and the need to secure international recognition, in de Valera's words, 'of Ireland as an Independent Irish Republic'. The outcome of the 1917 Sinn Fein Convention was, in effect, something of a compromise. Michael, among others, was not happy at the socialist complexion of Griffith's programme; de Valera, however, agreed to accept this so long as Griffith backed his proposals for a republic.

Two days later, at the annual Volunteer Convention, de Valera was again elected president. He was now the leading figure on both the political and military fronts. The immediate aim of this meeting was that the Executive was empowered to declare war on the British government if and when the latter extended conscription to Ireland. At this convention Cathal Brugha was appointed Chief of Staff, with Dick Mulcahy as his Deputy, while Michael became Director of Organisation, in recognition of his sterling work in drafting the revised Volunteer Constitution.

As 1917 drew to a close with de Valera in supreme control, the battle lines were drawn. It seemed as if the separatist movement was unstoppable, but early in 1918 it received some serious setbacks. In three successive by-elections Sinn Fein candidates were defeated. In South Armagh on 1 February, Dr Patrick MacCartan was beaten by the IPP candidate who was helped not only by the support of the Ancient Order of Hibernians but also by the fact that the Unionist candidate (who really had no chance) stood down in order that the anti-Sinn Fein vote should not be split. This pattern of tactical voting, rather than any change of public opinion towards Sinn Fein, accounted primarily for the defeat of MacCartan, a prominent member of the IRB who would later play a major international diplomatic role.

At Waterford on 22 March Sinn Fein suffered its second reverse, but on this occasion the circumstances were quite exceptional. The by-election was caused by the death of John Redmond, who had succumbed to a heart attack earlier that month. The IPP leader, whom Frank O'Connor grossly caricatured as 'hook-nosed, spineless and suave',[6] had done as much as as he possibly could to represent the Irish viewpoint within the framework of Westminster. On 18 October 1916, for example, he had moved a resolution in parliament charging ministers with maintaining a system of government in Ireland inconsistent with the principles for which the Allies were fighting in Europe. This, of course, was thrown out. The following year he threatened a return to the traditional obstructionist policies of the IPP and it was his threats that finally induced Lloyd George to summon the Irish Convention and release the prisoners. In the deliberations of that Convention Redmond played a conciliatory part, but as he witnessed the negotiations foundering on Orange intransigence his health broke down. The seat was contested, for the IPP, by Redmond's son, and undoubtedly the strong sympathy vote carried the day, leaving Dr Vincent White in a poor second place. Ten days later, at the East Tyrone by-election, Sean Milroy was defeated by the IPP candidate, but when a by-election arose in Offaly in mid-April, the Irish Parliamentary Party candidate stood down and the Sinn Feiner was elected unopposed.

What brought about this dramatic change was the supreme folly of the British government, whose new Military Service bill was enacted on 16 April, raising the age limit for compulsory military service to fifty-five but, more importantly, extending conscription to Ireland. This decision flew in the face of all the agreements so far reached in the Irish Convention and had the immediate effect of destroying that body's credibility. The balance of power now swung back in favour of the Nationalists, who mounted a massive anti-conscription campaign. Leaders of Sinn Fein and the IPP sank their differences; even the nascent Irish Labour Party joined in the joint resolution condemning the measure and, on 25 April, called a one-day general strike in support. Significantly, the Catholic hierarchy (which, hitherto, had stood on the sidelines even if not overtly hostile to separatism) now threw its weight behind the movement. Sermons against conscription were preached from every pulpit and fund-raising went on at every church door. Enormous crowds signed a pledge in furtherance of the joint resolution and the National Defence Fund rapidly raised a six-figure sum, despite the strenuous efforts of the British authorities to suppress newspaper support for it.

The man chosen by Lloyd George to be his instrument was Field-Marshal Viscount French of Ypres. He had been Chief of the Imperial General Staff immediately before the war but had vacated this post at the time of the Curragh Mutiny in 1914. On the outbreak of war, however, he was restored to favour and commanded the British forces on the Western Front, being largely responsible for the costly conduct of that campaign. Resigning in December 1915, he was 'kicked upstairs' with a peerage and the appointment of Commander-in-Chief in the United Kingdom. Now he was sent to Ireland the the resounding title of Lord Lieutenant-General and Commander-in-Chief, with almost dictatorial powers and a mandate from Lloyd George to give the rebels hell – providing, of course, that the rebels could be induced to strike the first blow. Johnnie French would remain in this position of supreme power until early 1921; then in his seventieth year, he would retire with an earldom to his native Kent.

Even before the passage of the Military Service bill and the appointment of French, the political climate in southern Ireland was rapidly deteriorating. The German submarine campaign had entered its bitterest phase, taking a terrible toll of Allied shipping as part of the campaign to starve the British into submission. Britain consequently relied more and more on the foodstuffs produced in Ireland, and from late-1917 onwards, the bulk of this produce was directed across the Irish Sea. The farmers of Ireland, North and South, had never had it so good, and as demand continued to rise, so the economy boomed. Sinn Fein perceived twin dangers in this: the general rise in living standards had a generally enervating influence on the separatist cause, and the drain of foodstuffs out of Ireland was deemed an insult to the memory of all those who had perished during the Hungry Forties. A directive was sent from Dublin by Diarmuid Lynch, Sinn Fein's Food Director, to the local Sinn Fein clubs to counter this by rounding up cattle and driving them off into the hills. At the same time the cattle pastures were to be ploughed up to prevent further grazing. To back this two-pronged assault, squads of uniformed Volunteers, often accompanied by the local brass bands, were ordered to take the field. In many cases, however, the orders from Dublin were exceeded; there were instances of farmers being intimidated by armed gangs. Michael himself questioned the wisdom of this campaign; cattle-rustling, in his view, smacked of lawlessness, while the ruthless ploughing of grazing land had undertones of Bolshevism which he found repellant. Inevitably, the authorities reacted sharply; martial law was declared in County Clare on 27 February and restrictions were enforced in Tipperary and Galway. The most dramatic incident took place in Dublin itself, when Diarmuid Lynch ordered that a herd of pigs, about to be put aboard a freighter at the North Wall bound for England, should be seized and slaughtered on the spot. The carcasses were sold to local butchers and the proceeds paid to the farmers, but Lynch (an Irish-American) was arrested and sentenced to deportation. The authorities refused him permission to marry his fiancée but she was smuggled into Dundalk Gaol and a wedding ceremony hastily conducted by a visiting priest. The actual deportation was turned into a monster demonstration, orchestrated by Michael himself. He even paid a visit to the Dublin Bridewell to arrange communications between Ireland and the United States immediately before Lynch and his bride were escorted to the docks.

In March 1918 Michael had been in Longford again, doubtless combining business with pleasure; but as well as renewing his acquaintance with the Kiernan family at Granard, he was drumming up support for the anti-British food campaign. At Legga near Granard he made a speech that was deemed to be particularly inflammatory. The law finally caught up with him on 3 April when he stepped out of his office in Bachelor's Walk, straight into the arms of waiting G men. At first Michael strenuously resisted arrest, and the resultant brawl soon attracted a large and sympathetic crowd. The situation could well have turned nasty for the detectives, had not Joe McGrath turned up and calmed things down. In the end he persuaded the policemen to let Michael and himself walk ahead, across the O'Connell Bridge, to the police station in Brunswick Street where Michael could give himself up. From Dublin he was taken to Longford and formally arraigned at the Assizes. He was remanded in custody and from Sligo Gaol he wrote to Hannie a week later,

Sad! Sad! Sad! Before me the prospect of a long holiday . . . I'm very anxious to know what Lloyd George has done about Conscription for this country. If he goes for – well, he's ended.[7]

At the end of April, Michael was released on bail and drove straight to Granard for an emotional reunion with Kitty and her sisters. The local Volunteers had been apprised by Larry Kiernan of Michael's release and turned out to give him a warm welcome. Uniformed men lined the main street as Michael drove up to the Greville Arms. The following day, he took his leave of Kitty and returned to Dublin.

That very afternoon, 1 May 1918, Michael was strolling along Sackville Street when he bumped into Joe O'Reilly who had been with him in London, fought alongside him in the Rising, and had served in Stafford and Frongoch. For six months Joe had been kicking about Dublin without a job, and subsisting on hand-outs from the National Aid Association. Only a week earlier the youth, in desperation, had taken a job with the British military, and was now working as a labourer at Tallaght Aerodrome. Michael joshed him about this, but suddenly he turned serious. 'Chuck it and come in with me. I've a big job in front of me and I'll want your help.'

'All right,' said Joe after a moment. 'But let me collect me wages first.'

'No!' responded Michael firmly. 'I need you right now.'

Meekly Joe gave way. Like one of the Twelve Apostles answering the call of Jesus Christ, he turned around and accompanied Michael to his office. On the spur of the moment he began the most intimate relationship of his life. Slight of build and boyish in appearance, he would be the medieval page to Michael's paladin, and the stories that grew with the passing of the years would seem straight out of the pages of Mallory or Chaucer. O'Reilly's devotion to the Big Fellow knew no bounds: he was courier, clerk, messenger boy, nurse, slave. When Michael was in the mood for relaxation, Joe sang the old ballads Michael loved; when he was out of sorts, Joe put up with his foul moods. He would be out in all weathers on his ancient bike, shivering and soaked to the skin. His labours were never done, never fully appreciated or rewarded. He would endure imprisonment and suffer torture, yet he never complained and remained cheerful under the most trying circumstances.[8]

Failing utterly to sense the mood in southern Ireland, the British government now compounded its folly by inventing a German plot, despite the fact that German interest in Ireland (lukewarm at the best of times) had evaporated after the Easter Rising. Any vestigial German sympathy for the Irish cause disappeared the moment the United States came into the war anyway, but this did not prevent the British from coming up with such a patently ludicrous idea. All that mattered was that it provided the pretext for a massive round-up, between midnight and dawn on 18 May, of all Sinn Fein leaders that the police and military forces could lay their hands on. The German Plot, details of which were never made public, was merely window-dressing to appease American opinion. Those who were lifted that night included de Valera, Griffith, Cosgrave, Sean Milroy, Joseph McGuinness, Countess Markievicz and Count Plunkett, along with Dr Richard Hayes and Dr Brian Cusack, both prominent members of the Executive Council.

The capture of these prominent figures, as well as a number of men and women of lesser importance, need never have taken place, for Joe Kavanagh, Michael's mole in Dublin Castle, gave a list of the wanted men the previous day to Thomas Gay who had charge of the public library in Capel Street. In turn, Gay took the list straightaway to Harry Boland's tailoring shop in Middle Abbey Street and he took it to Michael Collins at Bachelor's Walk. Michael immediately despatched his faithful side-kick Joe O'Reilly to various addresses around the city, delivering verbal warnings to all concerned. As if this were not sufficient, Michael repeated the warning that evening at a meeting of the Volunteer Executive, while Padraig O'Keefe reiterated the dire message simultaneously at a meeting of the Sinn Fein leadership at 6 Harcourt Street.

In fact, the latter debated the matter at some length. There were three courses open to them: they could go into hiding, meet the arrests with resistance, or let the authorities take them into custody. In the end the last option was seen as affording the best advantage to Sinn Fein, partly because sufficient personnel would still be at liberty to keep the movement going, but mainly because they could make political capital out of the arrests. A new executive board was then selected and before the meeting closed all papers were bundled up and hidden away.[9]

The German Plot round-up had one unforeseen consequence. The removal of the diplomatic and statesmanlike section of Sinn Fein at this critical period left the militant wing, led by Cathal Brugha, in complete control of the organisation. Thanks to Brugha, the tactical error was made on the opening of Dail Eireann the following December of declaring a Republic in unequivocal terms. The declaration was later found to present extreme problems as, once proclaimed, the impossibility of going back on it was obvious. Had the status of Ireland been left undefined it would have been possible to work gradually towards it, unfettered by any previous definition. Ironically, this premature declaration of a Republic was to cause embarrassment to de Valera who would state vehemently, 'We are not Republican doctrinaires' and the famous words 'Get me out of the strait-jacket of the Republic'. This would set in motion a tragic chain of events during and after the Treaty negotiations in 1921.[10]

Michael himself was on the wanted list, but having eluded capture at Harcourt Street he went eventually to the home of his colleague Sean MacGarry which had been raided earlier in the night. Reckoning that lightning would not strike twice in the same place, he went to bed and slept soundly. The following morning he got up early and cycled to his office in Bachelor's Walk as usual. Smartly dressed, in a dark grey suit, starched collar and tie, and wearing a dark overcoat with a trilby hat and well-polished shoes, he looked like a lawyer or an accountant, certainly not the Shinner on the wanted list. For the first time, but by no means the last, he passed unobtrusively through the military patrols. This chameleon-like quality, of being able to blend into the crowd, would stand him in good stead in the years to come. He had a habit of blowing his nose ostentatiously as he exited his office on to the street, the handkerchief effectively covering the lower part of his face and preventing any watching tout or G man from getting a good look at him.

Despite the back-up plans arranged the previous evening, the round-up left Sinn Fein in total disarray and its rank and file demoralised. There was a general feeling that the struggle should be given up, or at least suspended. In the ensuing weeks Michael, ably assisted by Harry Boland, argued endlessly in a desperate bid to persuade the waverers to continue the fight. This was a testing time, and Michael rose to the occasion. Nor should the importance of Harry Boland be overlooked. He and the Big Fellow were a great team, but Boland has tended to be overshadowed by the towering personality of Collins. Harry, however, had a keen brain matched by tireless energy and indomitable will. He, too, would die in that tragic year of 1922, and Ireland lost a statesman and diplomat of consummate skill. Far less mercurial in temperament than Michael, it was he who buoyed up Collins when a black mood came over him, or brought the euphoric Michael down to earth, or coped with his sudden rages and boisterous good humour by turns. Boland came of a family with impeccable IRB credentials, both his father and uncle having worked for the Brotherhood. He himself took part in the Rising and had been imprisoned in Dartmoor and Lewes. Now thrust into prominence by the round-up as joint-secretary, with Alderman Tom Kelly, of Sinn Fein, he had his work cut out to restore the shattered organisation. The ensuing months would be the most challenging in the battle for the hearts and minds of the Irish people.

CHAPTER 6

The Work of Four Men, 1918–19

I am the very model of a modern Major-General.
WILLIAM S. GILBERT, *The Pirates of Penzance*

IN THE REORGANISED VOLUNTEERS IN THE SPRING OF 1918 CATHAL Brugha, as Chief of Staff, concentrated all his energies on meeting the threat of conscription, much of the day-to-day work devolving on the capable shoulders of Richard Mulcahy. Apparently the choice for this post lay between Mulcahy and Collins and in the end it was left to the two men to decide between themselves who should get it. Michael backed down, on the grounds that Dick Mulcahy had worked in Dublin for a number of years and, being familiar with the city, was better qualified for the job. Perhaps Michael also perceived that Brugha's deputy (whoever he might be) would never have the same amount of real power as he could by combining the two most important directorates. To this end he now stepped down from his job with the National Aid Association to concentrate on his military duties. The Headquarters Staff consisted of a number of directors, M.W. O'Reilly (formerly senior detainee at Frongoch) being Director of Training, Diarmuid O'Hegarty Director of Communications and Michael Staines Director of Equipment, as well as a number of staff officers and Dick McKee who commanded the Dublin Brigade. Michael Collins, on the other hand, was Adjutant-General, a function which would, in ordinary circumstances, have given him wide-ranging powers, but which he combined with two other posts, Director of Organisation and Director of Intelligence. Each of these would have been a full-time job for any general officer of reasonable intelligence and experience, but not only did Michael do all three, he carried out his disparate duties with his customary efficiency and attention to detail. As if this were not enough, he involved himself in a number of other tasks, notably the marketing and distribution of the Volunteer newspaper *An t-Oglach* which was edited by his friend (and biographer) Piaras Beaslai. Brugha was so preoccupied with harebrained schemes that he was unaware how Michael was quietly and unobtrusively taking into his hands effective control of the Volunteer Army. Later the Chief of Staff would say that Collins was merely a departmental head under his leadership, but there is no doubt that he resented the brash young man who effectively supplanted him. From March to May 1918, however, Brugha was totally embroiled in planning a spectacular assault on Westminster which would have made Guy Fawkes look like a choirboy. Cathal cherished the desire to get a hit squad into the House of Commons so that they could mow down the entire government front benches with machine-guns. During this period he even crossed to England to confer with Neil Kerr in Liverpool and Sam Maguire in London.

Security at Westminster was much more casual then than it is today, so the massacre was quite feasible; but in the end saner counsels prevailed and the plan was called off. Nevertheless, attacks on individual cabinet ministers remained an option that Cathal raised from time to time. On the other side, Brugha's counterpart and principal *bête noire* was Sir Henry Wilson, the Chief of the Imperial General Staff. A native of Edgeworthstown, County Longford, he was a rabid Orangeman with a blind, irrational hatred of Irish nationalism. He had nothing but contempt for the separatists and made the cardinal mistake of grossly underestimating his opponents. It was Wilson who coined the term 'murder gangs' to describe the Active Service Units which would prove to be the most effective formation in the coming conflict. Wilson had all the Irishman's fiery eloquence; it was a tragedy that so much of his invective was aimed at his fellow-countrymen in the Twenty-six Counties, whom he dismissed contemptuously as 'rats'. Till the day he died, he never grasped the fact that he was contending with an entirely new form of warfare. Ironically, he had served as a brigade major in South Africa during the Boer War and had been recalled to the War Office in order to apply the lessons learned in that conflict. Wilson, however, had a Bourbon cast of mind; he forgot nothing but learned nothing. The Volunteers of 1916 he dismissed as a disorganised rabble, and ever afterwards he had a mental image of his opponents as a Fred Karno's Army (a vaudeville act famous for its slapstick antics).

The tactics which Michael Collins evolved in the summer of 1918 produced a brand of guerrilla warfare that was without parallel or precedent. What the Volunteers lacked in numbers, equipment and weaponry, they would make up for in other ways. They were tight-knit, organised in 'circles', a cell system as a precaution against informers and breaches of security, and they fought on their own terrain, whether it might be in the alleyways of Dublin and Cork or in the moorland hills of Kerry and Tipperary. Their superior organisation and intelligence owed a great deal to the staff officer who controlled these matters. Their morale was very high and they were imbued with the justice of their cause. Far from being the murder gangs dismissed so cavalierly by Wilson, they had their own strict code of conduct and discipline.

Even more important, in the context of May 1918, the Volunteers were being transformed from a political minority into a national army. Michael dedicated a considerable amount of time and energy to achieving this, though it was done so subtly that the moderates in Sinn Fein (far less the British authorities) were not aware of it at the time. Even before the German Plot round-up, therefore, Michael (through his multifarious positions in the Volunteers) had taken over real power from Griffith. The British, by imprisoning de Valera, Griffith and the other political leaders, had, by default, presented the energetic young Adjutant-General with the real power in Ireland. The arrest and imprisonment of the Sinn Fein leaders was but the prelude to a campaign of repression and intimidation, employing such weapons as censorship and the curfew to cause the maximum inconvenience to the general public. The people of southern Ireland were demoralised and frightened, and more and more they began to turn to the Volunteers for protection and guidance. Even the Catholic priesthood was obliged to acknowledge the reality of the situation.

Through the summer of 1918 Michael pursued his various activities with the manic intensity of a demented leprechaun. He was now twenty-seven and at the peak of physical fitness; but he could not go on indefinitely punishing his rugged constitution with such demanding work that often kept him at his desk right through the night, railing constantly against 'all the hours we waste in sleep'. It was at this time that he stopped smoking and all but gave up alcohol, insisting that he would be a slave to nothing. In October he succumbed to a dose of Spanish influenza which turned into a bad attack of pleurisy from which only his incredible stamina saved him. Michael, who had never had a day's illness in his life until then, at first refused to leave his desk, and it was only when he collapsed in great pain and a high fever that he agreed to retire to bed. After a short while he felt a little better, so he struggled into his clothes and prepared to go out on his bicycle. Joe O'Reilly, alarmed at his chief's condition, tried to talk him out of it, but Michael ranted and raved like a man possessed and Joe quailed before the onslaught. He said no more as Michael feverishly buttoned up his overcoat and rode off; but Joe set off after him at a discreet distance. Michael's progress was decidedly erratic and, as luck would have it, he collapsed outside the police station in Store Street. Joe pedalled furiously towards his chief but already Michael was groggily picking himself up and staring in a daze at his bicycle whose pedal had been broken in the fall. When he clapped eyes on his subordinate he eyed him truculently.

'Here, Mick,' said the youth. 'Take my bike. I'll bring yours.'

With great difficulty Michael got his leg over the saddle and rode off unsteadily, but he frequently turned to glower at his faithful henchman who was doing his best to keep up on a machine which had lost a pedal and whose saddle had been adjusted for Michael's long legs. At Cullenswood House Michael had so far forgotten the pleurisy in his anger that he threatened to shoot O'Reilly if he kept following him like that, whereupon he fainted again and fell off the bicycle. Joe dragged Michael to the kerb and dashed off to the nearest pub for a tot of whiskey to revive him. Somehow he managed to get Michael to the house of MacDonagh's widow where the stricken leader was put to bed. Michael made a very bad patient, alternately cursing those who ministered to him and cracking boisterous jokes. He cursed everyone roundly when the doctor was summoned; reluctantly he agreed to take the mustard bath prescribed, but only if Joe alone gave it to him.

Twenty-four hours later, Michael was responding to treatment sufficiently to begin hollering for his clothes. He had important work to do, vital engagements to keep; but O'Reilly, in desperation, hid Michael's trousers and even went to Volunteer Headquarters to get written orders from Mulcahy confining the Adjutant-General to bed. The Chief of Staff, however, doubted whether any order from himself would have the slightest effect. When Joe returned, he found Michael out of bed, pacing up and down with a blanket round his shoulders. When Joe came into the room Michael grabbed him by the throat. 'It's my trousers or yours!' he growled.

Later that day Michael set off on foot for a meeting at Cullenswood House. Joe recalled that he had more than the usual jauntiness in his stride, as if to say 'I'll show you I can walk'. To Austin Stack he wrote on 12 October: 'It's the first time in 8 years I've felt it necessary to stay in bed . . . Of course I'll be all right tomorrow, but I'm very impatient.' By sheer willpower alone Michael overcame the pleurisy although it would have a debilitating effect on him for some time and leave him prone to colds.[1]

Someone with such an amount of nervous energy, who drove himself to the very limit of endurance, was a hard taskmaster to those who worked with him. He bicycled furiously round Dublin on his ancient Raleigh, charging like a whirlwind into the offices of his colleagues, or bounding up the stairs three at a time. The way Mick Collins charged around like a bull in a china shop, assessing the situation in a twinkling and barking out decisive orders, had a startling effect on subordinates. Half a century later veterans of the Anglo-Irish conflict would wryly recall the superhuman activities of the restless Adjutant-General. The word that came most readily to lips in describing him was 'magnetic': 'You became aware of his presence, even when he wasn't visible, that uncomfortable magnetism of the very air, a tingling of the nerves.'

In the latter part of 1918 Michael had no fixed abode. He had several offices in different parts of the city, but the nearest thing to home in that turbulent period was the dingy, cluttered office at Bachelor's Walk. Sometimes he spent the night there, if he was working round the clock; but more often

Michael Collins at the age of six

Members of the Collins family, about 1902 (from left to right): sister Margaret, grandmother O'Brien, sister Katie, mother Mary Anne, sister Mary and brothers Pat and Johnny

Michael's mother (left), sister Mary Powell, her baby daughter Nora, and Michael's maternal grandmother, Mrs O'Brien, about 1905

The Four Alls tavern, Sam's Cross

The humble farmstead in which Michael was born, restored in 1990

The remains of Woodfield farmhouse today

Collins as a staff captain of the Irish Volunteers, Dublin 1916

Prisoners of the Easter Rising in Stafford Gaol; Michael Collins is marked with an X

Officers and men of the Irish National Army, outside Kilmainham Gaol, 1922

LEFT: *Michael's fiancée, Kitty Kiernan (courtesy Felix Cronin)*

BELOW: *Hazel, Lady Lavery, painted by her husband as an Irish colleen, and featured on Irish bank-notes from 1928 to the present day*

OPPOSITE

TOP: *Griffith, de Valera, the Lord Mayor of Dublin and Collins at Croke Park, 1921*

BOTTOM: *Michael Collins and Harry Boland (far right) on the pitch, Croke Park, 1921*

Michael was an inconspicuous figure as he rode through the Dublin streets on his bicycle

than not, Michael never knew where he would lay his head that night. He was perpetually on the move. Sometimes he shared a room with Gearoid O'Sullivan or Diarmuid O'Hegarty, though more often with Piaras Beaslai or Harry Boland, sometimes both together. He was a difficult room-mate, always first to be up early in the morning and stamping around the room disturbing the others and hauling them out of bed. All the while he would be talking animatedly, perhaps bouncing the latest ideas (which had come to him in the night) off his long-suffering bed-fellows. He had a temperament impatient of all restraint, even that imposed from within, 'exploding in jerky gestures, oaths, jests and laughter; so vital that, like his facial expression, it evades analysis'.[2] Michael's words and actions, taken separately, might be commonplace, but the vibrancy and ebullience of the man was infectious. He exuded an aura of confidence that inspired others to tackle assignments more readily; they felt safer and stronger and more fearless when he was around.

Not everyone responded to his charismatic presence; there were some who considered him arrogant and insolent, stiff-necked and rude. To the ladies of the National Aid Association, irritated by his nonchalant manner when they interviewed him, would be added others who were repelled by his brusqueness and lack of common courtesy. In the summer of 1918 there would be many people, both men and women, who met Michael Collins and formed a rather poor first impression, merely because he neglected to shake hands or wish them good day; but this was a man in a terrible hurry with no time for social niceties. Robert Brennan, in fact, took an instant dislike to Michael which, in spite of a later appreciation of his infinite capacity for work, he never entirely overcame. 'Perhaps it was because he was ruthless with friend and foe; because he could brook no criticism or opposition. He drove everyone hard, but none harder than he drove himself.'[3] William Cosgrave was another who was not immediately impressed or charmed by Michael. His first impression was of an insufferably brusque young man; but this view later softened when he realised what a tremendous amount of work this human dynamo was achieving.

Michael knew that he was a difficult man, that he was often unreasonable, that his temper had an exceedingly short fuse; but he had a lot to do. In the vacuum left by the round-up the military and political power of the Republican movement was, for the time being, effectively in his hands. He knew only too well that he was now the most wanted man in Ireland. Later the myth would grow that Mick Collins led a charmed life, but his restlessness was his salvation. Constantly on the move, never sleeping in the same place two nights in a row, varying his movements and avoiding habits and routine, he succeeded in eluding the military patrols and the G men. He came and went as he pleased, or so it seemed, and must have put his hosts to considerable inconvenience not to mention danger, yet no one ever complained. Sometimes someone would protest at the way he mistreated his faithful stooge, O'Reilly. Then Michael would go puce with rage at the impertinence; but just as quickly his high colour would subside, his features would be calmed, and he would express contrition, with that little-boy smile that so often disarmed his critics. Sometimes, if he had transgressed in some way, he would make amends, despatching Joe for flowers or chocolates or a bottle of champagne for his hostess. For an instant he would be kindliness and attentiveness personified, though often the consideration came inopportunely and at random, like a misdirected kiss. But even those who would some day be his deadliest rivals could be mollified by the Collins attention to small personal details. He went to inordinate lengths to provide comforts for the Sinn Fein prisoners; he even noted the particular brands of tobacco they smoked and made sure that they got them regularly. When he could not get the brand that Austin Stack preferred he sent poor Hannie on a hunt round all the tobacconists of West London for it. On one occasion Joe O'Reilly, at Michael's behest, asked solicitously after a sick relative of the Chief of Staff. Momentarily the adamantine mask slipped and Brugha's eyes filled with tears. 'Mick is so kind,' he sobbed. 'He thinks of everybody.' The essential humanity of the man was evident in the warm personal notes and letters he wrote. He was an indefatigable correspondent; he had secretaries in each of his various offices and these girls sorted his mail, but often Michael would snatch the odd moment to pen a few lines that came straight from the heart. This attention to notes and letters of sympathy or encouragement is all the more astonishing when it is realised that Michael might deal with up to a hundred orders and directives a day to the divisional and brigade staffs then in course of providing the infrastructure for the forces that would soon take the field against the enemy. The archival material pertaining to this period, and now preserved in the Ministry of Defence archives at the National Library of Ireland, is documentary witness to Michael's daemonic energy. Nothing was too trivial for his personal attention, whether it be the resolution of a squabble between rival battalions in County Limerick or a sharp reminder to a brigade commander that his subscription to *An t-Oglach* was overdue.[4]

What Michael was to the Volunteer Army, Harry Boland was to Sinn Fein during these critical months. He, too, was in his late twenties, and had the same ebullient temperament. Both men could be aggressive one minute and utterly charming the next. They worked well together and, increasingly, spent their leisure hours together. They were Absolom and Achitophel, Roland and Oliver, D'Artagnan and Aramis. In the latter part of 1918, until Boland went off to the United States, they ate, drank, wrestled together and even slept in the same bed. They fought and argued, and then made up. There was an extraordinary bond between them; but they fell in love with the same woman and in the end Michael would be the one to win her heart. Although they were both constantly on the move, without any permanent refuge, they frequently stayed with Batt O'Connor and his wife, and the latter has left the most perceptive description of them. She would recall a furious argument that blew up suddenly, in which Harry proposed that Ireland could only attain independence from Britain by a long process of peaceful persuasion and political evolution, whereas Michael took the line that successive Home Rule bills from 1886 onwards had proved the futility of the political course. Only direct action would achieve their aims, and as they lacked the men and *matériel* they would have to wage war on the enemy by whatever means were available. In light of later events the stance taken in this argument by the protagonists seems ironic. Very early one morning Mrs O'Connor tiptoed round the house to check that all was well. The door of the bedroom occupied by Michael and Harry was ajar as a precaution against being taken by surprise, and as she passed along the corridor she noted a shaft of moonlight from the bedroom window fall upon the pillow where the two heads rested, side by side. It was a touching scene that roused the mother's instinct in her, until she was reminded of harsh realities, noting that Michael's brawny, naked forearm rested in sleep on the bedside table beside two long-barrelled Parabellum revolvers.[5]

Having imprisoned the Sinn Fein leaders, the British government sat back and wondered how best to proceed. Apart from the appointment of Field-Marshal French as Lord Lieutenant General with sweeping civil and military powers, the complexion of the executive in Dublin Castle was changed for the worse. In place of Henry Duke and Sir Brian Mahon, the Chief Secretary and Commander-in-Chief respectively, the hardliners Edward Shortt and General Sir Frederick Shaw were despatched from London to implement a new wave of restrictions, aimed at keeping the Irish in their place but, in fact, merely antagonising them even further. Now Irish language classes, athletic and sports meetings, even football matches and dances, were banned. Even worse, these restrictions were rigorously enforced. As relations between the people of the Twenty-six Counties and their political masters soured, one measure at least never materialised. In Britain itself the call-up was applied to more and more men in their late forties and fifties, and the combing-out process applied more ruthlessly in order to draft men who had hitherto escaped the net on account of health or reserved occupation; but the conscription of Irishmen remained a dead letter, thanks to widespread opposition within the Cabinet which was only too well aware that southern Ireland was a powder keg just waiting to ignite. Ironically, the most eloquent speaker, in persuading his colleagues, was General Smuts, the Boer leader during the South African War.

Jan Christiaan Smuts, born in Cape Colony in 1870, had a brilliant legal training at Cambridge and in 1898 became State Attorney of the Transvaal, but following the outbreak of the Boer War he joined the Boer field forces and, as

Commander-in-Chief in Natal and the Cape, played a major role in the peace settlement (1902). In the ensuing decade he worked for the creation of the Union of South Africa, serving successively as Treasury and Defence minister. During the First World War he commanded Imperial forces in East Africa and in 1917 represented South Africa at the Imperial Conference. As a member of Lloyd George's War Cabinet, he created the Royal Air Force and formulated the concept of the British Commonwealth. In 1919 he became prime minister of South Africa and in 1921 attended the Imperial Conference where he played a notable part in securing peace in Ireland.

Smuts pointed out that the Volunteer Army had been thoroughly overhauled and reorganised since the Easter Rising and, if all reports were to be believed, was now a formidable fighting force, far better trained, equipped and organised than ever before. The advice tendered by the man who had organised guerrilla warfare so effectively in the Boer War could not be ignored. In the end, only Lord Milner (who had headed the reconstruction of South Africa after that war) continued in favour of extending conscription to Ireland. As a compromise, the measure was still on the statute book when the Great War to end all wars ground to a halt on 11 November, but as the threat receded, the Volunteers were stood down. The men, organised along territorial lines, had trained part time and without thought of payment, but as the situation was normalised they returned to their farms and factories, their offices, schools and professions. There would be no respite for the Adjutant-General and his political counterpart Harry Boland, though.

Armistice Night in Dublin was not exactly the scene of jollification it was in London or Glasgow; it was the signal for a series of ugly brawls and running street battles. Rather smugly Michael reported to Austin Stack, still in prison:

> As a result of various encounters there were 125 cases of wounded soldiers treated at the Dublin Hospitals that night ... Before morning 3 soldiers and 1 officer had ceased to need any attention and one other died the following day. A policeman too was in a very precarious condition up to a few days ago when I ceased to take any further interest in him. He was unlikely to recover. We had a staff meeting so I wasn't in any of it.

Britain was exhausted, especially by the last months of the war. In July there had been a desperate strike of munitions workers in Coventry which spread like wildfire to Birmingham and Yorkshire, quelled only by the government's threat to draft the strikers into the army. There were further strikes in August, the most ominous being that which swept through the Metropolitan Police. The spectacle of London's policemen demonstrating and picketing police stations was regarded as a reflection of the moral collapse of the nation. Significantly in this crisis, Lloyd George relied very heavily on the Specials, the men over military age who had volunteered for part-time service as special constables. As the war progressed this force had become highly organised and extremely efficient. Hitherto special constables had been regarded as a joke; but now they had won the respect and gratitude of their hard-pressed country. Special constables would later be proposed by Lloyd George as one of the solutions to the breakdown of law and order in Ireland.

By September 1918 the outcome of the war was no longer in doubt, but the British people were reeling under far-reaching restrictions that altered their way of life and an ever-increasing range of rationing which accentuated the general war-weariness. Undernourished as a result of food shortages, the people easily fell prey to the epidemic of influenza. Many thousands throughout the United Kingdom died that autumn, though the global death-toll ran into millions. Since May 1915 the country had been ruled by a coalition ministry, but the cessation of hostilities meant a return to party politics. A fortnight after the Armistice, parliament was dissolved and a general election was called for 14 December. Lloyd George went to the country on an idealistic, rather sentimental programme of social amelioration based on the wartime spirit of comradeship. There was much talk of bringing the Kaiser to book and making the Germans pay for the war. The Welsh wizard insisted on pledged can-didatures for the election and all independent candidates were outlawed, although the Labour Party defied the ban and secured 57 seats. Independent Liberals succeeded in gaining 26 seats, compared with the 484 seats which went to Coalition supporters. Sinn Fein won all but four of the 77 seats in the Twenty-six Counties (the remaining four were the University seats held by Unionists). In the populous Six Counties of north-east Ulster, 26 Unionists were elected, while the Irish Parliamentary Party was reduced from 80 to a mere six MPs. In several instances, Sinn Fein leaders were elected in two separate constituencies. De Valera was elected in County Down as well as East Clare, while Griffith was elected in Tyrone-Fermanagh as well as East Cavan. To his three jobs in the Volunteer Army, Michael Collins now added a fourth, being elected MP in Armagh as well as his native county, where he had addressed the electors of South Cork:

> You are requested by your votes to assert before the nations of the world that Ireland's claim is to the status of an independent nation, and that we shall be satisfied with nothing less than our full claim – that, in fact, any scheme of government which does not confer upon the people of Ireland the supreme, absolute and final control of all this country, of all the affairs of the country, external as well as internal, is a mockery and will not be accepted.[6]

Curiously enough, this address made no reference to the actual form of government which would be established in the new Ireland. Whether by accident or design, the magic word 'Republic' was not used. Instead, Michael focused attention on the prisoners rounded up six months previously and also spoke emotively of the men who had faced the firing squads after the Easter Rising – 'sixteen of the noblest men that this or any generation in Ireland produced' who had 'by their calm and unflinching self-sacrifice redeemed the national situation'. He summed up his objectives as 'to subvert the tyranny of our execrable government, to break the connection of England – the unfailing source of all our ills – and to assert the independence of my native country'.

Described by *The Times* as an overwhelming victory for Sinn Fein, the dramatic outcome of the general election had not been achieved without a great deal of effort (as well as chicanery). To Michael Collins and Harry Boland had fallen the task of vetting the lists of Sinn Fein candidates which were compiled following the Ard Fheis in October. At that convention Michael had been disappointed to find a middle-of-the-road mood. Worse still, there were even delegates ready to speak out against him, criticising him for the extremism of the policies he was advocating. Michael mustered a bland smile at these attacks, but inwardly he was seething and determined there and then to ensure that never again would reasonableness and moderation rule the day. Michael, in particular, went over the lists of nominees submitted by the local Sinn Fein clubs and ruthlessly purged them of anyone regarded as a moderate. In the short term it was vital that the bloc of Irish MPs should be staunchly and uncompromisingly Republican, to show a united front against the British. In the long run this would create a problem, when the decision whether or not to accept the terms of the Treaty was being debated; but in the closing months of 1918 there was no room for political vacillation.

Ever since the German invasion of Belgium in August 1914, which had propelled the United Kingdom into the war, a central plank in Allied propaganda had been the rights of small nations. Of course, this was aimed primarily at the dismemberment of the Habsburg empire whose bombardment of poor little Serbia had started the war in the first place; but as the war escalated, and more and more countries were sucked into the vortex, the rights of small nations became a potent weapon. It proved to be a two-edged sword: what was good for the Czechs, Slovaks and Slovenes would surely be just as beneficial to the Irish, and they had a head start, in that the Home Rule which had been promised in 1914 could not be denied them in 1919. Undoubtedly, had there not been the little matter of north-east Ulster, Ireland as a whole would have made a bloodless transition, acquiring perhaps the status of Hungary in the Habsburg empire (Griffith's goal) or the status of Canada as a dominion (a notion with which de Valera toyed). The obduracy of the Ulstermen who were determined to remain completely within the British state was the stumbling block. In the 1780s the Protestants had made common cause with the Catholics in an Ireland which, for eighteen years, enjoyed its own parliament and a large measure of independence. This experiment failed mainly because power remained in the hands of a small Protestant clique and the Catholics were denied the vote. Wolfe Tone's United Irishmen sought an alliance with revolutionary France to create a democratic Irish Republic, but the Protestants, in alarm, formed the Orange Society and thus sectarianism reared its ugly head. An uprising led by Tone in 1798 was easily suppressed and in the aftermath Irish autonomy was swallowed up by the Act of Union in 1800 whereby Britain and Ireland formed the United Kingdom. Memories of this brief experiment, and the savagery of the Protestant reaction to it in the North, undoubtedly lay at the heart of the British government's thinking in 1919 when the question of implementing Home Rule could not be postponed any longer. The fact that the old Irish Parliamentary Party had been discredited and all but swept into oblivion, to be replaced by an apparently solid Sinn Fein, should have put the matter into sharp focus.

With the benefit of hindsight, it is probable that some form of partition was inevitable. The tragedy is that division among the Nationalist leaders allowed the Orangemen to secure the whole of the Six Counties. A Boundary Commission would eventually be established, with a view to deciding the frontier on politico-religious grounds, but it was powerless from the outset. Had partition been implemented by plebiscite, in the way that boundary disputes in the new Europe were settled, the area controlled by the Unionists would, in fact, have been rather less than half the area that became Northern Ireland.

Between 28 December 1918, when the election results were declared, and 4 February 1919, when the new parliament was due to assemble at Westminster, opinions in Ireland, North and South, were sharply divided on what course Sinn Fein would, or could, take. The mainly Unionist press in the North, predictably, denounced the Sinn Fein MPs as a revolutionary rabble which ought to be disqualified on account of their republican views; but throughout Ireland many of the provincial newspapers were controlled by the old IPP, and tended to dwell on the fact that the Sinn Feiners themselves were divided and unsure of how to proceed. The British press was overtly hostile; typical was the reaction of *The Daily Telegraph* which warned its readers that 'if the Sinn Feiners resort to histrionics . . . and proclaim themselves to be an Irish Convention or Parliament or some such name, the Government must deal with them with a resolute display of government and by no parleying with treason'. Other papers compared the proposed Dail Eireann (Gaelic for Irish Assembly) with the ill-fated Chartists' Convention of 1839. *The Globe* robustly dismissed the abstention of the Sinn Fein MPs as 'tomfoolery', pointing out that Britain could retaliate with a few differential tariffs 'on pigs and butter [which] would make Ireland bankrupt and raise in six months an overwhelming cry to be readmitted into the British Empire on any terms'. The consensus of opinion in Britain, as echoed in *The Daily News* of 1 January 1919, was that Sinn Fein would not go so far as to set up a provisional government, 'owing to the grave risks of such a movement ending in impotence and ridicule owing to its lack of force and funds'. The same paper conceded two days later, however, that Sinn Fein might set up a body similar to the Ulster Provisional Government which Sir Edward Carson had threatened to establish in 1913. It was felt that any move to establish a separate government would only have propaganda value, aimed at securing a hearing for Ireland at the Peace Conference. In general, there was a feeling that the proposed assembly was nothing more than a stunt, a piece of make-believe. By 15 January *The Times* pontificated that the attempt to create a separate parliament would be 'a hopeless fiasco'. By now other papers were either resigned to Sinn Fein abstention or were actually welcoming this move 'as a blessing' that would not disrupt the business at Westminster. Patrick Thompson, writing in *The Labour Leader*, alone appears to have foreseen that 'a bitter conflict between the Irish Government *de jure* and the British Government *de facto* will be carried on, perhaps to the logical conclusion of another armed revolt'.

The Sinn Fein MPs were resolutely committed to the policy of abstaining from Westminster. The decision to convoke the Dail had been taken at the Ard Fheis in October, when the matter was still purely hypothetical; but on 19 December, five days before the results were declared, the decision was reaffirmed. Sean T. O'Kelly was appointed chairman of a committee to set up the proposed assembly. A meeting of 'elected Republican members' (or at least those of them at liberty) was held on New Year's Day at the Mansion House. On this occasion it was resolved that 'Messrs Beaslai and Collins were deputed to issue the whip to the Republican members' who would be summoned to attend a 'publicly announced' assembly at Dublin City Hall in due course.

The delay in implementing this decision was due to the fact that the majority of the Sinn Fein MPs were in prison at the time. The Sinn Fein Executive Council discussed the feasibility of substitute members, but no decision was taken. Michael was reported as 'very much against' forming a parliament while so many of those who had won seats in the election remained in prison.[7] Another option was to extend membership of the Dail to leaders of national organisations, local government bodies, trade union leaders and the Catholic hierarchy, but in the end this ploy was rejected. It was essential that the Dail should be seen from the outset to be wholly representative of the wishes of the people, and therefore only those who had been duly elected by the existing parliamentary process could be eligible to attend.

In due course, those MPs who were not languishing in English gaols met at the Mansion House, Dublin, on 21 January 1919 to form their own parliament, known in Irish as Dail Eireann. In the interests of national solidarity the IPP and Unionist MPs were included in the summons, but none of them responded. Whether the Sinn Fein leadership, or such of it as was still at liberty, took the trouble to notify the authorities in Dublin Castle or Westminster of their intentions is not known, but it may be supposed that the Castle, and therefore London, were well aware of the situation. Even the *Times* report conveyed the impression that no one at Westminster was paying much attention to the antics of the Shinners. Three days earlier, Lloyd George had departed for the Versailles peace conference, to deliberate over the destiny of Poland, Czechoslovakia and the other small nation states which had emerged as a result of the war. If the Prime Minister pondered on events at home he was probably more concerned with the great strikes of miners and railway workers, among others, which erupted that month, or the seemingly insurmountable problems that had cropped up to delay the demobilisation of the vast wartime armies. Early in January Sir Edward Shortt gloomily predicted that 'while the Peace Conference is sitting it will be impossible to get Lloyd George to appreciate the situation' and he hinted darkly that his own powers to take the initiative were restricted: 'Obstruction, jealousy, stabs in the back all contribute to make the life of a Chief Secretary a rather heart-rending business.'[8]

By contrast, the world's press attached far more significance to the meeting of the breakaway Irish parliament; among the thousands who thronged the streets of Dublin to watch the comings and goings of the members were about seventy reporters and press photographers from the United States and Canada as well as many European countries. The dramatic effect of the inaugural meeting was heightened as the roll of members was called and in so many cases the response, in Irish, was, 'imprisoned by the English'. Only twenty-four members were, in fact, present on that auspicious occasion to hear Father O'Flanagan read a prayer before Cathal Brugha delivered the opening address in Irish.

The Provisional Constitution was read out, providing for a president and a cabinet of four ministers. In the document, the expression for the chief executive was *Priomh Aire*, literally 'first minister'. This would later be open to interpretation; de Valera, who was elected to this office in his absence, would regard himself not as the President of the Dail but as President of the Republic, although there was a world of difference. More importantly, he would be regarded in the latter role when he was in America. In the first Dail Michael was initially Minister for Home Affairs but, when the second session was convened in April, the key portfolios, of Defence and Finance, were apportioned to Cathal Brugha and Michael Collins respectively. While continuing his military duties Michael would be immersed in the running of a government department responsible for funding the embryo state. His greatest achievement in this particular role would be the raising of the National Loan; and as if this were not enough he was also involved in setting up two clandestine newspapers, operating a bomb-making factory and establishing his élite assassination unit, known simply as 'The Squad' or more fancifully as 'The Twelve Apostles'.

After the recital of the Constitution, Brugha declaimed in sonorous tones the Democratic Programme in Irish and English. Members and spectators rose to their feet during this emotionally charged ceremony and many wept openly. The rest of the two-hour session was something of an anti-climax, the assembly, having constituted itself a parliament, going on to discuss at some length the selection of delegates to attend the Peace Conference and press the claims of Ireland. At a meeting of the Volunteer Headquarters Staff two days later Cathal Brugha forcefully told his subordinates that a new situation had arisen:

> The Volunteers have become the army of a lawfully constituted government, elected by the people, and are entitled morally and legally when in the execution of their duty to slay the officials and agents of the foreign invader who is waging war upon our native Government.[9]

The inaugural meeting of the Dail was characterised by orderliness and decorum. The British authorities did not interfere, though Lord French took the precaution of sending an observer, George Moore, who sat in the gallery and reported back that the meeting represented the general feeling of the country. Looking round the gallery, he was also singularly impressed 'by the profound emotion of the spectators'. For many of them, sitting absolutely still and hanging on every word, it was manifestly a day of their souls' consecration, 'a day that they had never expected to see but whose coming moved them profoundly'. That evening, a reception and dinner were held in the Oak Room in honour of the visiting journalists. Thus, from the outset, the rebel government gave top priority to cultivating the foreign press, one of the most potent weapons in its arsenal during the coming conflict.

On that very day, a party of Tipperary Volunteers led by Dan Breen and Sean Treacy decided, on their own initiative, to raid the quarry at Soloheadbeg and seize a consignment of gelignite which was to be stored there. They ambushed the explosives wagon and its escort of RIC constables, two of whom were shot dead at point-blank range in the ensuing scuffle.

These shots triggered off the Anglo-Irish War.

CHAPTER 7

The First Dail, 1919

We, the Republican Members of the Irish Constituencies,
in accordance with the National Will, are empowered to
call together the Dail Eireann and proceed to act
accordingly.

RESOLUTION OF SINN FEIN MPS, 1 JANUARY 1919

ON THE MORNING AFTER THE DAIL WAS FORMALLY INAUGURATED, its members met again to organise its business. Cathal Brugha was elected 'President of the Ministry pro tem' and then proposed his ministers which the Dail approved: Eoin MacNeill (Finance), Michael Collins (Home Affairs), Count Plunkett (Foreign Affairs) and Richard Mulcahy (National Defence). The unanimity of the meeting was broken only by Piaras Beaslai who voted against MacNeill as Finance Minister on the grounds that the latter openly professed his ignorance of financial matters. Sean T. O'Kelly was elected as Ceann Comhairle (chairman), a secretariat of four was appointed, and the Dail then adjourned. It did not meet again until 1 April, by which time the political situation had changed dramatically.

Press reaction to the newborn parliament was predictable, if mixed. Reports in the Irish papers were mildly euphoric one moment and full of gloomy foreboding the next. Only *The Cork Examiner* appears to have been wholly positive in describing it as 'a political event of the first importance'. On the other hand, *The Belfast Newsletter* dismissed the proceedings as a farce and, having detected some reference to religion as one of the differences between Ireland and England, in the Message to the Free Nations of the World, went off at a hysterical tangent:

> Thus Ireland is alleged to be a Celtic and Roman Catholic nation, and all who are not Celts and Romanists are regarded as foreigners. It is because Ulster knows that this is what Home Rule means that it will not have it.

Actually, there was absolutely no reference to religion, or indeed to Home Rule, in the document. The British press was generally hostile. Even *The Manchester Guardian* condemned 'Republican theatricalism' and its 'absurd climax' which no one in Britain would take seriously. In contrast, *The Daily News* warned that it would be foolish to dismiss the new assembly as nothing more than a bunch of well-meaning idealists; and it rightly perceived that the outrage at Soloheadbeg was 'a message deliberately sent by the new invincibles to the talking shop in the capital'. In the days and weeks that followed, the inaction of the Dail reinforced the view that it was a fantasy. Arthur Griffith, then in Gloucester Prison, managed to smuggle out a long letter on 23 January giving sound advice: don't attempt too much, and concentrate on getting a hearing at the Peace Conference. Two men were, in fact, sent to Paris with £4,000 (half in gold sovereigns) but they achieved little and never filed a report, much to Michael's disgust; and he repeatedly queried how the money had been spent.

In the days preceding the assembly of parliament at Westminster there was considerable speculation in Britain regarding the abstaining Sinn Feiners. Fearing that they might change their minds and actually turn up, the London police were ordered to bar their entry and arrest any who happened to be on their wanted list. There was much talk in the discomfited IPP camp of the Sinn Feiners being invalidated and their seats handed over, by default, to the runners-up. In the end, the British government did nothing and the gap in the composition of the Commons was tacitly ignored. It is interesting to speculate that, had the seventy-three Sinn Fein MPs taken their seats at Westminster, they would have voted solidly with Labour, and consequently the ill-fated and short-lived Labour governments of 1923 and 1929 might have achieved a great deal more as a consequence – one of the great might-have-beens of history.

Meanwhile, Lord Haldane was sent by Lloyd George to Dublin to negotiate with Sinn Fein on the basis of Dominion status, provided that there was no repetition of the Soloheadbeg affair. The Sinn Fein leaders demanded the release of the prisoners but referred to a speech by de Valera in 1918 which implied that Dominion status would be acceptable. This would give Ireland full control of Customs and Excise but leave her without an army or navy. Charles Hathaway, an American diplomat in Dublin, reported to his government that 'the majority of Sinn Feiners would not stand out for a republic – that in fact Sinn Fein in demanding independence is following the Irish practice of asking the most in order to get much'.[1]

The Dail determined to try and get its views aired at the Peace Conference. On 10 February Sean T. O'Kelly arrived in Paris and began pleading the Irish case; but though the French newspapers reported sympathetically on the issue, the Irish 'delegate' failed to get an audience with Woodrow Wilson, far less make his views heard by the Conference as a whole. Had O'Kelly succeeded, and Ireland been placed on the agenda, pressure could have been brought to bear on Lloyd George and the British government; but the Conference restricted its deliberations to the aspirations of small nations emerging from the ashes of the vanquished empires, and studiously avoided any attacks on the empires of the victorious Allies. As international diplomacy foundered, where parliamentary procedure had failed so often in the past, Sinn Fein began to pay more attention to the views of the extremists and physical-force men.

It is not certain under which of Michael's many hats he planned the escape of Sinn Fein leaders from their places of confinement in England and Wales, but early in 1919 he and Harry Boland worked on a number of schemes. One of the more quixotic was a plan to remove *Lia Fail*, the Stone of Destiny, from the Coronation Chair in Westminster Abbey. Seized by Edward I in 1296, the stone had been transported from Scone where, for generations, it had been used in the crowning of the Scottish kings; but it had been brought from Ireland to Dalriada (Argyll) late in the sixth century, and it was believed to have been brought to Ireland by Queen Scota (ancestress of the Scots) in the Celtic migrations, and that it was the very pillow of stone on which Jacob slept when he dreamed of the angels ascending to heaven. In the end, Michael's scheme was aborted, and the stone would remain undisturbed until Christmas Day 1950 when a band of young Scottish Nationalists retrieved it for several months.

Instead, the young militants of Sinn Fein were ordered by Cathal Brugha to concentrate on an even more spectacular exploit which would have much greater practical benefit. Michael had previously (on 11 November 1918) taken advantage of the Armistice Day celebrations to organise the escape of Denis MacNeilis from Cork Gaol. MacNeilis had been imprisoned for taking a pot-shot at a constable in the RIC and wounding him. At a time when many other Irishmen were in prison for more serious offences under the Defence of the Realm Act, the springing of MacNeilis seems a strange choice; but he was a Volunteer, and therefore someone for whom Michael felt a responsibility. Besides, Cork Gaol was where Michael's uncles had been imprisoned almost seventy years earlier, so perhaps there was a personal element in this choice.

This was but a curtain-raiser for the much more ambitious and hazardous enterprise three months later, the liberation of de Valera from Lincoln Gaol. It was almost aborted when, on the day of the Dail's inauguration, four of the German Plot internees broke out of the prison at Usk in Monmouthshire. Michael was furious at this daring escape, fearing that the British would tighten security and jeopardise the escape which he was then planning. De Valera had managed to borrow the key used by the prison chaplain while he was saying Mass, and taken impressions in candle wax. Drawings of the key were actually sent brazenly out of the prison in the form of a Christmas card drawn by Sean

Milroy showing a cartoon of a drunken Sean MacGarry wielding a huge key outside his front door, with the caption 'Xmas 1917 can't get in'. The other side showed MacGarry in a prison cell looking at a large keyhole in his cell door, with the caption 'Xmas 1918 can't get out'. On the card was written the message:

> My dear Tommie,
>   The best wishes I can send are those de Valera wrote in my autograph book. Field will translate.

Field was Michael's *nom de guerre*. Then followed, in de Valera's handwriting, an explanation in Irish that the key in the picture was an exact drawing of the prison key and that the keyhole showed a cross-section of it. The message continued, asking for a key and some small files to be sent in a cake. De Valera asked for arrangements to be made for the escape and a date to be fixed, using a coded message 'Billie got up the –th of last month – is now quite well'. This would indicate a date in January when the escape should be attempted.

The card and wax impressions were sent eventually to Gerry Boland (Harry's brother) who had a replica key cut and smuggled into the prison inside a cake. This key was defective, so a second one was made and smuggled into the prison in another cake. The second key did not work either, because it was not a master key and therefore unable to override the key used by the chief warder to put a double lock on all doors. Next, a blank key and a set of small files, likewise smuggled in a cake, were delivered, but the blanks had a central slot which meant that they would not fit the prison locks. Finally, a fourth cake, delivered by Kathleen Talty, contained blank keys which proved very effective. MacGarry then sent a coded message to Michael Collins who was in Manchester with Harry Boland, finalising details for the escape with characteristic meticulousness. At 7.40 p.m. on Monday, 3 February, de Valera, standing anxiously at his cell window, saw the prearranged signal – a torch beam. For what seemed an age the beam stabbed the night sky and de Valera was sure that everyone would see it. Harry, in fact, was disconcerted to find that he could not switch off his torch and eventually thrust it deep into his coat pocket. De Valera responded by holding several matches together and lighting them to produce a momentary flare.

Immediately de Valera, accompanied by Milroy and MacGarry, calmly opened cell and corridor doors and made their way quietly to the back gate in the outer wall. This opened easily enough, but straight away they were confronted by a second gate. Outside this gate stood Michael Collins with a duplicate key; Harry had cut through the barbed wire of the perimeter fence to bring them thus far. Michael inserted his key in the lock and tried to turn it, but it jammed and then broke under pressure. Later, Piaras Beaslai would describe this tense moment:

> Boland . . . dwelt on the feeling of utter despair which seized him at this juncture. Collins said, in a heartbroken tone, 'I've broken a key in the lock, Dev.' De Valera uttered an ejaculation and tried to thrust his own key into the lock from the other side. By an extraordinary piece of luck, he succeeded in pushing out the broken key with his own and opening the gate.[2]

Harry threw his fur coat over de Valera's shoulders and donned a light raincoat as they sauntered down the lane, arm in arm, pretending to be a courting couple as they emerged on Wragby Road near the military hospital. They even exchanged good-natured banter with other couples, British soldiers and nurses who were kissing and taking fond farewells by the hospital gates. There was a worrying moment when Michael and Harry could not find the taxi they had ordered, but in the end it was located outside the Adam and Eve Inn. Here they parted company, the prisoners driving to Worksop, twenty-five miles away, and thence by Sheffield to Manchester, while Michael and Harry would head for London by train. It says a great deal for Michael's superb organisational skills that both the escape and the complicated journey afterwards were undertaken so smoothly, especially the hiring of cars at a time when vehicles and petrol were still subject to wartime restrictions.[3]

The escape was not discovered till 9.30 p.m. when the cells were being locked for the night; but by the time the hue and cry was raised the escapees were well away. The public first knew what had happened when the stop press columns of the late editions in Dublin broke the news the following day. The dramatic escape of the man who was universally regarded as Ireland's leader – the only commandant from the Rising to escape a firing squad – had a terrific impact on Irish morale and grabbed the world's headlines. Reported sightings of the fugitive were legion – everywhere between Skibbereen in County Cork and the Peace Conference at Versailles. In fact, de Valera remained in hiding in Manchester for several weeks. Meanwhile MacGarry and Milroy had travelled on to Liverpool. Michael, in London, avoided his sister Hannie and spent the day with Sam Maguire and other IRB members before catching the train to Liverpool. He had not eaten or slept in thirty-six hours when he was met by Neil Kerr but on learning that a ship was about to depart for Dublin that night he forgot about food and sleep and went aboard, anxious to make his report to Cathal Brugha as soon as possible.

Most biographies of de Valera state that he waited in Manchester, anxious to return home. In fact, within an hour of his escape, de Valera had dropped a bombshell. He had made up his mind to go straight from England to the

United States, where he had been born and where, he felt, he could best serve the cause of Irish independence by whipping up support there. In mitigation, he had the precedents of Masaryk and Paderewski who had marshalled the Americans of Czech and Polish descent to secure the emergence of their nations. Michael disagreed violently with de Valera, but the latter was obdurate. In Dublin Michael broke the news and Beaslai vividly recorded the response:

> The statement was received by all of us with dismay. We felt that de Valera's departure would be a fatal mistake, that the country would misunderstand his motives and regard it as a selfish, or even cowardly, desertion. When this view was expressed, Collins replied, 'I told him so, but you know what it is to try to argue with Dev. He says he had thought it all out in prison and that he feels that the one place where he can be useful to Ireland is in America.' The meeting took the view that the place for an Irish leader was in Ireland wherein the strength of the fight put up would determine the support in America, and it was decided to send Brugha to England to urge de Valera either not to go at all or, failing that, to show himself first in Ireland, so that the publicity value of his escape should not be dissipated.[4]

Accordingly, at great personal risk, Brugha crossed to Liverpool and arrived in Manchester on Friday, 7 February, to confer with de Valera at the presbytery of Father Charles O'Mahoney, chaplain of the Crumpsall workhouse. Cathal stayed there till the Sunday evening, haranguing, cajoling and wheedling by turns. In the end he convinced de Valera that, if he had to go to America, he ought to pay a token visit to Ireland in passing. At length de Valera yielded on this point, but decided to stay put until Michael Collins had made his usual thorough plans for a safe journey. De Valera's version of Brugha's visit is that, prior to 7 February, he had planned to go back to Ireland; but as a result of Cathal's visit, 'bringing him up-to-date with the progress to establish an Irish legislature and conditions in Ireland', he decided that his chances of getting a hearing at the Peace Conference were slim. Then – and only then – did it occur to him that the best place for him to further the Irish cause was in America.[5]

There may, of course, be some truth in the statement of de Valera's biographers that the enforced inactivity of hiding in Manchester was a greater strain than prison life. On 18 February word reached him from Michael Collins that arrangements had now been finalised for his return to Ireland. Michael was still in Dublin on 10 February, for he wrote to Austin Stack on that day; but probably the following week he returned to England to superintend the movement of the most wanted man in the British Isles. He arranged for de Valera, disguised as a priest, to be escorted by Paddy O'Donoghue, Kathleen Talty and Mary Healy by taxi to the home of a Mrs

McCarthy near Liverpool docks. The following night he was taken aboard the *Cambria* by Seamus O'Donoghue, the second mate, and Con Murray, an able seaman, and concealed in O'Donoghue's cabin.

At 1 a.m. on 20 February, like a thief in the night, de Valera landed in Dublin, wearing carpet-slippers and with a black silk handkerchief concealing the lower part of his face. He was immediately bundled off by Michael to the house of Dr Robert Farnan in Merrion Square. While de Valera gave an extensive interview to Ralph Couch, an American journalist, Michael and Harry combed the city for a more secure hiding-place. Eventually they hit upon the premises of the Dublin Whiskey Distillery on the north side of the city near Clonliffe College and, under cover of darkness, de Valera was brought to a disused gate in the college wall. Harry's imitation of a curlew brought Father (later Monsignor) Michael Curran from the dinner-table of Archbishop Walsh to open the gate. As de Valera parted from Harry Boland he asked him to procure a large fountain-pen for use on the voyage to New York. For the rest of February and much of March 1919 de Valera stayed in the Gate Lodge of the Archbishop's residence at Drumcondra, the Archbishop being unaware of his presence. During this period he worked on a declaration which he hoped to place before the Peace Conference.

On 6 March Pierce McCann, a prominent member of Sinn Fein from Tipperary, succumbed to Spanish influenza in Gloucester Gaol. Arthur Griffith, himself suffering from this deadly ailment, warned the British authorities that if there were further deaths in captivity Ireland would rise in rebellion. Hours later, all prisoners from the German Plot round-up were suddenly released. Earlier that week, de Valera had returned to Liverpool to lodge with Mrs McCarthy while arrangements for his voyage to America were being finalised. He was therefore in Liverpool when the release of the prisoners was announced. Although there was an outside chance that the British might move against him out of pure spite, de Valera felt that he could now return openly to Ireland, and receive the hero's welcome that had been denied him a month earlier.

Michael himself had returned to England towards the end of February, accompanied by Harry Boland, partly to make arrangements for de Valera's impending trip and partly to confer with Sinn Fein sympathisers in London. They had great difficulty getting accommodation there, and at first had to doss down on a mattress on the floor of a friend's house, but after a few days, made all the more uncomfortable by a mild attack of food poisoning, Michael obtained a room in the Regent Palace Hotel. The hotel was crammed to overflowing, with fifteen hundred people staying there, and Harry and Michael often had to queue for hours to get a seat at mealtimes. From an undated letter to Kitty Kiernan, written immediately after their return to Ireland about 8

March, Michael revealed that 'we had to combine a good deal of business with the maximum of pleasure'. The London conference lasted eight days, sitting from 10 a.m. to 5 p.m., and every day they were booked up with friends for theatres, concerts and even dances. 'On only one night did we have a proper rest.'[6] Michael returned to Ireland by a roundabout route, in a freighter which docked at Valentia Island off the Kerry coast, and accompanied by two of the released prisoners, Laurence Ginnell and William Cosgrave.

Shortly after his return to Dublin Michael began planning a great national homecoming for de Valera. The highpoint of the reception would take place at the Mount Street Bridge (which de Valera's battalion had so stoutly defended in April 1916), when the Lord Mayor would hand over the keys of the city. The freedom of the city had hitherto been confined to royalty, so this gesture was unprecedented and expected to turn into an event of great national rejoicing. De Valera prepared a fiery speech, paying tribute to Mick Malone and his other gallant comrades who had fallen in the defence of the bridge three years previously.

In the end, the speech was never delivered. Michael published an announcement, in the name of Sinn Fein, that the grand civic reception would take place on 26 March. Twenty-four hours before the monster demonstration, however, it was prohibited by Chief Secretary Shortt, backed by a massive military presence throughout the city; the British authorities might be prepared to turn a blind eye to de Valera's safe return, even though he was technically an escaped prisoner and therefore liable to re-arrest, but they could not countenance a triumphant spectacle. Michael, characteristically, was for going ahead with the reception (which would have involved a mass turnout of the Volunteers) and spoke very forcibly on the issue at a Sinn Fein Executive meeting which was chaired by the newly returned Griffith. When the moderate Darrell Figgis had the temerity to question the minutes of the previous meeting, at which the reception had allegedly been mooted, Michael rose to his feet and glowered at his challenger, who later produced a graphic account:

> Characteristically, he swept aside all pretences, and said that the announcement had been written by him, and that the decision to make it had been made not by Sinn Fein, though declared in its name, but by the 'proper body, the Irish Volunteers'. He spoke with much more vehemence and emphasis, saying that the sooner fighting was forced and a general state of disorder created throughout the country (his words in this connection are too well printed in my memory ever to be forgotten) the better it would be for the country. Ireland was likely to get more out of the state of general disorder than from a continuance of the situation as it then stood. The proper people to make decisions of that kind were ready to face the British

military, and were resolved to force the issue and they were not to be deterred by weaklings and cowards. For himself, he accepted full responsibility for the announcement and he told the meeting with forceful candour that he held them in no opinion at all, that, in fact, they were only summoned to confirm what the proper people had decided. He had always a truculent manner, but in such situations he was certainly candour itself. As I looked on him as he spoke, for all the hostility between us, I found something refreshing and admirable in his contempt for us all. His brow was gathered in a thunderous frown, and his chin thrust forward, while he emphasised his points on the back of a chair with heavy strokes of his hand. He was a great foeman when he fought thus – a worthier foeman than when he manipulated organisations. But, by his contempt of his audience, he had touched the combative in Griffith.[7]

Griffith strongly opposed the reception proposal, though he pointedly remarked that he would accept the decision of the meeting and 'no other body' – a side-swipe at the IRB. The meeting adjourned so that the views of de Valera himself could be ascertained. He, too, was adamant. In a letter to the Sinn Fein Executive de Valera stated that he did not consider it an occasion on which they would be justified in risking the lives of the citizens. 'We who have waited know how to wait,' he wrote. 'Many a heavy fish is caught even with a fine line if the angler is patient.'[8] So de Valera returned to Dublin unobtrusively and bided his time.

Michael's own version of the stormy meeting of the Sinn Fein Executive was summed up in a letter which he wrote to Austin Stack:

The chief actor was very firm on the withdrawal, as indeed was Cathal. I used my influence the other way, and was in a practical minority of one. It may be that all arguments were sound, but it seems to me that they have put up a challenge which strikes at the fundamentals of our policy and our attitude.[9]

Interestingly, news of the contretemps at the Sinn Fein Executive leaked out to the Royal Irish Constabulary, whose monthly intelligence report noted drily that 'the physical-force party has lately got the upper hand'.

Generously, Michael turned over his own office at Sinn Fein Headquarters to de Valera. Not aware of this, callers continued to come in enquiring after the Big Fellow. One afternoon de Valera flounced angrily out of the room, demanding, 'Who is this Big Fellow?' That evening there was a Sinn Fein meeting at which a place was left vacant for de Valera as chairman. When Michael motioned to him to take it, he replied, 'Let the Big Fellow take the chair.' The source of this story was Padraig O'Keefe, a fellow Corkman. Like Michael, he had no illusions about de Valera. On one occasion the latter took O'Keefe aside in the Sinn Fein offices and said, 'Paddy, did you hear they're sending me to America?'

'Bejasus, they are not,' replied O'Keefe. 'It's your own bloody idea to get over there out of the trouble.'[10]

On I April 1919 the second session of the first Dail was convened, and met on three occasions over the ensuing four days. At the opening meeting de Valera's position as *Priomh Aire* (First Minister) was confirmed. He appointed a Cabinet of seven which merely shifted individuals from one ministry to another. In this reshuffle Michael emerged as Minister of Finance, the others being Griffith (Home Affairs), Plunkett (Foreign Affairs), Brugha (Defence), William Cosgrave (Local Government), Countess Markievicz (Labour) and MacNeill (Industries). In addition, three non-Cabinet posts were created, Robert Barton becoming Director of Agriculture, Laurence Ginnell Director of Propaganda and Ernest Blythe Director of Trade. In June 1919 the Cabinet was expanded with the addition of Sean Etchingham (Fisheries) and J.J. O'Kelly (National Language), while Austin Stack was brought in as Home Affairs Minister in November when Griffith was promoted to Acting President in de Valera's absence. In this line-up Michael, at twenty-eight, was the youngest, while Count Plunkett, at sixty-eight, was by far the oldest. All but three (Plunkett, Griffith and MacNeill) had fought for Ireland in the Rising; one (Barton) had taken part in the Rising on the other side, as an officer of the British army.[11]

On Sunday, 6 April, de Valera made his first public appearance for almost a year. Ignoring a proclamation banning such gatherings, a huge Gaelic League football match was held at Croke Park to raise money for the National Aid Association. When the President made his grand entry as guest of honour, 30,000 spectators rose to their feet as one and greeted him with tumultuous cheers. To the surprise of RIC intelligence officers who were discreetly monitoring the occasion, de Valera made no attempt to address the crowd. At the Ard Fheis held two days later, de Valera declared emphatically that he was against any form of violence towards the RIC, a statement which (according to a police spy in the hall) 'was well received by moderate members, resented by extremists'. Darrell Figgis, on the other hand, formed the opinion that the meeting was packed by IRB and IRA men (a term now coming into widespread use for the first time) who had been instructed, by Collins, to vote against those members of the Executive who sought a constitutional solution. Figgis was, in fact, soundly defeated for the post of Secretary by Harry Boland, and felt ruefully that the militants had gained the upper hand. Nevertheless, Michael himself, only four weeks later, was complaining that the political activists were squeezing out the supporters of physical force in the party.

On 10 and 12 April there was a two-day session devoted to government policy. De Valera announced that he would continue to seek international support, co-ordinate the efforts of voluntary bodies in various national activities and resist British efforts to impose harmful legislation on the country. In a curious statement he touched on the relationship between his government and the Irish Volunteers (or IRA): 'The Minister of National Defence is, of course, in close association with the voluntary military forces which are the foundation of the National Army,' although the exact nature of that association was not defined.

Only two positive decisions were taken at this juncture; the first was the launch of bonds for the National Loan in the amount of £500,000, with half to be offered at home and half abroad; and the second was the social ostracism of the police, widely regarded as the instrument of British injustice and oppression. Sending individual constables to Coventry was one thing; perpetrating acts of violence against them was another, and 'official' Sinn Fein was resolute in its condemnation of the latter. Needless to say, the physical-force element regarded the police as a legitimate target. No attempt was made to discuss the Democratic Programme; when Piaras Beaslai raised the matter, de Valera told him that this was not the time for such deliberations. The Dail was then adjourned.

The Dail Loan was Michael's greatest single achievement; indeed, Griffith would later describe it without exaggeration as 'one of the most extraordinary feats in the country's history'. Many in the Cabinet, particularly Griffith, were sceptical at the outset; the most Sinn Fein had ever managed to raise in the past was a few thousand pounds, but now Michael was confidently promising to raise a quarter of a million. Griffith gazed askance at the young braggart, but when he soon found that Michael's words were matched by deeds he looked upon him with new respect. Nerve centre of the Dail Loan was Michael's office at 6 Harcourt Street where he controlled a battery of secretaries, clerkesses and typists. Though he was a tough boss he was always fair, and even if he seldom took time for a quick bite he always made sure that his staff had their proper meal breaks.

The Loan was launched at a great outdoor ceremony in the grounds of Padraig Pearse's school, St Enda's College. Michael, as Minister of Finance, made a particularly rousing speech. The immediate problem confronting him was how to get across to the public that money was being raised. When he placed advertisements in newspapers, the British authorities promptly suppressed the offending papers. They might turn a blind eye to the antics of the Dail, but fund-raising was definitely frowned upon. Ever resourceful, Michael had a propaganda film made by his friend John MacDonagh, and even compromised his innate obsession with anonymity by appearing in one scene himself. Copies of this film were taken round the cinemas by young men in trench-coats with ominously bulging pockets and projectionists were persuaded to show the Dail Loan promotion between the main features. Then the Volunteers would pocket the reel and slip away before the police arrived.

Michael made a series of personal appearances, making impassioned speeches on behalf of the Loan. In midsummer he paid a fleeting visit to Cork and took the opportunity to visit Johnny and Katty as well as his sister Mary whose sons Sean and Michael Powell long afterwards remembered their big, bluff uncle playing with them and their toy boat on the River Lee. Michael, who could not swim a stroke, was concerned when the boys tried to retrieve the boat from deep water. 'Ye young shcamps!' he would admonish them, in his broad Cork accent. Everywhere he went he was dogged by the RIC. A posse, backed by troops, lay in wait for him at Clonakilty station but Michael, dozing off in the train, missed his stop and evaded arrest. In Dunmanway he put his money where his mouth was, opening the contributions with £25 of his own cash, a month's salary.

By one means or another, by forceful eloquence and personal example as well as word of mouth, Michael got the fund rolling. Soon sums of money were trickling in; then the trickle became a flood. Raising the cash was one thing; what to do with it was something else. Accounts in various banks, both in Ireland and in Britain, were opened in the names of various Sinn Fein sympathisers and enormous risks were taken to ensure the deposit of funds therein. About half the funds were converted into gold, and a considerable amount of the precious metal was gathered together from the rings and trinkets of countless thousands. The gold, other than coins, was melted down and cast into crude bars concealed in a baby's coffin buried in the foundations of Batt O'Connor's house. Other caches of gold were concealed below the floors or within the walls of various other buildings in Dublin, including Maurice Collins's shop and the cellar of Kirwan's in Parnell Street. Almost as valuable as the money itself was the list of subscribers, which would have compromised the independence movement had it fallen into the wrong hands. On 12 September 6 Harcourt Street was raided; Michael barely escaped through a window and sat on the roof with the precious documents till the raiding party had left. His accounts of the fund, which eventually surpassed the £250,000 he had promised, have been preserved and are an eloquent testament to his attention to detail, as well as providing a vivid (and at times harrowing) picture of the struggle to raise such a huge sum against all the odds. It also sheds interesting light on the patchy pattern of fund-raising in different parts of the country. One district's niggardliness provoked Michael to write to Austin Stack: 'If you saw the bloody pack down there & their casual indefinite meaningless purposeless way of carrying on'. By contrast, Terence MacSwiney's indefatigable efforts in Cork yielded more than twice as much money per capita as any other part of Ireland. Significantly, this was an area that was suffering a greater degree of harassment from the RIC and the military than almost anywhere else.

During the first half of 1919 the ministries of the rebel government worked out of the old Sinn Fein offices at 6 Harcourt Street, described by the English journalist Hugh Martin as an 'extraordinarily shabby and mean-looking headquarters'. Today it is the headquarters of *Connradh na Gaelge* (the Gaelic League) and very much an ornament to this fine Georgian street, but in 1919 it was in a dilapidated condition. No government could operate for long in such down-at-heel surroundings and in July a much more commodious building up the road at 76 Harcourt Street (now the premises of the Foreign Ministry) was purchased for £1,130. Batt O'Connor, the master-builder who had often provided Michael and Harry Boland with a bed for the night, was called in to prepare a series of ingenious hiding-places in this building, not only for men on the run but for the secret documents of the rebel state. The Post Office was informed that the new occupants of the house were the Irish Club, a designation that fooled no one, least of all G Division, which discreetly examined the contents of all mail packets going in and out of both 6 and 76 Harcourt Street (unaware that the intelligence section organised by Michael Collins was doing precisely the same to all Castle correspondence).

On Sunday, 1 June 1919, at home in Greystones, de Valera prepared to sit down to a very special lunch, celebrating his wife Sinead's birthday, but at that very moment a messenger arrived from Michael to say that he must leave at once, as arrangements had now been completed for his departure. De Valera was upset, but he had no alternative but to grab his suitcase and accompany the messenger to Dublin where he met some of the Cabinet and then took the mail-packet to Holyhead. On board, he ran into Father McCarthy who had been the chaplain at Kilmainham in 1916. McCarthy was travelling with Sir James MacMahon, the Under-Secretary for Ireland, and wanted to take de Valera to MacMahon's stateroom to meet him. De Valera refused point-blank, and therefore missed an opportunity to meet with the most prominent of the Irish Catholic civil servants, a man who could have provided a conduit right to Lloyd George himself. But de Valera was now set on going to America, and nothing could deflect him from that course. At Holyhead, he gave McCarthy the slip and caught the train to Liverpool where Michael's friends were on hand to smuggle him aboard the SS *Lapland*. On 11 June the seasick stowaway awoke to the first sight of his native city since he had left it thirty-five years earlier – all 'straw hats and sunshine'. The visit to America was meant to have been a brief one; but it was to last eighteen months, and it was not until 23 December 1920 that de Valera returned to Ireland, by that time a country changed beyond all recognition.

CHAPTER 8

The Intelligence War, 1919

Tuar beannacht bheith i bpriosun
(If you want good wishes, go to gaol)
TRADITIONAL IRISH BALLAD

AFTER THE SPECTACULAR BREAK-OUT OF DE VALERA, MILROY AND MacGarry from Lincoln in February, Michael was involved in several other escapes which raised morale and gave the movement worldwide publicity. On 16 March he pulled off the daring escape of Robert Childers Barton from Mountjoy Gaol in Dublin. A member of a prominent Anglo-Irish family, with estates in County Wicklow, Barton was nine years older than Michael and had the conventional upbringing and education of his class. On the outbreak of war he had obtained a commission in the British Army and had been stationed in Dublin when the Rising erupted. This had the effect of converting him from Home Rule to the Nationalist cause and he was one of the Sinn Fein MPs elected in December 1918. The following February, along with several others, he was arrested and imprisoned. Before the war he had been chairman of a co-operative banking project and he therefore had considerable agricultural and financial expertise which would be particularly useful. When the Dail established Banc na Talmhan (the National Co-operative Mortgage Bank) in August 1919, Barton was appointed its first director. It was imperative that such a man, representing the Protestant element in Sinn Fein, should be set free at the earliest opportunity.

On this occasion Michael resorted to the traditional methods by smuggling into Mountjoy a stout file and a rope. On the third Sunday in March, when the moon was bright and Dubliners were at evening devotions, Barton propped up a dummy of himself, sawed through the bars on his cell window and lowered himself to the ground below. Swiftly he crossed the prison yard and called softly to Michael and his team outside. A rope ladder was thrown over the outer wall and finally Barton jumped from the top into a blanket. He was immediately driven to Batt O'Connor's house where he lodged for the night.

Mrs O'Connor recognised him immediately as the British officer who had been kind to her after Batt's imprisonment three years earlier. When Batt rejoiced at Barton's escape, Michael said, 'That's only the beginning. We're going to get Beaslai and Fleming next.'

Pat Fleming had been court-martialled and sent to Maryborough (now Portlaoise) Gaol in March 1917. Demanding political status, he had put up an obstreperous campaign, refusing to wear convict clothing and smashing up his cell. Eight warders were required each morning to force him into prison clothing, a daily exploit that earned him the sobriquet of Samson. Then the authorities changed tactics and left him in a bare stone cell totally naked; later they resorted to cruel restraints, such as the strong belt, the 'muffs' and the straitjacket. Nothing daunted, Fleming even managed to destroy his straitjacket by burning it off in the flame of the gas-jet that illuminated his cell. In the end the authorities gave way and transferred him to Mountjoy where political prisoners were held.

Early in 1919 Piaras Beaslai had been arrested on a charge of sedition. On 29 March Joe O'Reilly stood on the canal-bank outside the prison, holding three bicycles. At a signal from within, one of Joe's comrades, Paddy Daly of the Squad, threw a rope ladder over the wall. First to appear was Beaslai, followed by Fleming and eighteen others. A further five prisoners nobly remained behind as a rearguard, covering the warders with 'pistols' (spoons actually) in their pockets.

Michael was waiting impatiently in the lounge of the Wicklow Hotel for news when O'Reilly arrived after having seen to the concealment of the escapees. Michael's first question was, 'Is Fleming out?'

'The whole gaol is out,' cried Joe.

'What?' asked Michael. 'How many?'

'About twenty, when I came away!'

Michael stared blankly at Joe for a moment, then burst into hearty guffaws before rushing off to debrief Beaslai and Fleming. That evening Michael was at his desk in Cullenswood House, and Joe noted that every so often he would lay down his pen and burst into fits of uncontrollable laughter, the tears streaming down his cheeks as he recalled the great escape and tried to imagine the consternation of the governor when he arrived to find his prison practically empty.

Late in March 1919 the long arm of the law reached out and almost grabbed Michael himself by the collar. On 20 April 1918 he had been released on £50 bail from Sligo, bound to surrender later to stand trial for sedition under the Defence of the Realm Act at the next Longford assize; but he never did. On 6 February 1919, at the Hilary Sessions in Longford, the case of Rex v. Collins was resumed. As the defendant did not turn up, the bail money put up by

Michael Cox and Michael Doyle was forfeit and a warrant for the arrest of Michael Collins was issued by the magistrates; but in the confused situation of Ireland several weeks passed before the appropriate documents landed on a desk in Great Brunswick Street police station and the immediate arrest of the young Sinn Fein leader was ordered. Fortunately for Michael, he was forewarned by one of the detectives, Ned Broy.

Like Joe Kavanagh, Broy was increasingly troubled by the cruel dilemma of having to implement the policies of a foreign power against his own people. Through a close friend, Michael Foley, he sought an introduction to Michael Collins. A meeting on neutral territory, at Foley's house in Cabra Road, gave both men the opportunity to weigh each other up. In the finest traditions of the RIC, Ned was powerfully built, broad-shouldered and held himself erect in the approved military fashion. He had penetrating green eyes, which one English observer would later describe subjectively as hard and cruel one minute and shifty the next, as befitted a man who had so cunningly double-crossed his British masters. A native of Kildare, Broy had been reared in the Nationalist tradition, in which bitter memories of the atrocities of the Yeomanry in the 1798 rebellion died hard. Until 1916 Ned had obeyed orders and conscientiously carried out his duties as confidential clerk in the administrative section of G Division which had its headquarters at the police station in Great Brunswick Street (now Pearse Street); but the Rising, and the brutal execution of the ringleaders, had produced a sea-change. Through his daily routine, he was only too well aware that Sinn Fein and the IRB were riddled with informers and police spies. Then it had come to him that the only way for the Nationalists to beat the British at their own game was for him to act as a mole within the RIC. Unbeknown to him, Joe Kavanagh had come to this decision around the same time. Just as Kavanagh was distrusted by Sinn Fein as an *agent provocateur*, so also Ned Broy was frustrated when he found that the information he supplied to Sinn Fein, via the O'Hanrachain family (who had lost a son in the Rising), was being ignored or discounted. It was this sense of futility that had driven him to seek a meeting with the Big Fellow himself. Michael was a shrewd judge of character and was the first to realise the true worth of both Kavanagh and Broy, although he employed them separately and unknown to each other, a policy that enabled him to confirm and corroborate the material which they supplied to him individually.

Kavanagh would prove a most effective source of intelligence for almost a year before he became too ill from cancer to continue; but before his untimely death he recruited another man. James MacNamara was an unlikely choice, for he came from a prominent Unionist family and was regarded by the RIC as one of their best men. He would continue to supply Michael with vital information until early in 1921 when he was suddenly dismissed. The grounds for his dismissal were not stated, and MacNamara wisely did not seek an explanation. On hearing of the sacking, Michael told him, 'You're lucky. If they had anything on you you'd have been shot outright!'

Fortunately, by that time Michael had recruited a fourth detective. David Neligan, like the others, had become disillusioned and disaffected by what he saw going on around him, and in May 1920 he got in touch with Patrick Sheehan, then secretary to de Valera. Sheehan's reaction was to advise Neligan to leave the RIC, as his brother Maurice, a trade union leader, was also urging him. Neligan duly resigned and returned to his family home in Tralee, but when Michael got wind of this he immediately contacted him and requested that he return to Dublin. Michael said that it was imperative that he rejoin the RIC as soon as possible, but Neligan demurred, saying that he would rather join one of the flying columns, as the guerrilla bands were known. Michael riposted, 'We have plenty of men for the columns, but no one who can fill your place in the Castle.' With great reluctance Neligan eventually gave way. To pave the way for his re-enlistment, it was arranged for him to receive a series of anonymous threatening letters which he showed to the police. In due course he was reinstated in G Division, but a few months later volunteered to transfer to the Secret Service wherein he remained undetected until the British withdrew from the Twenty-six Counties in 1922. His position, at the very heart of the British intelligence machine, cannot be overemphasised; it was a master-stroke which would enable Michael to carry out the most devastating single blow of the entire war, in November 1920.

In the early months of the intelligence war, Michael met with his police agents personally and separately, but usually at the home of the librarian Thomas Gay in Clontarf. The information which Michael received was then passed to Liam Tobin, who was unaware of the source; but by the end of 1920 Neligan would be dealing with Tobin direct. Liam was a young Corkman who had fought in the Rising and been detained in Frongoch. In happier times, he had worked in a hardware store; but by 1919, aged twenty-five, he was Michael's chief executive in the Intelligence Directorate and it was he who had accompanied Michael on a pilgrimage to Westminster Abbey in order to assess their chances of removing the Stone of Destiny. Neligan later produced vivid pen-pictures of both men. Tobin, once a devil-may-care young rascal, had become:

> Tall, gaunt, cynical, with tragic eyes, he looked like a man who had seen the inside of hell. He walked without moving his arms and seemed emptied of energy. Yet this man was, after Collins, the Castle's most dangerous enemy.[1]

Michael Collins, on the other hand, seemed to have remained unaffected by the stresses of the period when Nationalist fortunes were at their lowest ebb:

> He had a winning smile, a ready laugh and cheerful manner. He had a trick
> of turning his head swiftly and then the resolute line of his jaw showed. He
> was a friendly man with the fortunate manners of putting one at ease.

Ned Broy's duties included the transcription of the daily reports of the G
men into a ledger; he was thus in a unique position to funnel information to
Michael, either through his cousin, Pat Treacy, or through Thomas Gay at the
public library. Ned was also in the habit of popping into a dairy in Parnell
Square for a glass of buttermilk, and here he would also pass on messages to
Sean Duffy, one of Michael's couriers who, as an electrician, moved freely all
over Dublin. Other 'drops' included Phil Sheerin's dairy near the railway
station in Amiens Street where agents in their role as railway employees could
bring reports from the North, Harry Boland's shop in Middle Abbey Street
and O'Hegarty's bookshop in Dawson Street.

Luck (and British ineptitude) was also on Michael's side when his cousin,
Nancy O'Brien, was personally selected by Sir James MacMahon as his
confidential clerk. At that time Nancy was still working for the Post Office
where her loyalty was never questioned; but it is a complete mystery to this day
why the authorities overlooked the fact that she was a close relative of the most
wanted man in Ireland. On hearing that Nancy's new duties would be the
handling of Dublin Castle's top-secret coded messages, Michael exploded, 'In
the name of Jasus how did these people ever get an empire?' Nancy was willing
to do what she could to ensure that copies of these messages should get to
Michael almost as soon as they reached Sir James, but at times Michael could
be unreasonable in his demands. The poor girl not only had to spend her meal-
breaks locked in the toilet making copies of decoded messages which she then
secreted in her corset and knickers, but she was also frequently called away
from her office in the basement of the General Post Office by a curt,
peremptory message from her cousin, to check out something in one of the
offices on an upper floor, far from her own workplace, and in a part of the
building where she had no right to be. When she complained about missed
lunches and all those stairs she had to climb, Michael playfully pinched her
bottom and said, 'Yerrah, ye can well afford to lose a bit of that.' Nancy's
apartment in Glasnevin became an important 'post office' where a veritable
army of informers called at all hours of night and day to drop titbits: postal
and telegraph clerks, postmen, railwaymen, dockers, seamen, civil servants,
warders from Mountjoy and even disaffected constables of the Dublin
Metropolitan Police. Daring and resourceful, Nancy was mercilessly used by
Michael; what little free time she had from her official duties was often utilised

as a courier, whenever Michael had some message or package that was especially important to be delivered. When her father died, and Nancy went home for the funeral, Michael callously exploited the situation by giving her a consignment of goods to deliver for him. On the train journey to Cork, a British officer gallantly helped the attractive young lady with her extremely heavy luggage, unaware that her cases were crammed with firearms and ammunition.

Tim Pat Coogan recounts a story which he received from Nancy's son, Michael Collins. On one occasion she got quite a grilling from her cousin over a message which he was expecting but which she denied receiving. The only message she had seen recently was some nonsense from an anonymous admirer referring to 'Angelus bells and the light glinting in her hair'. Michael immediately exploded: 'What sort of a Gligeen ejit are you anyway? That's the message I'm looking for. The warders change at six o'clock and our man will be in his room when the light goes on.' Nancy wept angry tears and told Michael where he could stuff his messages in future. In the wee small hours that night Nancy was awakened by gravel rattling on her window-pane. On peering out, she saw the burly figure of her cousin standing in the front garden below, and motioning to her to come down. Full of contrition and remorse, he apologised profusely, saying that he was 'under the most terrible strain'. To make amends, he said, 'Here's a little present for you,' and left a package on the garden wall before vanishing into the shadows. On the wall Nancy found a big bag of boiled sweets.[2]

Piaras Beaslai, too, had a cousin who was recruited into Michael's intelligence network. Lily Merin was a member of the Women's Auxiliary Army Corps and worked as a typist in the Castle. Through her Michael obtained vital information concerning field security and counter-insurgency operations, as well as personal details of British intelligence officers which enabled him to finger them with devastating accuracy. Lily would take the carbon paper from her office to a house in Clonliffe Road where she would retype intelligence reports, placed in sealed envelopes for one of Michael's intelligence officers to pick up after she had gone. Thus Lily never knew who collected the reports and he, in turn, never knew her identity either. She was also involved in a literally quite deadly game in the later stages of the Anglo-Irish War when Dublin was teeming with British intelligence officers, mostly in plain clothes. Lily would take a stroll down Grafton or Dame Streets, arm in arm with Frank Saurin or Tom Cullen, two of Michael's most trusted men. As they passed a man whom Lily recognised as a British agent, she would give her escort's arm a squeeze. Just how many British agents were targeted by means of this identity parade will never be known. Lily continued to work at the Castle until the middle of 1921 but shortly after the Truce came into effect she was summarily dismissed, proof that the British had only managed to breach IRA security when the clandestine forces came out in the open.

Not all of Michael's best operatives worked in the Dublin area. Josephine Marchmont was the chief clerkess at military headquarters in Cork covering the entire south-west of Ireland. She had impeccable credentials; her father had been a senior constable in the RIC and her Welsh husband had been killed in action during the war. One day a canteen orderly at the barracks noted Josephine, dejected and weepy, and discovered that she was pining for her two little sons in Barry, Glamorgan, in the custody of her mother-in-law who had refused to give them up. This titbit was passed to the adjutant of the First Cork Brigade of the IRA, Florrie O'Donoghue, who sent it on to Michael Collins. Shortly afterwards Josephine was told that, if she agreed to co-operate with the IRA, she would get her sons back. Josephine agreed, and Michael himself supervised the kidnapping of the boys, carried out by Florrie O'Donoghue and Sean Phelan. The children were spirited over to Ireland and lodged with the families of sympathetic farmers where Josephine could visit them. Thereafter she provided a vast amount of information on troop movements and military deployment, on imminent raids and round-ups and on individual intelligence agents, spies, informers and stool-pigeons. She was the eyes and ears of the IRA in the South-west, enabling the Volunteers to stay one jump ahead of the British at every turn. After the killing of three British intelligence officers in November 1920 she came under suspicion, but was tipped off by a friendly soldier that all female staff were to be searched on leaving the building that evening. She succeeded in getting rid of the copies of top-secret documents she had intended to smuggle out that night and was 'clean' when searched. After the Anglo-Irish War she married her spymaster, Florrie O'Donoghue.[3]

Although Michael was heavily involved, in the latter half of 1919, in launching and organising the great National Loan which eventually raised £380,000, his most spectacular achievement as Minister of Finance, it was as Director of Intelligence at Volunteer GHQ that he really came into his own. Through his IRB connections, Michael established a network of agents that extended throughout the length and breadth of the British Isles. He had his spies in the offices of the railway companies and shipping lines who tipped him off about troop movements; he had agents aboard coastal steamers and transatlantic liners which enabled the envoys of the infant republic to go to Paris and New York without passports or visas; he had a network of informers covering every level and aspect of Irish society, not only in Ireland itself but wherever there was an Irish community; and he was on particularly good terms with John Devoy and Daniel Cohalan, the leaders of the Fenian Brotherhood in America and old-style political bosses who marshalled Irish-American support. Michael's phenomenal talent for organisation was seen at its best in the seaports. On the surface it might appear that the British were firmly in control; but the IRB had so thoroughly infiltrated the port authorities and the dockers' union that wanted men were easily spirited out, and much-needed arms and ammunition poured in. Every morning Joe O'Reilly would cycle down to the North Wall to meet the incoming steamer. This gave new meaning to the 'Irish Mail', as Michael's secret channel was dubbed. Gelignite from the coalfields of the Rhondda and Lanarkshire carefully packed in tin trunks; rifles in wicker hampers marked 'China – Fragile' or, dismantled, in sailors' kitbags; revolvers, hand-grenades and ammunition in hand-luggage – all this and much more came ashore each morning under the very noses of the RIC and the military patrols.

Michael's agents permeated the postal and telegraphic services of the United Kingdom and were to be found in every government department in London and the provincial cities of Britain as well as all over Ireland. Eventually he would be able to count on the vast majority of the ordinary people of southern Ireland, as the British oppression scaled new heights. Michael was the spider at the centre of this vast and intricate web; he alone held all the secrets in his head, and many of his files were marked DBI ('Don't Butt In'). While this intelligence network eventually gave him a total overview of British activity in and out of Ireland, in the initial stages the most important element lay within the RIC itself.

On the evening of 7 April 1919 Ned Broy even managed to get Michael into the headquarters of G Division. Tiptoeing past the dormitory where the G men were sleeping, Michael was led into the record room where he spent the night sifting through secret police files, including his own which contained the information that 'he comes of a brainy Cork family'. Working diligently through the records until daybreak, Michael carried away an old detective daybook as a souvenir – and in his head the details of the RIC intelligence system. Now he knew exactly what he was up against and how he could best fight it. With the slender resources in men and arms at his disposal he realised that he could never hope to combat the British on their own terms; but if he could eliminate the enemy's intelligence he could paralyse its police and military or at least severely limit their effectiveness. It was Broy himself who told Michael, 'The RIC will have to be dealt with. You'll have to shoot.' This was a tall order, bearing in mind that the RIC was a gendarmerie with over ten thousand well-armed and highly trained men, but the notion of dealing with its key figures, especially the G men, seemed attractive. Attending a session of the Dail the following morning, and showing no evidence of fatigue after his busy, sleepless night, Michael pondered how he could deal with British Intelligence.

He now had a detailed list of all the detectives in G Division, their movements and whereabouts. At this time official Sinn Fein policy was resolutely set against acts of violence and the Soloheadbeg incident was, if not unanimously deplored, certainly widely regretted. Consequently Michael initially contented himself with verbal warnings to individual G men. Volunteers, acting under Michael's orders, would sidle up to a detective in the pub or the street and softly caution him to lay off. Many of them got the message: now that they were marked men their enthusiasm for arrests, interrogation and acts of intimidation and harassment generally waned. Of course, there were some who chose to disregard repeated warnings and in the end they would pay for their stubborn courage with their lives.

The campaign of friendly warnings began on 9 April and continued for several months, but as the British increased the frequency and severity of raids on houses and business premises, the seizure of property, the suppression of newspapers and magazines, and the arrest and detention of men and women for seditious acts, Michael gradually stepped up his counter measures. Constable O'Brien was gagged and bound to the railings outside his police headquarters. Unscathed by this terrifying ordeal he later commented to Broy that it was damned decent of Sinn Fein to leave it at that, and thereafter he took no further active role against the Volunteers.

Not surprisingly, the officers of G Division did not take kindly to being threatened. On 9 May they retaliated with a massive raid, timed to coincide with the visit of the Irish-American Delegation which was then on a fact-finding mission to Dublin. On that momentous day, at a public session of the Dail, the three Americans, Frank P. Walsh, Edward F. Dunne and Michael J. Ryan – the first Americans to address an Irish parliament since Benjamin Franklin in 1782 – received a heroes' welcome. Lest the delegates might be in any doubt that Ireland was suffering under an oppressive régime, the civic reception following the meeting was raided by the RIC backed up by heavily armed troops. Tim Healy, who was present while the police and military jostled and bullied the assembled dignitaries, later commented on this monumental act of stupidity: 'The stars in their courses fight in favour of the Sinn Feiners.'[4]

The principal objective of the raid, however, had been to arrest Michael Collins. Immediately after the morning session of the Dail he had taken his place for the civic luncheon with two other IRB comrades, but their meal was rudely interrupted by Joe O'Reilly who burst in breathlessly to say that lorry-loads of troops and police had cordoned off the streets round the Mansion House. Michael rushed to the rear door of the building, but a glance through the keyhole showed Daniel Hoey leading a squad of soldiers at the double up the lane. Joe got hold of a ladder from the janitor and Michael and his two comrades scaled the high wall from the rear yard into an adjoining building which was then empty and semi-derelict. They managed to climb through a broken window, and while Joe was replacing the ladder there was a mighty hammering on the oaken door at the front. The Lord Mayor himself opened the door, to be confronted by a chief inspector who announced that he had a warrant for the arrest of Michael Collins whom he knew to be in the building. The Mansion House was then invaded by swarms of police and soldiers who searched the building from cellar to roof. Perhaps because he was hovering too closely behind them, Joe himself was arrested at one point, but released on the intervention of the Lord Mayor. Meanwhile Michael and his friends crouched under the roof of the building next door and actually heard the detectives in the yard below debating whether it would be feasible to squeeze through the missing window-pane. After the longest three hours of Michael's life, the raiders gave up and departed. Covered in grime and dust, Michael emerged from his hiding place and dropped down through a trapdoor into a contractor's store. From there he returned, via an adjoining garage, to the Mansion House.

The Lord Mayor was determined that the reception for the American delegates should go ahead, despite the dramatic interruption and the fact that everything was in disorder. While members of the Dail and civic leaders mucked in to tidy up the mess left by the raid, Michael sent Joe home for a change of clothing. The reception was actually well under way by the time Joe returned with Michael's Volunteer uniform. There was a stunned silence when the door opened and in walked the wanted man, the man who had caused all the commotion earlier in the day. It was a large assembly, the men formally attired in morning suits and the ladies in their finest gowns, but Michael, resplendent as Adjutant-General, was the only person present in military uniform. The Big Fellow was received with thunderous applause. Michael, indulging his histrionic temperament and talent for self-dramatisation, savoured the moment to the full.

The nerve centre of Michael's intelligence operation was a house in Crow Street where Liam Tobin was installed with a small staff which included Tom Cullen and Frank Thornton. Tobin, in particular, had a genius for gathering and collating the seemingly unconnected trivia which enabled him to build up a picture of the enemy's movements and intentions. Using such unlikely sources as *Who's Who* and the social columns of *The Times* and *The Morning Post*, Tobin constructed elaborate profiles of the movements, haunts, hobbies, appearance and social connections of everyone remotely connected with the British administration of Ireland. From this building, virtually in the shadow of the Castle, the intelligence machine of the infant republic operated with deadly and devastating efficiency. There was nothing romantic or cloak-and-dagger about the way Michael conducted this aspect of his work. He himself came and went, smartly attired like a lawyer or bank manager; his staff might have been clerks in an accountant's office as they went quietly and unobtrusively about their daily routine. On this modest, pedestrian, almost banal organisation, Michael built up for himself a fearful reputation such as no Irish leader had ever enjoyed.

In midsummer Michael's sister, Katie Sheridan, came up from Mayo to Dublin on a visit. As she boarded the train, however, an informer had recognised her and as a result her description was wired ahead to Dublin where police and military lay in wait to pounce on a woman wearing a brown gabardine coat. Luck intervened; during a delay at Athlone, Katie was seen by a friend who, struck by her poor appearance (she had been ill recently), insisted that she take her fur coat and wrap up well against the unseasonably inclement weather. When the train reached Dublin around midnight the platform was swarming with armed troops. The passengers were ordered to remain seated while the train was searched. Word spread that the sister of Michael Collins was the object of all this activity. Having successfully evaded detection on account of the change of coats, Katie stepped out of the carriage and was horrified to see on the platform not only Joe O'Reilly but her kid brother himself, large as life. Her head swam and she almost fainted, but Michael, unabashed, ran up to her solicitously. When he asked a porter what all the commotion was about, and was informed that the arrest of Michael Collins was imminent, he made for the nearest British officer and blustered, 'That damned Collins again! This is the third time today I've been held up on that damned blackguard's account!' He indicated the tottering figure. 'Look at that poor lady; she's obviously very ill. What possible use can there be in detaining her?' The officer noted the fur coat and as this did not tally with the description he had been given he nodded curtly and let her go. Michael thanked the soldier courteously and shepherded poor Katie through the press of soldiery, still muttering imprecations against that damned Collins.

By the end of July, when wholesale arrests were the order of the day and individual acts of police brutality were becoming more numerous, Michael decided that the time had come to fight fire with fire. One G man, known as 'The Dog' Smith because of his brutal manner, was singled out on account of a specific case in which he was involved. At first he received the customary warning from the Volunteers, after he had arrested Piaras Beaslai for being in possession of seditious material which he had planned to publish in *An t-Oglach*. Detective-Sergeant Smith was approached with a reasonably polite request to drop the charge, but he retorted, 'I'm not letting young scuts tell me how to do my duty.' The 'young scuts' were Michael Collins and Harry Boland. At this juncture Michael approached Dick McKee, commander of the Dublin Brigade, to select a small group of men who would have no scruples about taking life. In this casual manner the Squad came into being.

Unlike most other Volunteers of the period, members of the Squad were full-time professionals, paid £4 10s a week. This élite team of trained assassins worked under Michael's direct orders though he himself never took part in any of their operations. It was led initially by Mick McDonnell, whom Michael had known in Frongoch, and later by Paddy Daly. In addition to these two, the first members of the Squad were Ben Barret, James Conroy, Sean Doyle, Joe Leonard, Pat McCrea, Joe Slattery and Bill Stapleton.

Having recruited a hit squad, Michael agonised for several days about ordering it into action. Commanding Volunteers in the General Post Office and leading men into action in the heat of battle was one thing; but Michael had never before ordered the death of another human being, in cold blood, and he became unusually silent and morose at the enormity of it. When the decision was taken, and the day named for the shooting dawned, those closest to him were aware of an extraordinary tension in him, a tension made all the more unbearable when, for reasons beyond their control, the hit-men reported back empty-handed. Joe O'Reilly watched fearfully as his chief paced the room, swinging his arms and digging his heels viciously into the carpet. For ten or fifteen minutes Michael continued in silence; then he snatched up a paper and tried to read, but his eye kept straying to the window with an empty, faraway look. When Joe tried to break the silence with some banal comment, Michael would turn and rage at the poor inoffensive youth. The Big Fellow, the pugnacious hot-head at whose very name the moderates quailed, was beginning to learn things about himself. He had a zest for the fight, whether in the political arena or the battlefield; but the responsibilities of life and death had a very sombre, sobering effect on him. 'I am a builder, not a destroyer,' he once remarked to Ned Broy. 'I get rid of people only when they hinder my work!' But though he ordered the deaths of many men he never became hardened to it.

In fact, members of the Squad lay in wait for The Dog for several nights before succeeding in intercepting him on the way to his home in Drumcondra on 30 July. Although hit by several bullets, Smith managed to draw his own revolver and return fire as he staggered into his house and bolted the door. He subsequently died of his wounds. Michael's reaction to the report from the Squad, that they were amazed to see the detective continuing to run after he had been hit, was to replace their .38 revolvers with .45 calibre weapons whose stopping power would never be in doubt.

Official reaction to the Smith killing was a total clamp-down on Sinn Fein, but this merely played into the hands of Michael and other extremists. Apart from that traumatic third session, on 9 May, when the Irish-American reception was so dramatically held up, meetings of the Dail that summer were conducted in private, the fourth session (17–19 June) being held in a room at Fleming's Hotel, and the fifth (19–20 August) in the Oak Room of the Mansion House. On 12 September the British authorities banned the Dail and carried out a massive raid on Sinn Fein headquarters at 6 Harcourt Street. The ban did not prevent the Dail meeting again on 27 October, when twenty-eight members met in the Oak Room, but it would not reassemble till the end of June 1920. An amazing amount of business was transacted during the brief meetings of this parliament, and the foundations of the counter-state laid, leading to Sinn Fein control of local government, the establishment of Sinn Fein courts and tax-raising in parallel with the British system which was increasingly ignored or boycotted. But there is no doubt that the inability of the Dail to function openly and continuously created something of a power vacuum on the Republican side.

In this situation Michael Collins and the physical-force element gained the upper hand. Ominously, there were many indications that the physical-force men in other parts of the country were increasingly a law unto themselves. The social boycott of the RIC was extremely effective, and by August 1919 Joseph Byrne, Inspector-General of Police, was officially admitting that the police could no longer enforce law and order throughout the country without the assistance of troops. Even so, this was not enough for the hotheads, particularly in southern and western districts. In Tipperary, the victors of Soloheadbeg, Dan Breen and Sean Treacy, urged the Dail to issue a proclamation ordering all British forces out of Ireland, and when this was refused they took matters into their own hands, initiating a campaign of violence against the RIC and, significantly, those who refused to ostracise them. In June an inspector of the RIC was shot in the main street of Thurles, County Tipperary. As the unfortunate victim lay dying, a crowd gathered and jeered, with cries of 'Up the Republic'. No sympathy was shown for the dead man or his family, the town council remained silent on the matter and scarcely a blind was drawn on the day of the funeral. Lord French was in England at the time and told a public meeting there that the Dail was 'a so-called, self-constituted, illegal, insane Government' which possessed 'a secret army which they called the Irish Volunteers'. This army contained 'a body of assassins', and he concluded that 'the result is a complete system of intimidation throughout the whole population', ruefully admitting that police efforts to track down the assassins 'are rendered absolutely abortive'.

Some time in May, Michael was elected president of the Supreme Council of the Irish Republican Brotherhood, a position he was to hold till his death more than three years later. Thereafter there was a gradual polarisation, subtle and imperceptible at first, but eventually so clear that even the British press were commenting on it. *The Daily News*, for example, reported:

> Both the official Sinn Fein Party and the unofficial groups of gunmen have their spy service in the very heart of the Government machine. The old position, where there was always a traitor among the Irish revolutionaries,

has been completely reversed. The conspirators are now well informed and the Government utterly in the dark.[5]

Just how effective Michael's intelligence system was can be shown by a single exchange of letters. On 4 November 1919 Frank Barrett, commandant of the Mid-Clare Brigade, wrote to Michael: 'We failed to decode police wires this month. Will you please let me have this month's code as soon as possible.' Michael responded four days later with the code, an indication of his complete mastery of the intelligence situation. Frederick Dumont, American consul in Dublin, reported to the US Secretary of State on 2 January 1920:

> Nothing occurs in Ireland that the wonderful espionage system organised by Sinn Fein does not cover. This very espionage system, supposedly unpaid, shows the hold that Sinn Fein has either through fear or affection . . . No conversation can be conducted over the public telephone without it being known or reported to Sinn Fein . . . With this all-encompassing system, the leaders of the political side of the movement must know who is conducting the campaign of the assassination of policemen.[6]

What Dumont had failed to comprehend was that the intelligence network was supplying information to Michael Collins in his capacity as Director of Intelligence, not to the Cabinet or officials of the Dail. After Harry Boland went off to the United States to prepare for the visit of 'the Chief' as he referred to de Valera, and thereafter stayed by his side during his protracted tour, Michael had sole responsibility for the intelligence war against the British and their supporters. More and more, he had the effective control of the campaign as violence escalated on both sides. Darrell Figgis, a supporter of the old, non-violent Sinn Fein, viewed this development with apprehension, seeing the campaign against the police as part of a cunning ploy on Michael's part to condition the people of Ireland to the use of physical force:

> The ground was well chosen, and the gains were many. The first gain was that the civil work of the RIC practically ceased . . . The second gain, from the point of view of those who planned this campaign, was that the people were being attuned to the thought of the appeal to armed force. The third gain was that the RIC were steadily withdrawn from all isolated barracks and concentrated in the larger, more central barracks, leaving large tracts of country to be controlled and policed completely by the IRA.[7]

After the assassination of 'The Dog' Smith in July, Michael did not order the killing of any other policemen until 12 September when, in response to the banning of the Dail and the raid on Sinn Fein headquarters, he authorised the slaying of Daniel Hoey, the G man who had fingered Sean MacDiarmada in April 1916. Hoey was shot down the very next day, outside police headquarters in Great Brunswick Street. A week later, with two killings under its belt, the Squad was formally inaugurated at 46 Parnell Square, headquarters of the Keating branch of the Gaelic League. In January 1920 Tom Keogh, Vinnie Byrne and Mick O'Reilly were added; thereafter the team was jocularly known as the Twelve Apostles. The hit-men were all young, just out of their teens, and probably regarded their assignment as a great adventure, though Michael controlled them rigorously. They were sworn to abjure alcohol and had to keep at the peak of physical fitness. Very strict rules were laid down for the shootings, both in the way they were carried out and in the care to avoid injury to innocent civilians. Michael regarded assassination as a last resort, and only after repeated warnings was a policeman targeted. When Daly had a personal grudge against a policeman who had maltreated Paddy's crippled daughter and it was thought that he might shoot the man, word of this reached Michael who gave Daly a severe dressing-down, with the words 'Any man who has revenge in his heart is not fit to be a Volunteer'. Michael was at pains to explain that the execution of policemen was a political act and must at all times be seen to be so. It was very important that the Squad should regard themselves as an élite force, a band of knights fighting a just war by the only method open to them.

Once the order was given, the Squad would study the locale carefully and work out when and where the shooting would take place. Up to eight men would be involved, including look-outs and back-up, but the actual execution would be carried out by two men who would saunter up to the victim. A body shot at point-blank range from one gunman would be followed immediately by a head shot by the other as the victim fell to the ground.

By the end of 1919 some eighteen policemen had been killed, though not all were victims of the Squad by any means. Breen and Treacy killed two while helping Sean Hogan to escape from Knocklong Prison in County Limerick, and an abortive attempt to free a Volunteer prisoner from Limerick Gaol resulted in a further two deaths. Most of the shootings came after the suppression of the Dail in mid-September. This followed the policy advocated by Arthur Griffith who had earlier declared that there should be no violence unless and until Dublin Castle proscribed the Dail. When the British authorities obliged, the need for restraint on Michael's part disappeared.

Piaras Beaslai was re-arrested in May. This time, the authorities were taking no chances with the Sinn Fein propagandist and promptly shipped him over to England, where he joined other prominent political prisoners then being held in Strangeways, Manchester. Some of them, including Austin Stack, had been held previously in Crumlin Road Gaol, Belfast, and had staged a prison riot there at Christmas 1918 which had lasted a fortnight and provoked Orange mobs to go on the rampage outside the prison, hellbent on lynching any Catholics who fell into their hands. Alarmed at the prospect of triggering off a pogrom, the authorities had the Republican prisoners transferred to Strangeways.

This was even more hazardous than the prison break at Lincoln the previous February, and in planning the escape to the last detail Michael even put his own head in the noose, by crossing to England and brazenly visiting Stack under an assumed name. The resultant escape on the night of 25 October was audacious and carried out on a grand scale, involving Volunteer units from Liverpool and Manchester whose task was to disrupt traffic in the vicinity. Some of the top brass from Volunteer GHQ in Dublin, including Rory O'Connor and Peadar Clancy, took part in the actual rescue. Beaslai, Stack and four others broke out, using a wooden ladder which had been propped up against the outer wall. Stack was suffering from a septic leg, aggravated by his exertions in climbing the ladder. When he returned to Dublin via the 'Irish Mail' he was confined to bed at Batt O'Connor's for several weeks. Michael visited him every day, revealing a surprising tenderness and solicitousness.

On the very day that Stack and Beaslai arrived back in Dublin, Michael had a very narrow escape when the police and military raided 76 Harcourt Street. Fortunately, one of the precautions Michael had taken was to save him the day. On his instructions, Batt O'Connor had installed a light ladder which could ingeniously be hauled up to the roof. By this means Michael escaped through the skylight even as the detectives were clattering up the staircase. Coolly closing the hatch, Michael crawled across the roofs of neighbouring buildings until he came to the skylight of the Standard Hotel where he had arranged a similar ladder in permanent readiness. But the ladder was missing, and as he lowered himself gingerly through the aperture he found to his horror that he was dangling over the stairwell with a thirty-foot drop to the lobby of the hotel. He needed all his strength and stamina to swing back and forward until he had sufficient momentum to leap towards the landing. He managed to clear the railing but caught his foot and fell awkwardly, injuring his knee badly. Calmly he picked himself up and dusted himself off as he descended the stairs to the lobby and exited on to the street. In the meantime, several members of the Squad had been alerted and were now occupying discreet vantage-points, watching for the emergence of the military from 76 Harcourt Street with the Big Fellow in their hands. Imagine their surprise when, instead, they saw him stroll insouciantly out of the Standard and hail a cab.

Suspicion for the tip-off about Sinn Fein's new headquarters fell on Harry Quinlisk, formerly a corporal in the Royal Irish Regiment who had been captured on the Western Front and was one of the handful of prisoners-of-war recruited by Casement into his Irish Brigade. Stranded in Germany after the Armistice and the subsequent civil disturbances, he had only recently returned to Dublin where he had soon made contact with the Volunteers. Tall, well built, with cadaverous features, he was a vain man with an exaggerated idea of his own importance. The fact that he had military experience and spoke German fluently, however, attracted Michael to him, feeling that he might be useful as a training officer. He provided Quinlisk with fresh clothing and even took him in at his own lodgings in the Munster Hotel, but it soon became apparent that Quinlisk was a whingeing windbag, always looking for a hand-out. He and an associate haunted Michael's office and were incensed when he refused to see them. On the very day of the raid, Quinlisk and his pal were turned away at the door by Joe O'Reilly who told them that his boss was away in the country. After the raid, of course, Quinlisk was regarded with the gravest suspicion and no one would have anything further to do with him. He then approached several members of the Dail to complain of the monstrous behaviour of Mick Collins towards him. He told them that he planned to go to America and complain of Mick's treatment to none other than John Devoy himself. In the end he changed his mind but continued to nurture his grievance against the Big Fellow. Working himself up into a passion of hate, he decided to turn informer. On 11 November 1919 he wrote to the Permanent Under-Secretary at Dublin Castle, stating that he had been connected with Sinn Fein and was now prepared to tell all he knew of it:

> The scoundrel Michael Collins has treated me scurvily and now I am going to wash my hands of the whole business. If you accept my offer then please send a man, one who can be trusted, to the above address on tomorrow evening at four o'clock.[8]

The Castle authorities jumped at the opportunity to recruit an informer so close to their most wanted man. At the appointed hour Quinlisk met with officials who subsequently reported back, at great length. Within hours, a transcript of the interview was in Michael's hands. Quinlisk now approached his intended quarry with a plausible tale of having been to the Castle to obtain a passport to go to America. Michael appeared to accept this story, but, acting on the information in the transcript, he got Cullen to telephone Quinlisk's controller, Superintendent O'Brien of the RIC. Disguising his voice and pretending to be Quinlisk, Cullen arranged to meet O'Brien in Parliament Street. The Squad took up positions shortly before the appointed hour. In due course a squad of detectives appeared but something alerted them for, fearing an ambush, they halted at the top of the street and turned back. Later the G men accused a dumbfounded Quinlisk of trying to doublecross them. Quinlisk now swung back in the opposite direction, writing a self-pitying letter to a friend of Michael and following this up with a long, highly coloured account which he sent to *The Freeman's Journal*, describing in lurid terms how the Castle had tried to bribe him with £50 if Collins were arrested, and a much larger but unspecified sum if he would give evidence leading to the terrorist leader's conviction for the murder of policemen. Quinlisk concluded on a sanctimonious note:

> In giving this account of how Dublin Castle endeavours to do their nefarious work in Ireland, I am actuated only by the desire to open the eyes of our own people and of the English. That Mr O'Brien should calmly suggest to me that I swear falsely against my own countrymen, and be rewarded by immunity and monetarily, shows what respect these very people have for the law, which it is their duty to uphold and maintain.[9]

This extraordinary letter was never published; it may have been censored by the British authorities, of course, but the fact that a copy very quickly came into Michael's hands seems to point to his own agents within the newspaper's organisation. Clearly, Quinlisk was not a man to be trusted by either side, though both would continue trying to use him for their own purposes.

About the same time as the Castle was trying to trap Michael with the help of Quinlisk, it was using another rather more effective tool. In November 1919 there arrived in Dublin a small, plump gentleman with sharp features and a plausible air. He was clad in breeches and knee-boots and claimed to be a travelling salesman for a company that marketed musical instruments. He checked in at the Granville Hotel under the name of Jameson, and he passed the time reading the thrillers of Edgar Wallace and catching small birds which he installed in cages in his bedroom. His real name was Burn, and though his father had been a police inspector in Limerick he himself had been raised in England and took care to conceal his Irish antecedents. With the British Army he had seen service in India and the Western Front before being recruited into the Secret Service. Posing as a communist agitator, he had been an *agent provocateur* during the London Metropolitan Police strike. This had led him to the Irish Self-Determination League whose secretary, Art O'Brien, had given him an introduction to Michael Collins. On 9 December Michael wrote to O'Brien: 'Jameson has duly arrived and been interviewed by 3 of us. I shall report developments later on.'[10] At this interview, held in Mrs O'Keefe's restaurant in Camden Street, Jameson had promised to supply arms and ammunition, as well as foment mutiny in the British armed forces. He claimed to represent the Bolshevik government which was looking for some way of exacting revenge for British intervention in the civil war then raging in Russia, and also had good contacts inside the Birmingham Small Arms factory. Although Joe O'Reilly took an immediate dislike to the smooth-talking English communist, Michael merely growled and kept his own counsel, for the time being.

While Dublin Castle was trying to infiltrate the rebels' intelligence organisation, Michael was pressing ahead with his own campaign of intimidating or eliminating G men. His most daring project, as the year drew to a close, was the assassination of none other than Lord French himself, but the attempt, on 19 December, was abortive. Michael had got word that the Lord Lieutenant-General was due to leave his country estate at Frenchpark, Co. Roscommon earlier that day, travelling back to Dublin by train. He and his entourage alighted at Ashtown Station, two miles from the vice-regal lodge at Phoenix Park on the north side of the city. An ambush was hastily organised at a convenient point in the road. As it happened, the train reached Ashtown ahead of schedule, so that French's cavalcade took the ambushers by surprise. Tom Keogh, Martin Savage and Dan Breen were actually in the process of wheeling out a farm-cart to block the road when a constable appeared and curtly ordered them to clear the way. One of the Volunteers lobbed a grenade at the policeman who was knocked to the ground and stunned by the blast but otherwise unharmed.

At that juncture the cavalcade arrived but, alerted by the explosion, the leading car (with Lord French in the passenger seat) sped off towards Dublin. Assuming that the first car contained only bodyguards, the ambushers let it go and concentrated their gunfire on the second vehicle, wounding the driver, Detective Sergeant Halley. Martin Savage was shot by one of the soldiers and was the only casualty on the Republican side. French himself, though badly shaken, was unhurt. Later on, of course, the ambush was a technique that Michael would raise to perfection – ironically, in the long run.

In November the Irish Convention finally issued a secret report coming to the conclusion that 'a sincere attempt be made to deal with the Irish question once and for all'. Nevertheless, it recognised that the British government would not permit Ireland to leave the Empire, and that Ulster must not be forced under the rule of an Irish parliament against its will. On 24 November the Convention recommended the establishment of two parliaments in Ireland, linked by a Council of Ireland. This led to the Home Rule Act of 1920 which divided the island into two parts. While this statute transferred the administration of Ireland, North and South, to Irish hands, it left the great bulk of taxing powers in the hands of Westminster. The province of Northern Ireland, comprising the six counties of North-east Ulster, alone came into existence, its parliament at Stormont being formally inaugurated by King George V on 22 June 1921. So far as the rest of Ireland was concerned, however, the passing of the Home Rule Act merely aggravated a situation already at breaking point. In the three-year period (1917–19), there had been a total of 12,589 raids on private homes by the RIC and military forces; in the course of the following year this would increase to over a thousand a week.

CHAPTER 9

The Year of Terror, 1920

One man with a dream, at pleasure,
Shall go forth and conquer a crown;
And three with a new song's measure
Can trample a kingdom down.
ARTHUR O'SHAUGHNESSY, *Ode: We are the Music Makers*

DESPITE THE MISGIVINGS OF JOE O'REILLY, MICHAEL COLLINS WAS keeping an open mind on the loquacious Mr Jameson. Around the New Year Michael arranged a second meeting, this time over tea and buns in the house of Mrs O'Kelly in Ranelagh. This was followed by a third meeting, at Batt O'Connor's house in Brendan Road where Michael lunched most days with Austin Stack, still convalescing from his leg wound. Tobin and Cullen, who shared O'Reilly's distrust of Jameson, were ordered to collect him and bring him out to Donnybrook on the tram for the meeting. Batt's wife, who opened the door to the trio, was immediately taken aback at the sharp-featured Jameson; some sixth sense warned her to be on her guard and she drew Michael aside to air her views, but he growled and waved his hands impatiently. He seemed to have taken a tremendous liking to the plump little man who had such a fund of jokes and witty anecdotes. Another interview was arranged for the following day, when Jameson would meet Cathal Brugha and Richard Mulcahy as well as the other top brass in the Volunteer Army. Jameson was positively euphoric as he took the tram back into the city and made a beeline for the Castle to report his impending master-stroke.

Michael finally began to suspect a trap when it was reported to him that a G man had been seen maintaining a discreet watch on the O'Connor home that day. When Jameson left the house with Liam Tobin, this detective was seen to ride off on his bicycle in the direction of Waterloo Road to alert a party of police and troops lying in wait around the corner that the bird had flown – though, unbeknown to them, the bird was still ensconced in Batt's parlour. One of the G men in the ambush party was James MacNamara who relayed this

141

information to Michael shortly afterwards. As a consequence, Michael wrote at length on 20 January to Art O'Brien in London on the subject of Mr Jameson:

> What I have to say with regard to him will probably be somewhat of a thunderbolt to you. I believe we have the man or one of them. I have absolutely certain information that the man who came from London met and spoke to me, and reported that I was growing a moustache to Basil Thompson. I may get some more information. In the meantime will you get in touch with him somehow and show him my paragraph on himself in the other memo.[1]

Sir Basil Thompson was, in fact, Chief Commissioner of the Metropolitan Police in London. The casual reference in this letter shows that Michael even had agents in the highest echelons of Scotland Yard. The handwritten memo referred to in the letter infers that Michael was, for a time, genuinely taken in by Jameson, and other senior officers of the Volunteers were similarly deceived, despite the fact that the man was allegedly English. Tom Cullen, however, had no illusions about 'that crooked English bastard' and he began to prepare a trap with Tobin and Thornton.

MacNamara had also been present at a meeting of G men in Dublin Castle the previous day, when the political detectives received a pep talk from their new commander. Chief Superintendent William Redmond was a Belfast man, now promoted to Assistant Commissioner with a mandate to put new fight into the demoralised force. An ardent Orangeman, he had an innate distrust of the Dublin detectives whom he considered inefficient and corrupt. In the course of haranguing his new command, Redmond said, 'You were supposed to have been looking for Collins. You have been after him for months and never caught sight of him, while a new man, just over from England, met him and talked to him after two days.' This chance remark, made in the hearing of MacNamara, would shortly seal the fate of both Redmond and Jameson.

When MacNamara passed this information to Michael the latter decided to test Jameson. Having warned Mrs O'Connor that he would not be in for lunch the following day, Michael, accompanied by Joe O'Reilly, cycled up Morehampton Road as usual. As they came towards the detective who was keeping the house under surveillance, Michael suddenly accelerated away from his companion and sped round the corner into Brendan Road, then just as quickly round the next corner to the left. Meanwhile Joe, in puzzlement, stopped at the house and told Mrs O'Connor that Mick was not coming in for lunch. Still baffled by Michael's strange behaviour, Joe got on his bike and went off round the corner. He found his boss waiting at the end of the side road.

'See anything?' asked Michael.

'No.'

'Cycle up now and have a look.'

Joe cycled off round the corner. As he did so, he saw from the end of Morehampton Road a military convoy driving at full speed towards him. Pirouetting on his rear wheel, Joe pedalled furiously back round the corner and dodged into the side road just as the lorries screeched to a halt outside the O'Connor house. Amid the clatter of troops and the barking of orders, Michael calmly strolled round the corner to watch the fun. In a minute he was back in the side road, chuckling to himself.

'We have the laugh on them now.'

An unsuspecting Mrs O'Connor opened her door to the urgent knocking, to be confronted by Assistant Commissioner Redmond himself, brandishing a revolver. Without a word, he swept past the startled woman and kicked open the dining-room door. When he saw the table covered with a green baize cloth, obviously not set up for lunch, he could not smother a cry of disappointment. He then charged upstairs in a rage. In one of the bedrooms he chanced upon a framed portrait of Dail members and made to confiscate it, but Batt's wife begged him to leave it alone, saying that he could easily obtain a print of it for a few pence in any souvenir shop in town. Redmond then recovered his composure. Returning his pistol to its holster, he told Mrs O'Connor that he would not be troubling her again, although that night he kept a freezing vigil outside, with his trusted henchman MacNamara for company.

While the raid was in progress, Michael and Joe were cycling down Herbert Park. At first Michael could not help seeing the funny side of it, and periodically threw back his head and laughed aloud; but presently he stopped in his tracks and glowered at Joe, growling and muttering under his breath in a manner that betokened no good for Jameson.

Ironically, while waiting for his quarters in the Castle to be made ready, Redmond was staying at the Standard Hotel, through whose skylight Michael had made his perilous descent. MacNamara reported to Michael that this would be his only chance to get close to the Assistant Commissioner, and he warned that the man wore a bullet-proof vest. Michael went to extraordinary lengths to identify Redmond correctly, after the Squad nearly killed an innocent civilian by mistake. Frank Thornton was sent to Belfast to liaise with Sergeant Matt MacCarthy from Kerry who was stationed in the RIC barracks in Chichester Street. MacCarthy, who seems to have been the Belfast counterpart of Ned Broy, passed Thornton off as his cousin, and installed him in the office of the District Inspector when he and other officers were attending the police boxing championships. Coolly, Thornton went through the personal files until he found Redmond's, complete with an excellent photograph which he promptly purloined. Within twenty-four hours, the picture was in Michael's hands.

The following day, having learned that Redmond's quarters at the Castle were now ready for occupancy, Michael ordered the hit. It was carried out by Paddy Daly that evening as the Assistant Commissioner was mounting the steps of his hotel. Unbeknown to the Squad, Redmond had forgotten to put on his body armour that day, but they took no chances anyway and aimed at his head. The first shot smashed his jaw but Redmond tried to draw his own weapon before the second shot, through the forehead, finished him off. He was only yards from the door of the hotel when he fell and, as he was rather short in height, the Dublin wags explained gravely that he did not come up to the standard.[2]

Next day, 25 January 1920, the Castle retaliated by offering a reward of £10,000 for information leading to the apprehension and conviction of those who had by now perpetrated the murder of fourteen members of the Dublin Metropolitan Police and the Royal Irish Constabulary. From this has grown the myth that the reward was offered specifically for the capture of Michael Collins. This was not strictly true, although effectively that was what it meant.

About this time Jameson reappeared on the scene, having gone to England over the Christmas and New Year holidays. He renewed contact with his rebel friends and showered them with appropriate gifts, in the form of revolvers and automatic pistols which filled a heavy leather portmanteau. Jameson handed over this case to Frank Thornton who promptly lugged it down to the basement of the tobacco firm Kapp & Peterson at 56 Bachelor's Walk. Jameson, of course, was not to know that the weapons were spirited away within seconds and lodged several doors along the street at number 32 where Sean MacMahon had his clandestine quartermaster's stores. Shortly afterwards MacNamara tipped off Michael that a raid on Kapp & Peterson would take place at three o'clock. From a safe distance across the river Tobin, Cullen and Thornton watched the police and troops ransack the Kapp & Peterson premises and depart empty-handed. Intriguingly, the detectives were seen to return to the basement at midnight, armed this time with picks and shovels. So certain were they of their information that they now tore up the floor in quest of the cache of weapons.

Jameson had pressed on Liam Tobin an iron cross which he averred was a decoration conferred on him by the Bolsheviks; later it would hang from the wall of Tobin's office as a grim memento. Jameson had also given him a pass which he declared would enable Tobin to enter a barracks at any hour. He now requested its return, and Michael saw an opportunity for another frame-up. Tobin was instructed to tell Jameson that the pass was in the house of X, a prominent Loyalist. That night, Michael and his closest associates watched with glee as the house was raided and the unfortunate Orangeman was kept shivering in his nightshirt on the doorstep. Jameson was now getting desperate and even urged Tobin and Cullen to open fire on a military patrol as they raided another house. As an *agent provocateur* he was having remarkably little luck. In February he returned to England to confer with his masters, but by the end of the month he was back in Dublin. For several days he made futile attempts to renew his contacts, but to no avail. Then, one day, he ran into Joe O'Reilly in the street. Joe did his best to avoid the little man, but Jameson ran after him, calling out his name at the top of his voice. In that split second he signed his own death warrant. Joe stopped and turned towards his pursuer. Jameson, panting for breath, blurted out that he had to see Collins urgently. Joe tried to fob him off, but the bird-fancier was persistent.

'But I want to see him. I must see him. Can you take a letter to him?'

'He's not in town,' countered Joe. 'It will take a couple of hours to reach him.'

'Never mind. I must try and see him. I'm leaving on the boat tonight.'

Joe nodded slowly and agreed. As he feared, Michael was mad at him when he delivered Jameson's message. Meekly he stood silent while the Big Fellow ranted and raved at him. Promising to keep out of Jameson's way in future, he made a hurried exit – and ran slap into the little man yet again. This time Jameson, carrying a canary in a cage, nagged him for an answer. When could he meet Collins again? What was the reply to his letter? Feeling miserable, Joe said that no answer had come yet. Eventually, he agreed to meet Jameson again at five o'clock that evening at a draper's shop near the General Post Office.

The storm he had faced before was nothing to what took place when he returned with this news. Michael was beside himself with rage, pacing up and down the room like a caged animal and cursing the luckless Joe. Then he stopped suddenly and his face resumed its normal colour.

'When did you say you'd meet him, and where?' he snapped.

'At five –'

Michael scribbled a brief note and sealed it in an envelope. Joe knew by his grim expression what this meant. Wordlessly, he took the envelope and delivered it.

At the appointed hour, Joe met Jameson and presently handed him over to the four young men, grave and taciturn, who would escort him to Michael's latest hiding-place. Joe accompanied them as far as the tram-stop and waved them off. From the platform, Jameson thanked the lad for his trouble. Joe's last sight of him was taking his seat with his escort as the 19 tram clanked off up Sackville Street towards Glasnevin. At Ballymun they alighted and Jameson was taken to the rear entrance of the Albert College. Here the chief escort, Paddy Daly, told him that he was to be shot. Jameson tried to bluff his way out, warning the Squad, 'You fellows will get hell if anything happens to me. Collins will deal with you! And Tobin happens to be a particular friend of mine.' But when he realised that the four young men with drawn pistols meant business, he stood to attention and clicked his heels smartly as the hammers of the .45s were cocked. They asked him if he wished to pray, but he declined.

'We are only doing our duty,' they told him.

'And I have done mine,' he said. As the guns were levelled at his head he smiled and said sardonically, 'That's right. God bless the King. I would love to die for him.' After they shot him they searched his pockets but found only a well-thumbed novel by Edgar Wallace. His hotel room was equally barren, revealing only birdcages and two cases of jewellery.

Burn/Jameson's return to Ireland was all the more courageous in view of the fact that Quinlisk had already come to a sticky end. Kathleen Napoli Mac-Kenna, visiting Sinn Fein headquarters one day in December 1919, recalled seeing 'a well-dressed young man, with frank open countenance and nonchalant air sitting smoking, his legs dangling, on a console-table in the inner hall',[3] and was afterwards told by her friend Anna Fitzsimmons that this was Quinlisk. 'Darn nice lad, that,' she had remarked. 'Pity he's up to no good in here.' A few weeks later Michael set him up, telling him that he was heading for Cork where he would be staying at Wren's Hotel. Predictably, Michael's intelligence unit intercepted a coded message from the Castle to the RIC District Inspector at Cork ordering him to raid Wren's Hotel and arrest Michael Collins. Quinlisk himself went hot-foot to Cork, determined to be in at the kill to collect his £10,000 blood money. Instead, he was waylaid by the Cork IRA; his bullet-riddled corpse was found in a ditch on 18 February. Kathleen MacKenna noted:

> The event impressed me deeply and threw a new light on the bitterness of the struggle in which I was now taking part. From it I realised . . . how ruthless Collins could be when necessary. He had played up to, and trapped, this Irish Judas who for hard cash was prepared to betray one of Ireland's most valuable leaders.

The tragedy of Ireland is that there has never been a shortage of such Judases. Next to try his luck in betraying Michael for pieces of silver was Fergus Brian Mulloy, a sergeant in the Army Pay Corps stationed at Parkgate Street. Through a Sinn Fein MP named Ferran, Mulloy was introduced to Batt O'Connor. Over tea, he informed Batt that his superiors wanted him to join the Secret Service. He was willing to do so, provided he could supply Michael Collins with information about its activities. After the Jameson affair Batt was understandably wary, but he promised to see what he could do. Thereafter

Tobin, Cullen and Thornton would meet Mulloy from time to time at the Café Cairo or Kidd's Restaurant. Mulloy was full of brag-talk, but it never amounted to anything positive – not a single firearm or military pass, despite his oft-repeated promises to steal revolvers from the Parkgate Street armoury.

Although one or other of Michael's most trusted lieutenants continued to meet Mulloy on an almost daily basis, they heartily distrusted him. At best, he was a fantasist and a time-waster; at worst he was a dangerous enemy agent. They watched and they waited to see what he would do. One day, Mulloy offered to smuggle Cullen and Thornton into Dublin Castle after dark and let them copy some of the most secret documents (about whose contents he was remarkably vague). Cullen and Thornton politely declined this offer; instead, they suggested that Mulloy help them to assassinate Colonel Hill Dillon, head of the Military Intelligence department (and actually Mulloy's commanding officer), who lived in rented accommodation outside the military base. Mulloy's poker face never flinched when this was put to him; but the very next day Colonel Dillon moved into secure quarters. Mulloy was blissfully unaware that his true identity had been revealed to Michael at the very outset, by Beaslai's cousin, Lily, who was Dillon's confidential typist.

Mulloy overstepped the mark when he asked Liam Tobin to write down the names and addresses of some prominent Sinn Feiners, such as Count Plunkett and Countess Markievicz. When he produced a sheet of Dail Eireann headed notepaper, which had been seized in the September raid, Liam smelled a rat. Three days previously Tomas MacCurtain, Lord Mayor of Cork, had been shot dead in front of his terrified wife by a group of men with blackened faces pretending to be IRA. A week earlier, MacCurtain had been one of several prominent figures in Sinn Fein to receive a death threat, written on Dail Eireann notepaper. Liam felt the fine hairs on his neck rising at the prospect of Plunkett and Markievicz in a ditch, with an incriminating sheet of paper – in his handwriting – pinned to them. Lloyd George would then disseminate his propaganda about a Sinn Fein 'murder gang' settling old scores, and thus spread disunity in the movement. The meeting ended inconclusively, but that evening Tobin told Michael that Mulloy would have to be killed. Michael nodded briefly and told him to get on with it. The following evening, 25 March 1920, Mulloy was shot dead outside the hotel on Wicklow Street.

William Doran, the hall porter in the Wicklow Hotel, was a notorious informer who had been responsible for the arrest of many Republican sympathisers. Michael ordered his execution but the Squad was foiled on several occasions. In the end Liam Tobin instructed Joe Dolan, who knew him well, to carry out the shooting. 'Dan McDonnell and myself entered the Wicklow Hotel one morning about nine o'clock, shot him dead in the hall and walked away. I was back there at 1 p.m. having my lunch,' wrote Dolan.[4]

Unaware of her husband's clandestine activities, Mrs Doran applied to Sinn Fein for a widow's pension. For the sake of her children, Michael gave instructions that she was to be paid.

Local government elections had last been held in Ireland in 1913, before the outbreak of the First World War. They had been due to be held again in 1917 but the rise of militant nationalism led the British government to postpone them repeatedly. This situation had reached the stage where Sinn Fein was openly taunting the authorities for lacking the stomach for such a plebiscite. By the end of 1919 the government could delay the local elections no longer, although it took steps to make matters more difficult for Sinn Fein by moving the goalposts. Instead of a simple 'first past the post' result, it now introduced the system of proportional representation with a single transferable vote.

Proportional representation was an electoral arrangement devised early in the nineteenth century with the object of securing a representative assembly which would truly reflect the voting strengths of the various parties among the electorate. Every shade of opinion, however slight, would thus be represented in the legislature as near as possible to its proportional mathematical claim. This, according to the political philosopher John Stuart Mill, was true democracy. The appeal of this system, especially to minority groups, has been widespread and nowadays there are few democratic countries which are not without some such system, although Britain continues to be a notable exception, clinging to the 'first past the post' tradition.

Various methods of implementing the system have been tried. The second ballot system, as used in France, is open to corruption and abuse owing to the wheeling and dealing between first and second rounds. The alternative or preferential vote, used in Australia, entails the voter marking the candidates numerically in order of preference. Both methods have been used to remedy the defects of a single-member constituency. Germany, however, pioneered large constituencies with several representatives, and the device known as the single transferable vote. The voter is free to indicate his preference by numbers against the long list of candidates. The returning officer then distributes the surplus preferences of successful candidates and those with no chance among those who are designated by the preferences, until all the seats are filled by those with quotas. A variation of this was adopted for the Northern Ireland elections held in the summer of 1996. This system was previously tested in a special municipal election in Sligo in January 1919 and resulted in the failure of Sinn Fein to secure a majority of seats. Thus heartened, the government fixed January 1920 as the date for municipal elections in urban districts, to be followed in March by elections in rural areas. In January the voters turned out in unprecedented numbers. Apart from ugly scenes in Cork where Volunteers and ex-soldiers slugged it out on the streets with revolvers, hand-grenades, crowbars and hurling-sticks (remarkably, no lives were lost) the elections passed off fairly peaceably. The result was a moderate victory for Sinn Fein which took 560 seats, compared with Labour's 394, the Unionists' 355, the Home Rulers' 161 and municipal reformers' 108. This result applied to Ireland as a whole and it should be noted that, even in the Six Counties, the Unionists won only 255 seats, compared with 318 by their opponents. Not only was Sinn Fein now the dominant force in all the major towns and cities of southern Ireland, but the second city of Ulster, Londonderry, now had a Nationalist lord mayor. In the elections for the county councils, postponed yet again and not actually held till June 1920, Sinn Fein had a landslide victory, reflecting not only their traditional strength in the country areas, but a marked swing of public opinion in their favour in the interim. The party won handsome majorities in twenty-nine of the thirty-three county councils, including Fermanagh and Tyrone, wrested from the Unionists for the first time.

The British government took these electoral results very badly. Having already imposed a curfew in the Dublin metropolitan area between midnight and 5 a.m., the authorities now tightened the screw. Following the urban elections, Dublin Castle decreed a ban on fairs and public meetings in the Twenty-six Counties. In retaliation, Richard Mulcahy gave approval for Volunteer attacks on police barracks. Local brigades responded enthusiastically with co-ordinated assaults on police posts everywhere. By the end of March 1920 the RIC had been forced to abandon many of its stations and barracks. During the first six months of 1920 the Volunteers destroyed 424 empty barracks, 47 courthouses and 22 tax offices; on a single day, 315 deserted police barracks – 'tombstones of British prestige' – were burned to the ground by jubilant Volunteers in a carefully orchestrated demonstration of national solidarity to mark the fourth anniversary of the Easter Rising. Sixteen occupied police barracks were also destroyed and 29 others severely damaged in prolonged attacks.

Having survived an ambush in December 1919, a virtual prisoner within his vice-regal lodge at Phoenix Park since the Volunteers had made his country mansion in County Mayo uninhabitable, and acutely embarrassed by his sister, Charlotte Despard, one of the more outspoken critics of Dublin Castle, Lord French was determined to combat the rising menace of Sinn Fein by military means. He was now hand in glove with another blimpish dinosaur, Field-Marshal Sir Henry Wilson; as early as 2 February 1920 the London correspondent of *The Irish Independent* was claiming that Wilson was operating 'a sinister dictatorship in Irish military affairs'. Massive swoops and monster round-ups, detention without trial, midnight raids and the 'lifting' of vast numbers of individual suspects became the order of the day. On 4 February huge military parades took place in Dublin and Limerick, characterised by *The Irish Independent* as 'a needless, irritating and stupid proceeding, but it is just what we might expect from rulers animated by spleen and not guided by reason and common sense'. Even in Britain, the more independently minded newspapers were beginning to speak of Ireland as 'the new Belgium', alluding to the repressiveness of the German occupation in 1914–18.

On 5 April, some two hundred prisoners in Mountjoy Gaol went on a hunger-strike. Lord French said that they could die so far as he was concerned. A week later the Irish Labour Party and Trade Union Congress began a general strike. Within twenty-four hours the British authorities caved in and Dublin Castle announced the immediate release of the prisoners. This was allegedly an amnesty to mark the appointment of a new Chief Secretary, Sir Hamar Greenwood, and a new Commander-in-Chief, General Sir Nevil Macready, son of the celebrated actor. These changes had been precipitated by the resignation, in frustration and disgust, of Ian Macpherson who had served as Chief Secretary since the beginning of 1919. His successor, Hamar Greenwood, was a Canadian bullshitter of the first magnitude who would raise 'economy with the truth' to a previously undreamed-of level; 'to tell a Hamar' would pass into everyday language. His subordinates in Dublin Castle very quickly got the measure of him; even Lloyd George admitted in November 1920 that, after seven months in the job, Greenwood 'knows nothing at all about Ireland'. Sir Nevil Macready, appointed at the same time, was a former general who had then become Commissioner of the Metropolitan Police. The scourge of the striking miners of Tonypandy in 1913 was now Commander-in-Chief of the British forces in Ireland. Two months later, the RIC, now more than 15,000-strong despite the campaign of murder and intimidation, got a new Commissioner. Major-General H.H. Tudor had just retired from the army and had absolutely no police experience, but it rapidly became apparent that he had no intention of running a police force anyway. The demoralised constabulary, soon to be reinforced, were derided as Tudor's Toughs. Nominally the military were there to back up the police, but there was no unity of command, which would prove a severe handicap. After G Division was rendered impotent by the Squad, the British appointed Brigadier-General Ormonde Winter as Intelligence chief, despite the fact that he had no previous experience in this field and was devoid of any administrative ability. Consequently he had very little success in combating Michael's intelligence machine; a blimp of the old school, derisively known as 'Colonel O', he vented his spleen on his unhappy subordinates, five of whom committed suicide within months. His only success in his new-found role as a detective was to locate some of the Dail Loan bank accounts and to discover that Michael Collins was sleeping with a girl once a week. Whether there was any truth in the gossip that linked Michael's name with Moya Llewelyn Davies has never been satisfactorily resolved. Michael was on very close terms with both Moya and her husband, Crompton. She herself never concealed her affection for Michael. Rex Taylor, when working on his biography of Collins in the mid-1950s, had a bundle of Moya's letters which implied a love affair. In a telephone conversation with Valentine Iremonger of the Irish Embassy he promised to send this material for copying and deposit in the National Library of Ireland; but he was forestalled by 'two men in bowler hats' allegedly representing the Llewelyn Davies family who repossessed the documents. Taylor's biography has only a passing reference to Mrs Llewelyn Davies, a quotation from a letter she wrote to J.M. Hone (biographer of Yeats) in 1942 which described Michael as:

> a man with a great and tender heart, who loved the beautiful in nature and in art as far as he had time or opportunity to find it. His friends who wrote about him have distorted him as much or more than his enemies.

Moya wrote her autobiography and showed it to Batt O'Connor, whom she had helped with his own memoirs. He and his wife were aghast when they read in the manuscript very revealing details about Michael and Moya. In a country where the censorship of books was notorious, Batt and his wife decided on a little censorship of their own. They confided the matter to Liam Tobin and Frank Thornton who, in time-honoured fashion, sent Moya death threats if she proceeded with publication. The book was never published, and the manuscript itself has apparently vanished. The matter reared its head on 23 August 1987 when *The Sunday Press* aired a rumour that Michael and Moya had had a child.

In mid-1920, the police, and to a lesser extent the military, did as they pleased. For over a year there would be a complete breakdown of law and order, on a scale and savage intensity that people in Britain could not comprehend; even now they have never grasped the enormity of the crimes perpetrated in Ireland, in their name, in 1920–21.

The civil service was just as inept and ineffective as the police and the military, with the bonus of departmentalism, that quaint form of tribalism which traditionally infects British government services. Their new head in Ireland was the Scottish career bureaucrat Sir John Anderson, best-remembered today for the air-raid shelters of the Second World War named after him. Twenty years earlier, however, his ignorance of Ireland soon had him immobilised in a bureaucratic bog just as deadly as the real thing in Connemara. Among his subordinates were some able, not to say brilliant, young men but they, too, rapidly became disillusioned by what they observed around them. Mark Sturgis compiled a diary which indicates that his mordant wit kept his grip on sanity, while Alfred (Andy) Cope confided to his Irish girlfriend, Kathleen Napoli MacKenna (who promptly told Michael Collins), that he and his chums 'made sorties all over the country. When they got outside Dublin or any other big town they put a Sinn Fein flag on the bonnet of the car. Thought this a great joke.'[5] Cope's main task was to try and establish some sort of contact with the Dail. Quite early on, he began exhibiting a marked sympathy for the other side, and told his girlfriend wistfully that he wished he was one of them: 'it must be a great adventure and very exciting' was his naïve comment. In London, however, the wave of new appointments, coupled with concessions to prisoners, was regarded somehow as giving in to the rebels. *The Morning Post* was not untypical when it howled of 'a situation of unparalleled ignominy and painful humiliation' when the hunger-strikers in Dublin were set free. In Wormwood Scrubs, 172 Irish prisoners began a hunger-strike on 20 April, but without general public support in England this failed to achieve similar results. In the end, these prisoners were released on individual merits; on the brink of death they were removed to nearby hospitals, and released from there when they were fit enough to travel. In Dublin, Michael believed that they should have stuck it out: 'it was a great mistake on their part to come out'. When apprised of violent victimisation of Irish prisoners by the other convicts, Michael argued that this would 'greatly increase the members of the various Irish organisations. Wormwood Scrubs will form the rallying point for the hitherto lost or unknown members of our exiles abroad.'[6] The situation got out of hand when bands of Irish men and women, praying at a candle-lit vigil outside the prison, were set upon by unidentified gangs armed with crowbars and sledge-hammers and badly beaten up, while the stalwarts of the Metro-politan Police looked the other way.

At a time when the Nationalist side should have been closing ranks to meet the rising tide of oppression, there was already dissension. Harry Boland returned home briefly on 27 May 1920 and had a boisterous reunion with his closest comrade. Michael quipped that de Valera might be the GS (Great Statesman) but Harry was the GSS (Great Social Success). Harry lost no time in rushing off to Granard to renew personal ties with Kitty Kiernan, to whom he had been writing regularly from America. A letter from Dublin to Kitty on 17 June indicates that something stronger than mere affection had been kindled between them as a result of Harry's four-day trip. Indeed, one of the closing sentences, 'Yet I long to be in Ireland, more so than ever that I have hopes to win the girl I love best in all the world . . .'[7] implies that Harry was seriously contemplating marriage. In the meantime, he would shortly be returning to America to be with the Chief.

De Valera had been extremely successful in drumming up financial support;

in all, he would raise over $6,000,000 in eighteen months. But on the political front he was less successful. He failed to grasp that Irish-Americans were primarily Americans, and that American political considerations took priority. He soon fell out with the leading figures, John Devoy and Judge Cohalan, old-style Tammany Hall political bosses. Cohalan had presidential aspirations and cynically used the Irish vote in his bid to oust Woodrow Wilson. Wilson, of Scots-Irish and Covenanting descent, needed Lloyd George's support in getting the League of Nations going and went out of his way to avoid embarrassing his ally, hence his refusal to meet Irish delegations at the Peace Conference. Cohalan, who had unwisely espoused the German cause up to 1917, was now advocating Self-Determination for Ireland, a vague term that fell well short of outright independence. De Valera, whose title of *Priomh Aire* had been misunderstood, was often hailed as President of the Irish Republic wherever he went, and as time passed he got to liking the notion. Cohalan and Devoy had their differences, but on one thing they were united: they were anxious to take this uppity maths professor down a peg. When de Valera imprudently said in an interview that he would be in favour of some form of association between England and Ireland similar to that which then existed between the United States and Cuba, Devoy openly denounced him for letting down the Irish cause. Stung by this vehement reaction, de Valera did exactly what he did later in the Treaty debates when his Document 2 met with disfavour – he beat a hasty retreat to extreme republicanism. Ironically, Cohalan and Devoy also backed down from their rather perilous republicanism and became more emphatic in favour of Self-Determination. As would occur in 1921–22, a microscopic amount of principle provided the excuse for a torrent of viciousness and folly. It was a foretaste of the Treaty split. Behind the mask of solidarity there was a world of difference between the extreme republicans and the vast majority 'demanding the Republic in the tone in which a farmer at the fair declares before God that nothing less than fifteen pounds will he take for a beast which all know he will be glad to sell for ten'.[8]

It was characteristic of the American split that neither faction gave a toss for the men who were actually fighting against desperate odds at home. To John Devoy, Michael Collins was merely a stick with which to beat de Valera. Devoy, as leader of the Fenian Brotherhood, was bound to support Michael as the head of the IRB. In Ireland itself, however, Michael was now locking horns with Cathal Brugha. As Minister of Defence, Brugha was demanding that the Volunteers should take an oath of allegiance to the Republic, effectively making them subordinate to the Dail. Griffith heartily endorsed this, with the aim of bringing the extremists into line. Michael, on the other hand, sensed that what Brugha really had in mind was to smash the power of the IRB, which Michael controlled. The Volunteers and the IRB were not quite synonymous but they were close enough for Michael to resist Brugha's demand as strenuously as possible. The IRB's allegiance was to its Supreme Council which it regarded as the *de jure* government of Ireland. Michael, by this time *was* the Supreme Council, and in exchange for that absolute authority he was being asked to content himself with such questionable authority as his position in the ramshackle Cabinet afforded him. On this occasion, however, Michael was outflanked; the oath to the Dail had become mandatory in August 1919, and there was little he could do about it, though the situation left him seething with resentment. Brugha, for his part, realised with indignation that though the power of the Brotherhood had been curbed, this secret society had not been destroyed, and increasingly he was aware that Michael Collins was bypassing him and using the IRB to further his own aims. Thus Brugha the idealist and Collins the realist were forced farther and farther apart.

In the spring of 1920 this clash of personalities was submerged by the steadily worsening situation. The British counter-attack took many forms, from harassment and arbitrary arrest to random killings, torture and savagery of the most bestial kind. A policy of commercial warfare was initiated; at one extreme numerous creameries, dairies and bacon factories were burned down to cripple Ireland's agricultural economy; at the other, a more subtle tactic was aimed at nobbling the great National Loan which Michael had so successfully organised. Aware that Sinn Fein was collecting large sums of money, the British authorities set about tracking down these funds. Alan Bell, a former magistrate, was brought out of retirement and sent down from Belfast to Dublin with extraordinary powers of search and arrest in order to get to the bottom of this money. He quickly established his own interrogation unit in Dublin Castle, whither bank managers and accountants were summoned, or brought under duress, for extensive grilling. Bell's team went through bank accounts and deposit ledgers with a fine-tooth comb, and Michael realised that, sooner or later, Bell would get his hands on the National Loan. This money, collected in dribs and drabs from poor farmers and shepherds, 'the tips of servant girls and baccy money of old men', was not only hard cash but symbolic of the national will, and Michael was damned if he would let Mr Bell get his sticky fingers on a single penny. When Bell succeeded in uncovering a massive deposit in the Munster and Leinster Bank Michael concluded that the man would have to go, and he promptly issued the requisite order to the Squad.

Ironically, Bell proved remarkably hard to pin down, for exactly the same reason that Michael himself continued to elude the authorities. In his smart business suit and Homburg hat he was innocuous in appearance. The Squad were convinced that such a high-powered executive must live within the Castle precincts and move outside only with a heavily armed guard. Michael, however, discovered that unobtrusive Mr Bell took the tram each morning from

Monkstown to Nassau Street. To be sure, a G man was assigned to escort him from his lodgings to the tram-stop while another detective collected him at his destination and walked him to the Castle gate. On the tram itself he travelled alone. One morning, as the Squad lay in wait at the top of Sandymount Avenue, a 'littler' (one of the boys used for errands) cycled up and said that a man answering Bell's description was on the tram heading into town. Four members of the Squad boarded the tram and took seats behind the inoffensive little man, the only occupant who remotely answered Bell's description. What did they think of that horse in the two-thirty, one asked casually. Someone said that he doubted if it was the favourite, but another snapped that it was a dead cert, and to back his words suddenly locked his arms around Bell's throat. In vain, the magistrate struggled violently; he was dragged kicking and screaming off the tram and shot in full view of the terrified commuters: one shot through the heart at point-blank range and a second through the temple. Bell's death had the desired effect, and the National Loan was no longer molested. Tragically, Alan Bell's brother was the very doctor in Gloucester Gaol whose humanity had secured the release of the republican prisoners during the flu epidemic the previous year.

When Joe O'Reilly brought Michael the news, the latter jumped up like a coiled spring suddenly released. He had been more than usually tense that morning and for some inexplicable reason released his tension by taking it out on the lad. Joe, who was worn out by fatigue and sleepless nights, broke down under this uncalled-for tirade, and wept like a child. Between angry sobs he told Michael that he was going, and would not come back. Michael heard him out, then said that he might as well deliver some despatches on his way. Joe flounced out of the room, as good as his word, but he ran into a girl who, seeing his tear-stained face, wormed the story out of him. She immediately stormed into Michael's office and gave him the rough edge of her tongue, saying that he had treated O'Reilly abominably. Predictably, Michael was astonished at the very idea and wondered what all the fuss was about. Joe, having gone off in high dudgeon, slept on it and was back on duty the following morning as usual. The incident was never mentioned, but it remained seared in O'Reilly's memory till the end of his days.[9]

During the first six months of 1920 British rule in Ireland virtually collapsed. Of course, civil servants continued to turn up for work but as time passed their workload dwindled to vanishing point. In this regard Dail Eireann made astonishing strides in setting up the counter-state. The Sinn Fein landslide in the rural elections completed the process which was, by midsummer, well established in the towns and cities. People dutifully paid their rates to the republican local authorities, and ignored the tax demands of the British Inland

Revenue. The wholesale destruction of stamp offices and tax offices, as well as a spectacular raid on King's Inn, the repository of government tax records, made British tax-gathering unworkable. Similarly, the Sinn Fein land courts, to which people now took their cases, proved far more effective and prompt in settling disputes than the old British system ever was. In one instance, a dispute that had lasted twenty-seven years was amicably settled by the Sinn Fein land court. As the RIC withdrew from large parts of the country and were besieged in their heavily fortified barracks in the chief towns, the role of policing the countryside passed more and more to the Volunteers. The demoralisation of the RIC was hastened by a policy of intimidation against the families and elderly relatives of policemen. Meanwhile, the Squad widened its scope; having virtually wiped out G Division, it now diversified into the systematic killing of detectives from other divisions and the settling of old scores. One of the casualties as this campaign escalated was Lee Wilson who had grossly maltreated Tom Clarke in 1916. Now a District Inspector in Gorey, County Wexford, he was gunned down by the Squad. Soon afterwards, the Squad also shot Constable Ashe in the same town, who had been identified by Michael's intelligence network as one of the men who had murdered Lord Mayor MacCurtain in March. Head Constable Cahill, another perpetrator of this monstrous deed, was actually given away by a chance remark made by his ten-year-old son, who was overheard in the Monaghan police barracks to say 'When I grow up, I won't murder lord mayors'. On its own, this was not sufficient to convict Cahill, but other evidence (much of it circumstantial and all of it hearsay) was enough to mark him down for the Squad's special attentions.

The jury at the coroner's inquest into MacCurtain's death had returned a verdict of wilful murder against David Lloyd George, Lord French, Ian Macpherson and Acting Inspector General Smith of the RIC. More specifically, Divisional Inspector Clayton and District Inspector Swanzy, together with 'some unknown members of the RIC', were named. Sergeant Matt MacCarthy, Michael's mole in the Belfast RIC, tipped him off that Swanzy had been transferred to Lisburn, County Antrim. Although this was a Loyalist stronghold, swarming with armed Orangemen, the men of Cork No I Brigade IRA were determined to avenge the death of MacCurtain (who had been their commandant) and begged Michael to authorise them to send their own hit squad to Lisburn. Michael vetoed the proposal, on the grounds that their strong Cork accents would have betrayed them. In the end, though, he compromised and permitted Sean Culhane, the Brigade intelligence officer, to travel north armed with MacCurtain's own revolver, and liaise with Belfast Volunteers. On Sunday, 22 August 1920, Culhane and two Belfast men took a taxi out to Lisburn and waited for Swanzy to emerge from church after the morning service. Amid a large throng of worshippers, Culhane spotted his man and fired the first shot. Swanzy was felled immediately and Culhane and one of his guides jumped back into the taxi. The other man, Roger McCorley, paused long enough to make the usual head shot before leaping on to the running-board of the car as it sped off. 'I was forced to grab the handle of the door on my side, open the car and throw myself in,' he later reported. 'As I still had my finger on the trigger of my gun as I landed in a heap on the floor I accidentally fired a shot in the car.'[10] Inevitably, Swanzy's death at the church door triggered off a Protestant frenzy in which many Catholic homes were burned and their inhabitants savagely mauled.

A month earlier, there had been an orgy of killing, rape, burning and looting at Banbridge, another predominantly Protestant town, and the home of Colonel Bruce Smyth VC. This fire-eating war hero had become Divisional Commissioner of the RIC for the province of Munster, and on 19 June he had delivered a pep-talk to the police at Listowel in such violently murderous language that it provoked a mutiny. Perhaps the last straw had been his reference to an emigrant ship which had departed recently 'with lots of Sinn Feiners on board'. The gallant colonel assured his men that it would never reach port. The ship was the *Viknor* which did, indeed, sink in very mysterious circumstances, to the chagrin of Admiral R.C. Hall, head of British Naval Intelligence, who was annoyed that he was denied the opportunity to seize the papers of some very important passengers who went down with the ship. Days before the Swanzy shooting, an IRA gunman walked into the County Club in Cork, calmly approached Smyth and said, 'Your orders were to shoot on sight. Well, you are in sight now, so make ready.' Smyth tried to escape but was shot in the back of the head.

In midsummer the wave of pogroms reached new depths of depravity in the Six Counties. Thousands of Catholics, who had found work in the Belfast shipyards during the wartime boom, were chased from the yards amid a hail of red-hot rivets. Thousands more were driven from their homes; the process of ghettoisation that continues to this day was thus initiated in a storm of furious bigotry. In Londonderry towards the end of June, where the two communities were more evenly matched, the Catholic Nationalists fought pitched battles in the streets with the Protestant Loyalists. On 15 July the British government's euphemistically named Irish Situation Committee met in London and agreed that Loyalists in the Twenty-six Counties were saying that 'they felt the time had come when they must know whether the Government intended to master the country or they would be forced to make terms with Sinn Fein'. This sounded terribly like the invitation to a showdown. A few days later W.E. Wylie, legal adviser to Dublin Castle, bluntly opined that 'within two months the Irish Police Force as a Police Force would cease to exist' and so far as the courts were concerned 'the entire administration of the Imperial Government had ceased'. Wylie admitted defeat when he added that the murderers of policemen were 'not real criminals, but political fanatics' and 'after seeing the marvellous organisation which Sinn Fein had built up, he was of the opinion that the Irish were capable of governing themselves'. General Tudor underscored this by reporting that the authorities were up against a well-organised body, and to restore order would be a very lengthy business, which he ventured to think could not be done in the time at their disposal.

In July 1920, therefore, the British government was faced with despair in the upper echelons of its Irish administration. It is probable that, at this stage, Lloyd George first entertained doubts that the struggle could continue, or that imperial might would prevail, but mindful of the ultimatum from the southern Loyalists, he was prepared to give the Irish situation one last shot. It would be the foolhardy action of a desperate man.

CHAPTER 10

The Black and Tans, 1920–21

Cry, 'Havoc!' and let slip the dogs of war.
WILLIAM SHAKESPEARE, *Julius Caesar*, III, i, 273

LATE IN 1919 SIR HENRY WILSON NOTED IN HIS DIARY THAT HE had been urging Lloyd George 'with all my force the necessity for doubling the police and not employing the military'. At that time active hostilities on the Irish side had consisted largely of taking pot-shots at policemen as they moved about the countryside. On the British side the war consisted mainly of raids and round-ups, in which troops were used to back up the police. Fearing that incidents in which soldiers had run amok were bound to escalate, and wishing to protect the reputation of the army, Sir Henry proposed an ingenious alternative. There was no point in trying to attract new recruits for the RIC among the Irish themselves. Instead, he recommended that a ready supply of men, trained in the use of firearms and toughened by four years of trench warfare, lay readily to hand among the many thousands of unemployed ex-soldiers in England. Lloyd George was attracted to this idea, and shortly before Christmas advertisements began to appear in the British press. Men who were ready and willing to undertake 'a rough and dangerous task' were sought for a special constabulary to assist the regular officers of the RIC. The new men were paid at the rate of ten shillings a day, all found. Recruits quickly found that they were expected to implement an unofficial 'shoot-to-kill' policy. After a cursory training in police procedures, the first batch of Specials was despatched to southern Ireland at the end of March 1920.

Many of them were young men unable to settle down to civvy street after years in the forces, and a good proportion of them appear to have been brutalised by their previous military experience. They were by no means all the sweepings of the English gaols as Sinn Fein propaganda made out, though not a few of them did, indeed, have prison records. As a group, in the words of Piaras Beaslai, they were physically and morally depraved. In pursuing their mandate 'to make Ireland hell for the rebels' they arrogated to themselves the right to shoot, burn, torture, loot and pillage at will. For some unaccountable reason they were kitted out in a motley assortment of uniforms. Officially it was stated that they were so impatient to get to Ireland that they could not wait for the proper uniforms; but throughout their time in the Twenty-six Counties (about fourteen months) they continued to be dressed in a peculiar fashion: either khaki military tunic and navy-blue police trousers, or navy-blue police tunic and khaki trousers or breeches, with the same apparently random choice of headgear. This strange garb certainly set them apart from the regular police and the military (which may have been the intention all along), but in no time they were dubbed the Black and Tans, after a famous pack of foxhounds, and the name was even adopted semi-officially. For example, *The Weekly Summary*, a propaganda newsletter produced by Dublin Castle, contained an editorial on 27 August which stated that the Black and Tans would 'go on with the job of making Ireland once again safe for the law-abiding, and an appropriate hell for those whose trade is agitation, and whose method is murder'.

This reflects the attitude of the beleaguered authorities in the Castle, not to mention a curious naïvety regarding the Black and Tans. In short order this rough, tough, unruly mob numbering several thousands was let loose on southern Ireland. Armed with rifles and revolvers, with seemingly unlimited supplies of ammunition, they roared round the streets after curfew in lorries, Crossley tenders and powerful Lancia armoured cars. They believed in the safety of numbers, usually operating in gangs of forty or fifty rather than in small patrols. They would descend on pubs and restaurants like a swarm of locusts or ravening wolves, disregarding the legal opening hours. Drunk and disorderly more often than not, they terrified the law-abiding populace and had the effect of driving decent Irish people into the arms of the Volunteers. They created a hatred of all things English in areas which had hitherto been quite neutral, and hardened the resolve of the extremists. As a fighting force they were useless; as a police force they were a joke. These mercenaries were terrorists of the very worst sort, hated by the ordinary people of Ireland and despised by the constabulary they were supposed to be augmenting.

In the popular mind the Tans were often confused with the Auxies, a quite separate force serving much the same purpose. The Auxiliary Cadets were originally intended to be embodied in the RIC but from the outset formed a separate force. They wore police tunics, navy-blue breeches, knee-length boots and navy-blue Tam o' Shanter bonnets. They were recruited exclusively from ex-officers of the army and navy and received a minimum of a pound a day, twice as much as the Specials. If the Black and Tans were the Waffen SS, then the Auxiliaries were the *Leibstandarte*, a black-clad élite unit numbering about fifteen hundred in all. Their minimum rank in the armed services would have been captain or equivalent, but they included many young bloods who had

Gearoid O'Sullivan (in the dark jacket) with members of the Squad

Members of the first Dail, 1919

18. This instrument shall be submitted forthwith by His Majesty's Government for the approval of Parliament and by the Irish signatories to a meeting summoned for the purpose of the members elected to sit in the House of Commons of Southern Ireland, and if approved shall be ratified by the necessary legislation.

Decr 6th 1921.

On behalf of the British Delegation.

D Lloyd George

Austen Chamberlain

Birkenhead.

Winston S. Churchill

L. Worthington Evans

Hamar Greenwood

Gordon Hewart.

On behalf of the Irish Delegation

Art Ó Gríobhtha (Arthur Griffith)

Mícheál Ó Coileáin

Riobárd Barton

E. S. Ó Dúgáin

Seoirse Gabhán Uí Dhubhthaigh

ABOVE: *The last page of the Treaty, bearing the signatures of the British delegation (left) and the Irish delegation (right). The latter wrote their signatures in Irish, Griffith alone adding the English version of his name in brackets*

RIGHT: *Michael Collins as Chairman of the Provisional Government, with members of his cabinet*

Erskine Childers

Robert Barton

Eamonn Duggan

George Gavan Duffy

David Lloyd George

Winston Churchill

Lord Birkenhead

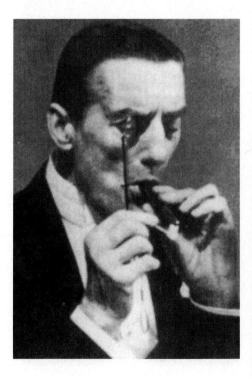

Sir Austen Chamberlain

Field-Marshal Sir Henry Wilson

Sir Hamar Greenwood

Sir James Craig

Sir Edward Carson

The Black and Tans were there to 'make Ireland a hell for rebels to live in'

General Richard Mulcahy

Michael Collins in pugnacious mood, addressing an election rally, 1922

ABOVE: The opening shots of the Civil War, fired from Free State 18-pound artillery supplied by the British government

RIGHT: General Collins, Commander-in-Chief of the National Army, on a tour of inspection shortly before he died

Troops of the new Irish Free State search for Republican anti-Treaty forces during the Civil War

Meeting of pro- and anti-Treaty officers at the Mansion House, Dublin on 8 May 1922 (from left to right): Sean MacEoin, Sean Moylan, Eoin O'Duffy, Liam Lynch, Gearoid O'Sullivan and Liam Mellowes

attained field rank, and there was a tendency for them to retain their recently demitted military titles. Like the Volunteers, they elected their officers and NCOs. They wore their medal ribbons with fierce pride, and included many a Military Cross and Distinguished Service Order. They were the product of the finest English public schools and a good percentage came from old Anglo-Irish families; but otherwise they differed only from the Black and Tans in their ruthlessness and ferocity. Utterly fearless, especially when cornered, they often earned the respect of their opponents; but they also included a sinister sprinkling of sadists and psychopaths who delighted in devising ever more fiendish methods of torture, mutilation and death. The outrages committed by the Tans and the Auxies, and they were legion, were either played down by the authorities or denied altogether, and it was in his role as official repudiator of all wrong-doing that Sir Hamar Greenwood really came into his own.

The decision to fight violence with violence was not properly thought out. Lloyd George, the instigator of this half-baked policy, baulked at Sir Henry Wilson's idea of applying the terror tactics which had apparently been so effective in subduing the Boers in the latter stages of the South African War. Wilson was an enthusiastic advocate of laying waste the countryside, erecting blockhouses, rounding up civilians, including women and children, and confining them in concentration camps. To these tried and tested methods which had brought the Boer commandos to their knees in 1902, Sir Henry proposed to add the shooting of hostages by roster, the aerial bombardment of disaffected towns and villages and even the use of poison gas, but Lloyd George drew back from all-out warfare, afraid of alienating world opinion (particularly in the United States). In the end, he compromised, and tacitly gave the counter-insurgency forces a completely free hand. The war, such as it was, would be fought in the alleyways of towns or the country lanes, between relatively small bands on both sides. In this form of guerrilla warfare the advantage should have been with the British, with their vast experience of such operations from India to South Africa; but lack of co-ordination between the various forces, squabbling between rival departments of the civil service and a demoralising sense that what they were doing was plain wrong and unjust, combined to rob the British of victory. On the other side were two or three thousand poorly armed boys, led by a twenty-nine-year-old ex-audit clerk; but there were other factors: an unquenchable national spirit, inspired leadership and a charismatic commander with an unrivalled genius for organisation and intelligence. Small wonder that at least one of Britain's senior figures, the Cabinet Secretary Thomas Jones, would ask rhetorically, 'Where was Michael Collins during the Great War? He would have been worth a dozen brass-hats.'

But in the second half of 1920 the war steadily escalated. If the Volunteers executed a 'tout' (and there were plenty of these spies and informers in every community) the Tans and Auxies would retaliate with random slayings. If the Volunteers raided a police post and captured arms and ammunition, the forces of law and order would destroy a village in the vicinity. The bullet and the Mills bomb were the preferred weapons of the Volunteers, but in their arsenal of fiendish atrocities the Black and Tans had the knife and the bayonet, the rope and the pyre. The pikes and pitch-caps of the Yeomanry of Ninety-Eight were as nothing to the stomach-crunching savagery of the Tans. Prisoners were hideously tortured and mutilated, ears, noses, tongues and genitals cut off, eyes gouged out, limbs set alight. The literature of the Troubles is replete with the ghastly litany of murder and mayhem. From individual atrocities the Black and Tans rapidly graduated to wholesale destruction of property. This policy was actually given Cabinet sanction on 31 May 1920, being described as 'a plan whereby Irishmen were made to feel the effect of the campaign of murder and arson along economic channels'. In dry civil service jargon in the corridors of Downing Street the mandarins of Whitehall calmly discussed 'the best method of imposing fines on Irishmen in affected areas'. The consensus of opinion was that there was little point in imposing fines when the authorities lacked the means to extract the money. Instead, the destruction of creameries was an excellent objective, but in the ensuing months any agricultural or industrial concern would become a legitimate target.

On 20 September, as a reprisal for a pub brawl in which two Tans were shot, the town of Balbriggan was subjected to a horrific attack, in which a hosiery factory, four public houses and forty-nine dwelling-houses were burned to the ground, two people were killed and many others wounded in a prolonged orgy of looting, torching and shooting. The following day the towns of Ennistymon, Lahinch and Miltown Malbay were subjected to similar attacks, Lahinch Town Hall and many other public buildings being destroyed in the process. Fermoy, Galway, Lismore, Mallow and Thurles were also sacked in ensuing days, in reprisal for IRA attacks. Even Sir Henry Wilson, the bloodthirsty advocate of such extreme action, was beginning to have his doubts when he noted in his diary (23 September) that 'the local people' (presumably the Black and Tans) 'marked down certain SFs ... and then coolly went out and shot them without question or trial'. Then he commented, 'Winston saw very little harm in this but it horrifies me.' In the course of 1920 the forces of the Crown killed over two hundred unarmed civilians including women and children: 'Sixty-nine were persons deliberately killed in the streets or in their own homes; thirty-six were men killed while in custody, the rest were victims of indiscriminate firing by military and police.'[1]

Then there were the regular troops of the British Army in Ireland which had a strength of 36,000 by April 1920. Reinforcements were promised but by the end of the year numbers had only risen to 40,000, though a further 10,000 were added in the early months of 1921 as the war reached its bloody climax. The troops were, for the most part, only lightly armed, though latterly they had armoured cars and field artillery, heavy machine-guns and mortars. This impressive military power, however, was largely neutralised, partly by its very poor communications, and partly because of the tactics employed by its opponents. For both of these factors, Michael Collins was largely responsible. Apart from disrupting telephone and telegraphic communications on a large scale or intercepting calls and telegrams, the Volunteers became adept at raids on post offices (not only for much-needed cash but also to seize mailbags). After examination, letters were usually forwarded, with a handstamp CENSORED BY THE I.R.A. applied boldly across the front of the envelope to explain the delay in transit. In June 1920 a mail train in County Cork was held up and after the removal and destruction of all police and military correspondence the rest was delivered to Bantry post office with appropriate censor marks. The most spectacular raid took place at the General Post Office in Dublin in July, leading *The Pall Mall Gazette* to comment sarcastically that if the country's chief post office were no longer secure, 'it would really save time if official correspondence were forwarded direct to Sinn Fein', while *The Irish Times* noted sourly: 'We seem to be approaching the day when British authority in Ireland will be shaken to its base by the laughter of two hemispheres.'

When, in September 1920, the British authorities were forced to use aircraft for the delivery of its despatches, Michael Collins swiftly countered. Five Volunteers in stolen British uniforms stood around a white circle painted on the ground and the pilot of one of the military planes, mistaking this for his dropping zone, jettisoned a sack of letters and despatches in the middle. The intelligence recovered in this coup proved invaluable, but also gave Michael the idea of adopting a similar means of communication. Scotland Yard would later report that Michael's London contact, Art O'Brien, was trying to purchase aircraft and train pilots as the nucleus of a Sinn Fein Air Force. Commandant James Fitzmaurice, a former RAF pilot, did fulfil this role later on, though he is best remembered nowadays for his spectacular transatlantic flights in 1927–28.

On other fronts, the British forces fared even worse. The trade unions were mobilised effectively to hamper the movement of military and police by road, rail and sea, and for many months on end the dockers paralysed all attempts to land stores at Dublin, Kingstown (Dun Laoghaire), Queenstown (Cobh) and other major ports, forcing the army to tie up thousands of men and vehicles on this essential task when they should have been out hunting for Shinners. Michael also organised the railway workers so effectively that at one stage the British government seriously considered closing down the railway companies altogether. In the interim the military were obliged to move troops and stores by road. In southern Ireland country roads turned and twisted through ever-varying scenery, their high banks and hedgerows providing unlimited scope for ambushes. This was a tactic much favoured by Michael. After the débâcle of the attempt on Lord French the previous December, the road ambush had become a vital part of Volunteer strategy. It was a tactic that worked extremely well, the element of surprise making up for the lack of manpower or heavy weaponry. In the narrow country roads the destruction of the leading vehicles in a line of trucks could hold up a military convoy for hours on end. Even the employment of the lightly armoured Crossley tenders failed to give protection to these convoys. By the time their Lewis guns raked the hedgerows the damage had been done and the Volunteers had melted away, to attack again at will in some other place. The ambush, as an essential part of IRA strategy, was first mooted at a GHQ staff meeting on 1 August 1920. Brugha, who seems to have had little concept of what was actually going on in the countryside at the time, argued against ambushes, preferring set-piece battles, which would have been disastrous. Even when he was outvoted, the Minister of Defence felt that the ambushers should call on the enemy to surrender before opening fire on them if they refused. The Corkmen present, Terence MacSwiney and Michael Collins, rubbished this outmoded chivalry, saying that the element of surprise was all-important. Brugha finally fudged the matter, leaving it to individual commanders to decide how they should operate. Brugha continued to argue that indiscriminate use of ambushes provoked reprisals against innocent civilians in the vicinity. Others argued against the ambush on moral grounds; it was sneaky to take the enemy by surprise like that. Michael's response to such mealy-mouthed objections was predictably robust, yet he would meet his death in just such a skirmish.

Above all, Dublin Castle failed utterly to penetrate Michael's intelligence organisation, whereas the Castle was so thoroughly riddled with Michael's agents that the British almost gave up in disgust. In December 1920 Archbishop Clune of Perth, Western Australia, made contact with Michael with apparent ease, impelling Mark Sturgis to wonder how the Australian archbishop could have such easy access to Ireland's most wanted man, when 'our own intelligence fails to find him after weeks of search'. Long before December, however, Sturgis and his colleagues had been forced by the escalation of Volunteer activity to abandon their civilian lodgings and move into rooms within the Castle precinct. Thereafter a doom-laden atmosphere not unlike that within the Hitler bunker in the spring of 1945 increasingly prevailed.

By 28 August 1920 army officers were being advised to wear civilian clothes off base, and three days later they were warned to send their wives and children back to Britain, as their safety could no longer be guaranteed. During

September civilian clothes were extended to all drivers and Intelligence personnel wherever they were operating and shortly afterwards all remaining Irish personnel were posted out of the island as a matter of security and political expediency. Even this seemed a doubtful move, in the aftermath of the June mutiny of the Connaught Rangers in India when 350 soldiers refused to obey orders. Seventy-five were convicted of mutiny and fifteen sentenced to death, but only one man, James Daly, was hanged. The others were still serving sentences of penal servitude in military prisons some time after the Irish Free State came into being. In October British officers in Kerry were told that it was no longer safe to go fox-hunting. Now this was really too much, and the Sixth Division exacted a terrible revenge by reimposing a ban on *all* sporting activities in the county, from hurling to dances, from football matches to race meetings.

By August few British officers would dare to ride or drive out into the countryside anyway; but even in Dublin, which was thronging with troops and police, the Volunteers moved with impunity. Frederick Dumont reported to the US Secretary of State that Sinn Fein took 'great delight in acts that tantalise the Government' which, for its part, adopted a very heavy-handed approach. Dumont deplored as childish 'the driving of armoured tanks through the streets of Dublin after any except great outrages in order to awe a peaceful population'.

As the days got colder and the nights longer, an unreal air of optimism infected the Castle; believing that somehow they had Sinn Fein on the run, the authorities stepped up the number and severity of raids. In truth, this was a desperate gamble to bring matters to a conclusion before winter set in. Michael Collins wrote to Sean Nunan in New York on 30 September saying that the British were losing the last few friends they had in Ireland. 'Positively some of the things they do are almost inconceivable, even to those who thought they knew them well', and he grimly noted that advertisements for the Black and Tans continued to appear in the newspapers, showing that 'their recruiting in spite of all their talk is not so brisk as they would like it to be'.

In the autumn of 1920 the number of raids rose sharply. In addition to the haphazard savagery of the Tans and the Auxies there was the horror of the torture chambers in the Castle, more sinister since the infliction of intolerable pain therein had become an instrument of government policy. Officers of the regular army were swift to emulate this, applying their own brutal methods in the interrogation of captured Volunteers before summarily executing them. One of the worst offenders was Major A.E. Percival of the Essex Regiment whose role as a torturer of suspected Shinners has been well documented.[2] For this he was selected as a very special target of the Squad which, having failed to assassinate him in Ireland, even went so far as to trail him to England when he went on leave in March 1921. Percival must have had a premonition, for he remained in barracks the entire time. The Squad were waiting to shoot him on the platform at Liverpool Street Station when he arrived from camp, but were compelled to withdraw hastily only minutes before the appointed time when tipped off that a police swoop was imminent.

Major Percival also incurred Michael's personal wrath when he led the raid on Woodfield, the Collins farm, one of four in the neighbourhood destroyed on 16 April 1921 as a reprisal for an IRA raid on Rosscarbery. The farmhouse and most of the outbuildings were razed to the ground and the occupants, an unmarried sister of Michael, a servant-girl and Johnny Collins's eight children (his wife Katty having recently died) were thrown out in foul weather. Johnny himself was absent from home that day, attending a meeting of the county council in Cork. This outrage was capped later that day by Johnny's arrest as he alighted from the train at Clonakilty; he was detained without trial at Spike Island and as a result of medical neglect lost the use of his right hand.[3] What goes round comes around. Twenty years later Lieutenant-General Percival, commanding British and Allied forces in Malaya, would suffer the supreme humiliation of surrendering the supposedly impregnable bastion of Singapore after a seventy-day campaign, followed by four years of unspeakable horror in a Japanese prison camp.

Amid the mounting terror in the autumn of 1920, Michael Collins continued to go about his multifarious duties in Dublin, made all the more arduous because others around him were losing heart and giving up the struggle. It is worth noting, for example, that Cathal Brugha, nominally Minister of Defence, never gave up his job as manager of Lalor's religious candle-making company throughout the Troubles. His main contribution to the fight at this time seems to have been to undermine his Director of Intelligence at every turn, and to continue proposing hare-brained schemes which were quite impracticable. From exterminating the entire government front bench in the House of Commons with machine-guns, he moved to the more feasible ploy of mowing down the densely packed queue outside a London cinema, but Michael told him coldly, 'You'll get none of my men for that!' To which Cathal had riposted, 'That's all right, *Mister* Collins. I want none of your men. I'll get men of my own!' When Brugha persisted with this crazy scheme Michael persuaded Richard Mulcahy, the Chief of Staff, to countermand the orders of the Minister of Defence – an episode which only intensified Brugha's hatred of Collins.

The officer selected by Cathal Brugha for this project was Sean MacEoin, the blacksmith of Ballinalee, County Longford, who became a legend in his own lifetime. Michael, however, had other, more practical uses for the fighting blacksmith. In September 1920 he came down from Dublin to Granard and stayed with the Kiernans at the Greville Arms. There he conferred with

MacEoin whom he appointed commandant of the Longford Brigade and director of operations for the neighbouring counties of Leitrim and Cavan, with a remit to form full-time active service units or flying columns whose mobility, coupled by intimate knowledge of the terrain, would prove very effective in the closing phase of the war. One of MacEoin's first targets was District Inspector Philip Kelleher of the RIC, a native of Macroom, County Cork, who often lodged at the Greville Arms. Kelleher, a famous footballer in happier times, was alleged to have insulted some women during a raid on a house in Ballinalee. He had been sent to Longford 'to spill blood, and he fully intended to do so', as he lost no time in informing his new parishioners. Approval for the slaying was given by Michael Collins at GHQ, but made conditional on the death of Terence MacSwiney or Kevin Barry, who were then in custody.

MacSwiney, MacCurtain's successor as Lord Mayor of Cork, died on 25 October after a hunger-strike lasting seventy-four days, while Kevin Barry, an eighteen-year-old medical student who had been caught during a raid in which three soldiers were shot dead, was hanged on 1 November after all attempts to secure a reprieve failed. With MacSwiney's death, Kelleher's fate was sealed. Shortly before midnight on 31 October two Volunteers went into the hotel bar and found their victim drinking at the counter with members of the North Longford Sinn Fein executive and a local priest. He was shot on the spot, the priest giving him the last rites as he fell. Larry Kiernan and his sisters were arrested and interrogated at Longford barracks. All were released the following day, except Kitty who was detained a further two days. On 2 November Constable Cooney, reconnoitring Ballinalee, was shot and fatally wounded. Near midnight on 3 November eleven lorries crammed with Black and Tans entered Granard and sacked the town, burning down the hotel in the process. The girls salvaged what they could, giving priority to the things that meant most to them. Characteristically Chrys took all the religious objects and a spool of thread, Kitty grabbed the silverware, Helen the dresses and Maud the account-books. Later, if a customer claimed to have settled an account in full, Maud would produce the relevant ledger and confront the client with the truth. The hotel was rebuilt with compensation money, though it was well into 1922 before it was open for business again.[4]

The orgy of destruction went on for several hours before the Tans, most of them by now quite drunk, clambered aboard their trucks and returned to their barracks in Longford. On the way, however, they were ambushed by Sean MacEoin and twenty Volunteers who, though outnumbered by five to one, killed at least a score and wounded about sixty. Exact casualties were never published, but this ambush was undoubtedly one of the greatest coups of the campaign.

No further reprisals were wreaked on Granard, but Michael, very concerned at the killing of Kelleher in the hotel and the manner in which the Kiernans were made to carry the can, summoned MacEoin to Dublin a few days later for a full debriefing on the series of incidents. Why Kitty Kiernan was singled out for more severe treatment than her brother and sisters is not known; but it is likely that her connection with Michael Collins and Harry Boland was common knowledge.

Michael was not the man to allow personal considerations to deflect him from his aim of dealing with the British and their lackeys. Frank O'Connor speaks of new demands on his mighty will-power:

> He had to concentrate. He took up Pelmanism. No one but Collins would
> have answered such a challenge with Pelmanism. It is one of the most
> illuminating slants we have on his peculiar view of the revolution.[5]

Pelmanism was a system of mind-training fashionable at the time; one would have thought that that was the last thing Michael needed.

Remarkably, he continued to go about his businesses on his bicycle as usual. Much has been made of the charmed life he appeared to lead, Ireland's most wanted man evading detection. It seems incredible that the British authorities had never succeeded in obtaining a good photograph of him. The only picture was a group shot of the April 1919 session of the Dail; everyone is staring benignly at the camera except the Big Fellow, putting on a malevolent snarl that totally distorted his features. While this confirmed the impression the British had of their deadliest adversary as a typical thug, it would prove utterly useless in identifying the smartly dressed businessman innocently cycling around the city. Several other photographs of the period do exist, but in them Michael is invariably shown with his eyes down, presenting the top of his head to the lens. His legendary camera-shyness does not entirely explain his ability to evade capture and the truth was probably more prosaic. Many of the Dublin Metropolitan Police actually knew him well enough. Mrs Leigh Doyle, walking across O'Connell Bridge with him one day, saw a constable salute him and wink conspiratorially. Michael never batted an eyelid, merely commenting to his companion, 'Sure, now – isn't that a queer thingeen!'

Of course, he did have several close shaves. On one occasion he was surrounded by a band of Auxiliaries in the street and bluffed his way out, pretending to be drunk. On another, he was seized and his head turned roughly from side to side, while an Auxiliary compared his profile with a photograph of the most wanted man. This was where the extreme mobility of his features saved his life. Once, while Michael was riding in a car with Broy, Neligan and MacNamara, they were stopped by a military patrol. Michael, who was carrying a revolver but had no pass to be out after curfew, could have been shot on the spot and compromised the others; but Broy saved the day by flourishing his pass and referring loudly to the big man in the shadows as the Sergeant. Apart from cycling around Dublin quite openly Michael seems to have made no secret of his whereabouts. At one stage he stayed at Miss McCarthy's private hotel, 44 Mountjoy Street; letters written by him to Austin Stack from that address are still extant. They must have been censored by the prison authorities, and this probably led to the raid on the street with a view to apprehending him; but luck was on Michael's side. The house had the numerals 44 gilt on a glass lunette above the doorway but with the passage of time one of the figures had worn off. Incredibly, the raiding party could not find a number 44 Mountjoy Street and returned to barracks empty-handed.

There was a curious grey area in Dublin that centred on the Café Cairo and Kidd's Restaurant (commonly called Kidd's Back) where some of the most wanted men, Michael among them, habitually rubbed shoulders with G men, Military Intelligence and the Secret Service. Considerable mystery to this day surrounds 'Lieutenant G', supposedly an Intelligence officer with whom Michael was on remarkably good terms. Rex Taylor produced substantial documentary evidence, in the form of cryptic notes in Michael's diaries and day-books, to meetings with 'G'; but Dave Neligan denied that any such officer existed, and subsequent writers have tended to go along with that view. Of course, 'G' could have been a letter picked at random, rather than an actual initial, and there is evidence to suggest that this man was, in fact, either someone called Reynolds or Thomas Markham, highly placed in the British intelligence system. In the murky world of intelligence and counter-intelligence, of spies and double or treble agents, anything was possible; and Michael was certainly adept at 'turning' officers in the RIC and the military to his will. It should also be noted that British intelligence officers and members of the Secret Service deliberately cultivated 'touts', minor figures in the rebel movement who could be leaned on or bribed to pass on scraps of information. After Neligan joined the Secret Service he introduced Michael's chief intelligence officers, Tobin, Cullen and Thornton, to his colleagues as men who had their ears to the ground and were worth cultivating. Eventually the trio from Crow Street became regular habitués of the British Intelligence crowd that used to hang out in Kidd's Back or Rabbiatti's Saloon in Marlborough Street. On one occasion a British officer who was having a drink with the gang said to Cullen: 'Surely you fellows know Liam Tobin, Frank Thornton and Tom Cullen. These are Collins's three officers and if you get those fellows we should locate Collins himself.' The trio nodded sagely and stared hard into their beer glasses.

Despite considerable restriction on movement, and the constant threat of being identified and arrested, Michael seems to have lived life to the full. He even attended race meetings at Phoenix Park, one of the few public events which were not proscribed (mainly because they provided recreation for the military). Michael would go with Tobin or Cullen, or perhaps a visiting officer from one of the country brigades, and always had a flutter. On one occasion he backed a rank outsider called Irish Republic which astonished everyone by coming first at 50 to I – a good omen. Although the curfew had now been extended from dusk to dawn, this did not prevent Michael from attending concerts and the theatre whenever he could get the opportunity to escape from one or other of his many desks.

During this period Michael, with one or more of his closest associates, often stayed at Vaughan's Hotel. Vera Neary, whose husband was one of Michael's bodyguards, recounts that the outside window-sill of the bedroom which they used had large nails embedded, on which they suspended their revolvers by the trigger guards; in the event of a raid they would not be found in possession of firearms, yet could get to them easily enough through the window which was left slightly ajar. While the Tans and Auxies were sleeping off last night's debauch, Michael would already be up and about, cycling from Vaughan's Hotel to Bachelor's Walk or Harcourt Street before sun-up. The morning would be spent in his intelligence office, initially mopping up any paperwork left unfinished from the previous day. Then Joe O'Reilly would arrive with all the newspapers, both Irish and British, and Michael would go through them. A very rapid reader, he could take in a paragraph at a time, swiftly marking passages of particular military or political interest. While he was thus engaged, Joe would be opening the mail, stamping the contents with the date and pinning them neatly to the envelopes. Again, Michael would rapidly scan these despatches, marking passages in blue ink. The rest of the morning would be taken up with dictating replies to one of the girls. He dictated rapidly and articulately, never repeating himself and never making mistakes. His letters were masterpieces of brevity and precision, incisive and straight to the point. Around midday he dealt with matters which came within his purview as Minister of Finance, chiefly in connection with the National Loan. After a brief lunch (over which he dealt constantly with his intelligence contacts) he would cycle to Bachelor's Walk and visit his Finance Office to grapple with the accounts. He was quite meticulous about this, so it angered him all the more when Cathal Brugha quibbled about small amounts of cash in Defence funds which could not always be accounted for. This nitpicking was aggravated by the fact that some of Michael's accounts were among papers seized during a raid, and he felt (probably with justification) that Cathal had pounced on this because he knew full well that Michael, for once, could not produce the necessary vouchers and receipts.

For a man on the run, Michael did not behave as he should. Perhaps it was the open manner in which he held court at Vaughan's Hotel which confused the enemy. In an alcove on the ground floor he received hosts of people, couriers with National Loan money to be deposited, intelligence officers with reports, brigade commandants from Kerry or Limerick demanding better arms or more ammunition, churchmen and gunmen, politicians and place-seekers, journalists and important foreign visitors. Michael dealt with them all in turn, nodding from time to time, taking the occasional note, giving decisions in staccato fashion. He had a diabolical memory for names, places, occupations. He could recall the duty hours of friendly postmen, and from his experience in West Kensington he knew precisely the movement of postal packets, and therefore where they might be located and intercepted. He gave dozens of interviews and dealt with hundreds of supplications.

His colleagues were accustomed to his habit of suddenly diving into a pocket for his notebook, as he jotted down details or dashed off a hurried note on the spot. Orderly in everything, he habitually used a fountain pen and abhorred a pencil. He would never use one himself and he became tetchy if anyone addressed a letter to him in pencil. What annoyed him most of all was letters signed with a rubber stamp. He ran a tight ship in his various offices and had an absolute fetish for punctuality. Woe betide the person, regardless of rank, who was a second late; Michael would greet them at the door, swinging his pocket-watch ominously in his hand and glowering furiously. To Michael, time was the most precious of all commodities; so often the success of his operations depended on split-second timing. With all the odds stacked against success, the only hope was in an organisation perfected to the tiniest detail. In one letter he summed this up: 'What a little detail causes a disaster often – in fact, it is usually the details that do it.'[6]

There was always an austere, almost puritanical atmosphere. On one occasion a staff officer was snatching a cuddle from one of the typists when Michael suddenly entered the office. The startled officer virtually hurled the poor girl across the room and buried his face in his papers to conceal what he had been doing. Had Michael realised it at the time, he would have slung the errant officer out on his neck.

And yet this was the same man who never tired of japes and schoolboy pranks, who anticipated the Goons by several decades with his surreal humour or sudden lapses into an exaggerated Cork argot with strangulated vowels that were well-nigh unintelligible. He invented nicknames and diminutives for friend and foe alike: Beaslai, Brugha and Mulcahy would become Piersheen, Cahileen and Dickeen, though not always to their faces. He had a genius for repartee and the stories of Michael's witty one-liners are legion. Underneath the humour, however, there was a roughness, and sometimes the comradely banter turned to merciless teasing. Joe O'Reilly was often the butt of this cruel humour, but so too was Tom Cullen. 'Schoolboyish jokes and bubbling high spirits made him an uncomfortable companion. After a time one grew to expect nothing but the unexpected from him, in word and act.'[7] Late at night, the tension of the day would be released in the sort of boisterous high-jinks for which he was notorious at Stafford and Frongoch. Many a room, in hotel or private house, was thoroughly wrecked by Michael in maniacal high spirits. Liam Devlin, who kept a pub near the Rotunda, often provided accommodation for Michael and his chums:

> When Devlin met Collins he handed over a neatly furnished room. Within a month it was a wreck. There was scarcely a chair with a back to it, the delf had disappeared. Yet when one of the gang, hearing a rumble and thunder from the sitting-room in which Collins was lashing out with a chair, apologised to the Devlins, they merely smiled and said, 'It eases his mind.'
>
> They spoke with the understanding of love, for it was in this savage lashing and straining that all the accumulated anxiety was released.[8]

The wrestling bouts and no-holds-barred scrimmages on the floor with Gearoid O'Sullivan, Liam Tobin and the other senior officers of the Republican Army were the horseplay of desperate men engaged in the deadliest of conflicts, always conscious of the fact that a clatter of boots on the stairs, the ramming of the door and a burst of gunfire might end their lives at any moment.

CHAPTER 11

Bloody Sunday, 1920

In prison we are their jailers;
On trial their judges,
Persecuted their punishers,
Dead their conquerors.

EOIN MACNEILL

THE BRITISH HAD NEVER FOUGHT A WAR LIKE THIS BEFORE.
Hitherto, even in the Boer War, the army had been accustomed to taking on an
enemy that could readily be identified; now it was confronted by an enemy it
could seldom see, and never distinguish from the mass of the populace. By the
winter of 1920, some 50,000 troops and 15,000 RIC were in conflict with
about 3,000 Volunteers. Eventually it would dawn on Lloyd George and his
ministers that they were in conflict not with a few rebels but an entire nation,
and to combat this menace General Macready established two enormous
concentration camps at Ballykinler, County Down, and at the Curragh, County
Kildare, where many thousands could be detained without trial. The small
bands of guerrillas, roaming the countryside and attacking at will, were but the
tip of the iceberg. The vast bulk of the Republican Army continued to live at
home and go about their everyday jobs. Kevin Barry, the medical student
executed on 1 November, had taken part on a raid on an army bread detail
during a break between exams. The Volunteers wore no uniform, their
preferred weapons were easily concealed, and their ability to strike suddenly
from any or every direction had a paralysing effect on police and military alike.
The British response, of arbitrary looting, arson, assault and murder by bodies
of men recruited specially for these purposes, had little effect on Sinn Fein or
the Volunteers, but it provoked disgust and contempt throughout the civilised
world.

The actual numbers killed in the Anglo-Irish War were very small – a few
hundred at most – and pale into insignificance when compared to the millions
slaughtered in Cambodia, Rwanda, Bosnia and Chechnya in recent times.

Nevertheless, the killings in Ireland were of such ferocity and violence that they haunt the nation to this day. The brutal murders of Lord Mayor MacCurtain of Cork, Mayor O'Callaghan of Limerick and ex-Mayor Clancy of Limerick, all shot in the presence of their wives, created shockwaves that reverberated around the world. Similarly, the murders of Canon Magner, Brother Prendergast and Father Griffin and the attempt to murder Bishop Fogarty at Killaloe by throwing him into the Shannon in a sack were greatly magnified by the fact that these were much-respected men of the cloth. The shooting of eight-year-old Annie O'Neill, mistaken for some young men 'running away', and young Mrs Quinn with her baby in her arms might fall into the category of unfortunate incidents brushed aside by Lloyd George or Sir Hamar Greenwood, but these killings were multiplied many times over by the injuries inflicted on people who survived their ordeal (even if many were so traumatised by the experience that a bitter hatred of England and all things English would endure for generations).

Indubitably, the sense of outrage felt by the Irish was also magnified by the fact that these foul deeds were condoned, if not actually ordered, by the men democratically elected to rule over them. On 1 November 1920 Sir Hamar calmly told the House of Commons: 'There is no charge with one exception of which I know urged against a policeman or soldier for murder.' No fewer than twenty-two coroners' inquests had returned verdicts of wilful murder or unjustifiable homicide against Crown forces, before the government stepped in with its solution – coroners' inquests were suppressed.

On 9 October at Caernarfon and on 9 November at the Guildhall Banquet, Lloyd George defiantly justified the policy of terror in Ireland. On the latter occasion, regarding reprisals by the RIC and its allies, the Prime Minister said:

> There is no doubt that at last their patience has given way and there has been some severe hitting back . . . let us be fair to these gallant gentlemen who are doing their duty in Ireland . . . it is no use talking about this being a war and these being reprisals when these things are being done [by Sinn Fein] with impunity in Ireland.
>
> We have murder by the throat . . . we had to reorganise the police and when the Government was ready we struck the terrorists and now the terrorists are complaining of terror.

Even as he spoke, Lloyd George was probably congratulating himself on the fact that he had already set in train elaborate plans to get Michael Collins, the one man above all others who was identified as the driving force of the rebellion. All the usual police and military intelligence methods having failed to track down this elusive chameleon, the Prime Minister had given directions that the elimination of this man must take top priority. To this end, a special squad of assassins would have to be formed from the best material then available. It was decided to recruit this élite band from the senior ranks of British Intelligence in the Middle East. No matter that these officers had no first-hand, up-to-date knowledge of the Irish situation; they had been dealing with the ethnic and religious problems in the newly mandated territory of Palestine which had given rise to a very similar type of warfare. This squad, numbering sixteen in all, came to be known as the Cairo Gang, partly because they had been recruited by GHQ in Cairo and partly because the Café Cairo in Dublin would become one of their favourite haunts.

These men began arriving in Dublin early in September 1920, in ones and twos on different dates, under assumed names, sometimes accompanied by their wives as additional cover to their real activities. They were attired in civilian clothes and posed as commercial travellers. They took rooms in Mount Street or Pembroke Street or booked in at various hotels in the city. They had one objective, to destroy Collins and his intelligence organisation, and they very nearly succeeded. For a few weeks they got themselves settled in but studiously avoided the established intelligence networks of the police and military. The first phase of their campaign was to demoralise the enemy and spread terror and dissension in the ranks of Sinn Fein by a series of killings. The first victim was John Lynch from Kilmallock, County Limerick, who was shot in his bed at 2 a.m. in the Royal Exchange Hotel on 23 September. Later it was announced by the Castle that Lynch had resisted arrest and fired on police. Lynch was not a Volunteer and never carried a weapon; he was in town merely because he was a National Loan organiser and had £23,000 to hand over to Michael Collins. It may be that the murderers had mistaken him for Liam Lynch (no relation), the Cork IRA leader; if so, it said very little for their intelligence in either sense of the word. Michael was outraged by this senseless slaying and determined to get to the bottom of it. Within twelve days he had ascertained the facts, which he reported to Arthur Griffith. He gave precise times and even named names. Captain Baggelly, an officer of the General Staff at Ship Street barracks, had received a phone call at 1.35 a.m. requesting a car to pick up the hit squad. Both RIC and military personnel were involved in the back-up, and at 2.15 a.m. a telephone call from the Headquarters of Dublin District to College Street police station passed the information that the RIC had called at the hotel and shot a man named Lynch. Michael's report ended chillingly, 'There is not the slightest doubt that there was no intention whatever to arrest Mr Lynch.'

On 11 October the Cairo Gang had a major coup when they broke into the home of Professor Carolan at Whitehall in the north of the city and cornered Dan Breen and Sean Treacy in bed. Unlike John Lynch, however, these were two of the most dangerous gunmen in the Republican movement, with a formidable string of successes ever since the Soloheadbeg incident. They shot their way out, killing two of the undercover men in the process. One of the dead officers was Major Smyth, brother of the colonel who had provoked the RIC mutiny at Listowel; he had been serving in Palestine when his brother was shot, and had volunteered with alacrity when the Cairo Gang was formed. Dan Breen was badly injured in this incident, having been cut by glass when he crashed through a conservatory roof.[1] Despite severe loss of blood he staggered to a nearby house whose occupants sheltered him until Michael could arrange for him to be moved to the Mater Hospital where the nuns concealed him in the maternity ward. Treacy got clean away but Professor Carolan was put against the wall, shot through the head and left for dead. The authorities maintained that the professor had been shot by Dan Breen (whose revolver was used for the deed), but Carolan lingered long enough to make a deathbed statement of the true facts. Treacy, who had shot Major Smyth, felt some compulsion to attend his funeral and pray for his soul, but he was recognised in the doorway of Peadar Clancy's gents outfitter's shop. In the raid that followed, Treacy and one of the Cairo Gang were killed, while Joe Vize, a former British naval officer who was Michael's Director of Purchases and head of arms smuggling, was arrested.

Some days later, when Breen was sufficiently recovered, Michael had him moved to a safe house, but when he learned that this building was about to be raided by a gang of Black and Tans, Michael mustered the Squad and personally took command of the rescue attempt. This was one of those rare occasions when recklessness overruled his usual common sense, but fortunately by the time the Squad reached the house the police and military had moved on. They had raided every other house in the locality but inexplicably overlooked the one Breen was hiding in. From his window, Dan had watched the fun, and even observed Michael and 'a few of the boys' on the fringe of the military cordon.

During the same month Frank Thornton was 'lifted' and detained for ten days before being released. Tobin and Cullen were arrested in Vaughan's Hotel (where Michael was then living), but allowed to go after a very intensive interrogation. Only the fact that, in all three cases, they were carrying false papers, in the names by which they were known to their buddies in British Intelligence, saved them from a bullet in the head. It was another close shave, and Michael knew that next time it would be himself, and he would not escape detection so easily. Once again, though, his superb intelligence network came to the rescue.

Frank Thornton later prepared a memoir on the sequence of events.[2] It was clear that the British were now operating a quite separate intelligence network on 'proper continental lines, with a Central Headquarters and other houses forming minor centres scattered all throughout the city'. In one of these, the sister of a Volunteer told her brother that some of the lodgers spoke with refined English accents, went out after curfew and kept odd hours. Then one of John Lynch's killers got maudlin in his cups and told a girl what he had done, and she promptly got the details to Michael. Finally, Sergeant Mannix of the Dublin Metropolitan Police, stationed at Donnybrook, got hold of a special list of British Secret Service officers, complete with their addresses. Armed with this, Michael infiltrated one of his men into the main lodging house as hall porter, and succeeded in obtaining duplicate room keys from the lodgings of all the others. Frank Thornton brought all his skills to bear on compiling detailed reports on each officer. Michael's intelligence officers intercepted their telephone calls and correspondence and even closely examined the contents of their wastepaper baskets.

In the end, Thornton was brought before a special session of the Dail Cabinet and Army Council at which he had to justify the proposed elimination of each and every man in his report. Top of the list were Colonel Aimes and Major Bennett. In addition to the Cairo group, two Irishmen named Mahon and Peel, and Major MacLean, the Chief Intelligence Officer at the Castle, were included for good measure. Frank had done his work well, and the meeting authorised the synchronised killings of the Cairo Gang, to take place early on the morning of Sunday, 21 November. This date was chosen partly because it was only a few days off, and partly because a major football match was scheduled for that afternoon and the city would be thronging with people. On 17 November Michael sent a note to Dick McKee, commandant of the Dublin Brigade:

> Dick – Have established addresses of the particular ones. Arrangements should be made about the matter. Lt. G. is aware of things. He suggests the 21st. A most suitable date and day I think. M.[3]

Here we have the mysterious English intelligence officer whom Michael trusted implicitly. All attempts to identify this man have failed but he must have been either one of the great unsung heroes of the war – or one of the worst double-dyed villains, depending on one's viewpoint.[4]

On the evening of Saturday, 20 November, Michael, with Dave Neligan and some friends, went to the Gaiety Theatre. During the interval Michael said to Dave that he wondered what kind of men he had sentenced to death. Dave casually told him to cast an eye over the people occupying the adjoining box! After the show, Michael and his intelligence chiefs conferred with McKee, Peadar Clancy (vice-commandant of the Dublin Brigade) and others in a room at Vaughan's Hotel to finalise details of the executions. The meeting broke up around midnight, McKee and Clancy going off to their hideout in nearby Gloucester Street.

Some time afterwards, Vaughan's Hotel was raided by a large posse of Auxiliaries. None of the plotters was captured, but the raiders arrested a young Gaelic scholar named Conor Clune from Clare who just happened to be in Dublin at the time to see Piaras Beaslai about Irish language projects. This unfortunate young man, who had no connections with the Volunteers, was whisked off to one of the interrogation rooms in the cellars of the Castle. During the night, Captain J.L. Hardy led a raid on Gloucester Street and captured Clancy and McKee, though not before the latter succeeded in destroying the hit-list. Hardy, whom Michael himself would describe as 'a notorious murderer', was the liaison officer between Dublin Castle and Scotland Yard and principal torturer. After the Troubles he found a lucrative career as a writer of lurid thrillers based loosely on his experiences; but without doubt his worst night's work was at hand. The innocent Clune as well as two of the leading figures in the Volunteer movement were subjected to several hours of the most excruciating torture. In the annals of man's inhumanity to man, the savagery of the Inquisition and the Gestapo must rank high, but that night both were surpassed by the sadism of Captain Hardy and his associates of F Division of the Auxiliary Police.

Michael was unaware that two of his best men had been arrested and tortured, and the elimination of the Cairo Gang went ahead as planned. On a bright, cold Sunday morning, shortly before 9 a.m., groups of Volunteers from the Dublin Brigade, each headed by a member of the Squad, silently made their way to eight separate locations in the city centre. A discreet knock and they are admitted by a servant, startled by the revolver brandished in her face. A guard left at the entrance, the others tiptoe upstairs. A key is slowly turned in a lock and a bedroom door eased open. In the twinkling of an eye the scene is surveyed and the target identified. The bells of the city's churches, tolling for nine o'clock Mass, had just fallen silent when the first shots rang out.

In the space of several minutes nineteen officers were shot. Not all of them belonged to the Cairo Gang, and at least one, a young officer of the Royal Army Medical Corps, was killed by mistake at the Gresham Hotel. All of the victims were still abed at the time of the assault, some in the arms of wives or sweethearts. A few were dragged out and put against a wall, but most were shot where they lay. Mick O'Hanlon's squad were scrupulous about not firing until they could separate their target from his girlfriend who valiantly tried to cover him, but having prised the terrified girl away, Mick Flanagan shot her lover. Great care, in fact, was taken to ensure that the women were not injured, although one wife miscarried moments after seeing her husband murdered beside her; and Joe Dolan, enraged at missing Hardy's colleague Major King, when he burst into the bedroom, took it out on the major's mistress whom he thrashed with King's sword-scabbard before setting fire to the room. Mick White calmly scoffed the breakfast of the elderly major he had just shot. One man died halfway through the bedroom window, with revolvers blazing over his screaming wife's shoulder. Another officer managed to jump out of the window in his bare feet, but was shot down in his pyjamas in the back garden. Michael's secretary, Anna Fitzsimmons, who had only been released from gaol the previous day and had gone to that very house for a good night's rest, was rudely awakened by shots and was a horrified eye-witness of this execution. Captain Baggelly, cut down at 119 Lower Baggot Street, went to his Maker not knowing that one of his assailants was Sean Lemass who would one day be *Taoiseach* (prime minister). Several officers made a grab for their guns before they were shot. In one case an officer's servant escaped and fired back at the house with a .22 pistol. Charlie Dalton recorded the shooting of 'three or four men' who were lined up against the wall in the hallway of their hotel:

> Knowing their fate I felt great pity for them. It was plain they knew it too. As I crossed the threshold the volley was fired . . . the sights and sounds of that morning were to be with me for many days and nights . . . I remembered I had not been to Mass. I slipped out, and in the silence before the altar, I thought over our morning's work and offered up a prayer for the fallen.[5]

The raids took the British completely by surprise, and the hit squads, for the most part, managed to escape without incident. Those engaged in the raids on Mount Street and Pembroke Road, however, ran into bands of Auxiliaries and this led to a series of ferocious running battles. Though heavily outnumbered and outgunned, the Volunteers succeeded in getting away, dragging their wounded with them. Only one man, Frank Teeling, fell into the enemy's hands, and Michael organised his escape before much harm could befall him.

In fact, almost half of the Cairo Gang escaped the massacre, either because they were elsewhere than expected or because their whereabouts had not been pinpointed in the first place. More importantly, a cursory examination of the bedrooms failed to reveal any papers of real significance. Nevertheless, the raids, though incomplete, struck such panic in the heart of the British intelligence machine that there was an immediate rush of survivors and their womenfolk in a fleet of taxis to the sanctuary of the Castle. Most fled from their lodgings without bothering to pack or dress properly.

Meanwhile, Michael Collins was impatiently waiting at Devlin's for reports on the raids. In due course Joe O'Reilly rode up on his bicycle and breathlessly reported. Later he would describe his boss as 'white and defiant with no expression of pleasure' as the news was given. Michael's reaction was swift.

'There'll be no football match today,' he said, and sent Joe off to the Gaelic Athletic Association to urge them to cancel the match, between Dublin and Tipperary. The Association said that it was impossible to cancel the match at such short notice; already vast crowds were thronging the area around Croke Park. As the morning wore on, Michael suddenly realised that there had been no word from Dick McKee or Peadar Clancy. With mounting apprehension he sent O'Reilly off to Gloucester Street to find out what had happened. Near their lodgings, Joe was met by a littler who told him that he had a message for Mick Collins.

When Michael heard that the two men had been captured, he collapsed in a chair and moaned, 'Good God! We're finished now. It's all up.' Frantically, he sent messages to MacNamara and Neligan to locate the prisoners. MacNamara discovered that two men had been taken to the Bridewell during the night and Neligan, at immense personal risk, went there and checked every cell, telling the sergeant-gaoler that he was looking for a cousin. Had the prisoners been there, it might have been possible for the Squad to mount an escape raid, but when Michael learned that they had, in fact, been taken to the Castle, he realised that they were done for. Like a man in a trance, he cycled across town to lunch at Mrs O'Donovan's as usual, and could not take his eyes off the empty place beside him, which had been set for Dick McKee.

After lunch Michael cycled back across the city, with a sense of impending doom. His gloomy forebodings were only too well justified. The British authorities reacted coldly and deliberately to the massacre of the morning. Instead of Black and Tans being turned loose in the white-heat of the moment, the British bided their time. Lorry-loads of Auxiliaries and soldiers drove up to Croke Park that afternoon and surrounded the athletic grounds. A large crowd was intently watching the match when the Auxiliaries opened fire on the packed stadium with rifles and machine-guns. Thirteen spectators were killed instantly and also the Tipperary goalkeeper, Hogan, while several hundreds suffered gunshot wounds or were trampled in the stampede. Later in the day a group of Auxiliaries and RIC rounded up a group of civilians in Lincoln Place near Trinity College and then ordered them to run for their lives. Seven of them were shot in the back and two, a man and a boy of ten, died of their wounds.

A few hours later the majority of prisoners in detention at the Castle were hastily transferred to the barracks at Beggar's Bush. Those left behind included Clancy, McKee and Clune, all in a badly beaten state. They were put into the Castle guardroom at the gate beside the canteen where, MacNamara reported, a crowd of Auxiliaries were drinking heavily without slaking their thirst for vengeance. Some time during the night all three prisoners were shot 'while trying to escape'. Neligan later reported that when their corpses were being loaded into a truck, the officer in charge went berserk and personally smashed their faces to a pulp with his torch.

Eye-witnesses are unanimous in describing Michael's anguished reaction on getting this terrible news, pacing up and down the room and repeating endlessly again that it was all over with them. He tortured himself by reliving their tortures. His burly body swayed with emotion and the revolver that dangled from his right hip kept tapping ominously against the leg of the table. Michael caused great consternation when he insisted that the battered corpses be taken to the Pro-Cathedral where they lay in state in the mortuary chapel dressed in Volunteer uniforms. Even the bravest of his comrades thought that Michael had gone off his head when he insisted on going to the chapel in person to examine the bodies and assist in their cleaning and dressing. The three men had been severely battered; their bodies were covered in terrible bruises, punctured by the stab wounds of bayonets and swords as well as the tell-tale bullet wounds, but they had been spared the horrific mutilations of some earlier atrocities and their various organs were intact. He wished his dead comrades to lie in state, but eventually gave way to the urgings of the priests that, in view of the dreadful state of their faces, it would be human decency to close the coffin lids first. The following morning Michael attended the Requiem Mass, and even stepped out of the crowd of mourners to deliver the oration, each second expecting the Auxiliaries to burst in and arrest him. It was while carrying one of the coffins afterwards that Michael was targeted by a press photographer. His portrait duly appeared in the first edition of *The Evening Herald*, but members of the Squad visited the printing-works and removed the block from the later editions. Then they toured all the newsagents' shops in the city and purchased or impounded every copy of the first edition they could lay their hands on, to prevent such a good likeness of the Big Fellow coming before the notice of the Castle.

The funeral, at Glasnevin, took place on 25 November, the very same day as the executed British officers were buried with full military honours in London. The perpetrators of the murders of Clancy, Clune and McKee were never brought to justice. Some years later, J.L. Hardy published his novel *Never in Vain* and had his hero, Andrew Kerr, receive a death threat 'for the brutal murder of Clancy and McKee', for which he himself had been responsible.

The deaths of the three men affected Michael very deeply; for some time afterwards he went about the city quite recklessly and fatalistically, almost as if he were daring his enemies to come and get him. Dublin in the aftermath of Bloody Sunday, however, wore an air of unnatural calm as people were afraid to venture out of doors, lest they be massacred by marauding bands of Auxiliaries. When Michael heard that a small flying-column led by Tom Barry (and including his brother Johnny) had slaughtered seventeen Auxiliaries in an ambush at Kilmichael near Macroom on 28 November, the black spell on him was broken. He burst in on his colleagues once more with the old exuberance, sweeping hats, caps and coats off hallstands in his glee and proclaiming triumphantly that Cork could show them how to fight. For several Sundays the Squad lay in wait for the remaining G men and gave up only when a newspaper-boy cheekily called out, 'Hi, gentlemen, ye're late again.' At the end of the year Shankers Ryan, the tout who had fingered Clancy and McKee, was found in a ditch with bullet holes in his chest and head.

In the wake of Bloody Sunday the British government put out bland statements concerning the identities of the murdered officers. The crime appeared to be motiveless, though some of the victims had allegedly been engaged in preparing cases for courts-martial. The massacre was therefore shrugged off by Sir Hamar Greenwood as 'an endeavour on the part of desperate criminals to strike back at the men who were thought to be specially concerned in bringing them to justice'.[6] Hamar pulled out all the stops, however, in dealing with the massacre at Croke Park and the murders of Clancy, Clune and McKee. The raid had been carried out to capture

> men belonging to the Tipperary units of the Irish Republican Army . . . most desperate characters in that organisation. The police were fired upon by armed Sinn Fein pickets at the entrance of the field . . . the police returned the fire . . . there is no doubt that some of the most desperate criminals in Ireland were amongst the spectators. The responsibility for the loss of innocent lives must rest with those men, and not with the police or military who were forced to fire in self-defence . . . and three prisoners who were being detained in a guard-room at the entrance to Dublin Castle were shot while trying to escape.

This was the bleakest and bloodiest moment of the Troubles. On one side, the nineteen officers; on the other, the fourteen at Croke Park, the Castle three, and the man and boy shot and killed in the street brought the death toll on Bloody Sunday to thirty-eight. In the following days, when news of Sunday's dreadful doings was splashed all over the front pages, the government got a generally bad press. *The Irish Independent* commented that 'Dublin has just passed through a weekend the like of which it has not experienced since 1916', while *The Times* in London was appalled that 'an army already perilously indisciplined and a police force avowedly beyond control have defiled by heinous acts the reputation of England'.

Sir Henry Wilson, however, commented in his diary about 'These poor murdered officers' and fulminated against the 'rats' and 'murder gangs' who had shot them. He was furious with Winston Churchill who 'insinuated that the murdered officers were careless fellows and ought to have taken precautions'. On 26 November, returning to the subject, Wilson wrote of Lloyd George, Greenwood and Churchill: 'I wonder they did not hide their heads in shame.' For once Sir Henry was close to the mark. On 22 November Patrick Moylette, a prominent Irish businessman in London, had an audience with the Prime Minister to see whether some sort of truce could be negotiated between the warring factions. The meeting had been arranged beforehand, and Moylette doubted whether Lloyd George would even give him the time of day, but was pleasantly surprised when he was ushered in.

'I suppose this ends all further hope,' said Moylette, referring to the murder of the officers.

'Not at all,' said the Prime Minister. 'They got what they deserved, beaten by counterjumpers.'[7]

Lloyd George's immediate reaction to Bloody Sunday, in fact, had been to instruct Andy Cope to get a message to his Sinn Fein contacts

> to ask Griffith for God's sake to keep his head, and not to break off the slender link that had been established. Tragic as the events in Dublin were, they were of no importance. These men were soldiers, and took a soldier's risk.[8]

Michael Collins himself later prepared a document alluding to the matter. It was typed on Dail Eireann headed notepaper, though Anna Fitzsimmons could not recall having typed it. Michael, in fact, probably typed it himself, and it bears annotations and additions in his neat handwriting:

> My one intention was the destruction of the undesirables who continued to make miserable the lives of ordinary decent citizens.
>
> I have proof enough to assure myself of the atrocities which this gang of spies and informers have committed. Perjury and torture are words too easily known to them.
>
> If I had a second motive it was no more than a feeling such as I would have for a dangerous reptile.
>
> By their destruction the very air is made sweeter. That should be the future's judgement on this particular event. For myself, my conscience is clear. There is no crime in detecting and destroying, in wartime, the spy and the informer. They have destroyed without trial. I have paid them back in their own coin.[9]

Fearing reprisals, some of the Sinn Fein leaders went into hiding. William Cosgrave, disguised as a priest, took refuge at a boys' home run by the Christian

Brothers at Glencree. Arthur Griffith, who got wind of a scheme by the British 'dirty tricks' brigade to spread lies implicating him in a homosexual affair with an ex-soldier, stood his ground. At the time of the hunger-strike in Brixton Prison, which would end in the deaths of Terence MacSwiney and two other Corkmen, Griffith appealed on 12 November to the remaining nine hunger-strikers to end their suicidal protest. Frederick Dumont was very sceptical about a premonition of Griffith that the British planned to assassinate him and other Sinn Fein Leaders. Dumont, who was also on the receiving end of information from the Castle, felt that Griffith was more likely to be killed by extremists on his own side, and thought it possible that the British authorities might even take him into protective custody for his own good. Where Michael Collins was concerned, however, the situation was quite different. 'It is quite probable that should Michael Collins, Sinn Fein Minister of Finance and head of the Irish Republican Brotherhood, and reputed leader of assassins, be captured in a night raid, he would be shot at once by his capturers.'[10]

In the last week of November there were mass arrests, bringing the total for the month to over five hundred and including Arthur Griffith, Eoin MacNeill and Eamonn Duggan. The American consul, Dumont, had been assured that Griffith would not be arrested, as the authorities regarded him as a moderate and 'almost a friend'. Griffith's arrest, in fact, had been ordered by Major-General Boyd, the British military commander in Dublin, on his own initiative, using the feeble excuse that had he not there was no telling what angry regimental officers would have done, and hinting that they would gladly have lynched the Sinn Fein leader. Dublin Castle was furious and Lloyd George was intensely annoyed, but neither lifted a finger, for Griffith remained in prison until the Truce in July 1921. When Mrs Griffith went to visit her husband in Mountjoy Gaol, however, she was pleasantly surprised to find him holding court with his Cabinet ministers and important foreign visitors and was treated with great courtesy and deference by the prison staff. MacNeill summed up the situation in the quatrain quoted at the beginning of this chapter; it could now be only a matter of time before right would prevail.

During one of the raids the security forces seized the papers of Chief of Staff Dick Mulcahy which indicated that he was contemplating a campaign of bacteriological warfare, specifically to infect British cavalry horses with glanders. To the horsey set in the Castle and Parkgate (British GHQ), this proved beyond a shadow of doubt the utter frightfulness of the rebels.

Six days after Bloody Sunday, the IRA took the fight to the enemy by mounting a wave of arson attacks in England. Seventeen warehouses in Liverpool were destroyed by fire but the real damage was done to Michael's intelligence network in Britain, when many of the Irish activists were rounded up as a consequence. Cathal Brugha's madcap schemes were anticipated by the

British who now closed the public gallery of the Commons and erected barricades in Downing Street. On 27 November Parkgate issued a directive to all military units to be 'prepared to offer resistance to any attempts on their persons'. The following day came the Kilmichael ambush, followed inevitably, on 11 December, by the most spectacular reprisal of them all, when a large part of the city of Cork was destroyed in a very selective conflagration. Many fine municipal buildings, including the City Hall, were razed to the ground, and the principal shopping thoroughfare, St Patrick's Street, was gutted. Sir Hamar Greenwood stated in the Commons that there was no evidence that the fires were started by Crown forces and stretched credulity beyond breaking point when he claimed that the flames had leaped from St Patrick's Street to the City Hall – five hundred metres (including the river) – without marking a single building in between. The Auxiliaries were immensely proud of the arson, and strutted round the city with burnt corks protruding from their cap-badges.

On Christmas Eve the unthinkable happened. Michael was hosting a dinner in the Gresham Hotel for some of his closest associates, including Tobin and Cullen, Rory O'Connor and Gearoid O'Sullivan, when the hotel was raided by the Auxiliaries. Michael was searched at gun-point and held his breath as one of the officers studied the little notebook in his pocket. The notes were fortunately so cryptic as to defy interpretation, but the word 'Rifles' on one page caught the Auxiliary's attention. Quick as a flash, Michael explained that the word was actually 'Refills' and begged to be allowed to go to the toilet. Not satisfied with this explanation, the Auxiliaries took him away under escort. When the rest were allowed to go, Tobin was concerned that Michael had not returned, and went off to the lavatory to investigate. To his consternation he found his chief being held under the brightest light while one of the Auxiliaries studied his face and compared it with a photograph. Michael was on the point of making a grab for the officer's revolver in its open holster when Tobin's appearance distracted the interrogator. Then, suddenly, Michael was released and he and Liam returned to the dining-room. By now the other Auxiliaries were making short work of the bottle of whiskey which had been in Michael's pocket. Michael promptly ordered a second bottle of Jameson's and on the stroke of midnight Volunteers and Auxiliaries alike drunkenly toasted the season of peace and goodwill to all men before they went their separate ways. In the wee small hours, despite the curfew, Piaras Beaslai found Michael and Rory O'Connor 'sitting on the ground embracing one another and Gearoid [O'Sullivan] half-lying on a chair'.[11] That night, for the first and only time, Eileen O'Donovan (daughter of Michael's landlady) saw him intoxicated.

As that dreadful year drew to a close, both sides in the conflict felt that enough was enough.

CHAPTER 12

Peace Process, 1921

And I shall have some peace there, for peace comes
dropping slow
W.B. YEATS, *The Lake Isle of Innisfree*

MOST OF THE PEOPLE WHOM MICHAEL RIBBED AND JOSHED TOOK
it in good part. A few did not, and nurtured a resentment which festered with
the passage of time. One of these was Austin Stack, whom Arthur Griffith
appointed Minister of Home Affairs. During a Cabinet meeting in August
1920 Michael had the temerity to poke fun at Stack's Rent Restriction Bill.
After the meeting, Stack said, 'That's a nice way you treated me.'

Michael, who probably regretted his flippancy but was unwilling to back
down, growled, 'Well? You deserved it.'

'All right,' warned Stack. 'I'll get even with you.'[1]

On another occasion, Michael punctured Stack's rodomontade with the
quip, 'I hope you won't make a mess of this the same as you did of the
Casement landing,' implying that it was Austin's fault that Casement was
captured, and that, as commandant of the Volunteers in that area, he had failed
in his duty to mount a rescue bid.[2] Thereafter Stack, who had once been one of
Michael's closest friends, transferred his allegiance to Cathal Brugha. The third
member of this triumvirate was Liam Mellowes, an IRB veteran who had gone
to America but returned in time to command the Volunteers in the west of
Ireland during the Easter Rising. Later he became one of the chief organisers
of de Valera's American tour. On his return to Dublin in the summer of 1920
he took over from Michael as Director of Purchases, with special responsibility
for the procurement of arms and ammunition. Michael had no particular
enthusiasm for this job and it appears not to have been performed with his
customary efficiency and dedication. On the other hand, it is only fair to point
out that it often involved disbursing sums of money to seamen and others
charged with the task of buying guns in foreign seaports, and sometimes these
seamen either vanished with the cash or failed to deliver the goods. At any rate,

the accounts of this directorate were less than satisfactory and gave Cathal Brugha more than enough ammunition to accuse Michael of certain irregularities, not so much a charge of outright embezzlement as a diversion of funds from the Ministry of Defence into the IRB. In the ensuing brouhaha Mellowes staunchly supported Brugha.

The latent friction between Michael Collins and Cathal Brugha came into the open at the end of November, when Michael was appointed Acting President of the Dail following Griffith's arrest and detention. Most of the Cabinet backed the Big Fellow, but Brugha and Stack were united in sniping at him whenever the opportunity arose. This dissension, concealed from the world at large, could not have come at a more critical time, for, at long last, the British were beginning to weary of the war and were putting out the first tentative feelers towards the other side. Lloyd George began with the discussions he held with Patrick Moylette and soon afterwards had talks with Joseph Clune, Archbishop of Perth (and uncle of the unfortunate Conor Clune so brutally done to death by Captain Hardy). These gentlemen soon found Lloyd George to be an extremely slippery character, a will o' the wisp who said one thing one day and the complete opposite the next. One minute he was adamant that he would never talk to rebels unless they surrendered unconditionally; the next day he would negotiate with them on equal terms without precondition. One day he would deal with Collins; the next he would insist that Collins must be handed over. One day he would be all sweetness and light; the next, some slight, real or imagined, would send the fiery Welshman back behind the barricades once more. The news from Ireland was contradictory and confusing, and whenever Lloyd George thought he detected a wavering in the enemy's ranks he would dig in his heels again. The well-meaning intervention of the Sinn Fein pacifists Roger Sweetman and Father O'Flanagan gave the impression that the rebels were on the point of caving in, and induced the Prime Minister to insist that the Volunteers must surrender their arms before talks could be considered. An uncannily similar argument would be used by the Conservative government of John Major seventy-five years later. Secret talks between the British and Sinn Fein dragged on through December 1920 but foundered on this condition. As a result, the war would continue a further six months, escalating in violence and atrocities.

Small wonder, therefore, that Michael was exceedingly wary of the Welsh wizard. When Lloyd George issued a statement to the effect that it was entirely due to Michael Collins that negotiations were stalled, Michael swiftly rebutted this: 'No person in Ireland or anywhere else had authority to use my name. My personal safety does not count as a factor in the question of Ireland's rights. I thank no one for refraining from murdering me.'

At this juncture the Chief himself returned to Ireland, after an absence of eighteen months. During his tour of America, de Valera had been hailed as the President of the Irish Republic, had received two honorary doctorates, and raised six million dollars (though only half that sum was actually remitted to the hard-pressed Dail). He was smuggled aboard the SS *Celtic* by two of Michael's agents, O'Neill and Downes, who had the hazardous job of moving him from one hiding place to another during the voyage to evade detection. When the ship docked at Liverpool on 22 December, Special Branch detectives were waiting to interview them in connection with the arson attack on warehouses the previous month, and as a result de Valera was almost captured; but in the end O'Neill and Downes were released and they hustled the Chief ashore disguised as a common seaman. On the Dublin steamer de Valera was concealed in the cabin of the second mate who told him he was just popping ashore to 'deliver some despatches for Mick [Collins]' – an announcement that did not improve Dev's humour. In the second mate's absence de Valera was discovered by the captain and first mate who, not unreasonably, wondered who the hell he was. De Valera pretended to be drunk, but was livid when the second mate returned hours later, very much the worse for alcohol, though the second mate's story that the big man in his bunk was his drunken brother-in-law was accepted by the skipper. In the early hours of 23 December the ship tied up at the Custom House Quay and de Valera was greeted by Tom Cullen and Batt O'Connor. De Valera asked how things were going.

'Great! The Big Fellow is leading us and everything is marvellous,' said Cullen with a broad grin, which vanished at de Valera's reaction.

'Big Fellow! Big Fellow!' He pounded the guard-rail with his clenched fist and spat out, 'We'll see who's the Big Fellow . . .'

Michael himself had been up since five o'clock after a night of sleepless anticipation. He made sure that everything was ready for de Valera's reception at the home of the eminent gynaecologist Dr Robert Farnan in Merrion Square (where the talks with Archbishop Clune had been held), but for some unaccountable reason he did not see the Long Fellow till early on the morning of Christmas Eve. The first Cabinet minister to confer with the Chief, therefore, was Cathal Brugha, who lost no time in shoving his oar in. Brugha complained that Michael Collins and his IRB group had got a stranglehold on power. Cathal weakened his case, however, by saying that he had been offered the Acting Presidency but had not taken it. 'And why did you not?' asked de Valera sharply. 'It was only at your refusal that the others came in.'[3]

Why Michael did not rush to meet de Valera and, in fact, let the initiative pass to Brugha, has never been explained. By delaying their reunion by twenty-four hours he not only gave Cathal the advantage, but offered a slight to de Valera which could hardly have improved his humour. It was an oversight for which Michael – and Ireland – would pay very dearly. Rather naïvely, Michael had high hopes that de Valera's intervention would terminate the silly squabbles between himself and the Brugha–Stack clique. It was eighteen months since they had parted company, eighteen months which, for both of them, had been packed with incident and high drama. In America de Valera had been treated right royally; in Ireland Michael had been a desperate man on the run. De Valera had returned with his ideals intact; Michael was a hard-headed realist and pragmatist. De Valera had retained sentimental views of Ireland and the Dail entertained sentimental views of its Chief. Now the sentiment was about to be rudely shattered on both sides.

De Valera interviewed his Cabinet one by one. It soon became apparent that he was not concerned with getting their views of the situation so much as imposing his will on them and reasserting his ascendancy. In particular, this entailed putting Michael Collins firmly in his place. Of secondary importance were continuing control of the Irish-American lobby and assuming control over the peace process. For the moment, however, Collins would be useful; de Valera ordered him to find him a safe house, and Michael dutifully procured a fine Georgian mansion called Loughnavale, set discreetly in its own grounds on Strand Road. Here de Valera was installed with Maeve McGarry as housekeeper and Kathleen O'Connell as private secretary. Sinead de Valera and their children remained out at Greystones (where Michael had cycled each week to give her £25, de Valera's salary as President of the Dail). As late as 3 February 1921 de Valera was admitting to a correspondent that he had not had the opportunity to see his children, 'though I saw Madame a few times'.[4]

De Valera, in fact, spent most of his time attacking the military strategy that had been adopted in his absence. Most of his criticism was levelled at Dick Mulcahy as Chief of Staff and, of course, Michael Collins. On Christmas Eve, he told Mulcahy that the 'odd shooting of a policeman here and there' was having a very bad effect, from the propaganda viewpoint, in America. 'What we want,' he said, 'is one good battle about once a month with about five hundred men on each side.' Michael's reaction to this failure to understand or appreciate the nature of the guerrilla war is not recorded, but it may be imagined. De Valera had apparently learned nothing from the débâcle of 1916 when static warfare had doomed the Rising from the outset. Even worse, de Valera had no time for the flying-columns and the road ambushes. Too late it dawned on Michael that he had been nobbled by Brugha. Michael knew only too well how pitifully short of arms and ammunition the Volunteers were, and of the tremendous logistical problems involved in equipping even the typical flying-column of sixteen men. Even when it was possible to provide every man with a rifle or revolver, there were seldom more than a few rounds of ammunition available. In vain Michael tried to point this out to the Chief, hinting gently at the folly of set-piece battles in which the British could swiftly marshal a thousand seasoned troops to every Volunteer; but de Valera was deaf to his entreaties.

The Dail was hastily summoned to hear the great man's views, but at the last moment de Valera, acting on Brugha's advice, failed to show up. Brugha also absented himself, and Michael (whether to save de Valera's face or his own) likewise stayed away. Understandably, the members of the Dail were infuriated and whatever favourable impact the Long Fellow had hoped to make was negated. A second meeting was convened at short notice in Walter Cole's house. On this occasion de Valera deigned to put in an appearance, although he commented sourly on Michael's men grouped at a table outside the room, playing cards and smoking, their revolvers beside them. To de Valera it looked like a set from a cowboy film. The mood of the meeting was belligerent and de Valera was told in no uncertain terms that there was no room for pacifism or moderation. Michael, characteristically, lashed out, saying that Cork, which had fought best, had suffered least, whereas Galway, which had fought least, had suffered most.

De Valera kept harping on about how grandly he had been received in America. The repetition of this eventually got on Michael's nerves, on one occasion interrupting the Chief in full flood with the remark, 'Oh, I have it off by heart!' To others, it seemed as if Mick Collins was behaving in a surly, even despondent, manner; in fact, the scales had fallen from his eyes and he was thoroughly disillusioned with de Valera. The latter, however, had no illusions about Collins; he was a dangerous rival. He alone had the skill and the ability to get things done, and for that reason he had become a powerful adversary. To be sure, Michael did not regard de Valera in the same light; his attitude was still tempered by a residual devotion that went back to 1916. The wily de Valera decided that he would have to get Collins out of the way. His proposal that Michael should go to America to continue the good work there was not entirely novel. Months previously, when there was a dangerous split in the ranks of the Irish-Americans, it had been suggested that a tour by Michael Collins would help patch things up; but now Michael was convinced that Brugha and Stack had put the notion to de Valera, and that the three of them were ganging up against him. When this suggestion was put to him Michael reacted with vehemence. He would resign from the Cabinet and General Headquarters and go off to Cork to join the flying-columns there who were doing such great work. He would sooner take up a rifle and fight under Tom Barry than remain in Dublin. Other senior officers felt just as strongly on the subject and spoke out. It was to de Valera what the Curragh Mutiny had been to the British government in 1914. On one occasion Mulcahy went to de Valera in exasperation and threatened to resign as Chief of Staff if he could not control Brugha. De Valera nodded sagely: 'Cathal is jealous of Mick,' was all he said, but never remonstrated with his tetchy Minister of Defence. Posing as the disinterested observer, de Valera essayed to hold the balance of power between the two opposing factions, but in his bid to enhance his own prestige he played one off against the other and left them bitterly divided.

As if this split in the ranks of Sinn Fein were not enough to contend with, Michael was hard hit when the British raided Eilean McGrane's apartment on New Year's Eve and collared a mass of Michael's intelligence files, including copies of Castle top-secret documents and the old daybook from G Division which he had kept as a souvenir of his visit to Great Brunswick Street. The British were astounded to find several letters addressed to Lord French among this haul and dutifully forwarded them to the Lord Lieutenant almost a year after they had been posted. French took this delay in his mail with remarkable *sangfroid*. Mark Sturgis, who handed the letters to French, recorded in his diary (3 February 1921) that His Excellency 'said he always saw a strong likeness between this war and South Africa; that all we now say of Michael Collins they said then of Smuts – and look at him now!'.

Mere possession of these papers was enough to have Eileen arrested and transported to England where she was harshly treated in prison. This damning cache immediately set the authorities on to tracking down the mole in their midst, and led them eventually, by a process of elimination, to Ned Broy who was arrested and interrogated by his senior officers. Michael promptly got word to Broy's immediate superior and dropped the hint that if he didn't want to be added to the Squad's hit-list he had better destroy anything that might incriminate Ned. Next, Michael persuaded (by a judicious mixture of bribes and threats) a colleague of Ned's to flee the country in circumstances that immediately transferred suspicion to him. And finally he wrote out and signed a letter addressed to an unnamed agent in the Castle, and arranged for this incriminating letter to be found there. In it, Michael asked what was all this fuss about the man named Broy who had never been any good and was always an enemy of the IRA. The combination of these ploys eventually got Ned off the hook. Though held in detention, he was spared a bullet in the back of the head, which would have been his fate had he been unmasked. He was eventually released at the Truce in midsummer.

Then James MacNamara was summarily dismissed. Somehow he had come under suspicion, but the authorities had nothing concrete. When told to get out he feigned indignation and his inspector, upset at losing such a good man, shook his head sadly.

'It's a conspiracy!' declared MacNamara vehemently.

'No, MacNamara, merely a mistake, I assure you! Merely a mistake.'[5]

Only Dave Neligan escaped detection, thanks to having faked a bitter feud with Broy, and he would continue to give sterling service to the cause until the Troubles came to an end.

On New Year's Eve Christy Harte, a porter at Vaughan's Hotel, was arrested and held in the Castle interrogation chambers for five days. Threats and physical violence failed to break him, but he was then brought into a long room, curtained at one end. The lights were switched off and out of the darkness, from behind the curtain, came a voice which reminded Harte that the rebels were virtually defeated and the leaders in prison. Only one man was still at large and that was Collins. If Harte would betray him, the sum of five thousand pounds would be placed to his credit at any bank of his choice and a free passage to any country. Christy was a poor man, and the temptation was enormous. Yet he protested his ignorance. 'Well,' said the voice, 'if you get to know Collins all you have to do is ring Dublin Castle, ask for extension 28 and say that the portmanteau is now ready.' He was then released – and promptly reported his experiences to Michael. Subsequently the police leaned on Harte but he continued to play dumb.

In the early months of 1921 Michael continued to work as usual, yet he had the feeling that the net was tightening around him. The police and military raided a house in Donnybrook and the detective in charge rifled through a bundle of love letters, until the girl to whom they were addressed protested vociferously. The detective apologised and, in his embarrassment, accidentally dropped the sheet of paper bearing a list of the houses to be raided. After the police had departed, the girl picked up the list and saw that the only house not yet crossed off was 23 Brendan Road. The following morning she passed the list to Batt O'Connor who was staggered to see that this was the very house where Michael had slept that night. The detective, on noting his loss, had rung up the Castle, but they had refused to repeat the address over the telephone for fear of being overheard.

Mrs O'Donovan's house was raided, but the bird had flown. The raiders almost grabbed him when they swooped on the nurses' home in Gardiner Row run by Linda Kearns. Michael was dining there when the Auxiliaries burst in. He grabbed his plate and dived under the table whose cloth concealed him. With bated breath he watched the boots of the raiders clatter past, only inches from his head, but they went off empty-handed.

On another occasion Michael was actually stopped and searched in the street. He was carrying £16,000 of National Loan funds at the time, but the Black and Tans who frisked him were too befuddled with drink to find it.

A few weeks later, on 1 April 1921, the Auxiliaries raided 5 Mespil Road, one of Michael's intelligence centres. The householder, Eileen Hoey, was arrested when a revolver was discovered in a desk drawer. She spent some very uncomfortable hours in one of the interrogation chambers at the Castle, but stuck to her story that the gun must have been left behind by one of her lodgers. Eventually she was taken home, but the Auxiliaries concealed themselves there, convinced that this was a Collins safe house and that, sooner or later, he would walk into their trap. In fact, Michael had been scheduled to call at the house at nine o'clock that Saturday morning. Knowing that Michael would cycle up to the house, push his bike round to the side and stride in through the back door in his usual fearless manner, Eileen was frantic with worry. She struggled to think of some way of warning the Big Fellow and finally hit upon the idea of getting her elderly mother to fake a heart attack. A female physician who was known to be sympathetic to the cause was duly summoned and agreed to get word through to Michael, by way of a Fianna boy who intercepted him only yards from Mespil Road. Michael made his getaway in the nick of time, but this raid was a devastating blow nonetheless, for the police seized a vast cache of documents. Eileen herself was sent to prison as a consequence, and suffered cruelly for several months before her release after the Truce.

During the early months of 1921 the war escalated on both sides. The British poured more and more troops into Ireland, while the hard-pressed Volunteers got a powerful boost when the first consignment of Thompson submachine-guns arrived in May. A second and much larger consignment, despatched from America by Clan na nGael, was impounded by US Customs on 16 June. With the first tommy guns had arrived Captain Cronin and Major Dineen, Irish-Americans who had served in the First World War and who had volunteered to help the cause as weapons instructors. During this period the assassination tactics which had proved so effective against the G men and British intelligence in Dublin were applied throughout southern Ireland; more than seventy executed spies and informers were found in ditches or by the roadside, shot through the head and heart, and invariably labelled. Not all of these victims were the handiwork of the IRA, however; a group of Auxiliaries led by Head Constable Igoe have been blamed for mock-IRA executions against innocent civilians. Be that as it may, there were other cases in which people were shot in particularly barbarous circumstances. A sign of the ugly turn the campaign was taking was the murder of several women, including an elderly Loyalist landowner named Georgina Lindsay who, along with her chauffeur, was shot as a reprisal for the execution of six Volunteers captured when Mrs Lindsay gave away an IRA ambush. Tim Pat Coogan cites the case of his own father being ordered by Michael Collins to execute two girls who had been consorting with British soldiers and giving away information. Eamon Coogan, however, decided that the girls 'were very young and very beautiful' and disobeyed the order. For once, Michael was not unduly concerned about the non-fulfilment of a 'job' and Coogan was transferred to more congenial duties.[6]

One of the worst incidents occurred in February at Clonmult when a band of Volunteers was besieged in a thatched cottage by police and military forces. When the Volunteers surrendered on the promise of fair treatment, they were set upon by Auxiliaries and Tans and nine of them beaten to death before a regular army officer intervened and rescued the other six; they were subsequently executed by order of a court-martial. On the day of their execution, by firing-squad at fifteen-minute intervals, six young British soldiers in various parts of Cork were shot as reprisals. Michael's sister and niece were in Cork at the time and gave him their eye-witness accounts of both atrocities.

While all this murder and mayhem was spinning faster and faster out of control on both sides, Michael was being harassed by Cathal Brugha. The Minister of Defence had now got his teeth into the accounts concerning weapons and ammunition which had been purchased in Glasgow. This squabble was not without an element of grim farce, as both Brugha and Collins were communicating with Michael Staines, then a prisoner in Mountjoy, in the vain hope that he would be able to shed light on the missing money. While Brugha was quibbling over petty sums he was withholding cash that was urgently required for the purchase of ammunition from Glasgow, a matter that precipitated a bitter feud between Richard Mulcahy and Liam Mellowes. The bickering eventually reached a point at which de Valera himself stepped in, convening an enquiry at which both sides put their case. Sean Dowling later got an eye-witness account of the incident from Austin Stack who allegedly found it all very distasteful and embarrassing:

> Collins was so upset by the accusation that he openly wept. 'Now,' said de Valera, 'it is quite clear that these charges are groundless.' Brugha arose without a word and left the room. Stack rushed after him: 'Come in, shake hands.' But Brugha angrily turned from him: 'You'll find him out yet,' he spat. He stamped out.[7]

There is abundant evidence that Brugha's venom was directed at Michael at this time because of the tremendous publicity the latter was receiving in the world press. Quite frankly, Cathal was as jealous as hell. De Valera once commented on this to Mulcahy, saying that it was a great pity that a man with Brugha's many fine qualities should be guilty of 'a dirty little vice like jealousy'.[8] Hardly a day passed without Michael's exploits, real or imaginary, getting more column inches in the newspapers than Brugha got in his entire career. Michael was faintly amused by these press stories and wrote on 5 March to his sister

Helena (Sister Mary Celestine) at her English convent following a highly coloured report in *The Daily Sketch* concerning a skirmish near Rosscarbery on 2 February in which he was said to have ridden a white horse into battle, just like Emiliano Zapata, and been killed in the fight:

> 'Mike', the super hater, dour, hard, no ray of humour, no trace of human feeling. Oh lovely! The white horse was an exaggeration. I have not ridden a white horse since I rode 'Gipsy', and used her mane as a bridle.[9]

It was after this shoot-out, at which Michael was not even present, that Major Percival's men raided Woodfield and burned out the Collins family. Woodfield was by no means the only farmhouse destroyed by the military; there was now a systematic policy of burning farms in the vicinity of IRA activities.

The IRA retaliated by burning the mansions of Loyalist landowners. Through March, April and May there was an orgy of arson all over the south and west of Ireland until the Loyalists appealed to the government to abandon its policy of burning the houses and farms of Sinn Fein sympathisers. In the end, an order was passed down the military chain of command to the effect that King George himself had intervened personally. It is doubtful whether His Majesty was involved, but it saved Lloyd George's face to convey that impression.

Late in March Sean MacEoin, the fighting blacksmith of Ballinalee, was seized on a train at Mullingar, shot through the lung while attempting to escape and savagely beaten by the Black and Tans. Brought to Dublin more dead than alive, he was incarcerated in Mountjoy where Michael made several attempts to set him free. On one occasion he managed to saw through the bars of his cell, but his exertions gave him a high temperature, and the well-meaning prison doctor had him transferred to a more comfortable cell, where he had to start this laborious task all over again. Then there was the ambitious plan to seize a British armoured car and raid the prison. Emmet Dalton and a group of the Squad succeeded in capturing the car while it was visiting the city abattoir. Dressed as British officers, Dalton and Joe Leonard bluffed their way past the prison gates in their commandeered vehicle, blocked the space between the inner and outer gates and made a beeline for the governor's office where MacEoin was supposed to be that morning on some pretext. Dalton (who had been an officer in the British Army during the war) was on the point of convincing a sceptical governor that he had authority to take MacEoin to the Castle, when suddenly shots rang out.

In the yard, a group of women delivering parcels to their menfolk had been arranged as a diversion, engaging the duty warder at the gate in an argument to distract him, but the warder was in a foul mood and made to slam the gate in their faces. As a back-up, two of the Squad now appeared with their revolvers drawn and covered the gateman. Seeing this, the sentry in the courtyard opened fire on the Squad. Tom Keogh shot the sentry and held up a squad of soldiers, despite the fact that a machine-gun in the gate turret was now raking the armoured car. For several days MacEoin had contrived, by one pretext or another, to be in the governor's office at ten o'clock, but on this crucial day the ruse failed. The changing of the guard was late, and he was told to remain in his cell till this was effected. As a result, Dalton and Leonard, faced with a suspicious governor who was on the point of telephoning the Castle for confirmation, overpowered him and his staff, using their own neck-ties as fetters, then calmly walked out, scrambled aboard the Lancia and drove off past a platoon of infantry who saluted smartly when they recognised the officers' uniforms.

Although Dalton and Leonard had seized two machine-guns and a quantity of rifles and revolvers in this raid, Michael was very upset that the main purpose had not been achieved. The release of MacEoin was extremely important to him. Apart from the fact that MacEoin was one of his most valued field commandants, time was not on their side, for the British were holding courts-martial in Mountjoy and executing many of the prisoners who were alleged to have been inculpated in the murders of the British officers on Bloody Sunday. None of them, in fact, had been involved in that affair, other than Frank Teeling, who escaped with Ernie O'Malley and Simon Donelly from Kilmainham. Michael even considered smuggling a revolver into the prison so that MacEoin could shoot his way out of the courtroom when he came up for court-martial, but this would have been suicidal, so the idea was rejected.

As harassment increased at a furious pace, to the point at which the Auxiliaries were riding round Dublin with members of the Dail lashed to posts in their lorries as a precaution against bomb attacks, Michael decided to retaliate by taking the fight to the very heart of the enemy. Having firmly rejected Brugha's various schemes as verging on lunacy, Michael now essayed an attack on the British Cabinet as a reprisal for the seizure of Dail deputies. To assess the feasibility of seizing Cabinet ministers, Michael sent Frank Thornton, George Fitzgerald and Sean Flood to London to work with Sam Maguire and Reggie Dunne. This was a prodigious task but Thornton rose superbly to the challenge, eventually compiling a massive dossier on twenty-five MPs who were regular and dependable in their habits. Each of these men was then identified by IRA men in London, so that, when the precise moment came, they would be seized simultaneously. This was an elaborate project, complete to the smallest detail, and undoubtedly it would have been a major coup had it been carried out. But perhaps the British authorities got wind of it, for they suddenly abandoned their policy of taking hostages in Ireland, so the kidnap plot was quietly dropped.

Oddly enough, Thornton and Flood suddenly had an opportunity to strike a devastating blow, quite by chance. They were in the underground station at Westminster, missed the lift and raced downstairs to the platform when, all of a sudden, they ran round a corner and collided with two of four men going in the opposite direction. They picked themselves up and helped to his feet the man whom Sean Flood had knocked over. To their amazement the other two men drew revolvers and ordered Flood and Thornton to put their hands up. The IRA men more or less ignored this command and continued to brush down the little man they had crashed into, when it suddenly dawned on them that their victim was none other than Lloyd George himself. The Prime Minister ordered his bodyguards to put away their weapons, but they were extremely reluctant to do so, saying that the assailants were obviously Irishmen.

'Well, Irishmen or no Irishmen, if they were going to shoot me I was shot long ago,' snapped Lloyd George, accepting the profuse apologies of the two IRA men who made a hasty exit and took the first tube east instead of west, and spent the rest of the day looking furtively over their shoulders in case they had been followed.

While the plan to seize two dozen British MPs was maturing, Michael had plans to seize upwards of sixty British agents in Dublin, in a spectacular rerun of Bloody Sunday. These men had been recruited as replacements for the Cairo Gang and their movements were carefully monitored from the instant they stepped off the boat. For the moment, though, Michael bided his time.

Meanwhile, de Valera got his way. On two occasions set-piece battles were fought. The first took place at Crossbarry in County Cork on 21 March when Tom Barry, the victor of Kilmichael, led a company of about a hundred men who fought their way out of a trap which had been sprung by a British military force amounting to two battalions of regular infantry with supporting artillery and armour. The battle raged all day long, Flor Begley giving encouragement by playing his bagpipes. The Volunteers managed to get away more or less unscathed, but inflicted heavy casualties on their attackers. Once again, Michael crowed that the Corkmen were doing more than everyone else to combat the enemy.

De Valera was determined on having a reprise of the Easter Rising and ordered the destruction of the Custom House on 25 May. Five years had elapsed since the Volunteers had fought a full-scale battle in the Dublin streets, and in the interim they had perfected the technique of the hit-and-run raid. Now they were ordered to enter one of the main public buildings of the city and set it alight, while a new formation, known as the Active Service Unit and comprising fifty hand-picked men, would give cover outside. The ASU, like Michael's Squad, were full-time operatives, paid up to five pounds a week, and were the élite of the Dublin Brigade. The men were given strict instructions not to open fire on British troops unless fired on first. On this occasion, the IRA went into action armed only with revolvers, each man having no more than four or five rounds of ammunition. The operation was carried out by men of the second battalion of the Dublin Brigade, commanded by Tom Ennis.

Michael was alarmed at this stunt and at first refused to have anything to do with it; but later he relented and allowed the Squad to assist the ASU outside the building. As they set out, he cycled to the start point on Strand Street and wished them luck. Inevitably, the conflagration attracted the unwelcome attention of the military and in a matter of minutes several armoured cars converged on the Custom House. Soon, both Black and Tans and regular troops were engaged in a series of running battles with the Volunteers who, having discharged their revolvers, withdrew as best they could. From the publicity viewpoint, the destruction of the Custom House was a spectacular success. Apart from the loss of one of the city's most imposing landmarks, the battle had crippled the British tax system. But the other side of the coin was the loss of six Volunteers and the capture of about seventy, several of whom would subsequently be executed. Within a week, moreover, Michael suffered a severe blow when his intelligence operation and the Squad were amalgamated with the Dublin Brigade, and transferred from his personal command. The Squad was absorbed into the ASU to become the Guard, later renamed the Dublin Guards when the Irish National Army was formed in 1922.

The day after the Custom House raid, Michael had the closest shave of his life. He was expected at his office in Mary Street at the usual time, but failed to materialise. The typist, Alice Lyons, and the office messenger, Bob Conlan, thought this was very unusual, but some sixth sense prevented Michael from turning up. Earlier that day he and Gearoid O'Sullivan had lunched at Woolworth's and the waitress, attracted by Michael's appearance, had given them excessively good service. 'We'll have to stop coming here,' growled Michael to his friend as they left the restaurant. 'She has us taped.' They went to a pub and then Michael escorted O'Sullivan to his office. There they chatted a while and Gearoid was surprised when Michael said casually that he would not be going to Mary Street. 'There's something wrong there,' he said.

Michael was thirty minutes overdue when a squad of Auxiliaries suddenly dashed upstairs. Alice met them on the landing, but an Auxiliary pushed past her, covered Conlan and demanded the key to the back room. 'We know Collins is in there,' he shouted. Then, distracted by scuffling on the landing above, he left her for a moment. In a trance, Alice walked downstairs past the sentries and, though hatless and coatless, vanished into the crowd before the alarm was raised. Joe O'Reilly was nearby when the Auxiliaries drove up, and immediately cycled off down Liffey Street where he ran into Michael. Together, they went to the office in Bachelor's Walk. 'The game's up,' said Michael despondently. 'There's a traitor in the camp.'

Only the previous week, the Auxiliaries had raided the shop adjoining Michael's Mary Street office. Convinced that the enemy were going to come into the office, Joe O'Reilly had squeezed out through a rear window on to the glass roof high above the street and had crashed right through it. For some time he had hung by his fingertips from a girder, while terrified girls in the workroom below had rushed off in a panic. Michael, however, had calmly watched the raid from a shop across the street. It occurred to him that the Auxiliaries had been acting on a tip, but had chosen the wrong number. Now the second raid confirmed this.

O'Reilly was startled to see Michael in such deep despair. He had never seen him in such a black mood before, one moment deathly pale, the next extremely agitated. Normally Michael was a man of few words, but now he paced up and down speaking rapidly for over an hour. Later, in Devlin's, he broke down completely and wept bitterly, repeating over and over again, 'There's a traitor in the camp.' After the Truce, when Michael was being entertained at the Castle, one of the British officials there raised the matter of the Mary Street raid, but Michael cut the man short, saying that he did not want to know. To his closest friends, however, he always maintained that he knew the informer, and even the amount of money – five hundred pounds – which had been paid. He even commented sardonically on the fact that the informer had given the authorities the Mary Street address on condition that there would be no bloodshed.

Michael was also unduly upset at the loss of a favourite fountain pen; again, his comrades were taken aback at the way in which such a trifle got to him. In fact, Michael, who had been working twenty hours a day and whose nerves were taut as a drawn bowstring, was on the verge of a complete mental breakdown. Then, suddenly, he stopped his ranting and raving and by some fantastic effort of will pulled himself together. Later, when he ran into Alice Lyons, he shrugged off the raid as a bit of a joke.

To the British, though, it was no joke. In the office the Auxiliaries found the personal effects of Major Compton Smith who had been taken as a hostage and shot by Cork No I Brigade. In captivity, Smith had greatly impressed his captors by his courage and dignity. In a letter to his wife he had stated that he was being treated 'far better than Englishmen would treat an Irishman in the same circumstances', and in a letter to General Strickland, shortly before he was shot, he begged that there should be no reprisals, adding that those who held him were no murder gang, but men filled with a sense of high duty. These last letters were sent to Michael for onward transmission, along with his personal possessions, a watch, cigarette case, signet ring and fountain pen. Michael had tried to prevent Smith's execution but was too late, and then tried to make amends by ensuring that everything was done to give him a decent burial and return his property to his wife. The discovery of Major Smith's pathetic relics sent the authorities into a towering rage, and made them more determined than ever to find Collins. General Macready even suggested to Sir John Anderson that a price of £10,000 be put on Michael's head. The only other Sinn Fein leaders to merit such a large amount were Cathal Brugha and Richard Mulcahy. By contrast, William Cosgrave, Gearoid O'Sullivan, Austin Stack and Joseph McDonagh rated a mere £3,500 apiece, while de Valera was not mentioned at all. Griffith and other leading figures, of course, were already in custody by this time. In actual fact, Anderson turned down this suggestion, but it does cast an interesting light on the importance of the respective leaders then at large.

Despite the setback of their grievous losses in the Custom House attack, the Volunteers continued to pursue an aggressive policy. Better weapons and more ammunition gradually made their task easier. The flying-columns ambushed and harried the military in the country districts while the urban Volunteers, in twos and threes, caused panic and disorder in the streets of Dublin and Cork before melting away again. During this period when the pace of raid and reprisal quickened, there was a resumption of the peace process, although it moved very slowly.

Ever since the passage of the Government of Ireland Act in 1920, which effectively set the Six Counties on a separate course, Sinn Fein had been operating a boycott of goods manufactured in Belfast, with wholesale seizures of 'contraband' organised by Joseph McDonagh. The arrest of Desmond Fitzgerald in February 1921 meant that his place as head of the Propaganda Department needed to be urgently filled. De Valera selected for this delicate but vital role the Englishman, Erskine Childers, whom Michael had introduced to de Valera and who, since the beginning of 1919, had been actively involved in the creation of the alternative government, first as a press aide in Paris, then as director of the Land Bank, a judge in the Dail courts and lastly as a consummate publicist. His articles in the British press, savagely indicting Dublin Castle, its policies and actions, did more to mould British opinion than anything else. As a result, British public opinion was increasingly sympathetic to the Irish cause, and Lloyd George, mindful of the fact that another general election might be called before long, decided at long last to give the Irish question the serious attention it demanded.

By the spring of 1921 the British government was under attack from all sides, at home and abroad, for its Irish policy. Not only the Asquith Liberals and the burgeoning Labour Party, but the press, church leaders, intellectuals, writers and other influential people, and latterly even members of the government itself, were joined in condemnation of British actions in Ireland. As if this were not enough to contend with, Lloyd George was confronted by a very serious coal strike which threatened to draw in the railwaymen, transport workers and dockers and paralyse the country. This growing industrial unrest put a severe strain on the armed forces, already stretched to the limit with commitments on the Rhine as well as in Ireland. Sinn Fein was 'very bobbery', according to Mark Sturgis over the miners' strike, and it was obvious that the Dail was kept remarkably well informed (by British Labour leaders) on the deteriorating situation in England.

By April Sir Hamar Greenwood was being forced to eat his words, admitting to the Cabinet: 'I was much too optimistic last December than I ought to have been.' That month, Lloyd George despatched the Earl of Derby to Dublin. Under an assumed name, he checked in at the Shelbourne Hotel and soon made contact with de Valera who dismissed him as merely a political scout. Despite this rebuff, Lord Derby, through mutual friends, sought to organise a meeting between Griffith and de Valera on the one hand and Lloyd George at the Derby home in England. This ploy likewise fell through, and Derby returned to London almost, if not quite, empty-handed. From him Lloyd George learned that de Valera and Michael Collins had quarrelled. The Prime Minister wrongly deduced that this was a disagreement over policy and was unaware that it was a clash of personalities. His assessment was that the moderate de Valera was in the hands of the gunmen led by Collins. At a Cabinet meeting on 27 April this matter was thoroughly ventilated. Lloyd George went so far as to tell his colleagues that 'de Valera cannot come here and say he is willing to give up Irish Independence, for if he did he might be shot'. Austen Chamberlain agreed: 'De Valera is at the mercy of Michael Collins.' This led Lloyd George to speculate that it would be advantageous to talk to Collins: 'No doubt he is the head and font of the movement. If I could see him a settlement might be possible,' though he doubted whether 'the British people would be willing for us to negotiate with the head of a band of murderers'.

The debate on whether to negotiate or not continued to rage in London and Dublin for several weeks. An influential body of Unionist businessmen in Britain, calling themselves the Irish Businessmen's Conciliation Committee, laboured earnestly from March till late May to bring the two warring sides together, but to no avail.

Meanwhile Lloyd George himself was taking steps to open a conduit to Michael Collins. Whatever else is said about him, he certainly had a nose for talent in the unlikeliest of places. It was in the Ministry of Pensions that he discovered Alfred (Andy) Cope who was then employed in its investigations branch. Cope was sent to Dublin in 1919 and assisted Sir Warren Fisher in the compilation of his report into the state of the administration of Ireland. This had brought Cope in contact with Sir James MacMahon and other senior Irish Catholic civil servants. Thereafter Cope became more and more sympathetic towards the Irish side of the argument and by the spring of 1921 had succeeded, through mutual friends, in putting out feelers towards Michael Collins. This approach was made by Cope at the behest of Lloyd George himself, although it was done in the utmost secrecy so as not to compromise either side. Cope hobnobbed with such prominent figures as Judge O'Connor who numbered many of the Sinn Fein leaders among his personal friends. One of these, Mrs Larry Nugent, records that, late in April or very early in May, Cope expressed a wish to meet de Valera, Stack and Brugha. When she asked, 'Do you not want to meet Michael Collins?', he replied, 'No. I meet Michael every night.'[10] On the face of it, this is an astonishing state of affairs: Cope, a prominent figure of the British establishment, and Collins the Irish leader, should have been poles apart. In fact, both men were very similar in outlook and temperament. It is not known how, when or where they first came face to face, but they seem to have had an immediate rapport. It was almost like a poker game, each man playing for very high stakes. In April 1921, when Michael was asked why he was continuing to turn down Dominion Home Rule status and sticking out for a Republic, he replied that the same effort that would get Home Rule would get a Republic. To the American journalist Carl Ackerman, he said:

> I am still of that opinion and have never had so many peace moves as we have had since last autumn. Our Army is becoming stronger every day, its morale is improving and its efficiency is increasing.[11]

A few weeks later, on 11 May, Lloyd George himself went public. In an interview with the New York *Herald Tribune* on 11 May, he said, 'I will meet Mr de Valera or any of the Irish leaders without conditions on my part and without asking promises from them. It is the only way a conclusion can be reached.' Cope was asked to set up a meeting between de Valera and Sir James Craig. The leader of the Ulster Unionists was escorted to the meeting by Emmet Dalton but the talks were inconclusive. Afterwards, Craig told Dalton that de Valera was 'impossible'.

Elections under the Better Government of Ireland Act took place on 24 May. On the eve of polling, Lloyd George replaced Lord French as Lord Lieutenant by James Talbot, Lord FitzAlan, the first Roman Catholic to become a viceroy. As a conciliatory gesture, however, it was too little and too late. In north-east Ulster, Craig's Unionists, by a blatant campaign of intimidation, gerrymandering and impersonation, swept the board, winning forty seats. Elsewhere in Ireland the Nationalists (both Sinn Fein and the IPP) did well, and all the Sinn Fein leaders, including Collins and de Valera, were returned with increased majorities. Sinn Fein, in fact, took all 124 seats in southern Ireland, plus the four seats allocated to the National University. The only seats held by the southern Unionists were, in fact, the four seats allocated at Trinity College. As a result of this election the Six Counties officially became Northern Ireland, and Sir James Craig prime minister at Stormont, the Northern Irish parliament. Ireland was now effectively partitioned and the political situation sharply polarised.

Lloyd George was now faced with declaring all-out war on Sinn Fein, with a total imposition of martial law in the Twenty-six Counties, or giving in and making the best of a bad job. Churchill urged the first course, and continued to advocate 'the most unlimited exercise of rough-handed force', even when other moves towards a peaceful solution were being considered. There then ensued a carrot-and-stick period when raids escalated while peace feelers continued to reach out. During the late spring and early summer of 1921 Michael was as ruthlessly hunted as ever. After the loss of his Mespil Road office he had worked mainly from 22 Mary Street but the day after the Custom House fire it too fell to the enemy. An office at 29 Mary Street, whither he had moved in the nick of time, was raided a few weeks later. Thereafter Michael operated from his old office at Bachelor's Walk or from Batt O'Connor's home before renting an unobtrusive house at 17 Harcourt Terrace where he continued unmolested until the Truce. This house was in a sedate, middle-class neighbourhood whose residents were believed to be staunch adherents to the Crown. It was the perfect hideout.

Early in June 1921 Tom Casement, brother of Sir Roger, contacted his old friend Jan Christiaan Smuts, the Boer general-turned-political leader and member of Lloyd George's War Cabinet. Smuts had given the British a merry run for their money during the Boer War, but was later the architect of the Union of South Africa and a widely respected Allied leader during the recent war. Smuts was now in London again, as Prime Minister of South Africa, to attend the Imperial Conference. Tom Casement decided to travel to London to see Smuts and enlist his aid. On 14 June 1921 de Valera met Casement and said he would be prepared to meet the South African statesman if Tom could arrange it. During this conversation Casement told de Valera that Smuts

> could not stand for an Irish Republic as he was Prime Minister of a Dominion. De Valera frankly told me that a Republic was out of the question. All he wanted was a Treaty between two nations. I saw that point and told him that I would put it before Smuts.[12]

Interestingly, de Valera would later deny this. Needless to say, there is no mention of it in de Valera's authorised biography by the Earl of Longford and T.P. O'Neill. Smuts had an audience with King George at Windsor on 12 June and gave sound advice on the speech His Majesty was due to make ten days later in Belfast when he ceremonially inaugurated the Northern Ireland parliament at Stormont. In his speech, the King spoke to the people of Ireland as a whole and pleaded for a spirit of reconciliation. The statesmanship of this speech and the goodwill that it engendered were set at nought by the crass stupidity of the British forces who, on that very day, arrested de Valera. So inept were they that they did not realise who they had lifted. When Cope found out, he had de Valera immediately moved from the detention cells to the officers' quarters and secured his release the following day. Meanwhile Casement had seen Smuts and the South African delegation, and Smuts was 'raising hell' with Lloyd George. This was followed by Cabinet meetings and top-level talks involving the senior military officers and civil servants. Andy Cope was summoned to air his views and spoke so forcibly that Hamar Greenwood butted in and told him to 'curb his Sinn Fein tendencies'.

As a result Lloyd George sent a message to de Valera, asking him to come to London with any colleague he chose, and meet him and Sir James Craig. De Valera replied on 28 June saying that a lasting peace could not be reached if the British denied the essential unity of Ireland. On 30 June Casement returned to Dublin, accompanied by Captain Lane, Smuts' private secretary, whom he introduced to de Valera. Casement suggested to Cope that Barton, Griffith and MacNeill should be released to help the negotiations. These three, along with Eamonn Duggan and Michael Staines, were duly set free. Subsequently the five men joined de Valera at Dr Farnan's house to meet Smuts himself. Michael was not present on this historic occasion.

Thereafter the peace process accelerated dramatically. The leading southern Unionists had meetings with Lloyd George in London and with de Valera and Griffith in Dublin, but Craig held aloof. Next, General Macready and Colonel Brind had a meeting with Duggan and Barton at the Mansion House and negotiated a truce. Both sides agreed to back off; there would be no attacks or reprisals, no provocative displays of force, armed or unarmed, and no actions calculated to disturb the peace. The Volunteers were allowed to retain their arms, a complete reversal of the policy enunciated seven months earlier when the peace process had begun. Had the British government conceded this point originally, seven months of the hardest fighting, with considerable loss of life and destruction of property, would have been avoided.

At 11.45 a.m. on Monday, 11 July 1921, a cavalcade of armoured cars, tanks and troop-carrying lorries began converging on their barracks. The streets of Dublin thronged with sightseers anxious not to miss this spectacle. It was a beautiful sunny day. At noon the bells of the city's churches rang out as the British troops in full combat gear filed silently through the gates and withdrew entirely from the scene. The men, women and children who looked on did so silently but with tears of joy. These khaki-clad figures with their tanks and guns represented seven centuries of tyranny and oppression. The silent onlookers stared through their tears as the massive gates of barracks and camps clanged shut. That evening, for the first time in years, Dubliners promenaded in the streets, still unable to believe that it was all over.

That night, Michael Collins was still at his desk in 17 Harcourt Terrace, working.

CHAPTER 13

Treaty, 1921

———

Agree with thine adversary quickly, whiles thou art in the
way with him.
ST MATTHEW, v, 25.

THE WORDS USED BY WINSTON CHURCHILL WERE UNCANNILY
similar to those used by Michael himself when, on the eve of the Truce, he
advocated 'a regular, all-round, thought-out onslaught' on all organs of the
British administration if the Truce did not hold. The Dail Cabinet agreed,
though fortunately it never became necessary to implement such a ruthless
scheme. Such a distrust of British intentions was justified. When General
Macready told Sir Henry Wilson that he had been summoned to a Cabinet
meeting and gathered that they were going to come to a 'gentlemanly
undertaking' with de Valera for a month's truce, he noted in his diary on 6 July:

> Valera has done well; a month's delay makes it impossible to take on
> murder-gang seriously this summer, as weather breaks in September-
> October. Valera knows this well enough.

Wilson reckoned that he would need '100,000 to 200,000 men, and one or
two years, to stamp out the murder gang and re-establish law and order'.[1]
Michael, on the other hand, felt that if things had been tough previously, they
could still get far worse. To Moya Llewelyn Davies he confided his feelings that
the Truce was 'only the first move. The days ahead are going to be the truly
trying ones and we can only face them with set faces and hearts full of hope and
confidence'.[2] During that summer, in fact, both sides made hectic plans for the
onslaught they felt was inevitable. Volunteer GHQ embarked on a mammoth
campaign of reorganisation, recruitment, training and equipment, increasing
strength from about 15,000 to five times that number. All over the country
training camps were set up at which Volunteers received intensive drill and
instruction in fieldcraft, small arms and infantry tactics. On the other side, the

British forces, though largely confined to their barracks, stepped up their preparations for full-scale war and laid plans for block-houses and concentration camps along the lines practised during the Boer War.

If Michael had been working hard before, he was now busier than ever, travelling all over southern Ireland conferring with local commandants, inspecting camps and, above all, overhauling and expanding his intelligence network. In Dublin he organised frequent and much larger shipments of weapons and ammunition, the first of which reached Arklow in August. Now and then, he managed to slip away into the countryside, going for long tramps along the country lanes around Howth, or picnicking with the Leigh Doyle family at the Devil's Glen, Rathdrum. Even in that seemingly tranquil setting he could not relax, but practised revolver shooting with his comrades. In July he paid several visits to Granard to see Kitty Kiernan. She came up to Dublin during Horse Show Week and they danced together far into the night, celebrating the lifting of the curfew and falling madly in love all over again. By the time Kitty returned to Granard she was certain that Michael was the man she would marry.

While the military on both sides laid their plans, the populace as a whole was oblivious to the perilous situation. There was a general feeling of euphoria as people savoured the sudden improvement in their lives. The deadening weight of apathy and despair, bred of generations of being terrorised by land agents, bullied by policemen, magistrates and soldiers, or shipped off to America like cattle, was suddenly lifted. The ordinary, everyday life in town and country may not have improved, but everywhere there was evidence of a new spirit abroad in Ireland. Wanted men came out of hiding and were fêted as heroes when they returned to their native towns and villages. The Volunteers began to appear on the streets in their new uniforms and cut a dash with the girls at dances and ceilidhs; commandeered cars ostensibly for Volunteer work and dashed up and down the winding country roads that beautiful summer with admiring girls beside them; were treated to free drinks in the pubs and generally strutted and swanked about the place. Thousands of youths flocked to enlist in the Volunteers, now that the fighting was over. These newcomers were derisively known to the old sweats as Trucileers. In this strange, unreal interim period even the Black and Tans and the dreaded Auxiliaries continued to make whoopee, and in the country pubs and city bars there was a great deal of fraternisation.

Both Michael Collins and David Lloyd George would have liked to proceed with all speed to a definitive agreement, a treaty; but that was never de Valera's style. Someone who could agonise for days over a single interview would not be hurried in such an important matter as this. It would be October before actual discussions commenced, and December before the British, running out of patience, forced the issue and delivered an ultimatum. Michael early on realised the dangerous situation; he and his comrades in the IRB hoped that some compromise could be reached. Brugha, on the other hand, was blind to the dangers and paid no attention, confining himself to vague advice to the Treaty delegates to keep talking.

As a first step, the British released all the imprisoned Sinn Fein leaders, with the exception of Sean MacEoin who had been convicted of murder. Michael dug his heels in and demanded that there be no discussions till MacEoin was liberated. He went further and exhorted the Dail to suspend sessions until MacEoin was released. In the end he took the matter into his own hands and published a statement in *The Irish Times* on 8 August. This provoked an immediate rebuttal from Erskine Childers who circulated a press notice that the Collins statement was 'wholly unauthorised'. As the fighting blacksmith was set free that very day the bitter disagreement was overlooked in the consequent jubilation. A few days later Michael had a boisterous reunion with him at Vaughan's. Michael was on the landing when MacEoin crossed the lobby; he was in such a hurry to greet his comrade that he vaulted the banisters in a flying leap and crashed down on MacEoin, still suffering from his wounds, and knocked the poor man to the ground. Michael took him to a session of the Dail where he was given a standing ovation.

Michael himself was suffering one of the greatest disappointments of his career. In going to London de Valera had pointedly excluded Michael from his entourage. Instead, he took Barton, Childers, Griffith, Plunkett and Stack. De Valera later told his biographers that the reason Michael was excluded was because it was important that the British should not have the opportunity to take the Big Fellow's photograph, blithely overlooking the fact that, had Michael gone to America as Dev had wanted, his photograph would have been taken thousands of times. This was a feeble excuse, and fine Michael knew it. On 13 July, the day before de Valera was due to meet Lloyd George, Michael sat at his desk in Harcourt Terrace and began drafting a letter, possibly to Harry Boland who was still in America at the time:

> Agreement is a trifling word or so I have come to look on it as such. At this moment there is more ill-will within a victorious assembly than ever could be anywhere else except in the devil's assembly. It cannot be fought against. The issue, and persons, are mixed to such an extent as to make discernibility an utter impossibility except to a few.
>
> It is a trust which is rapidly breaking for the rank and file of men and citizens theirs is a misplaced trust. For the trusted ones, far from being in accord, are disunited. This is a time when jealousy and personal gain count for more than country.[3]

Boland was certainly the recipient of a letter warning him of the changes in Dublin since the Truce had come into effect:

> There's something about which I don't like, and I have the impression that the whole thing is pressing on me. I find myself looking at friends as if they were enemies – looking at them twice just to make sure that they really are friends after all. I mention no names. After all it may be a wrong impression that's got into me. Frankly, though, I don't care for things as they are now.[4]

In the post-Truce euphoria there was a great deal of excess. Tom Barry was disgusted by what he found when he came up to Dublin. The General Staff had ensconced themselves in luxury suites at the Gresham where whiskey and brandy were constantly on tap: 'I went in and told them they should be ashamed of themselves.' The Shelbourne housed the IRA liaison office. P.J. Matthews, a staff officer, observed sourly that the office became 'a centre of entertainment' for Volunteers up from the country, as well as being besieged by job-hunters, place-seekers and people trying to sell things to Ireland's new rulers. Visitors charged bills to the office for food and drink totalling £20,000. Cope was a frequent visitor who 'often had late-night sittings with high IRA officers' and the rumour would soon get around that he and Michael Collins got roaring drunk together. There seems to have been no truth in this malicious gossip. Reporting to de Valera on 16 July, Michael wrote, 'Although there was a little more relaxation than I should have liked, everybody is working fairly hard again.'

Characteristically, Michael put the lull to good use. 'I have made millions of discoveries, and have been confirmed absolutely in certain things.' In de Valera's absence Michael got to grips with wildcat financial schemes by getting the Dail to approve the appointment of a registrar of companies. 'We are starting now what is a new order in Ireland,' he announced, 'and one of the first duties of the national Government is to secure that thrifty people shall not be deprived of their savings by any kind of schemer, or any kind of society, or group of individuals.' De Valera urged that until the registrar was appointed, no Dail deputies should lend their names to promote investment schemes. 'I never did allow my name for any such and never intend to,' countered Michael primly.

In mid-July Michael took time out to go down to West Cork and visit his family and friends. He was appalled to find some British soldiers acting in a manner that was 'arrogant and provocative', but generally speaking the British troops behaved themselves and kept a low profile. The only ugly incident occurred at Galway in October when a bunch of Tommies burst in on a fund-raising dance organised by the Republican Prisoners' Defence Fund. In the ensuing fracas a British officer was killed.

Though busier than ever in his role as Minister of Finance, Michael spent a great deal of his time in August and September on tours of military inspection. He would be up at five on a Sunday morning to embark on an exhausting round of these trips to the military camps, and not get out of his clothes till 4.30 a.m. on Tuesday. 'I was on the road again at 7.30 a.m. that morning,' he wrote to Moya Llewellyn Davies on 31 August from Wicklow. 'This will show you what the peaceful restfulness of the Truce is.'

At the beginning of September Michael decided to visit Armagh and address his constituents there in a great rally for Ireland. The night before, he worked late in his office preparing his speech which Alice Lyons typed out for him. Later, they left the building and were walking along the street when they were suddenly challenged by two armed men. Michael smashed his fist into the face of one, and then he and Alice ran for their lives, pursued by revolver shots. The gunmen were drunken Volunteers on a joy-ride.

The following morning, Sunday, 4 September, Michael went to Armagh, accompanied by Harry Boland who had returned from America on 21 August. Michael's partisans in the ancient cathedral city gave him a rousing reception, as he pleaded passionately for Loyalists to 'join with us, as Irishmen to come into the Irish nation, to come in and take their share in the government of their own country', but on the way home their car was surrounded by irate Orangemen and they were pursued by rocks and stones. The bodyguard seated alongside the driver had his tommy gun at the ready and itched to have a go, but Michael restrained him, saying, 'Thompson guns aren't fair against stones.'

They stayed overnight with Eoin O'Duffy at Clones, County Monaghan, left at seven o'clock on Monday morning and arrived back in Dublin at 5 p.m., having detoured to see the head of the Blessed Oliver Plunkett at Drogheda. There, Michael lit candles for himself and Kitty Kiernan, as he told her in a letter written on 6 September. At that time, Harry Boland was still in the running and he, too, wrote to her two days later about the Armagh visit, followed by a trip to Roscommon to visit his own constituency. On 2 October, however, at de Valera's behest, he set sail for America again, leaving the field clear to Michael. As late as 14 October Harry was writing from America hinting at marriage; but on the very same day Kitty was pressing Michael about the seriousness of *his* intentions.

The Dail had reassembled on 16 August, and de Valera was then formally elected President of the Republic, a position that had not existed until then. This gave Dev the status he craved, and which, to a large extent, he had been enjoying while in America. As de Valera saw himself as a president in the American idiom, he combined it with the office of prime minister, telling the

Dail 'I more or less concentrate in myself the whole Executive responsibility'. He also dampened down political aspirations, saying that (a) no one abroad would recognise the Republic, (b) if they persisted in this, they would face all-out war, and (c) that he would be in favour of giving each county power to vote itself out of the Republic if it so wished. By this time, he realised that Britain would never accede to Ireland's wishes for complete sovereignty. By mid-September he was warning the Dail that 'as far as he was concerned his oath of allegiance was to do the best he could for the Irish nation. That was the only allegiance he acknowledged'.[5]

This was an allusion to one of the sticking points, the oath of allegiance to the King. Lloyd George was on holiday at Gairloch in Wester Ross that autumn, and on 6 September he motored across to Inverness, close to where the King was staying, and whither the Cabinet had been summoned for an emergency session. The following day he wrote to de Valera saying that he was ready to begin talks 'to ascertain how the association of Ireland with the Community of Nations known as the British Empire can best be reconciled with Irish national aspirations'. On 14 September Joe McGrath and Harry Boland brought Dev's answer: 'The Irish Republic would be glad to discuss this question with the Community of Nations, known as the British Empire.'

During the ensuing five days negotiations almost broke down when Lloyd George tried to have de Valera's reply suppressed. The Irishmen countered by saying that, in that case, he would publish his reply in the evening papers – which he promptly did. There was dead silence for several days, and then Lloyd George sent an invitation to 'a Conference in London on October 11th' which the Dail accepted. At this time, the feud between Cathal Brugha and Michael Collins was coming to the boil. Brugha was issuing orders through the Chief of Staff, Mulcahy, to get at Michael. Mulcahy found this distasteful and protested so vigorously that Brugha sacked him – twice – but then was forced to reverse his decision, though Mulcahy also threatened to resign on several occasions. This uneasy situation was aggravated by the IRB which claimed to be a law unto itself. Four of the top generals (Mulcahy, O'Sullivan and O'Duffy as well as Michael himself) were members of the Brotherhood, and several brigade commandants were high in the organisation. To curb the powers of the IRB, Brugha decided to recommission the army and bring it firmly under civil control. The Dail Cabinet took this decision on 15 September. At the same time Austin Stack, who had been Deputy Chief of Staff in name only, now began attending GHQ meetings, and Brugha insisted on an office of his own at GHQ, though these matters were never discussed with the Staff. On 4 November the Cabinet reaffirmed these decisions and ordered the recommissioning to go ahead immediately. All staff officers and divisional commanders were given the rank of major-general. Michael, then in London, viewed these antics with amusement, likening Brugha to Napoleon.

Mulcahy was now virtually at Brugha's throat and complained to de Valera about the high-handed Minister of Defence. A meeting of the antagonists was convened at the home of Mrs Humphries in Ailesbury Road; Brugha and Mulcahy stormed at each other and almost came to blows before de Valera forced them apart. Cathal then burst into tears of anger and flounced out. Dev patched up the squabble somehow, but bad feeling continued to fester between the Minister of Defence and the Chief of Staff. Late in October war between the Brugha and Mulcahy factions flared up again, this time over Austin Stack. Brugha wanted him to continue as Deputy Chief of Staff, whereas Mulcahy wanted Eoin O'Duffy (who had been doing the work anyway). The matter was only resolved on 16 November when O'Duffy was shunted sideways to become Director of Organisation. O'Duffy (later to gain notoriety as leader of the fascist Blueshirts) regarded this move as 'a personal slight and a grave dishonour'. Finally de Valera made a judgement on 25 November: O'Duffy would be Mulcahy's Deputy Chief of Staff but Stack would also be a Deputy Chief of Staff, acting as 'Cathal's ghost on the Staff'. This farce was compounded by his omitting to pass this decision on to the Staff.

De Valera's involvement in negotiations with the British was merely preliminary and purely ceremonial. During August and September they were conducted mainly by correspondence, and many times the British found de Valera exasperating to deal with. By the end of August the Dail had produced a set of proposals which baffled Mark Sturgis: 'The Shinns themselves confess that after days of public and private deliberation they have succeeded in producing a document which no ordinary brain can interpret.'[6]

In the end a conference was convened in London in October. De Valera decided that he would not head the delegation this time, feeling that he should be held in reserve as a symbol of the Republic. This was greeted with consternation, and in the end only his casting vote produced agreement. Griffith, Cosgrave and Collins were opposed and urged de Valera to change his mind, but he refused to budge, saying that he believed that if external association was accepted, he would be in a stronger position to secure approval from hardline Republicans in the army and the Dail if he was not a direct party to the agreement.

That settled, there was the vexed question of whom to send. Griffith was an obvious choice, but he was no Republican and was prepared to settle for dominion status. De Valera told Griffith bluntly that scapegoats might be needed later on, and Griffith said that he was willing, if necessary, to play that role. Michael was another obvious choice, but he had no desire to go. De Valera, however, insisted, and later told the Dail why Michael was such an excellent choice:

It was felt from the personal touch and contact he had with his mind that he felt and he knew the Minister for Finance was a man for the team. He was obviously vital to the delegation.[7]

Neither Brugha nor Stack was chosen. Neither man had the intellectual capacity for negotiation. Stack would later declare, 'It consoles me to feel that from the outset I instinctively and openly set my face against negotiations in London; so did Cathal.'[8] Herein lay the seeds of tragic future dissent; no matter what terms Michael and his colleagues brought back, Brugha and Stack were bound to raise objections and snap at the heels of their *bête noire*. It is singularly unfortunate that no one, least of all de Valera, foresaw this problem. The other negotiators were Robert Barton, the Minister of Economic Affairs, Eamonn Duggan, a member of the Dail who seldom had anything to say for himself, and George Gavan Duffy, son of an Australian premier, the lawyer who defended Sir Roger Casement at his trial and a consummate Dail diplomat. Barton's cousin, Childers, was appointed delegation secretary.

At this juncture the long shadow of the Declaration of Independence, published in January 1919, lay across them. It was inevitable that, following the Truce, there would have to be some sort of compromise. De Valera realised this, and reminded the Dail that he was no doctrinaire Republican. He refused to let the Dail place restrictions on the delegates, and would not even permit the Dail to debate beforehand the sort of terms which Lloyd George might offer, and whether they would be acceptable or not. In fairness to de Valera, he was concerned lest word of such wrangling got back to Westminster, and thereby weakened the Irish bargaining position. On the other hand, no limit was ever laid down beyond which Collins and Griffith must not go in accepting an agreement. It was never defined – until Collins and Griffith returned from London with less than expected. But in October 1921 de Valera was imploring Michael 'not to mention the word Republic'. To Griffith, the President likewise besought some way to 'get him out of this strait waistcoat of a Republic'.

Michael had grave misgivings about his abilities as a negotiator and moved heaven and earth to get out of this assignment; but de Valera was adamant. In the end Michael caved in, and said that he was going to London 'as a soldier obeying his commanding officer'. It was abundantly clear to him that he had been selected for this invidious task because he would have to make the concessions which de Valera himself, as President of the Irish Republic, could not make. Michael would later reveal that he had gone against the sound advice of his friends, particularly Tim Healy. In an undated letter to his London friend John O'Kane, Michael wrote:

I was warned more times than I can recall about the ONE. And when I was caught for this delegation my immediate thought was of how easily I had walked into the preparations. But having walked in, I had to stay.[9]

Cynically, de Valera hoped that Michael, with the IRB in his pocket and the Volunteers eating out of his hand, would be able to persuade others to accept the climbdown when it became inevitable.

De Valera's subtle, mathematical mind would gradually evolve the concept of external association with the British Empire as a way out of the dilemma; he did not realise that his words and actions might be open to misinterpretation. This added to the mischief created in the Cabinet by the open disagreement between Collins and Brugha. Michael went to London naïvely believing that Dev was staying behind in order to keep Brugha and Stack in line, and dismantle the improvised Republic. Stack and Brugha, on the other hand, believed that Dev was staying behind to uphold the Republic and prevent Collins and Griffith from making concessions.

This confusion of aims was compounded by the fact that none of the team of delegates and secretaries seemed to have the least idea of what the other fellows were thinking about, and all were equally bemused when it came to the question of what de Valera and the remainder of the Cabinet at home were planning. Frank Pakenham (Earl of Longford) later considered that de Valera showed 'a great flair for preserving harmony'.[10] O'Connor, on the other hand, thought this should have read 'a great flair for masking essential issues'.[11]

Meanwhile, the British delegation had also been drawn up. In addition to Lloyd George, there were Sir Austen Chamberlain (Chancellor of the Exchequer), Lord Birkenhead (Lord Chancellor), Sir Hamar Greenwood (Chief Secretary for Ireland), Winston Churchill (Colonial Secretary), Sir Lamington Worthington-Evans (War Secretary) and Sir Gordon Hewart (Attorney General). With the exception of Lloyd George himself, this team was upper-middle or upper class, the products of the public schools and universities. Birkenhead, formerly the leading advocate F.E. Smith, had been prosecuting counsel at the trial of Sir Roger Casement, and in this context had fought a hard courtroom battle with one of the Irish delegates, Gavan Duffy. Before the war, Smith had been the ardent champion of Carson's fighting Ulstermen; later he would do a U-turn and become Carson's most formidable adversary, especially in the debates in the House of Lords over the Irish Treaty.

Birkenhead commissioned a dossier on the Irish delegates, but whoever carried out this job made some curious mistakes. Griffith, who was a very able and confident negotiator, was described as likely to be 'ill at ease'. Apart from Duffy (whom Birkenhead already knew only too well) the delegates will be very nervous and ill at ease . . . They are leaders in Dail Eireann, which is a very nondescript assembly. They are absolutely without world experience, and considerable allowance will have to be made on this score . . . may be a bit rude and extravagant in speech . . . They recognise their responsibilities and this, of course, adds to their nervousness.[12]

This dossier included individual pen-pictures, of which the following give a sample. Duffy was described as a Catholic, 'son of the late Sir Gavan Duffy, Prime Minister of one of the Australian States, vain and self-sufficient, likes to hear himself talk'. Robert Barton, a Protestant, was described as a cousin of Erskine Childers: 'held a commission during the war; lost a brother in the war; educated at Rugby and Christchurch; has no outstanding quality'. Eamonn Duggan was said to be 'completely under the influence of Michael Collins . . . recognises that he is not one of the strong men'. By contrast Michael, by far the youngest of the delegation, was regarded as 'the strongest personality of the party' while Griffith, 'more clever than de Valera, but not so attractive', was regarded as 'the real power in Sinn Fein'. This gives the lie to an outburst of Brugha in the Dail on 7 January 1922 that the British government had manipulated the selection of Collins and Griffith, and that these were 'the two weakest men we had on the team'. Furthermore, Brugha averred, the British had very quickly discovered this, singling them out and ignoring the rest of the delegation when the most crucial discussions were held.

On Saturday, 8 October, the Irish delegation sailed from Dublin and took up quarters in London at 22 Hans Place. Michael, getting formally engaged to Kitty Kiernan that day, delayed his departure by twenty-four hours. According to Father Ignatius there was another good reason for Michael's delay:

> He was staying at the Grand Hotel, Greystones, while I was giving a Mission at the church there. It was coming near the close of the Mission. Michael was very busy in Dublin, worked and worried almost beyond endurance. He got to Greystones one night very late and very tired. It was the eve of his departure to London re the pact. He got up next morning as early as 5.30 a.m., came to the church and made a glorious General Confession and received Holy Communion. He said to me after Confession, 'Father, say a Mass for Ireland' and 'God bless you, Father'. He crossed an hour or so afterwards to London.
>
> I said to the congregation that day, 'You saw one of Ireland's hidden saints making no small sacrifice for the Master this morning.'[13]

Not only did Michael slip quietly into London a day after the others were given a tumultuous welcome by the city's Irish community, but he took up separate quarters, at 15 Cadogan Gardens. Ostensibly the reason for this was that Michael could receive his intelligence agents away from the glare of publicity; but this house also accommodated the delegation's PR machine run by Diarmuid O'Hegarty, as well as Joe McGrath, Dan MacCarthy, Sean Milroy and other officials. Michael's personal staff included Liam Tobin, Tom Cullen, Emmet Dalton, Ned Broy, Joe Guilfoyle and Joe Dolan, which must have compromised them as intelligence officers and would have undermined their effectiveness had hostilities with the British been resumed. Ironically, Dave Neligan was also in London at this time; in his role as a Secret Service man, he had been assigned the task of spying on Michael Collins!

At 11 a.m. on 11 October the Irish delegation arrived at 10 Downing Street. They were ushered inside and met at the door of the conference room by Lloyd George. He alone shook hands with each delegate, leading them to their places on one side of the table, and introducing each man to his counterpart on the other side. In this unobtrusive manner handshakes were kept to the absolute minimum. Thus the 'Envoys Plenipotentiary from the Elected Government of the Republic of Ireland', as cited in Griffith's credentials, at long last faced the most powerful men in Britain.

Michael found himself seated opposite Lord Birkenhead. There was a certain aloofness about the others in sitting down with 'Collins the murderer, the man with £10,000 on his head', but in Birkenhead Michael soon discovered a kindred spirit, the instant click of realist with realist. Both men treated life as a gallant adventure but they also had a great deal in common. At Wadham College, Freddie Smith had been a great athlete, and even now, approaching fifty, he kept himself in shape with golf, tennis and riding most days. There was a human side to him, which he always showed to youth. Many of his young friends had perished in the recent war, and perhaps he saw something of them in the young man, not quite thirty-one, who sat opposite him. At any rate, an amazing rapport rapidly developed between them. Above all, Birkenhead appreciated Michael's direct, forthright manner and his ability to cut through the verbiage and come straight to the point. 'I hate a slow mind,' he said feelingly. Austen Chamberlain later wrote that Birkenhead had succeeded in entering Michael's mind, winning his sympathy and gaining his confidence.

Others left very mixed impressions. Cope reported to Sturgis on 15 October that 'Michael Collins is showing frankness and considerable reasonableness', whereas General Macready found him 'a great disappointment, flippantly trying to get out of corners by poor jokes in bad taste'. The following day was Michael's thirty-first birthday, though when he wrote to Kitty that day he spoke of it as his thirtieth, a Peter Pan touch perhaps. Interestingly, one of the many friends he made in London at this time was Sir James Barrie, to whom he was introduced by Moya and Crompton Llewelyn Davies. Barrie recorded his first impression: 'He has completely charmed me. He is blazing with intelligence.' Michael, who had been pictured not so long before in the English press as a hatchet-faced thug, was now lionised by the cream of London's society to which he gained entrée through the Anglo-Irish Davies, Lavery and Londonderry families. Society hostesses fell over each other to invite him to dinners and soirées and found him devastatingly handsome and debonair. Michael's head was not turned by this adulation from a quarter where it had been least expected. 'The English people are so demonstrative and excitable,' he confided to Hannie. He had no illusions that he was nothing more than a nine-days' wonder, an object of curiosity to people who would have rejoiced at his death only a few weeks earlier. This made him value his English friends from his earlier London days all the more.

The protracted deliberations which led eventually to the Treaty have been the subject of a vast literature, so they may be summarised here. As plenipotentiaries, the delegates had full powers to negotiate and sign an agreement, but it was always understood that they would refer matters back to Dublin for affirmation. In later years the myth would develop that the delegates did not consult Dublin and came back from London with the Treaty as a *fait accompli*. In fact regular progress reports were drafted by Childers and sent to the Dail which back-pedalled its more extreme positions during this crucial period. The delegates returned to Dublin on a number of occasions for discussions on moot points, and Michael crossed the Irish Sea every weekend. Only at the very end, when the delegates were more or less given an ultimatum on 6 December, and returned briefly to Hans Place to consider the matter, did they not take the trouble to pick up a telephone and speak to de Valera direct.

There were seven full meetings between 11 and 24 October before the Plenary Conference was divided into three separate sub-committees, Financial Relations (which met once), Naval and Air Defence (three times) and Observance of the Truce (five times). There were, in addition, no fewer than twenty-four sub-conferences, between 24 October and the night of 5–6 December when the Treaty was actually signed. At these Arthur Griffith was present on twenty-two occasions, Michael Collins on nineteen, Robert Barton on three and the other delegates at two apiece. A further nine informal meetings, between 8 November and 4 December, took place between members of the Irish delegation and Tom Jones, the Cabinet Secretary. Only Griffith attended all nine, whereas Michael attended three and Duggan two. Neither Barton nor Duffy took part in these discussions.

The atmosphere during the first of the full sessions was tense, especially due to the presence of Sir Hamar Greenwood whom the Irishmen heartily detested. By the fifth meeting, however, the atmosphere was much more relaxed. A measure of the touchiness of the situation was the reaction to the exchange of messages between Pope Benedict and King George. His Holiness sent a message to His Majesty hoping for a settlement as a result of the conferences, and the King in response hoped for 'peace and happiness for my people'. This provoked de Valera into making a rather pompous statement. The gist of what he said was perfectly valid – that the Irish people owed no allegiance to the King and that the independence of Ireland had been proclaimed by elected representatives of the people – but the rather tendentious way in which he expressed it cast a blight over the ensuing discussions, the British delegates denouncing his statement as inopportune and in bad taste. Needless to say, the newspapers in Britain magnified and distorted Dev's actions, and even Michael was depressed that de Valera, having tried to get out of the straitjacket of the Republic, was effectively lacing them in again.

In a letter to John O'Kane on 17 October, Michael stated bluntly, 'You cannot create a Republic overnight,' adding that he doubted whether Ireland was sufficiently stabilised politically or sound economically to cut herself off so precipitately and completely from Britain. Might not this end in utter chaos, he asked rhetorically. Why waste all that had been gained for the sake of a symbol? By the beginning of November, if not earlier, Michael had come to the conclusion that dominion status was the best solution for the time being, so long as it was seen as no more than a stepping-stone to complete independence. On 25 November a document on Dail notepaper and headed 'Memorandum by M.C. (draft)' was sent to Lord Birkenhead by Chamberlain with a covering note which commented, 'This is extraordinarily interesting, though sometimes perverse and sometimes Utopian. Who (outside our six) would guess the name of the writer?' The preamble to this remarkable document recited British oppression of Ireland over the centuries before going on to state that British people did not recognise the change which had come about not only for Ireland and England but for the whole world. This led Michael to conclude that:

(1) The business of the Irish Conference is to form some sort of alliance in which both may be associated for equal benefit.
(2) The position of Ireland is entirely different from that of Britain's Colonies.
(3) Nevertheless, both England and Ireland, by nature of their nearness to each other, have matters of common concern.
(4) The only association which will be satisfactory to Ireland to enter will be based not on the present technical legal status of the Dominions, but on the real position they claim and have secured.

A development such as this might lead to a world League of Nations. From conflict (world conflict) to harmony.

If America were able to enter such a League, a further move would be made towards world peace. Consequently, in such an atmosphere – through improved relationship – to a condition of financial stability.

The invitation to the Irish representatives to consider how association with the nations of the British Commonwealth can best be reconciled with Irish national aspirations makes it necessary to consider how far the members of the group have attained to independent nationality.

What steps should be taken to secure such standard of independence?[14]

Utopian this may have been, but it uncannily anticipated by almost a decade the Statute of Westminster which redefined the relationship between the United Kingdom and the overseas dominions.

Meanwhile, the British were getting intelligence reports from their agents in Ireland that spoke of growing unrest and lawlessness. The Volunteers had expanded out of all recognition, from about 3,000 before the Truce to over 73,000. Michael himself viewed this expansion with some alarm, fearing that this army might fall under the control of 'certain elements' who might then use it for their own ends. It takes no flight of the imagination to guess whom he had in mind. Added to this was the worry that there was growing interference from Dublin which, he felt, might jeopardise the peace negotiations in London. This was a matter which greatly concerned Griffith, who protested to de Valera when the latter tried to curb the plenipotentiary powers which had been conferred on them by the Dail. In the end he drew up a strongly worded paper to this effect, and got all the delegates to sign it. Lloyd George, aware of the situation, tried to exploit it for his own ends, but Collins and Griffith fought tooth and nail. To O'Kane, Michael confessed:

I prefer Birkenhead to anyone else. He understands and has real insight into our problems – the Dublin one as much as any other. Dublin is the real problem. They know what we are doing, but I don't know *exactly* the state of their activities. No turning back now.[15]

Two days later Michael wrote to the same correspondent:

G. was particularly dour today. He said to me – 'You realise what we have on our hands?' I replied that I realised it long ago. He meant Dublin reaction to whatever happens here.

The thing is up and down, up and down – never steady.

G. is a good man. Only, I fear, much the worse for the strain of a life spent in toil and trouble.

I reminded him of how when I was young I thought of him *as* Ireland. To which he replied, 'We stand or fall in this together.' It is the one bright hope of mine in all this welter of action and counter-action.[16]

Years of poverty and privation had, indeed, taken a heavy toll on Griffith whose health broke down during the conference. Though he continued as nominal leader of the delegation, this role, in effect, passed to Michael. By mid-November Michael was admitting to O'Kane that he could not trust anyone in the delegation beyond Griffith himself. Ironically, he felt that the delegation should have been led by Erskine Childers: 'He is sharp enough to realise how things will have due effect in Dublin – and acts accordingly.'

By the end of November Michael was absolutely convinced that the most he could hope to secure was dominion status, but in the changing, post-war climate, this was no bad thing. Sir Robert Borden, Prime Minister of Canada, had claimed complete sovereignty for his country, in the Peace Treaty debate of 2 September 1919, and Smuts, in the same debate, had said that South Africa had secured a position of absolute equality and freedom, 'not only among the other States of the Empire, but among the other nations of the world'. Therefore, argued Michael, the dominions of the British Commonwealth were now free and secure in their freedom. Ireland should have the same status as Canada.

What concerned Michael most of all at this critical juncture was the military factor. The RIC had become 'a spent force', the Auxiliaries were little more than mercenaries and the Black and Tans 'a motley, lawless crowd', but the regular army in Ireland was an *organised* force, and there was no telling how it might act. Michael was well aware of the growing friction between Lloyd George and the Chief of the Imperial General Staff. Henry Wilson, now a field-marshal and a baronet, was at the zenith of his powers and viewing the progress towards a definitive peace with the Shinners with distaste. He was itching to unleash his forces, and closely monitored the situation in Ireland, watching and waiting for a pretext to strike back at the rebels.

Then, on 23 November, they played into his hands. That night a band of Volunteers staged a raid on Combermere Barracks at Windsor. It was regarded as an inside job and a Sergeant Roche of the Irish Guards immediately came under suspicion. Wilson jumped to the conclusion that Michael Collins was organising clandestine operations in England, under cover of the peace talks. In fact, the raid was masterminded by Cathal Brugha with the two-pronged intention of stirring up trouble with the British and causing intense embarrassment to Michael Collins. Not surprisingly, Michael was beside himself with rage. Subsequently Michael Brennan (who had been given a thousand pounds by Brugha to procure arms) revealed that he had contacted Michael Hogan and Ned Lynch who had lived in London for years and asked them to buy firearms. Hogan and Lynch met Roche in a pub, and it was the latter's idea to lift the weapons from the Windsor armoury. Brennan, commandant-general of the 1st Western Division, later wrote to Michael denying all knowledge of the raid: 'Neither Brugha nor I had any knowledge of the scheme.' Michael convinced the British that he was not implicated in the matter, and even managed to secure the release of Roche, Lynch and Hogan. The timing of this raid seems highly significant, taking place on the eve of the recommissioning of the Volunteer officers by which Brugha and de Valera sought to place the Irish army under civilian control.

While constantly watching the 'Dublinites', as he called them, for back-stabbing, Michael was keeping a very wary eye on Lloyd George. He himself told this anecdote to the other delegates. One day Lloyd George was alone with Michael in a room which had a large world map on the wall, the British Empire picked out in red. 'He put his arm around my shoulder,' said Michael, 'at the same time pointing to the map, and said, "You're a capable man, Mick, supposing you help us".'[17] This emotional appeal was very much in character with the little Welshman; but it certainly brought home to the Irish delegation what they were up against. By that stage the negotiations were sticking on two points, the oath of allegiance to King George, and the matter of Northern Ireland. Of these, of course, the latter was by far the more important; but the Irish delegation allowed themselves to be bogged down on the vexed question of the oath, so that the larger issue of partition was glossed over. It has become fashionable to put all the blame for this on Griffith, but in truth this was an intractable problem. Michael himself, in an undated letter to O'Kane, showed that he realised this only too well:

> Craig is the man of the moment. A wily bird – obviously. Said too much in
> the past. Afraid, I think, that Dev will out with it. Ireland is Ireland.
> Borderland is trouble and always will be.

The reference to de Valera alludes to the meeting between them when Sir James Craig is supposed to have asked de Valera to become president of a United Ireland. This curious assertion was confirmed by Oscar Traynor, Dublin Brigadier at the time, who said that Craig had told de Valera that he did not desire the partition of Ireland, and had come to Dublin to ask de Valera to become prime minister of a United Ireland.[18] Michael had no illusions about the true feelings of the Ulstermen. They were 'held in sway not by any patriotic alliance towards England'. He deduced that the Scottish element in the population and money interests accounted to a large extent for the supposed allegiance. Michael was also acutely aware of the religious question: 'Protestant element is in force. Catholic population subdued.'[19]

Again, Lloyd George outmanoeuvred Griffith, suggesting a way out of the impasse by appointing a boundary commission to define the area under Unionist control. Had a plebiscite been held, Tyrone and Fermanagh would have joined the Twenty-six Counties, along with parts of Armagh, Derry and Down. Not surprisingly, the Ulster Unionists opposed this ferociously and this had the effect of directing Griffith's animosity against the Craig administration. By thus giving the Protestants of North-east Ulster a permanent majority over their Catholic brethren, Lloyd George ensured that what, in 1921, seemed like a temporary expedient, would become a permanent bone of contention that bedevils Anglo-Irish relations to this day.

Michael's notes to John O'Kane, more or less day by day, shed an interesting light on the negotiations as they dragged to their close. On 29 November he wrote:

> More and more the responsibility rests with me. What responsibility it is. I find the strain of looking into Chamberlain's false eye the most nervy of all my experiences. Birkenhead sees this — smiles and shrugs his shoulders.

And the following day he wrote prophetically:

> The only names worth considering after this will be the names of those who have kept away from London.
>
> Integrity of purpose is defeated at all times by those whose star rests elsewhere. The advice and inspiration of C[hilders] is like farmland under water — dead. With a purpose, I think — with a definite purpose. Soon he will howl with triumph — for what it is worth.
>
> I think also that Birkenhead's integrity of purpose is foiled in other quarters. I can almost see the gloating that is so obvious among some of our opposites — whichever way it means trouble at home, an enjoyable spectacle for more people than one imagines.

A few days later Michael penned an undated memo when a faint glimmer of light was beginning to show at the end of the tunnel:

> (I) The Treaty will not be accepted in Dublin — not by those who have in mind personal ambitions under pretence of patriotism.
> (II) Am confident of achieving victory by election. Pro-Treaty element could be 55–60% of all concerned. (G. questions this because of what may have happened during our absence.)
> (III) Anti-Treaty element will possibly enlist aid of Volunteers disgruntled by present state of affairs — quiet after storm.

(IV) Believe that majority of people will welcome Treaty. There will be some suspicion, however, regarding oath.[20]

Other notes assessed the influence of de Valera whom Michael suspected would command a large part of the Volunteer organisation. Michael thought that the Dail would back the Treaty, though he thought the female deputies, hardline Republicans and staunch members of Cumann na mBan to the last, would be a problem. He even compiled a list of deputies who, he thought, would support the Treaty, including Con Collins and Harry Boland, both friends of long standing, but who subsequently voted to reject it.

Another document was an undated memorandum by Michael, to which Griffith added his comments. Both men speculated on what Britain might do if negotiations reached a stalemate. If Britain resumed hostilities world opinion would prevent all-out war. Significantly, they were more concerned on reaction at home to the Treaty. Michael argued that even if they returned to Dublin with a document guaranteeing a republic, some people would not be in favour. Griffith agreed, but commented, 'Sooner or later a decision will have to be made and we shall have to make it.' On I December Michael wrote to O'Kane:

> Things are working up to a pitch. Lloyd George was too preoccupied for my liking today. Didn't seem to take much notice of what was being said.
>
> I'll give you a forecast – something definite before the 6th. And where shall I be? Dead and numb or half-dead already by then.
>
> As a child I wanted things and had ambition for them. Now I have them, but not for long. Whichever way it goes L/G won't lose. 'Got my political life at stake,' he confided. I didn't answer him. My life – not only political – is at stake.

Meanwhile, it was becoming clear that the delegation was drifting apart, with Michael, Griffith and Duggan on one side and Barton and Duffy on the other. This rift came into the open at a meeting of the Dail Cabinet in Dublin on 3 December, at which the delegates produced the draft treaty. In a nutshell, the British rejected outright independence and an Irish Republic. They would not agree to the external association which de Valera had advocated, but were prepared to concede dominion status with the implication of future constitutional expansion. Moreover, the things that really mattered, such as police, army, legislature and taxation, were to be handed over, and Michael must have found the prospects exhilarating. There was just one snag; to get them, Ireland had to accept the suzerainty of a monarch she did not recognise. This was not a problem faced by Grattan in the 1780s when Ireland had her own parliament, for no one could conceive of any form of government that was not monarchical; but the American and French revolutions changed all that.

Partition and the oath of allegiance notwithstanding, Michael came to the meeting in a mixture of exuberance and euphoria – soon dashed by the lengthy and very acrimonious bickering.[21] Michael lost his temper as the interminable discussion went round in circles, everyone chipping in with his tuppenceworth but making no attempt to come to a definite conclusion. Michael felt that the British had conceded as much as they could, and Griffith supported this view; but Duffy and Barton thought that the British were only bluffing and that external association would be granted if the Irish pushed hard enough. Griffith was prepared to drop external association if a united Ireland materialised; de Valera, however, pointed out that Griffith had secured neither. Michael was in a foul mood as he drove back with Tom Cullen to catch the steamer. 'I've been there all day and I can't get them to say Yes or No, whether we should sign or not.'

The following day it became apparent that the delegates were divided in their views as to what had been decided. Barton and Duffy were sure that the Cabinet had authorised them to press for external association; Michael and Griffith were equally adamant that no such decision had been taken. Griffith was prepared to go along with the others in the interests of solidarity in face of the British; but a furious Michael refused point-blank to do anything of the sort.

When the conference was resumed, Griffith argued cogently for external association, but when Duffy conceded that 'our difficulty is coming into the Empire', Austen Chamberlain snapped, 'That ends it!'

For all practical purposes, the negotiations had broken down. Lloyd George asked to speak to Michael alone. Face to face, they picked over the points of difference again: Ulster, the oath, defence and fiscal autonomy. Lloyd George was prepared to renegotiate, and the conference was reconvened at three o'clock that afternoon. After some discussion it became obvious that the tête-a-tête had paid off. Michael's modified version of the oath of allegiance was accepted by Birkenhead, while Lloyd George conceded fiscal autonomy, which Michael knew to be crucial if he were to raise loans abroad to get the new state off the ground.

At that point, when the delegates were wavering, Lloyd George produced his trump card. Either they signed, or all-out war would be declared. Frank Pakenham would argue later that the delegates were blinded by Lloyd George's histrionic artistry and forgot that there was such a thing as the telephone to Dublin; but other writers are probably right in surmising that, after that unseemly wrangle in the Dail two days earlier, Michael felt that there was little point in contacting Dublin at this juncture. Churchill would later describe this pregnant moment: 'Michael Collins rose looking as if he was going to shoot someone, preferably himself. In all my life I have never seen so much passion and suffering in restraint.'[22] The dejected Irishmen adjourned to discuss Lloyd George's ultimatum. A reprise of that wrangle now took place as the delegates squared up to each other, Michael, Griffith and Duggan on one side, Barton and Duffy sternly opposed. The fierce arguments ebbed and flowed all evening and dragged on into the night, with no sign of resolution. In the wee small hours, and in utter exasperation, the three put on their coats and hats and got ready to tell Lloyd George that they would sign, but the others pulled them back into the room and pleaded with them, over and over again. Then Duggan burst into tears at the memory of the hangman he had seen in Mountjoy, and this unnerved Barton. At length he was resigned to joining the three, and Duffy soon caved in, not wishing to be the odd man out and bear the burden of precipitating a resumption of war.

Shortly after 2 a.m. on Tuesday, 6 December, the delegates shuffled back into the conference room. 'Mr Prime Minister,' said Griffith coldly, 'the delegation is willing to sign the agreement, but there are a few points of drafting which perhaps it would be convenient if I mentioned at once.'

At 2.20 a.m. they put their names to the historic document. There was no sense of elation as the five men trudged silently through the cold, deserted streets back to Hans Place, only too well aware of the enormity of their decision. Coffee and sandwiches had been set out for the returning delegation, but Griffith ignored all pleas to take refreshments. Instead, he spent the rest of the night pacing up and down the hallway, his head in his hands.

Michael's reaction was altogether more sombre. When Birkenhead appended his signature to the articles of agreement, he turned to Michael and said, 'I may have signed my political death-warrant tonight.'

The Big Fellow replied, 'I may have signed my actual death-warrant.'

CHAPTER 14

The Split, 1922

National unity was broken at the top. No power under
heaven could prevent the split from spreading downwards.
FLORRIE O'DONOGHUE, *No Other Law* (1956)

DE VALERA WAS ON A TOUR OF INSPECTION OF ARMY UNITS IN THE
west when the delegates set off to return to Dublin. At Euston a vast crowd
gathered to give them a rousing send-off and Michael was carried by exuberant
supporters. There was an incredible euphoria among the London-Irish
community. By contrast, the reception at Dublin the following morning was
subdued at best, but mostly sullen tinged with violent outbursts of anger.
Gearoid O'Sullivan, who came to meet Kathleen MacKenna, was fuming at 'the
so-and-so' (de Valera) and his buddies Stack and Brugha who would not accept
what the Big Fellow had signed; 'Nothing can prevent a split in the army, and
the outbreak of civil war!'[1]

Michael had not shared the general euphoria, and had been unusually silent
during the journey home. He knew in his heart of hearts that de Valera would
not accept the Treaty, if only for selfish reasons. It was a compromise, the best
possible in the circumstances, but it was not de Valera's compromise. Now, too
late, it dawned on Michael that de Valera had anticipated as much, and that was
the reason why he had refused to lead the delegation. Now he could pose as the
man of principle who had not given way. On the evening of 6 December de
Valera returned to Dublin and was getting ready to preside over a banquet at
the Mansion House commemorating the sixth centenary of the death of Dante,
when Austin Stack produced a copy of *The Evening Mail* which had published the
details of the agreement. This was premature, as both sides had agreed to make
the details of the Treaty public at 8 p.m., to permit the messengers, Eamonn
Duggan and Desmond Fitzgerald, to arrive from London with the official text.
In fact this document was handed to de Valera only minutes after he had read
the newspaper. Duggan noted that the President was in a 'towering rage' and
ignored the document. When Duggan asked him to read it, de Valera snapped,

'Why should I read it?' Nonplussed, Duggan reminded him of the eight o'clock arrangement and pointed to the clock approaching that hour. 'What,' said de Valera, 'to be published whether I have seen it or not – whether I approve or not?' Piaras Beaslai who was also speaking at the Dante commemoration, observed that de Valera was in a 'state of suppressed emotion'. Only afterwards did he learn, to his astonishment, that de Valera had not taken the trouble to study the document itself. 'Apparently the fact that a Treaty had been signed without first being referred to him was the source of his agitation.'[2]

De Valera called a meeting of the Dail Cabinet the following morning and peremptorily demanded the resignation of the three absent members, Collins, Barton and Griffith. Cosgrave immediately leaped to their defence, saying it would be better to wait and see what they had to say for themselves first. The thought that Cosgrave was not wholly behind him pulled de Valera up short and, instead, he decided to make a statement to the press. When Fitzgerald read it he thought that people might misunderstand it, as it seemed to convey the false impression that the President (whom he had regarded as a moderate) was opposed to the settlement. Fitzgerald was taken aback when de Valera turned on him and spat, 'That is the way I intend it to read. Publish it as it is.'[3] The statement read:

> In view of the nature of the proposed treaty with Great Britain, President de Valera has sent an urgent summons to the members of the Cabinet in London to report at once so that a full Cabinet decision may be taken. The hour of the meeting is fixed for 12 noon tomorrow, Thursday. A meeting of the Dail will be summoned later.

This had a most chilling effect when it was published, the more so as the initial reaction of the people of Dublin to the news that a treaty had been signed was extremely favourable, tinged with immense relief that the struggle was over. When Michael and Griffith disembarked from the mailboat at Dun Laoghaire they were met by an impressive guard of honour orchestrated by the IRB. Michael seized the opportunity to draw Tom Cullen aside and ask him how the army was taking it. 'What's good enough for you is good enough for them,' Cullen reassured him.

By the time Michael and Griffith reached Dublin, de Valera had worked himself up into quite a state. When he rose in Cabinet to speak he was quivering with rage. What upset him most of all was the fact that the delegates had not referred back to him before signing, as Griffith had promised they would. He himself would have gone to London had he realised that Griffith was going to disobey his orders. De Valera argued that he would have stuck out for external association which would not have precluded eventual republican status. But now everything had been thrown away, 'without an effort, without permission of the Cabinet, or even consultation', he declared theatrically. Robert Barton countered by saying that if it had not been for the President's vacillation, the situation would never have arisen. Michael chipped in, pointing out that in a contest between a great empire and a small nation the settlement was as far as a small nation could go. Kevin O'Higgins did not like the Treaty but he felt that now it had been signed it should be supported, and he made an eloquent plea for Cabinet unity. In the end Cosgrave, Collins, Griffith and Barton voted for acceptance of the Treaty and Brugha, Stack and de Valera opposed it.

Michael left this turbulent meeting in a state of great distress. He had not been prepared for the bitter confrontation – least of all the biting venom of de Valera to whom he was still loyal and on whose support he had naïvely counted. It was this bitter opposition from a quarter he had least expected that finally broke Michael. To a close friend that evening he unburdened himself: 'Poor Ireland, back to the back rooms again,' and he wept uncontrollably. If his Chief were against him, who would be for him? 'My own brother will probably stand against me in Cork,' he sobbed bitterly. When he and Johnny met, a day or two later, Johnny criticised not Michael's judgement or want of patriotism, but the moustache which he had developed while in London. 'Next time you're shaving,' said Johnny drily, 'don't overlook that thing as well.' Michael took the advice to heart; when he reappeared at breakfast the following morning, he was clean-shaven. In the trials and tribulations of the coming weeks and months, Michael at least had the unwavering support of his family. In that respect he was luckier than many others in Ireland.

Ignoring the advice of propaganda chief Diarmuid O'Hegarty as well as Kevin O'Higgins, de Valera decided to make a strong statement, denouncing the Treaty but wording it in such a way that he sounded the soul of moderation. Nevertheless, the reaction to this statement was to divide the nation, and accelerate the descent into civil war. It is ironic that the Treaty, which was worked out as a compromise between the British and the Irish, should, by its very nature, become the instrument that divided the Irish so bitterly. Had it offered a little more or a little less, it would probably have united the nation for or against it. The immediate squabble in Cabinet was later magnified in the unseemly rumpus in the Dail, brought the wretched divisions within Sinn Fein starkly into the open, and hastened the disintegration of the country.

The tragedy is that popular support for the Treaty was strong and widespread throughout the Twenty-six Counties, though this was more marked in the more prosperous east than in the west. *The Cork Examiner* echoed general sentiments when it commented on 28 December: 'The flowing tide in favour of ratification of the Peace Treaty is submerging all opposition in its course.'

On 9 January 1922 *The Irish Times* reaffirmed this: 'The whole Nationalist Press and, as we believe, the vast majority of Southern Irishmen have accepted it with joy,' but it added a sombre note: 'Now Mr de Valera steps between Ireland and her hopes.' Four days earlier, no fewer than 328 local authorities and statutory bodies had declared themselves in favour of the Treaty, and only five against. The Catholic hierarchy was unanimously in favour, as were the Southern Protestants, the trade unions, chambers of commerce and agricultural organisations. On 10 December the Supreme Council of the IRB met and, under the impassioned eloquence of its President, declared its support for the Treaty. In the subsequent elections, the people of southern Ireland overwhelmingly supported the Treaty.

But the fly in the ointment was de Valera, around whom the extremists rapidly grouped. The showdown actually came on Wednesday, 14 December, when the Dail came together at University College to debate the Treaty and vote for ratification or rejection. Over the ensuing days there were twelve public sessions, culminating on Tuesday, 10 January. The debates were a bizarre mélange of high drama and farce punctuated by dreary, long-winded wanderings off the subject. The deputies were barely controlled at times by the Speaker, Eoin MacNeill, and in the course of the protracted sittings the entire gamut of human passions was played to the full. The most remarkable outcome of these extraordinary twelve days was the emergence of Michael Collins the consummate politician, forceful in debate and in complete mastery of the situation. An eye-witness account describes how

> Michael Collins rose to his feet. In repose his eyes glimmer softly and with humour. When aroused they narrow – hard, intense and relentless. He speaks like this. One or two words. Then he pauses to think. His speech does not flow like a stream as it does in the case of Eamon de Valera. Yet not from one word is firmness absent.[4]

He was, in truth, the Big Fellow. By contrast, his deadly opponent, the Long Fellow, was shown up as a political pygmy, a poisoned dwarf who had no compunction about sacrificing his country on the altar of his own pigheadedness.

From the beginning Michael was targeted by the anti-Treaty faction and as the sessions wore on the issue became not so much the Treaty itself, but the personal standing of Mick Collins. In the end, and to a very large extent, the voting reflected the love of or hatred for him – there could be no half measures – of the individual deputies. During the stormy sessions, Michael was for the most part calm and dignified, even stoical at times; but now and then his famous temper would explode. Strangely enough, or perhaps characteristically, what seemed to rouse his ire most of all was the inability of deputies to arrive for each session on time, thereby delaying the start of proceedings. With immense forcefulness he reminded them that punctuality was a great thing. Two factors were immediately apparent: the disagreement was set to divide opinion right across the country, and if Michael were the chief target of opprobrium he was not going to take it lying down.

The opening round centred on the delegates' terms of reference, and Michael very rapidly countered de Valera's interpretation of this, demanding that the original terms given to each delegate should be read out. When he proposed to read this de Valera interrupted him, wanting to know whether that document had ever been presented to, or accepted by, the British delegation. Griffith's comment that he had no instructions to present it were brushed aside by Dev. Michael then confirmed that the originals were, indeed, presented. Having read out the instructions which had been signed by de Valera as President, Michael continued:

> Publicly and privately we did not prejudge the issue; we even refrained from speaking to members of the Dail. I have not said a hard word about anybody. I know I have been called a traitor – [He was interrupted by cries of 'No! No!']
>
> *De Valera*: By whom?
>
> *Collins*: If I am a traitor, let the Irish people decide it or not, and if there are men who act toward me as a traitor I am prepared to meet them anywhere, at any time, now as in the past.

He went on to explain that the honour of Ireland was not involved in accepting the document. 'Ireland is fully free to accept or reject,' he said. This turned the tables on de Valera who was compelled to explain why he chose not to lead the delegation himself. He asserted that, by remaining in Dublin, he acted as a brake against any possible hasty action by the delegates. This seemed to satisfy many of the deputies, though Michael saw through this ploy from the outset. This was a red herring anyway, and an attempt was made to bring the debate back to the Treaty itself.

The Dail reassembled on 19 December, by which time the chief protagonists had taken up entrenched positions fortified by speeches well prepared in advance. Even Michael, for whom speechifying was not his forte, excelled on that occasion. Arthur Griffith began by formally moving the ratification of the Treaty and ended movingly with the ringing words, 'By that Treaty I am going to stand.' MacNeill seconded the motion: 'I take this course because I know I am doing it in the interests of my country, which I love.'

De Valera, speaking against ratification, claimed that the Treaty would not bring peace with England. 'It will not even bring peace in Ireland.' Although de Valera was usually a far better public speaker than Griffith, on this occasion there was not the same patent sincerity. There was more than a hint of petulance in de Valera's conclusion, 'Time will tell, time will tell, whether it would be a final settlement.' He was seconded by Stack who stoutly claimed, 'I stand for full independence, and nothing short of it.' These few words neatly summed up all de Valera's periphrases.

After lunch, it was Michael's turn to speak in favour of ratification. He had come with a prepared speech; the typewritten sheets lay before him, and he pointedly ignored them. Michael had none of Griffith's calm, measured approach, and certainly none of de Valera's polished precision. But he spoke from the heart, with the eager impetuosity of youth, a natural warmth and a passionate belief in what he had to say. John F. Boyle described him vividly:

> He spoke passionately, eagerly, pervadingly. He had his manuscript before him. He rarely consulted it. He preferred to rely on his intuition – on the unfailing native power of the Irishman to move, rouse and convince his hearers.
>
> Now and again he felt his smooth chin. He tossed his thick black hair with his hands. He rummaged among his documents. Like Mr de Valera, he stands now upright, now bent, now calm, and now quivering with emotion.
>
> On a previous occasion I said Michael Collins spoke slowly. He does – until he is aroused. Then the words come in a ceaseless stream . . . From beginning to end of his speech no responsibility was shirked. 'I speak plainly,' he said. He did.[5]

Even his most obdurate critics sat up and took notice. Childers, who spoke immediately after Michael, called it 'a manly, eloquent and worthy speech'. Like Griffith, Michael stuck firmly to the point and never tried to duck awkward issues. His total integrity shone through, in contrast to the windy rhetoric of his adversaries. Uncompromisingly, Michael refused to resort to subterfuge or excuse, when he could so easily have lashed out at the back-stabbing and the politicking which had gone on, even in London, among the lesser members of the delegation.

It was, for Michael, a long speech, but he emphasised that he looked upon the Treaty:

> as a plain Irishman, I believe in my own interpretation against the interpretation of any Englishman. Lloyd George and Churchill have been quoted here against us. I say the quotation of those people is what marks the

slave mind. There are people in this assembly who will take their words before they will take my words. That is the slave mind.

In a nutshell, Michael believed that the Treaty gave Ireland two things: security and freedom. 'If the Treaty gives us these or helps to get at these, then I maintain that it satisfies our national aspirations.' He pointed out that the history of Ireland was not, as was popularly believed, a military struggle of 750 years' standing, but 'a peaceful penetration' because of its economic pre-ponderance. Britain's resources were infinitely more dangerous than military dominance. The Treaty was the means of breaking this stranglehold.

He attacked those who had made snide remarks about his conduct and behaviour in London, who had hinted at succumbing to the temptations of the flesh. On the other hand, he did not give way, as he might easily have done, to a self-pitying catalogue of all the trials and tribulations with which he and the other delegates had had to contend during their delicate mission. Instead he emphasised the positive benefits accruing from the Treaty, notably Ireland's status in the community of nations known as the British Empire. To him, the independence which Ireland had now acquired was 'real and solid'.

Childers did not directly rebut Michael's statements. Instead, he examined the Treaty, clause by clause. Ironically, in so doing, he ignored his own arguments which he had previously made in favour of dominion status. Unfortunately this potentially embarrassing *volte face* was overlooked in the heat of the moment.

Barton, whom de Valera would have so precipitately expelled from the Cabinet, surprised everyone by following his cousin closely. Although he had signed the Treaty, and therefore felt obliged to stand by it, it soon became apparent that his true feelings lay on the other side. The following day Michael wrote to Kitty, full of foreboding:

> Yesterday was the worst day I ever spent in my life but thanks be to God it's over. The Treaty will almost certainly be beaten and then no one knows what will happen. The country is certainly quite clearly for it but that seems to be little good, as their voices are not heard.

On 20 December Dr MacCartan tried to put matters in perspective by his scathing remarks on both factions; the Republic had been well and truly laid to rest by both parties. This was an indirect reference to the paper drafted by de Valera as an alternative to the Treaty, and popularly known as Document No. 2, in which Dev had studiously avoided republican language. On balance, however, MacCartan had 'more respect for Michael Collins and Arthur Griffith than for the quibblers here'.

When Gavan Duffy rose to speak there was a *frisson* of anticipation. A rumour was circulating that he would repudiate the Treaty which he had signed. In the end, though, his speech was a damp squib and he showed his ambivalence neatly in the sentence, 'My heart is with those who are against the Treaty, but my head is against them.' The effect of this was countered by Eamonn Duggan, the fifth signatory, who emphasised that he had not signed under pressure, as he was not present when it was allegedly applied, but calmly and deliberately, remote from the actual scene of the discussions.

Several eye-witnesses would later comment on the change that had come over Michael at this juncture. 'Deadly serious, and the fun gone out of him' was one description. Another observed a statesmanlike thoughtfulness unnoticed in the days before he went to London. Michael now realised that the younger element in the population, the generation which would have the responsibility of running the country in the years ahead, was no longer solidly behind him. Desmond Ryan was forcibly struck by Michael's demeanour, 'with a weary and defiant face'.

In the ensuing days the debate became bogged down in irrelevance and occasionally bitter slanging matches. Kathleen Clarke set the tone for the female deputies who, as Michael feared, proved to be the shrillest opponents of the Treaty. In this she was joined by Miss Mary MacSwiney and Countess Markievicz. The latter even managed to turn her secondment of Michael's motion (to adjourn the debate till after Christmas) into a vicious personal attack on him, hinting that he was worn out and weary when he negotiated with Lloyd George, and that this physical state was brought on by his nocturnal activities. Having done the damage, she eventually apologised and the debate was adjourned until 3 January.

In the interim William Cosgrave, the Minister for Local Government, persuaded twenty of the twenty-six county councils to pass resolutions endorsing the Treaty, and this probably reflected fairly accurately the feelings of the country at large. Unfortunately the ploys of Michael and Harry Boland in ensuring that only Sinn Fein candidates of the more extreme republican variety had been chosen for the Dail were now coming home to roost. In the words of Desmond Ryan, there now resumed 'the long wrestle between ghosts and realities with all the stored-up spleens of five years flaming through the rhetoric'.[6] Meanwhile de Valera had not been idle; during the recess he applied every conceivable pressure on those deputies who had signified that they would support the Treaty, even brow-beating them with threats of treason if they did not desist. From Dev's viewpoint, as he expressed it to the Irish-American leader, Joseph McGarrity, the action of the five delegates was

> an act of disloyalty to their President and to their colleagues in the Cabinet such as is probably without parallel in history. They not merely signed the

document, but in order to make the *fait accompli* doubly secure, they
published it hours before the President or their colleagues saw it.[7]

Tim Pat Coogan shrewdly draws attention to the use of the third person,
'indicative of the state of de Valera's ego at this period'.[8] De Valera was suffering
some kind of tunnel vision, and could not understand why everyone did not
leap at his Document No. 2 as the obvious way out of the morass.

Michael, too, had used the Christmas break to try and find a solution of his
own. Taking a short break with his family at Sam's Cross, he had recharged his
spiritual and emotional batteries. On Christmas morning he and Johnny
climbed to the summit of Carraig a' Radhairc (the rock of the view).
Contemplating the panorama of tiny fields and scattered hamlets stretching
down to the coast, Michael turned to his brother and said quietly, 'I've seen
more of my own country this morning than I've ever seen in my whole life.' He
returned to Dublin refreshed and more determined than ever to get the Treaty
ratified. The small but influential Irish Labour group eventually came up with
a ploy which would have defused the situation. They proposed that the Dail
should form a committee which would be empowered to act as a Provisional
Government. This would then draw up a Constitution, a requirement of the
Treaty. The Constitution would thus emanate from the Irish people themselves,
and not be imposed on them by Westminster. Thus it would be feasible to omit
references to the oath of allegiance. This proposal was aired in the press on 4
January 1922, but swiftly rejected by de Valera who clung to his Document
No. 2 which he had reworked over the Christmas holidays, and was hell-bent
on putting this as an amendment to the motion advocating Dail ratification of
the Treaty. Had this ruse been accepted, the ratification of the Treaty would
probably have been talked out, for it would have allowed everyone to speak to
the amendment, whether or not they had already spoken. Griffith, however,
pointed out that what they were now being asked to consider was something
quite different – Document No. 3, he styled it. Well might de Valera huff and
puff about choosing his own procedure. This merely roused Griffith to
unwonted anger. Rising to his feet, he said stiffly, 'I submit it is not in the
competence of the President to choose his own procedure. This is either a
constitutional body or it is not. If it is an autocracy let you say so and we will
leave it.' When de Valera blustered that he was going to propose an amendment
on his own terms, Griffith retaliated by giving the text of Document No. 2 to
the newspapers. When this was published in full it had little appeal to the
extremists in particular, and baffled the public in general, who, comparing it
with the Treaty, could not see what all the bother was about.

Others now tried to break the log-jam. Sean T. O'Kelly called a meeting of
both factions at his house that evening to try and evolve a peace formula

acceptable to everyone. It was resolved that in order that 'the active services of President de Valera should be preserved for the nation', de Valera should be respectfully recommended to advise abstention from voting against the Treaty. In return, de Valera would be recognised as President not only of the Dail but also of the Provisional Government. Both Collins and Griffith accepted this plan but de Valera reacted very violently against the proposal, flew into a rage and volubly urged acceptance of his own pet document.

The following morning *The Freeman's Journal* savagely attacked him for 'his criminal attempt to divide the nation' by his Document No. 2 which the paper regarded as 'much worse' than the Treaty. The article ended by urging Irishmen 'to put their fate in the hands of their own countrymen', that is Collins and Griffith. Michael chivalrously wrote a letter to the paper protesting at the slur on de Valera's good name, but this conciliatory gesture had no effect. By now everyone on the Treaty side had leaned over backwards as far as they dared to appease de Valera; yet when the Dail resumed in private on 6 January he banged the table angrily and shouted, 'I am not going to connive at setting up in Ireland another government for England.' And with that he delivered his bombshell.

> What I do formally is to lay before the House my resignation. Definitely as Chief Executive authority I resign and with it goes the Cabinet . . . We worked together as one team. Now we are divided fundamentally, although we had kept together until we reached this bridge . . . This House has got my Document No. 2. It will be put before the House by the new Cabinet that will be formed if I am elected. We will put down that document. It will be submitted to the House.

Stunned silence gave way almost immediately to pandemonium, Michael, Griffith, MacCarthy and others clamouring at this wilful disregard for parliamentary procedure. Michael, in particular, railed against Tammany Hall methods and, with his jaw thrust out purposefully, he glowered at de Valera as he said that the House would not be held to ransom by three or four bullies. De Valera interjected to ask the Speaker if that was proper. MacNeill asked Michael to withdraw the term. Michael riposted, 'I can withdraw the term, but the spoken word cannot be recalled. Is that right, sir?' He went on to say that he would be satisfied with a straight vote on the Treaty, 'and then the President can have his Cabinet that will work with him and for him'.

Cathal Brugha was on his feet, saying that Collins probably had him in mind when he referred to 'bullies':

> In the ordinary way I would take exception and offence at such a term being applied to me, but the amount of offence that I would take at it would be

measured by the respect or esteem that I had for the character of the person who made the charge. In this particular instance I take no offence whatever.

An unexpected outcome of Michael's outburst about Tammany Hall was a split with his old friend Harry Boland, who had only returned from America yet again on 5 January, and took the remark personally. This moved him to retort that if Michael had had a little training in Tammany Hall and had reserved some of his bullying for Lloyd George, 'we would not be in the position we are in today'. It is not known when precisely Harry realised that Kitty Kiernan had, by this time, transferred her affections to Michael. In contrast with the passionate, lyrical letters from America, is the curt note which Harry sent to Kitty on 10 January:

> Kitty,
>   I want to congratulate you. M. told me of your engagement, and I wish you long life and happiness,
>   Ever yours,
>   H. Boland[9]

The news of Kitty's engagement to Michael could not have come as a bolt from the blue. On 5 October 1921, on the eve of his departure for America, Harry had written to her speculating as to whether he was making a big mistake in not taking her with him. 'I would just love to have you come to America where we will spend our honeymoon in perfect bliss!' This letter concluded with a very revealing passage:

> Mick and I spent the last night together. He saw me home at 2 a.m., and as I had to catch the 7.35 a.m. I bade him goodbye – only to find him at Kingsbridge as fresh as a daisy to see me off. I need not say to you how much I love him, and I know he has a warm spot in his heart for me, and I feel sure in no matter what manner our Triangle may work out, he and I shall be always friends.[10]

The courtship of Kitty and Michael went into overdrive during the London negotiations. Before leaving Dublin Michael had promised to write to her every day, and did his best although the notes were often brief, scrappy and written 'in great haste', hence the title of Leon O'Broin's collection. Kitty, on the other hand, wrote long, passionate and extremely candid letters every day in response. This correspondence reveals aspects of Michael's character not evident anywhere else. Kitty was deeply devout, and with her encouragement and example, Michael's faith, or rather the observance of it, was rekindled. Kitty's letters reveal the intensity of their love – 'a sacred and profane love' as she admits – and in recounting details of past encounters, it is very obvious that this love was consummated as frequently as possible. It is also clear that the path of true love, in this case, did not run smooth. During the discussions Kitty came over to London and appears to have compromised herself in some way. As a result, deeply engrained feelings of guilt led to stormy scenes. The tension of the relationship was becoming almost unbearable, and could not have helped Michael's mental equilibrium at a crucial stage in the negotiations.

Rumours of the affair got back to Dublin and seem to have been common knowledge in political circles. Soon this would be used as ammunition to attack Michael. The relationship would not be allowed to remain a private matter, but as the slanging in the Dail plummeted to ever lower levels, it was dragged into the political arena. During the resumed debate on 3 January, Countess Markievicz went off at a glorious tangent to tell fellow deputies that Michael Collins had broken up a royal romance. None other than Princess Mary, only daughter of King George, 'is to be married to Michael Collins who will be appointed first Governor of Saorstat Eireann'. Princess Mary was, at that time, engaged to Viscount Lascelles (whom she subsequently married). Michael was deeply embarrassed by this crude innuendo and, in characteristic manner, he responded with a rather stiff statement that lashed out at the aristocratic pretensions of the former Miss Constance Gore-Booth in no uncertain terms:

> I do not come from the class the Deputy for the Dublin Division comes from; I come from the plain people of Ireland. The lady whose name was mentioned is, I understand, betrothed to some man. I know nothing of her personally, I know nothing of her in any way whatsoever, but the statement may cause her pain and may cause pain to the lady who is betrothed to me. [Hear! Hear!] I just stand in the plain way, and I will not allow without challenge any Deputy in the assembly of my nation to insult any lady either of his nation or of any other nation. [Loud applause]

Interestingly, Michael's name was linked romantically with a number of women from the same class as Constance Markievicz. Hazel, Lady Lavery (who would later have a passionate affair with Kevin O'Higgins), alleged that she and Michael were lovers, and Edith, wife of the Marquess of Londonderry, was another who claimed to have been bedded by the lusty young Irish leader. The allegation that Moya Llewelyn Davies was another of his mistresses was never denied by the woman in question, although, like the others, it may have been no more than wishful thinking on her part. On the circumstantial evidence of these society ladies the reputation of Michael as a philanderer and womaniser has grown over the years as part of a none too subtle character assassination. From this myth is projected the sinister connotation of a sanctimonious humbug, discussing religion with Kitty Kiernan while hopping from bed to bed in London and Dublin. This canard has been meticulously examined by historians of the calibre of Dr Ryle Dwyer (1989) and Tim Pat Coogan (1990) and shown up for what it is, yet it refuses to die down.[11] The publication of the Kiernan-Collins love letters in 1983 ought to have been a powerful corrective, but certain sections of the press on both sides of the Irish Sea are not noted for letting the truth get in the way of a lurid story.

On Saturday, 7 January 1922, the Treaty was ratified by the Dail. In the closing debate, about five o'clock in the afternoon, Cathal Brugha rose to address the deputies. What was intended as a reasoned argument against the Treaty rapidly degenerated into a virulent personal attack on Michael Collins, which climaxed with three questions: what real position Collins held in the army; what fights Collins had taken an active part in; and 'can it be authoritatively stated that he ever fired a shot at any enemy of Ireland?'. Brugha added that he approached this matter with great reluctance, and would never have brought it up had it not been for a remark by Arthur Griffith that Michael Collins was the man who won the war. At that point Griffith himself shouted, 'Hear! Hear!' and Fionan Lynch added, 'So he did!'

Ignoring these and other interjections, Brugha proceeded to answer his own questions. Collins was merely the head of one of the sub-sections of the Headquarters Staff, adding that none sought notoriety except one and 'whether he is responsible or not for the notoriety I am not going to say'. Relentlessly he carried on:

> One member was specially selected by the press and the people to put him into a position which he never held; he was made a romantic figure, a mystical character such as this person certainly is not; the gentleman I refer to is Mr Michael Collins –
> *Duggan:* The Irish people will judge that.
> *Milroy:* Now we know things.
> *MacCarthy:* Now we know the reason for the opposition to the Treaty.[12]

Sean MacGarry was appalled by Brugha's conduct and said gruffly, 'I think we've had enough'; but MacCarthy with tongue in cheek complained that 'I must protest against the Minister of Defence being interrupted. He is making a good speech for the Treaty'. Brugha's attempts to humiliate Michael in the Dail failed. In fact, as MacCarthy hinted, it boomeranged. Many deputies who were hitherto uncertain which way to vote now looked at both Michael Collins and Cathal Brugha with fresh eyes. Sympathy for the Big Fellow and what he had had to endure from Cabinet colleagues was evident, while Brugha undoubtedly weakened his own arguments (whatever they might have been) by his patently unfair attack on Michael's war record. Suddenly, the mighty Cuchullain, hero of the Rising, was seen for what he really was, a petty-minded, spiteful nonentity, insanely jealous of the one man who had kept the struggle going during the dark days of the Black and Tans. The Brugha performance certainly brought out into the open the vendetta, and probably made everyone in the Dail more aware of the unseemly wrangles that had been going on, behind the scenes, for so long.

Brugha's speech was therefore something of an anti-climax. In a rather homely touch, the House then adjourned for tea. When it resumed at 7.15 p.m. Harry Boland made a brief statement explaining the circumstances in which he had made two speeches in America recently, the first for the Treaty and the second against. At the end of his speech he said:

> Apart from the propriety of introducing a private conversation I find it necessary to make a personal explanation; I certainly hope we won't reproduce any more private conversations.
>
> *Collins*: You cannot stand them, Harry, You stood for the Treaty first.
>
> *Boland*: No! and you know it, Michael.

Arthur Griffith was one of the last to speak, impelled to do so because of an earlier fatuous remark by Brugha who had (on 3 January) urged him to repudiate the Treaty which he had signed. If he dishonoured his signature his name would live for ever in Ireland.

Griffith's response to this ludicrous suggestion was to be one of the best speeches he ever delivered. At all times dignified, it showed occasional flights of passion and, above all, demonstrated that he was indeed a man of unshakeable principles. He took the opportunity to rebut Brugha's attack on Michael by eulogising the latter:

> He was the man whose matchless energy, whose indomitable will, carried Ireland through the terrible crisis; and though I have not now, and never had, an ambition about either political affairs or history, if my name is to go down in history I want it to be associated with the name of Michael Collins.

The poet George Russell, who heard this speech, thought that it was 'extraordinarily fine, I did not think he could have spoken with such fire and on such a high level'.[13] Griffith sat down at 8.30 p.m. and de Valera immediately jumped to his feet to protest that the Treaty 'would rise in judgement against the men who say there is only a shadow of difference –' Before he could mention his precious Document No. 2, Michael cut him off in mid-sentence with: 'Let the Irish nation judge us now and for future years.'

The vote was then held, the deputies being called by Diarmuid O'Hegarty one by one, in alphabetical order of their constituencies. Outside the chamber, the hubbub of voices was stilled and everyone craned to hear the results. As luck would have it, County Armagh was the first. Michael rose in his seat and, facing the Speaker, spoke in Irish: '*Is toil* (for)'. O'Hegarty went through the 120 deputies, each standing to respond '*Is toil*' or '*Ni toil*'. Then the second constituencies were called. When Cork was called out, Michael rose in his place and said that he claimed no second vote. De Valera did likewise, but both Griffith and Milroy objected to the disenfranchisement of their second constituencies. In the end MacNeill ruled that each deputy should have only one vote. The votes were totalled and MacNeill read the result: 'Sixty-four for approval and fifty-seven against. That is a majority of seven in favour of approval of the Treaty.'

De Valera then rose and said that it was his duty to resign as Chief Executive, but Michael jumped up and protested against it. The younger man spoke with warmth and sincerity, and his voice shook with emotion as he urged the President to carry on. With his hand outstretched, Michael, in a highly emotional state, reaffirmed his love for Dev, but this momentary idyll was shattered by Mary MacSwiney who shrieked in vehement denunciation of what she termed 'the betrayal of this glorious nation'.

In his closing statement de Valera said:

> I would like my last word here to be this: we have had a glorious record for
> four years; it has been four years of magnificent discipline in our nation.
> The world is looking at us now . . .

At that juncture he broke down and sank tearfully into his seat. Brugha stepped into the embarrassing breach with what, in hindsight, were ironic words: 'So far as I am concerned, I will see, at any rate, that discipline is kept in the army.'

The Dail then adjourned.

On Monday, 9 January, it reassembled but the debate rapidly broke down into a babel of proposals, rejections, counter-proposals, interjections, violent interruptions and total chaos. It began with a moment of high drama when de Valera formally tendered his resignation as president of the Dail. This was a historic moment, which elicited considerable sympathy from both factions. In the ensuing vacuum, Michael proposed a joint committee of pro- and anti-Treaty groups to patch up the split, but he was interrupted by Sean MacEntee from Belfast who refused to subvert the Republic.

Kathleen Clarke proposed the immediate re-election of de Valera, and Liam Mellowes seconded this, but Padraig O'Maille and Michael Collins condemned it. This was the old pugnacious Collins once more. He leaped to his feet, his burly frame seeming to radiate nervous energy. His jaw thrust forward aggressively, he argued tersely for an end to the pointless discussion. The Dail had voted; he was impatient to move on and settle the outstanding business, but he was ignored as speaker after speaker rose to address the House, occasionally even dealing with the matter in hand, but more often straying from the point to some pet hobby-horse. Liam de Roiste warned that this perilous situation might delay the British evacuation, but Austin Stack, predictably, said that he was for a Republic and de Valera. Dr MacCartan nodded, but pointed out that Document No. 2 was hardly Republican in tone. Michael interceded: 'No tactics! Let's be honest.'

Then he proposed an amendment, 'that this House ask Mr Griffith to form a Provisional Executive'. His old comrade in arms, Sean MacEoin, seconded the proposal, remarking that he regretted that he could find no man on the opposite side with courage enough to support the decision of the assembly.

The vote on the resolution to re-elect de Valera was taken and defeated by two votes, fifty-eight for and sixty against. Both de Valera and de Roiste refused to vote, the latter claiming that he would not be a party to plunging his country into 'fratricidal strife'. The atmosphere subsided as the import of this sank in. De Valera, mustering something of the quality that would make him a statesman one day, assured the pro-Treaty faction that they would want the help of his party yet, and 'we will be there with you against any outside enemy at any price'.

The following day the debate swiftly mired in the question, raised by de Valera, whether Griffith would use the office of president, if so elected, to further the aims of the Treaty. Griffith refused to be drawn. In his usual blunt manner he promised to 'keep the Republic in being until such time as the establishment of the Free State is put to the people, to decide for or against'. And he concluded uncompromisingly:

> Let nobody have the slightest misunderstanding about where I stand. I am in favour of this Treaty. I want this Treaty put into operation. I want the Provisional Government set up. I want the Republic to remain in being until the time when the people can have a Free State election, and give their vote.

The raucous Mary MacSwiney jumped to her feet and pleaded with Griffith to promise not to merge the office of president with that of head of the Provisional Government. It was the ultimate nonsense, and even de Valera laughed heartily at this ridiculous entreaty. Michael chose this moment to move to the election of Griffith as president. At that, de Valera's mood darkened and he spoke with vehemence:

> As a protest against the election as President of the Irish Republic of the Chairman of the Delegation, who is bound by the Treaty conditions to set up a State which is to subvert the Republic, and who, in the interim period, instead of using the office as it should be used – to support the Republic – will, of necessity, have to be taking action which will tend to its destruction, I, while this vote is being taken, as one, am going to leave the House.

As de Valera got up and walked from the chamber he was followed by the great majority of his supporters. Michael, momentarily taken aback, jumped up and cried: 'Deserters all! We will now call on the Irish people to rally to us. Deserters all!'

Daithi Ceannt fired back, 'Up the Republic!'

'Deserters all to the Irish nation in her hour of trial,' shouted Michael. 'We will stand by her.'

'Oath-breakers and cowards!' screamed Countess Markievicz.

'Foreigners! Americans! English!' bawled Michael, a jibe at de Valera, Childers and the redoubtable Constance, who had been born in London and who had married a penniless Polish aristocrat.

'Lloyd Georgeites!' she riposted as she flounced out of the chamber.

Above the hubbub could be heard the steady voice of Cosgrave asking, 'Now, Sir, will you put the question?'

Thereupon, Arthur Griffith was elected President of the Dail. The roll was then called and sixty-one deputies answered their names. Almost immediately Griffith appointed his Cabinet: Collins (Finance), Gavan Duffy (Foreign Affairs), Duggan (Home Affairs), Cosgrave (Local Government), O'Higgins (Economic Affairs) and Mulcahy (Defence). Thus four of the five signatories of the Treaty were in this Cabinet; the fifth man, Robert Barton, had left the chamber with de Valera.

In this dramatic manner the Second Dail had its stormy birth. The following day Griffith had circulars sent to all deputies summoning them to a session on 14 January to ratify the Treaty. In the event, the anti-Treaty members boycotted the proceedings, just as assuredly as Sinn Fein had abstained from Westminster in 1919. The ratification of the Treaty was a mere formality, a curtain-raiser to the main business which was to select a Provisional Government. In this body Griffith had no position and Michael was appointed chairman. There was now an anomalous situation: Dail Eireann, with its President and his Cabinet, co-existed with the Provisional Government of which Michael was chairman. Several ministers held posts in both the Dail Cabinet and the Provisional Government.

It was now up to the Provisional Government to receive certain powers and functions from Westminster in order to draft a Constitution; and to call a general election so that the people of Ireland could decide on the Treaty. As its name implied, the Provisional Government (*Rialtas Sealadach*) was an interim arrangement which, at the end of the year, would be automatically replaced by the government of the Irish Free State (*Saorstat Eireann*). By inference, the Second Dail would also come to an end at that time, and transfer its authority to the Dail of the Free State.

CHAPTER 15

Civil War, 1922

―――――

> It was an episode which has burned so deep into the heart
> and mind of Ireland that it is not yet possible for the
> historian to approach it with the detailed knowledge or the
> objectivity which it deserves . . .
>
> F.S.J. LYONS, *Ireland Since the Famine* (1971)

TWO DAYS AFTER THE TREATY DEBATES OF THE DAIL CAME TO A stormy conclusion, Sinn Fein held an *Ard-Comhairle* (high council). Michael arrived at noon looking 'tired, worried and preoccupied'.[1] Something of his state of mind can be gleaned from those daily notes and letters to Kitty. On 9 January he had written, 'I'm absolutely fagged out and worn out and everything . . . If you knew how the other side is killing me – God help me.'[2] He hoped that she might have come up to Dublin in his hour of need but she was depressed and physically unwell with the worry of it all. Michael himself spoke of his own depression, in a letter of 11 January. Kitty's anxieties over the deteriorating political situation were compounded by getting Harry Boland's curt note. In the midst of all his other troubles, therefore, Michael had to reassure his fiancée: 'I did not tell Harry – just said to him that he had little chance in that quarter now, so you're not to worry about that.'[3] This note was written during the Sinn Fein council, Michael trying to snatch a moment:

> I can't write at this damned table as everybody is shaking it and, in addition,
> my pen is bad so I'm in a sad way for those two reasons. And further, this
> place is full of people and I'm wishing to God I was away with you.

Michael clung pathetically to old loyalties, little realising how far reciprocation had vanished. In misery and rage he lashed out at former comrades who now deserted him. Hearing some gossip about himself one day he flung his hat furiously across the room shouting, 'Anyone can talk of Michael Collins!' Another time he heard that an erstwhile friend was slandering him. 'But it isn't the label they attach to me,' he said quietly. 'It is the label I attach to myself that makes me what I am.'[4]

Griffith likewise was strained and withdrawn, while his haggard appearance betrayed the tremendous toll on his stamina over recent months. By contrast de Valera, having shot his bolt, appeared calm, almost ebullient at times. Those who attended this surprisingly cordial *Ard-Combairle* formed the impression that a great burden had passed from de Valera to the shoulders of Collins and Griffith. De Valera, now shorn of executive responsibility, felt free to criticise the new régime.

Michael, on the other hand, had never been so unsure of himself in all his life. He saw himself as a soldier, not as a politician and, as he confessed to John O'Kane on 21 January, 'The more the rigmarole of my life continues to encompass politics the more uneasy I feel.' Michael was, in political terms, a babe in arms. He was thoroughly, even desperately, sincere and patently so. He wore his heart on his sleeve and was touchingly naïve. The downright honesty, implacable integrity and bluff boyish charm which had got him where he was, fitted him ill for the position he now found himself in. He took the split very much to heart. It was a grievous tragedy for which he felt personally responsible, and as events rolled inexorably towards open conflict his depression deepened. At a time when he should have been basking in the acclaim of the nation for having achieved a practical deal from the British – if not actual freedom itself, then the freedom to achieve freedom – he was beset by worry and dread and this tended to have a paralysing effect.

On 14 January the pro-Treaty element of the Dail met again to elect the Provisional Government, but on this occasion Michael was not his usual forthright, decisive self. Indeed, he had to be almost goaded into action by Griffith and Cosgrave. They perceived that strong government was required at this critical stage, and looked to Michael to provide it. But now they could see the young man beginning to unravel as the enormity of his position dawned on him. During the ensuing days and weeks there was a very real fear that Michael might undo much of the good work of the Treaty because he was not prepared to be ruthless enough with his opponents. It was at this time that the close comradeship that had grown up between Michael and Griffith during the negotiations began to founder. Griffith saw all too clearly that civil war was imminent and probably unavoidable. It was imperative that the campaign should be as short, sharp and decisive as possible.

On the Treaty side was the IRB, firmly under Michael's control, which thus gave him the support of a large proportion of the Irish Republican Army, especially the veterans who had fought the British. Ironically, this element contained many of the young idealists who had enlisted to fight to the death for the Republic but never thought the day would come when they beat the

British into giving way. When the Truce came, however, and they found themselves in uniform, with pay in their pockets, the desire to die for the Republic evaporated. Nevertheless, there was a hard core of the old guard, including such prominent figures as Tom Barry, Tom Hales, Liam Lynch, Liam Mellowes, Ernie O'Malley and Rory O'Connor, who fiercely opposed the Treaty. One of the reasons for Michael's indecision was his extreme reluctance to take up arms against old comrades.

The veterans were not the only ones who were anxious for peace. The Church, the trade unions and big business were united in desiring an end to years of conflict, and the particular form of government did not interest them overmuch. To these bodies could be added the Southern Unionists who were prepared to throw their weight behind the Free State, as well as the great bulk of the ordinary people to whom politics meant little.

Ranged against this majority was the vociferous, highly politicised minority led by de Valera, Childers, Brugha and Stack. Barton (perhaps influenced by his English cousin, Childers) switched sides, as did Gavan Duffy. Then there were the female deputies who included the formidable Maud Gonne MacBride and the widow of Michael O'Callaghan, the murdered Mayor of Limerick, as well as Mary MacSwiney, Kathleen Clarke and Countess Markievicz. The last-named had founded and organised the powerful women's organisation, Cumann na mBan, and it, too, was solidly anti-Treaty. Opposition to Collins, ironically, was strongest in his home county which had a long history of Republicanism and which would become one of the chief battlegrounds in the conflict, while Kerry and Tipperary which had seen the fiercest clashes with the British were also anti-Treaty. In addition to geographic considerations there was a Marxist factor. The anti-Treaty faction attracted men and women who were on the far left of the labour movement and whose ultimate goal was a workers' republic. Liam Mellowes, the great disciple of James Connolly, came into this category but so also, surprisingly, in view of her aristocratic background, did Constance Markievicz.

In accordance with the terms of the Treaty, Dublin Castle was surrendered to the Provisional Government on 16 January. This was a historic moment and Michael savoured it to the full, expressing the wish that this symbol of English terror and oppression ought to be treasured as a national memorial to freedom. Michael, however, was late for the appointment with Macready, leaving the General fuming at 'this mark of disrespect'. No disrespect was intended, for Michael was delayed by a rail strike on his journey back from Granard, where he had spent the weekend with Kitty. It was a bitterly cold day as Michael drove up to the Castle without ceremony. The senior civil servants were lined up, apprehensive at meeting the man whose hands were 'stained with outrage and crime', but Michael instantly dispelled this feeling. He 'grasped their hands with his iron grip and shook them warmly with the greatest bonhomie'.[5]

Eight days later the 'Southern Parliament' was convened and comprised the sixty-four pro-Treaty members of the Second Dail, together with the four Unionist representatives of Trinity College. This parliament elected the Provisional Government which would pave the way for the Free State. While Arthur Griffith continued as President of the Dail, Michael was Chairman of the Provisional Government. Both had their own Cabinets, with overlapping membership, although it was strange that Richard Mulcahy, Minister of Defence in the Dail, was not a member of the Provisional Government. The retention of the Dail Government was deliberate: it had been established in the name of the Republic. The Provisional Government, on the other hand, was set up under the Treaty as a caretaker administration, unless the people should reject it at the polls. The first offices of the Provisional Government were in the City Hall, Dublin. The fact that the Provisional Government sprang from the loins of the Southern Parliament was a major reason for the anti-Treaty faction refusing to recognise its legality. They now formed Cumann na Poblachta (the Republic League) as the anti-Treaty political party, but before long the respective sides came to be known simply as the Free Staters and the Republicans. The latter agitated for a resolution of the legal question by putting the matter to the vote of the Irish people in the proper democratic manner. A general election was, indeed, held on 16 June, but by that time the political posturing had been overtaken by military events.

Over the weekend of 21–22 January Michael was again in London for meetings with Churchill at the Colonial office to go over the finer points of the Irish Free State (Agreement) Bill which Churchill and Birkenhead piloted through both Houses of Parliament so skilfully that it received the royal assent on 31 March. Churchill had arranged for Michael to have a private meeting that day with the Ulster Unionist, Sir James Craig. Churchill graphically described the historic encounter between the leaders of the two Irelands:

> On January 21 they met in my room at the Colonial Office, which, despite its enormous size, seemed overcharged with electricity. They both glowered magnificently, but after a short, commonplace talk I slipped away upon some excuse and left them together. What these two Irishmen, separated by such gulfs of religion, sentiment, and conduct, said to each other I cannot tell. But it took a long time, and, as I did not wish to disturb them, mutton chops, etc, were tactfully introduced about one o'clock. At four o'clock the Private Secretary reported signs of movement on the All-Ireland front and I ventured to look in. They announced to me complete

agreement reduced to writing. They were to help each other in every way; they were to settle outstanding points by personal discussion; they were to stand together within the limits agreed against all disturbers of the peace. We three then joined in the best of all pledges, to wit, 'To try to make things work'.[6]

According to Major Sir Ralph Furse, the 'etc' consisted of several bottles of Guinness, and he commented fulsomely on the inspiration that thus regaled the two Irishmen in the search for mutual goodwill. Nevertheless, the Craig–Collins Pact was negotiated in spite of, rather than because of, the liquid refreshment, for Michael loathed the very sight of porter. The five-point agreement called for a conference of elected representatives for all Ireland to draw up a constitution that would guarantee the North its autonomy. The Boundary Commission was to be scrapped and Collins and Craig would work together to sort out the boundary. Craig agreed that the 10,000 Catholic workers expelled from the shipyards should be reinstated. Collins agreed to call off the Belfast boycott. Finally both men agreed to find a solution to the problem of Republican prisoners in Northern gaols, some of them facing execution.

Amid the weighty affairs of state, Michael also found time to raise with the British the delicate matter of the Lane bequest. Sir Hugh Lane had bequeathed his collection of paintings to Ireland by a codicil in his will that was hotly disputed, most notably by Lord Curzon as a trustee of the National Gallery in London where the pictures then reposed. Lane's aunt, Lady Gregory, had been battling for Ireland in this vexatious matter since 1915 and at one stage had persuaded Ian Macpherson, then Chief Secretary for Ireland, to draw up a Bill to legalise the disputed codicil. Now, at the suggestion of Sir John Lavery, she had written to Michael personally on 14 January begging him to intercede: 'I agree with Lavery that you can best do what he has failed in doing through nearly seven years.' Michael wrote back to Lady Gregory on 23 January saying that he had raised the matter and found the British government's advisers 'not unsympathetic'. Michael promised to keep nagging the British on this and, in due course, Curzon was overruled and the paintings returned to Ireland, where they form the nucleus of the Hugh Lane Gallery in Dublin to this day.

The Craig–Collins Pact lasted barely a week. On his return to Belfast Craig ran into such a wall of acrimony over the boundary matter that he was compelled to renege on the deal. On 27 January he assured a large gathering that there would be no change that left 'our Ulster area any less than it is'. Only twenty Catholics got their jobs back and Craig was powerless to put pressure on the shipyards.

On Thursday, 2 February, Michael had a further meeting with Craig, this time in Dublin, to discuss sundry matters of mutual concern, but the meeting broke up as soon as Michael unrolled a map showing the portions of the Six Counties which, by right, ought to join the Free State. Both Michael and Sir James subsequently put out statements, rather simplistically accusing each other of bad faith and breaking their previous agreement. This provoked an immediate summons to both men from Churchill. On Monday, 6 February, and again on Wednesday, 15 February, Michael was in London for further meetings at the Colonial Office, but neither made the slightest headway. From their now entrenched positions Collins and Craig would not budge. The demarcation that exists to this day had now fallen across Ireland.

On the latter trip Michael also visited the House of Lords to examine the homosexual passages in the alleged diaries of Sir Roger Casement (executed for his part in the Easter Rising) before meeting Lloyd George at 10 Downing Street. These meetings were one-day affairs, Michael usually travelling overnight in both directions to save time. His letters to Kitty indicate that he was 'thinking and dreaming of you' during these all-night travels. A letter from Kitty, which he received on his return to Dublin on 16 February, contained a very perceptive warning against her former boyfriend, Harry Boland:

> I want to talk to you again. One of the things, about drinking with H.B. If he is *not* to be trusted in other things, I wouldn't take much of that particular thing with him. Enough said!

Michael's response, in a letter written that night, was

> That was rather severe, what you said about H. this morning but I'm not so sure that your keen womanly 'horse sense' is not right. I have noticed a very uncommon instinct in you in that regard. It's better than my own often. It really is.

A happier matter was recorded the following day. On 16 February Lord FitzAlan formally handed over the instruments of power to Michael as Chairman of the Provisional Government. On that date the administration of posts and telegraphs passed from London to Dublin, James J. Walsh being appointed Postmaster General. Like Michael, he was a Corkman who had passed the first ever examination for entry to the Post Office, a decade before Michael took the same step. During the Easter Rising he had been in charge of the Republican telegraph system. Sentenced to death for his part in the Rising, he was reprieved and given penal servitude for life. Elected to the First Dail, he led the Irish delegation to a conference at the General Post Office London at the beginning of February to sort out the transfer of powers. This included the use of British stamps overprinted in Gaelic script which went on sale on 17 February. Writing to Kitty that morning, Michael drew her attention to the fact that 'The stamp on this was the first Free State stamp ever licked by a member of the Free State Provisional Government. That much for you – it was, of course, licked by me for you.'

In the realm of external affairs some progress was made. After the breakdown of the Craig–Collins Pact at the end of January there had been a wave of attacks on Catholics in the North. Michael had countered by ordering renewal of IRA attacks in the Six Counties, as well as taking hostages of Ulster policemen whenever they strayed across the border. Churchill decried this hostage-taking as 'more suited to the Balkans than to Ireland'. Michael pressed Churchill to use British troops for the protection of the Catholic communities in the North. Instead, to his horror he found, on 15 March, that Craig was inviting that arch-enemy of Nationalist Ireland, Sir Henry Wilson, to take charge of the restoration of law and order in the Six Counties. Six days later Michael sent off a hotly worded letter of protest to Churchill, though he ended on a conciliatory note reminding the Colonial Secretary that he was 'most anxious for harmony with Belfast'. On 30 March an eleven-point agreement was signed by Sir James Craig, the Marquess of Londonderry and E.M. Archdale on behalf of the Government of Northern Ireland, and by Michael Collins, Eamonn Duggan, Kevin O'Higgins and Arthur Griffith on behalf of the Provisional Government. The treaty was countersigned on behalf of the British authorities by Churchill and Worthington-Evans. This agreement was designed to ease the tension between Catholics and Orangemen in the North, to call off the boycott of Belfast goods and to work towards the Boundary Commission that would delimit the northern state along religious and political lines. Sad to say, the agreement lasted only nine days.

Within the Twenty-Six Counties, problems were just as intractable. The points at issue between pro- and anti-Treatyites were the oath of allegiance, the defence commitments (leaving Britain in control of certain naval bases) and the vexed question of partition. Neither side was at all happy with any of these points, and the sole difference between them was that Michael was prepared to go along with them for the time being, as a stepping-stone to full independence. Ironically, de Valera would eventually accept the first two, when he came to power in 1932, and partition was a matter that everyone recognised was going to be the toughest nut to crack. At the end of the day, people would look back on 1922 and wonder sadly why it had ever been necessary to fight each other. The problem in the spring of 1922 was that Ireland had more government than she could handle. The Provisional Government had to contend with the Dail (which should have been adjourned *sine die*), while, on the other side, the anti-Treaty deputies were headed by de Valera who was largely ignored by the anti-Treaty element in the army.

The shape of things to come emerged as the British army began to evacuate its bases and hand them over to the Irish army. This force, however, was now beginning to polarise along political lines, often dictated by the outlook of the divisional or brigade commanders. Thus the First, Second and Third Southern Divisions, the Second, Third and Fourth Western Divisions and the Fourth Northern Division leaned to the Republican side, along with the influential Dublin Brigade led by Oscar Traynor, but the political outlook of army units was very difficult to assess accurately. The situation was confused by the fact that both factions (known to each other as Mulcahyites and Irregulars) were, theoretically, part of the IRA, and there was a move to take it out of civil control by summoning a Volunteer Convention, just as they had done in the old days; but this was forestalled. By the Convention of 26 March the anti-Treaty faction broke away from the Volunteer Army, repudiated both the Dail and de Valera, and formally assumed the title of the Irish Republican Army under the effective command of Rory O'Connor. Meanwhile, one of the first acts of the Provisional Government was to begin recruiting for the National Army, with Lieutenant-General J.J. 'Ginger' O'Connell as Chief of Staff.

The first clash occurred at Limerick early in March when pro-Treaty troops clashed with anti-Treaty forces. The latter tried to take control of the Castle and Strand barracks as they were vacated by the British army, and in a bid to prevent this pro-Treaty troops from Dublin were rushed to the city. There was also a territorial element to this struggle, the men of Clare and Limerick bitterly resentful of the Dubliners.[7] Shots were exchanged but Liam Lynch negotiated a stand-off. Thereafter there was an uneasy lull for several weeks, during which de Valera whipped up passions in a series of fiery speeches – at Dungarvan on 16 March, at Carrick-on-Suir and Thurles on St Patrick's Day, and at Killarney on 19 March. It was on the last-named occasion that he concluded his speech with the notorious words:

> If we continue on that movement which was begun when the Volunteers were started, and we suppose this Treaty is ratified by your votes, then these men, in order to achieve freedom, will have, as I said yesterday, to march over the dead bodies of their own brothers. They will have to wade through Irish blood.

Michael likewise was stumping round the country, addressing meetings in a frantic bid to counter the charismatic de Valera. He entered into this frenzied activity with no great enthusiasm, disliking such rallies where he was very much in the limelight; but once embarked on this course he gave it his all. Lacking the deviousness and circumspection of the born politician, he was forthright, backing his blunt speaking with dramatic gestures. What he may have lacked in natural oratory he made up for in his appearance and personality. The Big Fellow was every inch the leader. He had a happy knack of gauging the mood of a meeting very quickly. He never forgot that he was speaking to ordinary men and women, and he kept his message simple, with plain words that everyone could understand. He enjoyed the thrust and parry of the verbal duel with hecklers, providing his audience with instant entertainment, then despatching his interrupters with a telling phrase. At a vast rally in Cork on 12 March a Mrs Agnellis was standing near the front of the throng, and left an interesting account of the occasion:

> He was at one and the same time the youthful dashing leader we had learned to love and admire; and yet a figure on which strain, worry and overwork had taken their toll. There came a momentary lull in his speech, and I said, not loudly enough as I thought, 'God bless you, Michael Collins.' He looked down from the raised platform on which he was standing, and said quite plainly, 'I need it.'[8]

Returning from this meeting, Michael was met at a wayside station by a little group of ragged children who solemnly pressed a bunch of shamrock into his great paw. Michael's eyes brimmed with tears as he accepted the ragamuffins' good wishes. His stomach was playing him up again, and he was feeling the cold; but this spontaneous gesture put new mettle in him.

The Volunteer Convention took place at the Mansion House on 26 March in a futile bid to patch up the quarrel, but ended with differences unresolved. The Republican element of the Convention reassembled on 9 April with Liam Lynch as Chief of Staff in the chair. A General Staff was appointed and headquarters were established in the Gaelic League Hall in Parnell Square. For several days the Republican IRA maintained a precarious existence in this rather cramped building, and on several occasions they feared an attack by troops of the new National Army. Meanwhile, starved of funds from government sources, the Republicans took matters into their own hands by staging a series of bank raids. In the latter part of March and throughout April there were numerous clashes and skirmishes, as anti-Treaty elements tried to seize barracks, commandeer vehicles and disarm pro-Treaty forces, as well as generally intimidate Treaty sympathisers. Newspaper offices, in particular, were targeted. Michael himself had personal experience of this. At Cork on 14 March, for example, armed men roughly barred his entry to the Republican cemetery, and that night a would-be assassin, brandishing a pistol in his face, was overpowered by Sean MacEoin, who would have shot the man on the spot had Michael not said, 'Let the bastard go.' A few weeks later he was assailed outside Vaughan's Hotel by gunmen. Drawing his automatic, Michael tried to fire a warning shot but the gun jammed. Coolly he seized a rifle from one of his attackers and held him at gunpoint till he could be marched off to Mountjoy; the rest of the party fled in disarray. Michael bitterly conceded, in a speech at Wexford on 9 April, that 'our country is now in a more lawless and chaotic state than it was during the Black and Tan régime'. In vain, Griffith urged him to take action to stamp out this lawlessness. There was evidence that individual divisional commanders, notably Ernie O'Malley and Seamus Robinson, were in danger of becoming petty warlords.

Then, on the night of 13–14 April, a group of Volunteers commanded by Rory O'Connor seized the Four Courts in the very heart of Dublin. This fine eighteenth-century building, designed by James Gandon, was one of the great landmarks of the city. Having failed to learn a vital lesson from the General Post Office débâcle in 1916, the Republicans now proceeded to fortify the Four Courts. The massive building, built on four sides of a square, housed not only the law courts but the tax offices and records of the British administration. Thus its seizure was a symbolic blow against the establishment, both the old and the new. The Republicans put Paddy O'Brien in command of the garrison, with Sean Lemass, a future *Taoiseach*, as adjutant.

The Four Courts garrison sent written demands to the Dail: the Republic was to be upheld and no elections were to be held so long as the threat of renewed conflict with Britain existed. As this bellicose action was the very thing most calculated to bring back the British in force, Michael's Provisional Government was on the horns of a dilemma. In vain Griffith continually nagged him to take punitive action. Days passed into weeks, and still the Four Courts, with its sandbags and barbed-wire entanglements, maintained defiance of the constitutional authority. Matters became worse when the insurgents began directing their campaign from the Four Courts, organising a renewal of the boycott of Belfast goods as a reprisal for the pogroms in the North, as well as stepping up the frequency of raids on banks and post offices. There is no doubt that many of these robberies were examples of private enterprise. Raids sanctioned by headquarters were given a semblance of legality when the officers in charge handed over receipts for the money taken; but latterly no such niceties were observed and the country as a whole was antagonised by these acts of banditry.

Still Michael refused to act. After two weeks a half-hearted attempt at a peace conference was organised by Archbishop Walsh and the Lord Mayor, Laurence O'Neill. Griffith refused point-blank to have any truck with the rebels, and it was only through the mediation of the Labour group that the two sides could even be brought face to face. Inevitably, negotiations collapsed on 25 April, Michael and Griffith being adamant that elections must be held on the issue of the Treaty.

In a multifaceted personality like Michael's there were bound to be contradictions and paradoxes. No one could ever have doubted his keen sense of patriotism, yet he would later be branded as a traitor for having sold out to the British and signed the Treaty. But Michael was a pragmatist: the Treaty was as much as he would get out of the British in 1921 and it was, as he saw it, a stepping stone to the ultimate goal of an independent, sovereign Ireland. By signing the Treaty he implicitly accepted the partition of Ireland; but while he vehemently defended the Treaty in the Dail and on the hustings with all the powers of oratory at his command, he was secretly working to undermine a major part of its terms. His reluctance to take firm action against the Four Courts rebels, or indeed against the anti-Treaty Irregulars in general, was partly due to the fact that they were old comrades in arms, but partly also because Michael remained totally committed to his Nationalist ideals.

In desiring a united Ireland with its own parliament, Michael had the backing of the British Cabinet which had come to just such a decision as early as December 1919. The problem, of course, was the violent opposition of the Orangemen in the north-east. When the question of making some provision for Ulster was mooted, it was originally suggested that the entire province, comprising nine counties, should be administered separately for the time being, the assumption being that such an enlarged area would have a Nationalist majority which, sooner or later, would vote for incorporation in the Free State. Not surprisingly, only a few days later, the Unionists rejected this and settled for the six Protestant counties. It was Sir James Craig himself who suggested a Boundary Commission to decide which areas along the border should go to the Free State and which to Northern Ireland. Once this commission was set up, however, Craig and his supporters did everything to obstruct and undermine its operations.

It soon became apparent that the real issue in the North was not religion, but power, although the religious factor was used to distinguish between Nationalist and Unionist. Thousands of Catholics, who had obtained war work in the shipyards and factories of Belfast and Londonderry, were driven out by murderous Orange mobs. There was an outbreak of what the British press euphemistically termed 'incendiarism', disguising the horror of the families waking up in the night to find their houses well and truly ablaze, as 'the men with the matches' went about their deadly business. Thousands of Catholics were burned out of their homes and hundreds perished as a result. Ironically, the British government gave way to the twisted logic of the Loyalists who demanded to be armed and organised in order to prevent unorganised retaliation that might bring them into conflict with the British forces. Out of this argument came the A, B and C Specials, respectively full-time, part-time and only called out in extreme emergencies. The Specials also got around the criticism that the RIC was tainted because many Catholics served in its ranks; from the outset the Specials were little more than a government-sanctioned Loyalist paramilitary force, evolving out of the pre-war UVF, and carrying on the policies of the Black and Tans with grim enthusiasm. The harassment of Catholics escalated sharply after the Specials came into being.

The worst single atrocity took place on 23 March 1922 when a group of Specials disguised as regular RIC broke into the home of the MacMahon family, lined up the father, his four sons and a lodger, Edward McKinney, and shot them in cold blood. Four were killed outright but John MacMahon survived, though seriously wounded in the head and chest, while his youngest brother, a boy of eleven, emerged unscathed from his hiding-place under the table. It was common knowledge that this deed was perpetrated by the death squads organised by the RIC's counter-insurgency division, in which thugs like Captain Hardy, Constable Igoe and Prescott Decies played a prominent part.

It was to counter the alarming growth in what has now come to be termed 'ethnic cleansing' that Michael was compelled to equip and arm the Northern IRA, at a time when he was taking steps to combat the IRA in the south and west of Ireland. When he learned that the British government was footing the bill for the Specials (£5 million), Michael was goaded into the extraordinary situation of authorising the Northern Military Council headed by Frank Aiken – the man who would ultimately command the Republican forces in the closing months of the civil war! Even more extraordinary was Michael's arrangements to send weapons and ammunition to the Northern IRA from the materiel supplied to him by the British for combating the southern Republicans. This was an exceedingly dangerous game. Michael was walking a tightrope between the anti-Treaty elements and the British who were increasingly leaning on his Provisional Government to put its house in order.

There is no doubt that Michael's seeming inertia at this crucial time was also dictated by the state of his health. The stomach pains from which he had suffered intermittently over the previous three years now became much more frequent, reducing him to a bland diet of curds and whey, when he bothered to eat at all. He also seemed to lurch from one cold to another. Superficially, his physique was as magnificent as ever, but long hours, overwork, lack of sleep and exposure to the damp, cold weather inevitably took their toll. One of the few bright patches in this rather dismal period was the friendship struck up between Michael and Oliver St John Gogarty, the noted physician and urbane wit whose elegant memoir *As I Was Going Down Sackville Street* (1937) contains an

Piaris Beaslai

William Cosgrave

Cathal Brugha

Countess Markievicz

ABOVE: *Arthur Griffith shortly before his death*

LEFT: *Michael Collins and Arthur Griffith*

REME

THOS

CLARE'S

SOLDIERS ARE W

LIVES ARE PLEDGE T

Eamon de Valera, speaking in County Clare, 1917

De Valera under arrest after the Easter Rising and (right) in 1932 when he came to power

Michael Collins, Richard Mulcahy, Diarmuid O'Hegarty and Kevin O'Higgins at Griffith's funeral,
August 1922

ABOVE: Griffith's funeral cortège as it passes Oriel House, notorious headquarters of the special police

Generals Collins, MacEoin and O'Higgins at Griffith's funeral;
(inset) Joe O'Reilly

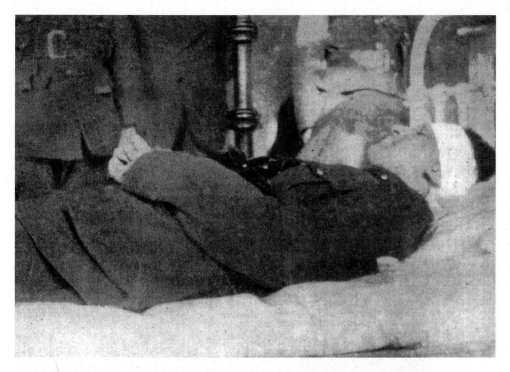

The body of Michael Collins at Shanakiel British Military Hospital, Cork, shortly after the ambush

Collins's funeral cortège passes the Government Buildings, Gardiner Street, Dublin (Hogan, Dublin)

Liam Tobin and Tom Cullen at Collins's funeral; (inset) Jock MacPeak, gunner of the Slievenamon

ABOVE: Bronze roundel by Seamus Murphy, Sam's Cross

*RIGHT: 30p stamp issued in October 1990, based on a
photograph of General Michael Collins taken a few days
before his death
(By permission of An Post, Dublin)*

affectionate portrait of Michael, then a frequent caller at the Gogarty residence in Ely Place. Gogarty's son Oliver recalls, as a boy, answering the door one night in those troubled times and anxiously calling out, 'Who's there?' From the darkness came a soft Cork voice: 'Never mind who it is. 'Tis good company you're in, anyway.'

At this point Harry Boland, now de Valera's private secretary, took centre stage. If his loyalties to his Chief and his old comrade-in-arms were sorely divided, now was the time to use his intimacy with de Valera and Collins to bring them together. On 20 May Harry eventually succeeded in getting the protagonists to agree to an electoral pact. Under the banner of Sinn Fein, the party to which both factions nominally adhered, the pro-Treaty element would nominate sixty-six candidates while the anti-Treaty group would put up fifty-eight. Thus the voters would still be electing Sinn Fein. Under the system of proportional representation which the British had foisted on Ireland in 1920, a pro-Treaty voter would give his first preference to a pro-Treaty Sinn Feiner and his second preference to the anti-Treaty Sinn Feiner, while anti-Treaty voters did the reverse. This pact was justified only by expediency and the rapidly worsening situation; but it was quite illegal, a carve-up that ignored the wishes of the smaller parties, such as the Farmers' Party, Labour and the Southern Unionists.

Subsequently Michael sought to justify his actions, in a lengthy statement which was afterwards republished in *The Path to Freedom*, the collection of his writings which appeared posthumously:

> The policy of the anti-Treaty party had now become clear – to prevent the people's will from being carried out because it differed from their own, to create trouble in order to break up the only possible National Government, and to destroy the Treaty with utter recklessness as to the consequences.
>
> A section of the army, in an attempt at military despotism, seized public buildings, took possession of the Chief Courts of Law of the Nation, dislocating private and national business, reinforced the Belfast Boycott which had been discontinued by the people's government, and 'commandeered' public and private funds, and the property of the people.
>
> Met by this reckless and wrecking opposition, and yet unwilling to use force against our own countrymen, we made attempt after attempt at conciliation.
>
> We appealed to the soldiers to avoid strife, to let the old feelings of brotherhood and solidarity continue.

We met and made advances over and over again to the politicians, standing out alone on the one fundamental point on which we owed an unquestioned duty to the people – that we must maintain for them the position of freedom they had secured. We could get no guarantee that we would be allowed to carry out that duty.

The country was face to face with disaster, economic ruin, and the imminent danger of the loss of the position we had won by the national effort. If order could not be maintained, if no National Government was to be allowed to function, a vacuum would be created, into which the English would necessarily be drawn back. To allow that to happen would have been the greatest betrayal of the Irish people, whose one wish was to take and to secure and to make use of the freedom which had been won.

Seeing the trend of events, soldiers from both sides met to try and reach an understanding, on the basis that the people were admittedly in favour of the Treaty, that the only legitimate government could be based on the people's will, and that the practicable course was to keep the peace, and to make use of the position we had secured.

These honourable efforts were defeated by the politicians. But at the eleventh hour an agreement was reached between Mr de Valera and myself for which I have been severely criticised.

It was said that I gave away too much, that I went too far to meet them, that I had exceeded my powers in making a pact which, to some extent, interfered with the people's right to make a free and full choice at the elections. It was a last effort on our part to avoid strife, to prevent the use of force by Irishmen against Irishmen.[9]

When news of this pact broke, it provoked very different reactions. In southern Ireland, it was generally greeted with relief, for the public were largely ignorant of the violent political undercurrents; but Hugh Kennedy, the chief Law Officer of the Provisional Government, was aghast at its blatant illegality, while Arthur Griffith was bitterly opposed to it and did everything he could to prevent the Cabinet endorsing it. At that meeting, when Griffith was asked if he favoured acceptance, he paused for fully three minutes, reflecting nervously, tugging at his tie and polishing his spectacles, as he struggled to find the right words. When he did reply, he abandoned the familiar 'Mick' and addressed his colleague stiffly as 'Mr Collins'. Churchill, anticipating that something of the sort might materialise, had actually written to Michael five days earlier, warning him that 'any such arrangement would be received with worldwide ridicule and reprobation . . . Your Government would soon find itself regarded as a tyrannical junta which, having got into office by violence, was seeking to maintain itself by a denial of constitutional rights.'[10]

Sir Henry Wilson, who had resigned as Chief of the Imperial General Staff to become military adviser to the Northern Irish Government, roundly condemned the Collins–de Valera Pact. At Liverpool on 25 May he stated that de Valera now had Michael Collins in his pocket – a jibe that may have signed his death warrant. The British government was furious and alarmed. Collins and Griffith were immediately summoned to London to explain themselves. Michael was extremely reluctant to go, and it was only on receipt of a handwritten letter from Churchill, pleading with him, that he changed his mind. In Downing Street on Saturday, 27 May, the Irish leaders, accompanied by Eamonn Duggan, Kevin O'Higgins and Hugh Kennedy, were told by Lloyd George that the meeting would have to be delayed because Birkenhead had a temperature. Michael burst out laughing. 'I never heard it called that before,' he said before dashing off to visit him. Birkenhead's butler confirmed that his Lordship was unwell, but Michael thrust his way into the hallway. Birkenhead, hearing Michael's voice below, came out on to the landing in his dressing-gown with a decanter in his hand. 'Come along up, Michael,' he said.[11] Meetings between Collins and Griffith on the one hand and Lloyd George and Churchill on the other continued intermittently until the middle of June, though only Griffith and Kennedy were present at the final meeting, on 15 June. During this period the draft of the Irish Constitution was discussed at great length, and any hopes Michael may have had of mitigating the worst aspects of the Treaty by injecting a Republican flavour into the Constitution were soon dashed.

In the meantime British forces halted their evacuation, strengthened the Six Counties border and made contingency plans for renewing the war. At the last moment, however, Michael, with Lloyd George giving him no option, broke the pact. On 15 June Michael was in Cork, when he received word of the outcome of the final meeting in Downing Street. In a speech to his constituents that day he said, 'Vote for the candidate you think best of.'

The text of the proposed Constitution, as heavily amended by the British, was only published on the very morning of the elections, leaving de Valera no time to prepare a denunciation of it. In fairness to Michael, it should be said that he fought to the very last moment in trying to get Lloyd George and Churchill to back down on their veto of the word 'Republic' which they had found so abhorrent, but they would not budge.

The elections took place on 16 June and were marred by riots and gunfights in many towns. At Castleblayney, Michael was addressing the voters from the back of an open lorry when an anti-Treaty supporter jumped into the cab and drove off at high speed. The general election was not without its moments of farce, too. Republicans in Cork were instructed to write Republican slogans on all available surfaces, but one election worker took this too literally and went round the city daubing the slogan 'Up the Republic wherever a small space presents itself'. In the same city anti-Treatyites seized a ballot box and altered 4,000 voting slips from first preference to Michael Collins to fourth preference. The clumsy forgery was readily detected as the thieves used the wrong kind of pencil.

As a result of the voting, fifty-eight pro-Treaty Sinn Feiners were elected, against thirty-six anti-Treaty Sinn Feiners, seventeen Labour, seven Farmers' Party, six Independents and the four Unionists of Trinity College. As the smaller parties and independents were solidly pro-Treaty, the result was a massive defeat for de Valera. The anti-Treaty vote totalled 133,864; all others lumped together amounted to 486,419, a resounding majority in favour of the Treaty.

The breaking of the pact and the terms of the Constitution widened the split; but two events on 22 June made civil war inevitable.

The first of these was the movement of a body of irregular troops into the Four Courts under Rory O'Connor. Hitherto the cluster of buildings had been occupied by a mainly unarmed group, but O'Connor now aimed at a military dictatorship. Significantly, both Liam Lynch and Cathal Brugha were opposed to this although, after swithering, they later joined the insurgents. From that day onwards the gates were kept locked and the armed Republican guards strengthened considerably.

The second event was the assassination of Sir Henry Wilson. On leaving the army he had entered politics, being elected unopposed as Unionist MP for North Down in the Northern elections of 21 February 1922 and appointed Military Adviser to the Craig administration. The immediate outcome was the replacement of the discredited RIC by a new gendarmerie, the Royal Ulster Constabulary, backed by militia forces known as the A, B and C Specials, and the introduction of harsh legislation, including flogging, for those convicted of terrorist activity. These and other measures coincided with the escalation of anti-Catholic pogroms in the North. It was in response to this terror campaign in the Six Counties that Michael had connived at IRA activity which consisted originally of beating off attacks by Orange mobs on Catholic districts of Belfast, but later used the methods of the Collins Squad to deal with the death-squads operated by District Inspectors Nixon and Harrison of the police. The shocking murder of the MacMahon family by the RUC on 23 March made even Churchill weep, and brought de Valera and Collins fleetingly together again. In direct response to the public sense of outrage in England at this atrocity, Lloyd George had summoned Collins and Craig to London to discuss 'every aspect of the situation'. Any compromise that might have been effected by this meeting was set at naught a month later when Wilson visited Stormont and furiously attacked Sir James Craig by demanding, 'Who is governing Ulster? You or Collins?' During May and early June the situation in the North continued to deteriorate and even Lloyd George found himself agreeing with Michael Collins that something had to be done to rein in the Die-hards. When Churchill refused to hold an enquiry into Protestant atrocities at Belleek and Pettigo, Michael telephoned him on 11 June and threatened to invade the North. The Provisional Government, he hinted, had 'a very definite policy to put into effect as a last resort against that demoniacal barbarism which is aiming at the extermination of their people in the Six Counties'.

Wilson was also scheming with Lord and Lady Londonderry to bring down the British Coalition government and restore Tory rule, which would place the Unionists in an even stronger position. Wilson was even being touted as a possible leader of this new Die-hard party. The situation of the Coalition moderates was not made any easier by the de Valera–Collins pact which Churchill described as doubling the forces of evil and halving the forces of good. To the members of an Irish businessmen's delegation, Churchill confided, 'You are being tortured by Wilson and de Valera.' But the field-marshal's days were numbered. He had been put on an IRB hit-list in June 1921 but removed a month later when the Truce came into effect. When the bloody pogroms in Belfast were at their height, in May 1922, Michael Collins angrily said to Liam Tobin, 'We'll kill a member of that bunch.' Sir Henry's intimate connection with every anti-Nationalist and pro-Unionist cause, from the Curragh Mutiny to the establishment of the B Special Constabulary, would have marked him out, even without his scurrilous personal attacks on Michael and his frequent tirades against the Treaty.

Nevertheless, the murder of Sir Henry Wilson, on his own doorstep on the afternoon of 22 June 1922, was as indefensible and inefficient as it was senseless; it had tragic consequences for Ireland that no one could have anticipated. Michael's old Post Office friend Sam Maguire had recently visited Dublin, and in the course of conversation someone had suggested that the elimination of Wilson would not only get rid of a thorn in their flesh but also help to heal the rift in the Nationalist movement. Maguire is believed to have had talks with both Michael and another old friend, Rory O'Connor at the Four Courts. It appears that on his return to London he organised the assassination, which was actually carried out by Reginald Dunne and Joseph O'Sullivan. The latter, a veteran of the Western Front, had lost a leg at Ypres. The fact that a one-legged man was the back-up for the assassination shows how hard the London IRA had been hit by the Treaty squabble. Dunne could have got away after the shooting, but chivalrously he delayed to help his crippled comrade and as a result both men were caught by an angry crowd and savagely beaten. In the course of this mêlée, a constable was shot, which did not improve the temper of the mob.

General Macready was immediately ordered to confine all British personnel in southern Ireland to their barracks and he himself was summoned to London that evening. The weapons used by Dunne and O'Sullivan, together with papers and other personal effects, were taken to 10 Downing Street, and as a result Lloyd George fired off a very stiffly worded letter to Michael. It was clear that the IRA was implicated in the murder:

> The ambiguous position of the Irish Republican Army can no longer be ignored by the British Government. Still less can Mr Rory O'Connor be permitted to remain with his followers and his arsenal in open rebellion in the heart of Dublin in possession of the Courts of Justice, organising and sending out from this centre enterprises of murder not only in the area of your Government but also in the Six Northern Counties and in Great Britain. His Majesty's Government cannot consent to a continuation of this state of things and they feel entitled to ask you formally to bring it to an end forthwith.[12]

Diarmuid O'Hegarty, Secretary to the Provisional Government, responded immediately, temporising by requesting the British to produce proof of the alleged conspiracy, such proof to be put before the newly elected parliament when it met on 1 July. Michael, at this time, was actually in Cork, holding an enquiry into the ballot-rigging that had almost cost him his seat. Churchill, via Andy Cope, informed Griffith that the information was of such a highly secret nature that it could not be disclosed, but he pressed the Provisional Government for a straight answer. The information appears to have been a letter from an IRA prisoner, smuggled out of an English prison, containing a reference to 'the Big Fellow' which inferentially involved Michael in the murder. There was no actual proof that he was in any way implicated, and all the evidence suggested that Maguire was either acting on his own initiative or in concert with O'Connor. If anything, the consensus of opinion at the time was that Wilson's murder was calculated to embarrass the Provisional Government. Nevertheless, purely circumstantial evidence, adduced by Coogan, cannot be ignored.[13] This alleges that Peig Ni Braonain took a top-secret document from Dublin to London where she was met at Euston by Liam Tobin, the inference being that the document contained orders for the Wilson killing. Tobin was back in Dublin when the assassination took place, and jubilantly told Mulcahy. The Defence Minister, however, was appalled and threatened to resign. This brought Tobin to his senses and, as the enormity of the crime sank in, he rushed off to Kingsbridge Station to intercept Michael on his return to Dublin from Cork. He was alarmed to see Michael looking so dejected, 'carrying the weight of the Republic on his shoulders'. He told him of Mulcahy's reaction and Michael replied, 'I'll make that all right.' The matter was never mentioned again.

The immediate repercussion was that General Macready was sent back to Dublin with instructions to prepare a British attack on the Four Courts. Macready managed to delay proceedings for several days until the Cabinet had cooled down and thought out the consequences which such an action might bring. In his memoirs, published two years later, Macready would pat himself on the back for his fabian tactics:

> On 25 June word came through from London that the Government had reconsidered their original decision and that no action was to be taken against the Four Courts – I never ceased to congratulate myself on having been an instrument in staving off what would have been a disaster.[14]

Meanwhile, a hysterical Tory press bayed for blood. *The Morning Post* of 23 June declared that 'Mr Lloyd George, Mr Austen Chamberlain and Mr Asquith all shared in the murder of Sir Henry Wilson and are bedabbled with the stain of his blood.' When the Commons debated the matter on 26 June it did so, in William O'Brien's telling words, 'hungry with anti-Irish fury'.[15] On that day Leo Henderson, a prominent member of the Four Courts staff, led a raid on Ferguson's garage in Lower Baggot Street, seizing trucks and fuel and thereby killing two birds with one stone: acquiring transport and operating the Belfast boycott. Henderson was promptly seized by Free State troops and placed under close arrest. The Republicans, by way of reprisal, kidnapped General O'Connell. This proved to be the last straw, so far as Michael was concerned. The question of the Four Courts and mounting British pressure was discussed in Cabinet the following day and an ultimatum was issued to the Republican garrison to vacate the Four Courts by 4 a.m. The British Coalition, faced with Conservative and Unionist anger, was on the verge of collapse, and might well have been brought down, had Collins not taken action.

Ironically, it can also be argued that the attitude of Lloyd George and Churchill at this critical moment did not help the Provisional Government. Churchill's statement about the 'band of men styling themselves the Headquarters of the Republican Executive', coming just before the Collins ultimatum, enabled the anti-Treaty faction to maintain that Collins was Churchill's stooge. Previously, in April, the British ship *Upnor*, carrying a large quantity of firearms, had been intercepted *en route* to Haulbowline and its cargo seized by anti-Treaty forces off the south-west coast. Michael was convinced that this incident was a conspiracy between the British government and his adversaries. Churchill, of course, stoutly denied the charge of collusion, but there were rumours around the corridors of Westminster during the preceding week, that guns were to be supplied to the IRA. There would always be the suspicion that pragmatists like Lloyd George and Churchill were prepared to do deals with anyone:

> Once they realised that there were other strong men in the country, apart from Collins, their policy seems to have been that of seeking out the strongest personality with the idea of backing him to the full, even against the legal Government.[16]

By 27 June the rebels had also seized the Kildare Street Club (a Unionist stronghold), the Masonic Hall (certainly not a Catholic haunt), the Fowler Hall and Kilmainham Gaol – all buildings with symbolic rather than strategic value. Significantly, de Valera, who had been keeping a low profile of late, now materialised to lend support to what he saw as a *coup d'état*. Another survivor of the Easter Rising was also prominent; Cathal Brugha, showing his contempt for politicians, joined the insurgents and in the ensuing days was in the very thick of the fray round the Hammam Building in O'Connell Street.

The ultimatum, in the form of a letter written by Thomas Ennis commanding the Second Eastern Division, was delivered by a Free State soldier at the main gate of the Four Courts at 3.40 a.m. on 28 June. The rebels had twenty minutes to comply, but spent the time in an impromptu church parade. The garrison, which consisted of about 150 men under Rory O'Connor, mustered under the dome and then received general absolution from a Franciscan monk, Father Albert. Then the men knelt by their rifles for the Lord's Prayer and three Hail Marys for Ireland. Most of the men, including their chaplain, were in tears as this short act of faith came to an end.

'Time's up!' shouted Rory O'Connor, snapping the case of his pocket watch. 'Take up your positions!'

At four o'clock precisely there was a burst of machine-gun fire, followed immediately by the boom and crash of an eighteen-pounder shell. The civil war had begun. Fighting would last eleven months, but the noise of the artillery, borrowed from the British, reverberates through Ireland to this day.

CHAPTER 16

Pass of the Flowers

Good luck be with you, Michael Collins,
Or stay or go you far away;
Or stay you with the folk of fairy,
Or come with ghosts another day.

SHANE LESLIE, ON SEEING SIR JOHN LAVERY'S PORTRAIT *Love of Ireland*, 1922

THE IRISH CIVIL WAR LASTED TEN MONTHS AND TWENTY-SEVEN days, but its brevity was matched by a ferocity on both sides, unparalleled in Irish history. Some 540 Free State troops were killed in action, but no official figures for losses on the Republican side were ever published, though they were probably much higher. Both J.M. Curran and R. Fanning[1] have suggested between 4,000 and 5,000 dead, but, based on conjecture, this seems to be an exaggeration. Nevertheless, it is a sad fact that losses were very much greater than those sustained in the 1916–21 period. Material damage amounted to £30 million and the cost of financing the war cost another £17 million. The costs of policing, not to mention the expense of keeping over 12,000 prisoners in detention, were an enormous drain on the slender resources of the new state. Conversely, the collection of rates and taxes was severely disrupted. The Irish Free State was almost bankrupted and its international credit grievously undermined. Only a massive loan from the Bank of Ireland to the Exchequer staved off total collapse. The agricultural economy was hard hit and millions of acres were left uncultivated.

It was the worst of all civil wars, with families split down the middle, with father against son, brother against brother. The manner in which so many met their deaths was far more horrific than the atrocities of the Black and Tan war. In many districts there was a complete breakdown of law and order and man's inhumanity to man plumbed new depths of depravity. It was a time when old scores were paid and family feuds settled under the cover of warfare, when every psychopath with a gun did his own thing in the name of whichever cause seemed the more convenient. Isolated acts of terrorism and despicable cruelty

265

were bad enough, but many of the cruel and inhuman punishments meted out were sanctioned by one side or the other. At Ballyseedy Cross near Tralee, County Kerry, Free Staters tied nine Republican prisoners together on top of a landmine, then detonated it. Eight men were blown to pieces while one, Stephen Fuller, was thrown clear and survived. The troops gathering up the fragments of bodies from the trees and bushes were unaware that one man had escaped. The following day four men were blown up in similar fashion at Countess Bridge near Killarney, and a few days later five blown up at Cahirciveen after first being kneecapped to prevent their escape. In one prison in the south-west castration was regularly employed as a method of torture, leaving the victims to die many years later in asylums without ever regaining their sanity.

In giving the order for the shelling of the Four Courts, Michael was taking a terrible gamble. For some time, to Griffith's increasing exasperation, he had been playing a double game, publicly extolling the Treaty but privately adhering to traditional Republican aims which became less and less tenable, especially after the outcome of the June elections. This explains his extreme reluctance to take action against the Four Courts. So long as the Republican Executive remained relatively passive he could turn a blind eye to its posturings, but the infiltration of armed men, the stockpiling of explosives and the creation of a bomb factory within its precincts alarmed him. Rory O'Connor's threat to attack the British and Churchill's threat to renew the war finally forced Michael's hand. One of the main reasons for his support of the Treaty was that it had been the means of British withdrawal. Anything that would reverse that process had to be avoided at all costs. Apart from the kidnapping of Ginger O'Connell which was the final act of defiance by Republican extemists, Michael was aware of divisions in the Republican ranks, and he now gambled on a pre-emptive strike on the Four Courts before O'Connor could patch up his differences with Liam Lynch, who was perceived as taking a more moderate view. There was hope that the conflict could be localised, and that the Four Courts could be retaken before Lynch's First Southern Division was mobilised to the rescue. Gearoid O'Sullivan informed Michael confidently that the fighting would be over 'inside a week or ten days'.

This is what is believed to lie behind the decision to permit Lynch and two of his senior staff officers to leave Dublin during the fighting. As it turned out, this was a fatal mistake, for Lynch was able to bring the IRA in Munster and Connaught into the conflict. The tragedy is that neither side wanted a civil war, and neither faction believed that it would ever come to that. Rory O'Connor, ensconced in the rotunda of the Four Courts, firmly believed that the attack, when it came, would be mounted by the British, and the resultant resistance would be good for Republican propaganda. Had General Macready not avoided this pitfall, the outcome might have been very different. But in the end it was Irish troops who took on the insurgents, and triggered off a bitterness which has tainted Irish politics ever since. Churchill's forecast that resolute action on Michael's part would, in fact, help to accelerate Irish unity has a hollow ring.

The battle for the Four Courts took three days and nights of heavy shelling, followed by an all-out infantry assault, before its garrison surrendered. Two eighteen-pounder guns were borrowed from the Royal Artillery and shelled the Four Courts from Bridgefoot Street. Unfortunately, the shrapnel shells which were all that Macready had available originally made no impact on the stout masonry. One shell passed right through the glass dome and exploded in Phoenix Park, close to British military headquarters, an incident that did little to improve relations between the Provisional Government and the British. The troops of the new National Army had had no training in artillery, and Michael urgently hunted around for ex-gunners from the First World War. In the end, Major-General Emmet Dalton, who had been an officer in the British army, had to take over one of the eighteen-pounders himself for three hours. When it became apparent that the Free State attack was having little effect, the British government offered Michael sixty-pound howitzers. Churchill even offered a squadron of RAF bombers, which, he argued, could very quickly be painted in the Irish tricolour to convey the impression of a Free State Air Force, but Michael declined this tempting offer.

There was no doubt that the fate of the Treaty and the Provisional Government now hung in the balance. The Four Courts emerged as a symbol of national defiance, a rerun of the General Post Office in 1916, and the longer the bombardment dragged on, the more the Provisional Government would be discredited and sympathy for the rebels would increase. Andy Cope reported to London that if Dublin were not effectively cleared of rebels, 'the PG is lost'.

Meanwhile, there were divisions both within the Four Courts garrison and in the Dublin Brigade. The latter received confusing orders and Oscar Traynor's intention of throwing a protective cordon round the Four Courts was frustrated by a complete lack of co-ordination between individual battalions and companies. Within the complex Paddy O'Brien of the Dublin Brigade was in charge of the garrison, but four of the Republican top brass – Joe McKelvey, Liam Mellowes, Ernie O'Malley and Rory O'Connor – outranked him. When O'Brien was badly wounded, Mellowes ceded command to Ernie O'Malley because of his war experience. O'Malley felt that they were like 'rats in a trap'.

The worst damage was caused not by the Free State bombardment but by the Republicans themselves. Two mines laid in the archives building, which was being used as a munitions centre, were detonated, causing a terrific explosion that scattered the accumulated documentary heritage of Ireland sky-high.

Seven centuries of precious writs, charters and invaluable historic material were scattered to the four winds. This was referred to by Churchill when he wrote to Michael after the fall of the Four Courts:

> If I refrain from congratulations it is only because I do not wish to embarrass you. The archives of the Four Courts may be scattered but the title-deeds of Ireland are safe.[2]

Disunity and a lack of total commitment within the Republican ranks brought this tragic farce to an end as much as the assault by the National troops. During the bombardment there was some haphazard attempt by the Dublin Brigade to hold various other buildings in the city, but not in such a way that made any sound military sense. On 29 June Traynor took over the Hammam and Gresham Hotels, along with two others on the east side of O'Connell Street – the wrong side of the street for any effective communication with the Four Courts. To these hotels repaired in due course the political leaders of the struggle. Sean T. O'Kelly turned up at the Hammam armed only with an umbrella. Quixotically, de Valera rejoined his old battalion as a private soldier, and released a lengthy press notice to this effect. For this he was roundly condemned by *The Irish Times*. Privately, Dev was in favour of the peace initiative launched by the Lord Mayor and the Labour Party, but this only brought him the disapproval of his loyal lieutenants, Brugha and Stack.

After the surrender of the Four Courts on 30 June, desultory fighting continued for several days on the east side of O'Connell Street. By 3 July all Republican strongpoints south of the river had fallen to the Free Staters, and the climax came in the fierce fighting around the four hotels. The following day de Valera and some others were smuggled across the river to Mount Street. On 5 July a white flag was hoisted above the Hammam Hotel, but when the Free Staters moved in to take the surrender, the rebels opened fire again. This, and their habit of firing from the cover of Red Cross vehicles, earned for the insurgents considerable opprobrium. Brigadier Paddy Daly commented that they were 'the dirtiest fighters I ever saw'.

Last to hold out was a small group led by Cathal Brugha himself. After he had ordered his men to surrender and seen them off the premises, Cathal ran out of the door, gun at the ready, and was instantly cut to pieces. Three versions of his death are recorded. The usual story has Cathal, a revolver in each hand, blazing away as he emerged into the street, to be cut down by a hundred rifles at point-blank range. Some other observers, however, have maintained that Brugha was unarmed when he fell mortally wounded. A more prosaic but detailed account was given by Lieutenant-Colonel Andrew J. McCarthy of the St John Ambulance Brigade who went into the Hammam after the others had exited.

There, in the foyer, he met Brugha and took him by the arm, but Cathal pulled himself away, drew a tommy gun from under his coat, and turned in the direction of the Lewis gunner who was covering the lane at the rear from Findlater's building, saying, 'They'll never get me.' Then he raised his machine-gun to his shoulder and took deliberate aim at the Lewis gunner and fired a burst. 'There was a quick burst from the Lewis gunner. They were both shooting it out. But soon Brugha was on the ground, wounded, and the firing ceased.'[3]

Michael took the news of Cathal's death very badly. Although they had become deadly adversaries, the venom was all on the older man's side, and Michael had reacted more in sorrow than in anger to his jealous outbursts. He never lost his admiration of Brugha; while condemning his pigheadedness, he admired his fanatical devotion to the freedom of Ireland. The tragedy was that, in seeking to attain that freedom, their paths should have diverged so violently.

Even when the street fighting in the city centre was at its height, Michael was seeking a way to end the war as honourably as possible. On I July he had a meeting with Archbishop Walsh, Cathal O'Shannon and the Lord Mayor, and recorded his impression of the discussion:

> Must make record of this – shows how reasonable our position is. We don't want any humiliating surrender. We want order restored. That only. Maintained for the future. Disgraceful acts must be put an end to. Archb. and L.M. agree that if arms kept by irregulars all the same things would happen again.[4]

Indeed, this concern for the decommissioning of IRA weaponry, a matter that would bedevil the peace process seven decades later, was now crucial. By 5 July the fighting in Dublin itself was at an end, but Liam Lynch (whom Eoin O'Duffy, on Mulcahy's orders, had permitted to leave Dublin) had issued a proclamation at Cork calling Republicans to arms. Mulcahy's decision to let Lynch and his staff officers leave Dublin seems, in hindsight, to have been incredibly naïve; but he believed that Lynch would use his influence to keep other areas from joining in the conflict. When Lynch raised the standard of Republicanism he was accused by the pro-Treaty faction of a breach of faith. The response to Lynch's appeal to arms was very patchy, its strength lying in the south and west of Ireland. From Cork, Lynch went to Limerick where he arranged a truce with the pro-Treaty garrison. Michael, however, refused to countenance this agreement and uncompromisingly ordered the Republicans to evacuate the town.

On 12 July, at a meeting of the Council of War of the Provisional Government, Michael was appointed Commander-in-Chief of the National Army. Contrary to belief, widespread to this day, Michael was not manoeuvred into this position by his Cabinet colleagues, eager to move him out of the political arena. As we shall see later on, Michael regarded as the top priority of his government the speedy conclusion of the war, and he felt that he was the man best equipped for this task. Consequently, he handed over to William Cosgrave as Acting Chairman, while he donned his general's uniform. The Minister of Defence, Richard Mulcahy, was back in uniform too, as Chief of Staff once more. Between them, these old comrades in arms revitalised the pro-Treaty forces, a curious amalgam of raw recruits – the 'sunshine soldiers' – as well as veterans of the Troubles, stiffened by an infusion of officers and NCOs who had previously served in the British or American armies. Arms and ammunition for this augmented army flowed in from Britain, together with artillery, armoured cars, light tanks and even aircraft (used mainly for reconnaissance and dropping propaganda leaflets). In addition to his duties as Chairman of the Provisional Government, Michael now shouldered the burdens of military command with immense cheerfulness. He was back where he really belonged, a soldier on active service, away from the political arena, yet he made sure that he never missed any important Cabinet meetings after taking over the supreme military command, and his voluminous papers indicate the breadth and complexity of the administrative matters of a non-military nature in which he continued to take a close interest.

Michael had a superhuman task. At the outset of the war, there was no doubt that the Republican forces, concentrated in Munster and the west, were numerically stronger and better equipped than the National Army – 13,000 against 9,000 effectives (the grossly inflated Trucileer army had largely been stood down). But from the middle of July onwards, the Free Staters received large consignments of arms and equipment from the British, whereas the Republicans had to make do with what they had, or could capture. While the Republicans had the initial advantage of operating in their home territory, with at least the tacit support of the bulk of the civil population in that area, the longer the war dragged on the more unpopular the fighting would become to most people, and this largely cancelled out any early strategic advantages. Memories of guerrilla warfare in the Troubles, with the dismal pattern of atrocities and reprisals, alienated the ordinary people, and the Republicans were ever mindful of the fact that they represented a viewpoint which had been resoundingly rejected at the ballot-box. It was all very well for de Valera to insist that there was a time when the minority were justified in acting against the majority, and this was it; but in the long run the cause for which they fought seemed less and less defensible.

The Republican campaign was greatly hindered by a lack of any central direction, coupled with very poor communications. Such strategy as there was seemed to consist of defending local territories, with no attempt to re-enter

Dublin or spread the conflict to other areas. Indeed, it rapidly evolved as a desire to hold on to Munster and abandon the rest. Ironically, this would have created another Six Counties situation in part of southern Ireland. By 9 July Liam Deasy was speaking of a fortified line between Limerick and Waterford, but in truth the Republicans never had the men or armaments for such an ambitious plan. Furthermore, the will to fight in a thoroughly professional manner was lacking. Frank O'Connor, who served on the Republican side, speaks of men who 'melted away' on Sunday mornings to attend Mass. When the National Army launched its offensive, attacking Republican barracks and strongholds along this defensive line, the Republicans withdrew with little or no fighting, putting their buildings to the torch as they went. Lynch himself moved his headquarters from Mallow to Limerick, and thence to Buttevant and latterly Clonmel, sowing confusion and despondency in the Republican ranks in so doing. Limerick fell to Government forces with little fighting, and the city of Cork capitulated without any resistance being offered. The Free Staters might be derided by the Republicans as mere mercenaries – many Scottish and English ex-soldiers were only too glad to serve in the ranks of the National Army as an alternative to unemployment in Britain – but the Republican troops were largely unpaid, seldom uniformed and tended to regard the war as a part-time adventure. While they were in control of Cork, they had the benefit of the customs revenue of the port; but by early September Lynch was reporting: 'We are very short of cash, as enemy issued orders to banks to refuse to release funds which they discovered were ours.'[5] Discipline was very poor and ancient territorial animosities between the several divisions did not improve morale. Nothing had been learned from Michael's experiences during the Troubles, and little attempt was made to build up an efficient intelligence system. Michael, on the other hand, was only too well aware of the value of good intelligence in the sort of war he was fighting, though he upset some of his old colleagues by bringing in Joe McGrath as Director, in place of Major-General Liam Tobin who was sent off to join an expedition against the rebels in County Cork.

There were deaths which affected Michael grievously. Harry Boland became a staff officer with the South Dublin Brigade but was soon forced to take to the hills. From there he wrote to Joe McGarrity on 13 July: 'It may very well be that I shall fall in this awful conflict,' but he ended on a defiant note: 'I am certain we cannot be defeated even if Collins and his British Guns succeed in garrisoning every town in Ireland.' The bitterness in these words was underscored by memories of old friendship and the failure to avert the conflict, though he had tried hard enough. On 25 July Harry wrote again to McGarrity: 'Can you imagine me on the run from Mick Collins?' Four days later, in fact, Harry received a *cri de coeur* from Michael himself:

Harry — it has come to this! Of all things it has come to this.

It is in my power to arrest you and destroy you. This I cannot do. If you will think over the influence which has dominated you it should change your ideal.

You are walking under false colours. If no word of mine will change your attitude then you are beyond all hope — my hope.[6]

The following evening, 30 July, Harry was in Dublin and dined with Anna Fitzsimmons at Jammet's Restaurant in Nassau Street. Anna (later Mrs Kelly) had been one of Michael's secretaries before the Treaty. During the course of the meal Harry urged her to 'Eat well', adding, 'because it may be your last meal with me'.

Twenty-seven hours later Harry Boland and Joe Griffin were getting ready for bed at the Grand Hotel in Skerries, a coastal resort to the north-east of the city, when a squad of National troops broke in and arrested them. The most widely accepted version of events states that Harry was shot while trying to escape from custody. Anna Kelly, however, gave quite a different story to the world sixteen years later. In this she told how Harry:

insisted on seeing the officer in charge of the raid. The soldier would not listen to him. Harry moved towards the bedroom door saying: 'I want to see your officer!' But a bullet in the stomach cut short his appeal . . . There had not been, could not have been, any attempt at escape. The stairs and hall were occupied by the raiding party. They were posted at the outer doors.

He was left in Skerries for four hours, and then taken to Portobello Barracks and from that to the hospital, where it was thought that an operation might save his life . . . When he was dying his sister, Kathleen, asked him, 'Who murdered you, Harry?' He would not tell. All he said was to bury him beside Cathal Brugha.[7]

When Michael was told of Harry's death he rushed into Fionan Lynch's room at 44 Mountjoy Street, crying helplessly. A letter from Kitty, which he received on 3 August, referred to Harry who was still alive when she wrote, but who died on 2 August. 'I see poor Harry is knocked out. Will I write to him? (Diplomacy.) I wouldn't do so without asking you.'[8] This letter crossed with one from Michael, in which he wrote, on 2 August:

I mentioned about Harry in yesterday's letter. Last night I passed Vincent's Hospital and saw a small crowd outside. My mind went in to him lying dead there and I thought of the times together, and, whatever good there is in any wish of mine, he certainly had it. Although the gap of 8 or 9 months was not forgotten — of course no one can ever forget it — I only thought of him with the friendship of the days of 1918 and 1919. They tell me that the last thing he said to his sister Kathleen, before he was operated on, was 'Have they got Mick Collins yet?' I don't believe it so far as I'm concerned and, if he did say it, there is no necessity to believe it. I'd send a wreath but I suppose they'd return it torn up.[9]

Kitty's next letter, which Michael received on 4 August, was almost entirely devoted to her anguish over Harry's death:

I realise I have lost a good friend in Harry — and no matter what, I'll always believe in his genuineness, that I was the one and only. I think you have also lost a friend. I am sure you are sorry after him. As for Larry [her brother], he was just going up to town to-day to see him. He will motor up to his funeral, I think, and if I get a seat I'll go for the day to see you. I hope you are well. When I think of the little whispering in my ear. *Always* when H. was saying goodbye, he'd say, 'Don't worry, Kitty, M. will be all right etc.' He seemed sincere saying that, and it used to make me happy, and then he'd say, 'Ah, I know how to make you happy.'

I'll wire you if I go up. It's very undecided yet. You wouldn't think it right for me to go to his funeral? I sent a wire to his mother; also I'll send some flowers, tho' they're not much good to him. He had my rosary beads: I have his.[10]

Kitty did come to Dublin on 4 August and she and Michael had lunch in a private room at the Shelbourne Hotel. A few hours later he wrote her a letter saying how much he had enjoyed her company, adding:

You will not misunderstand anything you have heard me say about poor H. You'll also appreciate my feelings about the splendid men we have lost on our side, and the losses they are and the bitterness they cause, and the anguish. There is no one who feels it all more than I do. My condemnation is all for those who would put themselves up as paragons of Irish Nationality, and all the others as being not worthy of concern. May God bless you always.[11]

In both this letter and the plea to Harry a week earlier, Michael was clearly referring to de Valera. In a war that had become personalised, the personalities took on a greater importance. The death of so many fine fellows, men with whom he had fought and played hard, with whom he had shared the privations of a prison camp and the dangers of the Troubles, was a matter which Michael took to heart. On 7 August he could only dash off a brief note 'in great haste' before setting off on a long and very tiring journey, a tour of military bases at Maryborough (now Portlaoise) and the Curragh. He did not get back to Dublin till very late at night, fatigued and frozen stiff, and went straight to bed. The low point of the day had been a Requiem Mass for nine soldiers who had been killed in action in County Kerry. Writing to Kitty on 8 August, Michael spoke of the really heartbreaking scene:

> The poor women weeping and almost shrieking (some of them) for their dead sons. Sisters and one wife were there too, and a few small children. It makes one feel, I tell you.[12]

Early in July Skibbereen fell to the Republicans who now had the whole of County Cork in their hands. For over a month this area had functioned like a mini-state; *The Cork Examiner* was edited by the Republican Frank Gallagher, ably assisted by Erskine Childers; the port authority was operated by the Republicans and tolls and duties provided much-needed revenue. There was even a set of postage stamps of an entirely distinctive design, unlike the Georgian overprints with which the Provisional Government had to make do. Sooner or later, however, the Provisional Government would have to deal with this Republican stronghold, and early in August Emmet Dalton was placed in command of an ambitious expedition sent from Dublin by sea. A flotilla of three ships, led by the *Arvonia*, set sail on 7 August with almost a thousand troops, an armoured car and an eighteen-pounder cannon aboard. This was an extremely foolhardy venture. As Frank O'Connor, who served on the Republican side, wryly pointed out: 'Technically, a landing from the sea is supposed to be one of the most difficult of military operations, but as we handled the defence it was a walk-over.'[13] Michael Hayes, Speaker of the Dail, reported the fall of Cork to Mulcahy with the memorable words that Dalton had succeeded 'by breaking all the rules of common sense and navigation and military science'. Although the approach to Passage West had been mined by the Republicans, Dalton was greatly assisted by the commander of the British naval base, H.C. Somerville, who gave him the precise location of the mines. The landings at Cork, Youghal and Union Hall were virtually unopposed, the tired defenders being taken by surprise. Although the city was liberated easily, the Republicans withdrew in good order. Many of them simply disappeared, back to their farms and homes, but a hard core continued at large in the more remote, mountainous districts, prepared to carry on the fight by guerrilla tactics.

This left Kerry as the most obdurate of Republican areas. Here the Republicans had a series of successes early in the war, capturing several towns and seizing the arms and equipment of the pro-Treaty garrisons. General Paddy Daly effected a landing with 500 men at Fenit on 2 August but ran into stiff opposition at Sammy's Rock and Farranfore, the latter leaving eleven Free Staters killed and 114 wounded. By mid-August the main centres of population were in the hands of the Provisional Government once more, although in the remoter districts the war was only just beginning. South Tipperary, the haunt of the redoubtable Dan Breen, was another hard nut to crack, Republican resistance stiffened by the fact that de Valera himself, serving as Director of Operations for the Second Southern Division, was active in Carrick-on-Suir and Clonmel during July and August. Government troops mounted an offensive in this area on 8 August and after an artillery barrage Clonmel capitulated on the evening of the following day. As the rebels withdrew they set the town alight. Thereafter the divisions split up into small mobile flying-columns, just as they had done during the Black and Tan war, and prepared to continue the fight in the hills.

On 5 August Michael sent a very up-beat memorandum to Cosgrave reviewing the military situation. He claimed that, apart from pockets of resistance in the west, 'no definite military problem' now confronted him outside the First Southern Division. If it were not for Munster, he averred, the Dáil could have been summoned 'and the question of Police, Courts and the necessary punishments for people found guilty of breaking Railways, cutting telegraph wires, looting, carrying arms unauthorisedly, etc. settled'. The army would then simply co-operate with the police in restoring law and order. He advocated the installation of garrisons in all the principal points to shake the domination of the Irregulars. 'The establishment of ourselves in a few more of these positions would mean the resurgence of the people from their present cowed condition.' One of the journalists from *The Irish Times* accompanying the pro-Treaty forces confirmed this optimistic view, arguing that if the Government troops moved quickly the war would be over in three weeks.

Before he set off to supervise military operations in Kerry, Michael was advised to settle the matter by negotiation. After a month of hard fighting, though, he was in no mood for compromise. After the capture of Cork, he was in Tralee on 12 August when he was dealt yet another body blow. That morning Arthur Griffith was getting dressed to go to work; while bending down to tie his shoelaces he suffered a cerebral haemorrhage and died almost immediately. He was only fifty-one, but the worries and anxieties of the past two years had taken a terrible toll. The hard bargaining with the British and all the travelling back and forward during the Treaty negotiations had broken his health. The eruption of the civil war was a blow from which he never recovered. Recently, at his doctors' insistence, he had been admitted to a private nursing home, but continued to work every day. 'In fear for the future of his country,' wrote Frank O'Connor, 'he had been going to pieces. He died a peculiarly lonely unknown man, as poor as the first day he entered Irish politics.'[14]

One of the canards that endures to this day is that, in accepting the post of Commander-in-Chief in mid-July, Michael unwittingly let himself be shunted sideways by 'a junta within the Cabinet into accepting what appears to be a military post of great importance, but one which in fact was bereft of political power'.[15] Sean MacBride, the source of this story, claimed that this step was taken because Michael's policy in the North was unwelcome to his Cabinet colleagues as well as to the British. MacBride hinted also that British Intelligence had a hand in this, in revenge for his policy of assassinating their agents during the Troubles. The story becomes even more convoluted for it appears that Michael was taking time out from his multifarious duties to track down the identity of 'Thorpe', the code-name for Dublin Castle's most trusted, important and long-serving informer, believed to have betrayed the Invincibles who carried out the Phoenix Park murders in 1882. Forty years later, Thorpe was still at work. Through his own highly placed moles, Michael was aware of a high-level informer on the British side and was determined to unmask him. By April he was asking 'G' (possibly Thomas Markham) to investigate this. Apparently G turned up some evidence, for Michael's pocket-book contains the cryptic entry on 4 August: 'Markham – Thorpe – Healy'.[16] MacBride's theory was that Michael had discovered that Thorpe was, in fact, none other than Tim Healy (1855–1931).[17] This would be comparable to discovering that Winston Churchill had been a Soviet agent for most of his life! Healy came from a prominent Cork family, had a brilliant career in politics and at the bar, and ended up as the first Governor-General of the Irish Free State. Curiously, Healy resigned his parliamentary seat in 1918 and was out of the public eye throughout the ensuing turbulent years. When his name was first proposed as a contender for the Governor-Generalship it was greeted with incredulity. He had the reputation of being an extreme Nationalist, the very man, in fact, who had split the Nationalist Party over Parnell in the year that Michael Collins was born. His cause was most eloquently promoted by his nephew, Kevin O'Higgins, as 'an old man of the people', and, indeed he turned out to be an excellent choice. As King George's personal representative he did nothing to embarrass the Free State Government, while he was also instrumental in cultivating the goodwill of the Protestant minority. At the time of the Invincibles trial, interestingly enough, he himself was in prison (1883), having been convicted on a charge of sedition.

MacBride furthermore maintained that, back in 1882, Healy was a member of the IRB and had conspired with an American agent of Clan na nGael to murder Captain Henry James Jury, proprietor of the celebrated Dublin hotel where the Clan agent was registered. Jury was allegedly caught going through the American's baggage. Tim Pat Coogan investigated MacBride's allegations and made some interesting discoveries, which point to Jury's death, on 29 May 1882, having taken in place in highly suspicious circumstances. The supposition is that the British discovered that Healy had murdered their agent and compelled him to work for them thereafter. One other piece of this strange jigsaw was that in 1920, shortly before Bloody Sunday, Michael suddenly developed a consuming interest in the history of the Invincibles and asked Art O'Brien for full details. This may have some bearing on the fact that, as soon as news of Michael's death reached Dublin, someone removed a top-secret file from his desk in Portobello Barracks. Whether this action was done *before* the order from the Provisional Government on 23 August to clear Michael's desk was carried out by Gearoid McGann, Michael's secretary, or as part of that directive, has been a matter of endless speculation for years.[18]

Markham did, indeed, find some documentary evidence which apparently linked 'Thorpe' to Healy; these papers passed eventually to T.P. O'Neill, de Valera's official biographer, who gave them only a cursory glance before depositing them in the National Library whence, surprise, surprise, they seem to have vanished. Markham himself developed paranoia, especially after his wife's death, and was convinced that there had been a cover-up following Michael's death.[19]

Consequently, the case is not proven. Moreover, Cabinet papers of 1922 indicate quite unequivocally that Michael was in total command at all times. Far from there being any evidence of a junta or a cabal ganging up on him, Michael's forceful personality left its stamp all over the Cabinet discussions and it was his decision, and his alone, that he should take over as Commander-in-Chief — because he wanted to lick the army into shape and win the civil war quickly. Michael's ultimate goal was to lead a strong army into the North and put an end to partition; but only a military strongman, of the calibre of a Pilsudski (who was then driving the Bolsheviks out of Poland) could achieve this. Michael was at all times conscious of his destiny, but never more so than in July and August 1922.

Michael returned to Dublin for Griffith's funeral, which took place on 16 August. The simple procession to Glasnevin was all the more impressive as the General Staff in their green uniforms marched behind the coffin, Collins and Mulcahy in front, the other generals in three ranks behind. Michael, on the right of the line, towering above his colleagues, made a tremendous impact on the throng of spectators. This was the gilded youth in whom all their hopes reposed, so handsome, so dashing, with the gold bars of a full general on his epaulettes. But the set of his jaw betrayed more than the cares of state. As he marched behind the coffin, Michael's thoughts were hundreds of miles away, in the condemned cells at Wandsworth Prison; on the very same day, Reggie Dunne and Joseph O'Sullivan went to the gallows. At the cemetery Michael lingered over the fresh grave, moving his old friend Bishop Fogarty to remark, 'Michael, you should be prepared – you might be next.'

Michael gazed back: 'I know,' he said simply, then added sardonically, 'I hope nobody takes it into his head to die for another twelve months.'[20]

A keen observer might also have noticed that the Commander-in-Chief's sombre visage concealed real physical pain. Irregular eating habits compounded by overwork and stress had given him a recurrence of the severe dyspepsia that had plagued him, off and on, for over three years. At one stage, it may be recalled, he had given up smoking and alcohol, but latterly he had begun drinking again. Reports of intoxication, often in the context of being drunk with Andy Cope, were probably nothing more than malicious gossip. The incredible volume of work which Michael got through in an average day, judging by the mass of letters, directives, memoranda and reports, invariably marked with the time as well as the date, was indicative of the workaholic, not the alcoholic. Manuscript reports, often produced very late at night, show no variation in Michael's meticulous clerkly hand and give the lie to the canard of heavy drinking. But, most of all, the fact that all the evidence of eye-witness accounts suggests that, by the summer of 1922, Michael was suffering from gastric ulcers, must surely rule out the frequent resort to Jameson's whiskey alleged by his detractors. This was merely part of the hard-drinking, womanising image which was got up to assassinate his character, just as assuredly as Michael the man was done to death. Apart from stomach problems, which may have included a grumbling appendix, Michael was particularly prone to colds. At the time, this was often blamed on exposure to the inclement weather in the indifferent summer of 1922, but this was a fallacy. The tendency to pick up any viral infection that was going around indicates that the Big Fellow, in the last weeks of his life, was physically and mentally at a low ebb.

Significantly, the daily letters to Kitty came to an end about the time Griffith died. Michael and Kitty met again, probably for the last time, after Griffith's funeral. Perhaps Michael had a premonition; on impulse he ripped the button off his left breast pocket and handed it to Kitty as a keepsake, a good-luck charm. Several photographs of him taken in the ensuing days show the Commander-in-Chief improperly dressed, a matter which would have earned any of his subordinates confinement to barracks. Although there was no break in the relationship, it seems odd that no letters on either side are extant after a long and very loving one from Kitty, written on 15 August, which Michael received two days later. In it she mused on mortality:

Poor Griffith's death is too awful for me to think of, RIP. Was he prepared, I wonder? When that hour comes what good is anything else? We are just all bits of dust, the great as well as the small. He will be a loss to you. I can picture it. How unfortunate it should happen just now. He was, poor man, evidently overworked, too, and took no holiday, or at least not in time. I am always thinking of you and worrying, and just to-night somebody said that if you go to the funeral to-morrow you'll be shot, but God is very good to you, and we must both go to Lough Derg some time in thanksgiving. Did you ever hear of it? It's very hard. I did it three times already.

Lough Derg referred to a place of penitential pilgrimage near Pettigo, County Donegal, close to the border with Northern Ireland. The letter ended poignantly:

Perhaps I'll take a run up to town from the North, and meet Mops [her sister Maud] there at the end of the week, if Chrys doesn't mind. Are you lonely for me or too busy and too worried to think? I send you a kiss with my love . . .
    Good bye Mícheál
        Your own loving me.[21]

Kitty's 'run up to town' would, indeed, take place, but in very different circumstances.

Probably on Thursday, 17 August, Michael was at Furry Park, the home of Moya and Crompton Llewelyn Davies, for a dinner party that included Sir John and Lady Lavery, Sir Horace and Lady Plunkett, Piaras Beaslai and Joe O'Reilly, to whom a boy messenger, Bill McKenna, brought word of an assassination attempt. Joe wanted Michael to keep well away from the windows but, careless of danger as ever, Michael flatly refused. In the end, Joe and Hazel Lavery sat in the window to shield him. Meanwhile a search party discovered a sniper ensconced in a tree with a high-powered rifle. The man, named Dixon, had been a marksman with the Connaught Rangers. While the gay hubbub of voices in the dining-room continued unabated, Michael's bodyguards took the luckless Dixon through the darkened fields, down to the sloblands, and shot him dead.

Dick Mulcahy recollected later how he had breakfast with Michael on Saturday morning, 'writhing with pain from a cold all through his body'. Later that day Michael drove out to Greystones to visit the Leigh Doyles. He presented them with a studio photograph of himself in his uniform but was in too much of a hurry to autograph it for them; he would sign it when he returned from his southern tour of inspection. Though not one prone to studied gestures, at the gate as he left Michael turned slowly and gave them an impressive military salute, an incident that remained sharply etched on their memory.

George Bernard Shaw was in Dublin for Griffith's funeral and met Michael at Furry Park, and also at Kilteragh House, the home of Sir Horace Plunkett in Foxrock, on that evening. The greatest living playwright of the English language was deeply impressed by the young man in his splendid uniform, but though Michael spoke pleasantly enough to him, Shaw noted that 'his nerves were in rags and he kept slapping his revolver all the time he was talking'. Michael carried his pistol in an open holster slung low, cowboy style, from his Sam Browne belt and secured by a narrow strap round his leg, just above the knee. This mannerism, of tapping it frequently to reassure him that it was still there, was quite subconscious, but apparently became more pronounced in the last days of his life. Driving back to barracks after the party that night, Michael was ambushed by a group of anti-Treaty Irregulars. A fusillade raked the car but no one was injured and Michael's driver had the presence of mind to put his foot hard down on the pedal and speed out of danger. Michael was too racked with pain to care at that precise moment. Frank O' Connor's description of Michael's last week on earth is probably accurate enough:

> He lived it in suffering, mental and physical. Though still full of ideas and enthusiasm he found it hard to work. He sat at his desk, scribbled a few lines, then rose and left the room, not in the old dashing way, but slowly and in dejection. The shadow had begun to fall.[22]

Michael seems, indeed, to have had some sort of premonition. To Cosgrave he said, 'Do you think I shall live through this? Not likely!', then turned to a typist and asked, 'How would you like a new boss?' The girl was so taken aback at this that she repeated it to Joe O'Reilly who kept pondering these words and worrying so much that, on the following day, when they were driving into the city together, Joe anxiously asked Michael how his health was.

'Rotten!' said Michael heavily. After a pause, he asked, 'How would you like a new boss?'

Joe's heart sank. 'No! I'd never work for anyone else!' he replied fervently. Michael merely gave a quizzical half-smile, but Joe saw that he was touched and gratified by the response. He still got irritable if Joe fussed over him, but he was obviously grateful for the solicitude.

Historians and biographers, with the benefit of hindsight, usually refer to Michael's last mission as ill-advised. In truth there was no shortage of advice, notably from his Director of Intelligence, Joe McGrath, telling him – in a letter written in red ink – that it was extremely foolhardy to go to County Cork, the area in which IRA activity was at its height. It was Michael's own decision, against the advice of everyone else, to go ahead. He would be travelling in his own home county, and he was convinced that, though the people of Cork might be anti-Treaty to the last man, they would not lift a finger against one of their own. The Headquarters Staff had the impression that Michael was confident that he would be able to resume contact with old friends and, by the force of his personality, win them over. This direct approach was surely worth any number of peace delegations in Dublin. The journey west was mainly a public-relations exercise, to raise the flagging morale of the National Army, to engender goodwill and to defuse hostility. He hoped to visit his birthplace and see his family.

Refusing to heed all the warnings showered upon him, Michael compromised by sending Frank Thornton ahead to make sure that Clonmel was secure by vetting the Volunteers manning the garrison. At the same time Thornton was empowered to offer safe-conduct passes to prominent Republicans in the area whom Michael wished to meet. These were Tom Barry and Tom Hales, two of the most senior IRA officers in the west. On the tour of inspection that was cut short by Griffith's death, Michael had visited Portlaoise Gaol and interviewed Tom Malone (otherwise known as Sean Forde), leader of the East Limerick IRA. Michael asked him if he would be willing to attend a meeting of senior officers 'to put an end to this damned thing'. As he went out, Michael slapped one fist into the other palm, crying, 'That's fine! The three Toms will fix it!'[23] Leaving instructions with Jack Twomey, the prison governor, to look after Malone, Michael promised to see him again.

Ominously, Thornton's entourage was ambushed and Frank himself severely wounded in the affray. According to Frank O'Connor, de Valera (who was in the Clonmel area at the time) was convinced that Thornton had been despatched on a mission to murder him. As a result, whatever peace feelers were intended at Clonmel never materialised. Similarly, the peace talks which Michael had hoped to organise at Cork never came about.

On the night before his departure for Cork, Michael retired to bed at 7.30, suffering from a bad chill and severe stomach cramps. Joe O'Reilly and Michael's batman got him into bed and administered medicine, then Joe went off to the Mess and got some oranges and made him a drink of hot juice. 'God, that's grand,' sighed Michael. Encouraged by these, the first words of gratitude which had passed between them, Joe tucked him in for the night, but that was too much. Gathering all his strength, Michael bawled, 'Go to hell and leave me alone!'

Next morning, Sunday, 20 August, he was up very early and struggled through his breakfast. Mulcahy and others urged him to cancel or at least postpone the trip; but he was adamant. He had to get to Cork, come hell or high water. He roused Joe Sweeney to say goodbye and join him in a farewell drink.

'You're a fool to go,' said Joe.

'Ah, whatever happens to me, my own fellow-countymen won't kill me,' said Michael moodily.

As he tramped downstairs to wait for his staff car he tripped, banged his low-slung revolver against the wall and accidentally discharged a round. The bullet narrowly missed his foot – an ill-omen if ever there was one.

Roused by the shot O'Reilly woke suddenly and rushed to the window, but was relieved to see Michael standing outside on the steps of the barracks, waiting for his open-tourer to arrive. He was carrying a small green kitbag over his shoulder, his head bent in gloomy meditation. Joe thought 'he had never seen so tragically dejected a figure as Michael who, thinking himself unobserved, let himself fall slack in the loneliness and silence of the summer morning'.[24] Joe hastily pulled on his trousers and rushed downstairs to say goodbye, but the car had already left.

Michael's first stop was at the Curragh where he inspected the barracks. After breakfast at Roscrea, the entourage drove west to Limerick accompanied by Fionan Lynch, arriving shortly before midday, where Michael was met by General O'Duffy. An army dance was in full swing in Cruise's Hotel; Michael and his retinue looked in on the jollification, but at the bar there was an ugly incident. A young priest called Michael a traitor. 'Immediately,' said an eye-witness, 'a young officer from Dublin hit the priest who fell to the floor and rolled under some stools . . . Michael Collins never said a word. He left the dance.' From Limerick Michael drove to Mallow and inspected the garrison under Commandant Tom Flood. Just after leaving Mallow they ran into a crowd at a crossroads. Michael's driver, a Dubliner, suspected an ambush, but Michael laughed heartily: 'Drive on, you fool. Don't you see? It's only the usual Sunday evening crossroads dancing!' It was in the wee small hours that Michael alighted at the Imperial Hotel in Cork. Finding the two young sentries on duty in the lobby fast asleep he banged their heads together and strode on.[25]

One of the reasons for Michael's visit to Cork was to recover a large sum of money, said to be about £120,000, which the IRA had appropriated from the Customs and Excise by the simple expedient of sending an armed squad to the Cistercian monastery at Mount Melleray where the Collector was 'drying out' on retreat, and forcing him at gunpoint to sign the necessary warrants. To a hard-pressed Provisional Government, the cash (worth in excess of £2 million today) had to be retrieved from the enemy at all costs. This money probably gave rise to the myth that, at the time of his death, Michael was carrying a hoard of IRB gold which had been hidden away in the Cork area. Certainly,

Michael spent some time on Monday, 21 August, with H.A. Pelly, general manager of the Hibernian Bank in Cork, in a bid to locate the missing funds, and later that day fired off a memo to Cosgrave on the subject. It appeared that IRA cash from the Customs and Excise haul had been laundered through some of the London banks where Erskine Childers had opened accounts. As a result, about £39,000 was eventually recovered. In this connection Michael met his sister Mary Collins-Powell and sent her son Sean (later Lieutenant-General Collins-Powell, Chief of Staff of the Irish Army) on a dangerous errand connected with the Pelly mission. The boy was hotly pursued on his bicycle by some IRA men, but managed to give them the slip. Sean hoped that his uncle would take him along for the ride the following day, but Michael refused, saying, 'I've got my job to do and you've got yours.'

At 3.30 p.m. Michael wrote to Cosgrave again, recommending that the new national police force, the Civic Guards, should be extended to Cork and Limerick in order to restore law and order as soon as possible. Afterwards, he drove out as far as Macroom, inspecting army posts and visiting relatives and old family friends. By the time he returned to the Imperial Hotel that evening he was in a much more equable state of mind than he had been the previous day. An old pal from Frongoch called at the hotel and urged him to make peace. Michael argued with him for a bit and then said, 'Very well, see me tomorrow night. I may have news for you.' Then General Collins challenged his old comrade to wrestle for 'a bit of ear' and the two of them ended up rolling around on the floor, to the alarm and embarrassment of the sentries. That night Michael shared a room with Joe Dolan who remembered the vigour with which the Commander-in-Chief hurled his boots outside the door before taking a flying leap into bed.

Up at dawn on Tuesday morning, Michael ate a hearty breakfast. As he stood in the lounge of the Imperial chatting to Emmet Dalton, by coincidence who should walk past but another survivor of the assault on Mountjoy, Pat MacCrea, who had driven the armoured car in the attempt to free Sean MacEoin. MacCrea had recently been ambushed and wounded in Wicklow.

'Ah, Pat,' said Michael. 'Your fellow-countrymen nearly did for you!'

That sunny summer's morning Michael and his entourage set off on a lightning tour of West Cork just after six o'clock. Tuesday, 22 August, had been the date that Kitty had selected for their wedding, but Michael had postponed it till after his crucial mission. It appears that the reason for this particular trip was a tryst with prominent Republicans with a view to opening peace negotiations. According to Sean MacEoin, the IRA even supplied Dalton with details of mined roads and bridges and generally speaking assured a safe conduct for the Commander-in-Chief. The IRA had warned the bulk of their forces in the area to stand down while this delicate mission was in progress, but, as a precaution, Michael had arranged an armoured escort just in case. Nevertheless, this explains why the escort on this occasion was pitifully small, given the fact that they were moving through the staunchest of Republican territory.

The cavalcade consisted of a motorcycle scout, Lieutenant Smith, followed by a Crossley tender commanded by two former Squad members, Commandants Joe Dolan and Sean O'Connell, and carrying eight riflemen and two machine-gunners. The next vehicle was also a Crossley tender containing ten men, some of whom were pro-Treaty IRA from Mayo who wished to join the new Civic Guards and who had been promised a lift back to Dublin if they agreed to come along on this jaunt expressly to clear felled trees and other obstacles on the road which might have presaged an ambush. Next came a Leyland-Thomas straight-eight-cylinder open touring-car. In front sat the driver, M.B. Corry, and Michael's personal bodyguard, M. Quinn. In the rear sat General Collins and Major-General Dalton. At the rear of the column was *Slievenamon*, a Rolls-Royce Whippet armoured car named after the famous 'Mountain of Women'.

They went first to Macroom, via Coachford, where Michael saw Florrie O'Donoghue, who was in detention in Macroom Castle. O'Donoghue, one of the top IRA leaders in the area, had been given a safe conduct by Dalton to visit his sick mother, but had been accidentally arrested by a Free State officer. A reflection of the casual nature of this strange war was the fact that Florrie had caught sight of Michael from his cell window, and got the sentry guarding him to take a note to the Commander-in-Chief, while Florrie looked after his rifle for him! Michael himself appeared at the cell, unlocked the door, and led him out for a crack, complaining to Florrie, 'I've been all over this bloody country and no one has said a bloody word to me.' He was pleasantly surprised 'that no one could stop him'. It was in this overconfident frame of mind that Michael went to his death.

From Macroom to Bandon by the back road the way was littered with felled trees. At various points the road had been dug up or bridges dismantled, so that progress was exceedingly slow and the party was obliged to hire a local taxi-driver to guide them through this maze. At Ballymichael Hill the Whippet armoured car stalled, and everyone had to get out and push it up the steep gradient. While this was going on Lieutenant Smith, the motorcycle scout, went ahead knocking on the doors of cottages and farmhouses along the road, calling out loudly, 'The Commander-in-Chief is coming!' What his motives were have never been ascertained, but this action was both foolish and provocative. Fortunately no one took advantage of the warning to take a pot-shot at the visitors. Then the tourer played up, its engine overheating twice and entailing unscheduled halts for water.

Eventually, about nine o'clock, the cavalcade reached the crossroads at the entrance to Beal na mBlath, a minor pass between the hills which doubtless derived its exotic name from the carpet of wildflowers on the hillside in high summer. The cabbie was unsure of the road and an enquiry was made at Long's pub at the crossroads for directions. Denny Long, known as Denny the Dane, obligingly pointed out the road to Bandon and sent the party on its way. Unbeknown to the cavalcade, Long was standing at the bat-wing doors of his saloon where he had been posted as a lookout while a top-level Republican meeting was taking place in Murray's farmhouse nearby. As soon as the military column had disappeared round the corner, Denny reported to Tom Hales who, reasoning that the party would return from Bandon along the same route, decided to lay an ambush. Flor Begley puts this in its proper context:

> It leaked out that Michael Collins was coming south and that some members of the Dublin Brigade were coming to protect him and that they didn't give a damn about the 3rd West Cork Brigade fellows. This 'got their goat' and they decided to have a go at the Dublin crowd.[26]

In other words, Michael was not so much the target as those dreadful Dubliners muscling in on Corkmen's territory. Liam Deasy, one of the most senior officers of the Cork IRA, regarded Michael as 'the greatest leader of our generation' and felt that this was no mere social visit. 'I rated it as the foolhardy act of a brave man.'[27] At that moment de Valera and Childers were only ten miles away, a fact which has led some writers to speculate whether Michael was trying to arrange a top-level meeting with them, and renew the de Valera–Collins pact; but against that must be weighed the fact that the first they knew of Michael's death was when they read of it in the newspapers.

What Michael was doing up a country lane in the first place, when there was a perfectly good main road from Cork to Bandon, untrammelled by trenches and road-blocks, is something of a mystery; but it is believed that he was hoping to visit Canon Tracey of Crookstown and open a conduit to prominent Republicans such as Alfred O'Rahilly and Sean O'Hegarty. The previous weekend, however, the Canon's housekeeper had blabbed in the village store about 'important visitors' being imminent, as a result of which another IRA ambush was laid on 21 August at Farran, a heavily wooded area near Crookstown, with a view to kidnapping the Free State leader. When he did not show up on that day, a girl was sent to the Imperial Hotel to glean what she could of the Big Fellow's movements, and got a detailed itinerary from some of the loose-tongued escort party in the hotel bar. As a result the Farran ambush was set up a second time and remained in place all day.

Unaware of this flurry of preparations to greet him, Michael and his party continued through Beal na mBlath on the way to Bandon. At one stage the touring car got separated from the other vehicles and took a wrong turning, with the result that Collins and Dalton found themselves in Newcestown. When the rest of the column caught up with him, they found Michael in the cemetery studying the inscriptions on the tombstones, a rather morbid occupation. At that moment Tom Hales was preparing the fatal ambush back at Beal na mBlath by blocking the road with a brewer's dray and placing mines on the road. Snipers took up positions on the high ground above the road, past Long's pub; on the other side of the road, in the bushes beyond a small stream, a second group of riflemen concealed themselves. The preparations were watched by de Valera himself. He had spent the night in a farmhouse less than two miles away. On hearing that the Commander-in-Chief had driven past, he is reported to have said, 'What a pity I didn't meet him,' and 'It would be bad if anything happens to Collins, his place will be taken by weaker men.' From this quirk of fate has arisen the myth that de Valera planned and orchestrated his great rival's assassination, but nothing could be farther from the truth. The most reliable evidence indicates that de Valera went to Long's pub and tried to prevent the ambush. With all his eloquence Dev argued that Collins was in the area to negotiate a peace settlement, and that this would be on much more advantageous terms there in Cork than it would be once he was back with his Cabinet colleagues in Dublin. De Valera, however, was reminded in no uncertain terms that, in this area, he was merely a staff officer under the area commander, Liam Lynch, and they did not take orders from anyone else. Furious, de Valera stormed off to Kilworth where the local doctor gave him a lift by pony and trap to Fermoy and thence, by car, to Fethard where he was staying that night when he learned of Michael's death. Eye-witnesses say that he was 'furious and visibly upset'.

While Dev was on his way to Fethard, Michael was on the road from Bandon to Clonakilty. About three miles from the latter the road was blocked with felled trees, causing a thirty-minute delay. Michael himself directed the work of clearing the road, and took a hand in it. 'Active and powerful in body and mind,' said Emmet Dalton, 'he handled axe and saw with the same vigour as he could exhibit in the direction of affairs of state, military or civil.'[28] They lunched with family friends in Clonakilty where the whole town turned out to greet the local hero. From there they went to Lisavaird and Sam's Cross, visited the ruins of Woodfield destroyed by Major Percival, met brother Johnny and other relatives, and congregated in cousin Jerry's bar, the Four Alls, where Michael stood drinks all round. The same scene was repeated at Rosscarbery and Skibbereen as the trip gradually turned into a triumphal progress. At the latter town they paused for further refreshments at Walsh's Eldon Hotel which still has on its wall probably the last photograph taken of the Big Fellow, stepping into his staff car and waving to the enraptured onlookers.

In the afternoon they called at Rosscarbery and Clonakilty on the return journey, again sampling copious draughts of the notorious wrastler. While Michael was temporarily absent on a private visit to an old friend of his mother, there was a bit of a fracas at Callinan's pub in Rosscarbery between local troops and the Dubliners when John McPeak, the Scotsman in charge of *Slievenamon*'s machine-gun, 'commandeered' a bottle of whiskey off the shelf. In the ensuing fight Captain Sean McCarthy of the local force disarmed six of Michael's escort and had them locked up. McCarthy was suspicious of them because they were ex-British army personnel whom he suspected of a plot against the Commander-in-Chief. When McCarthy voiced his suspicions to Michael, the latter thanked him warmly and said, 'I'm going to put an end to this bloody war as soon as possible.' By now the schedule had been thrown to the winds and the visit to Crookstown was cancelled due to the lateness of the hour. By the time they left Bandon at 8 p.m. the entourage in general was well oiled. Michael, on account of his stomach problems, may have been reasonably sober, but Emmet Dalton (who in later life had quite a drink problem) admitted privately that 'we were all arseholes'.[29] Billy Powell, commander of the Lissarda IRA, said that the members of the convoy were 'in no shape for fighting. They'd been on a bit of a spree all day. Mick Collins stood them drink wherever he stopped.'[30]

Incredibly, news of the ambush at Beal na mBlath was common knowledge around the district, and Michael was repeatedly given warnings at Rosscarbery and Bandon. Two farmers carting lime got involved with an argument with the ambush party when they tried to move the disabled brewer's dray in order to get past. One of the men, a relative of Michael's, contacted Paddy Callinan in Rosscarbery and the publican relayed the message to Collins. Captain Paddy Collins, another of Michael's cousins, was present when Callinan warned the Big Fellow, but Michael merely shrugged his shoulders and said, 'Yerra, sure they'd never attack me.' There is no doubt at all that Michael ignored every rule of guerrilla warfare that day. Cousin Paddy noted that he was 'the same old Mick, not under any strain'. Indeed, far removed from the stresses and strains of Dublin and back among his kith and kin, he was the bluff, hearty, easy-going Mick that everyone loved and remembered. In Bandon he took a bibulous farewell of Major-General Sean Hales, the Free State commander, and set off for Beal na mBlath where Sean's brother Tom and the local IRA were lying in wait to kill him.

Meanwhile, at Beal na mBlath itself, the ambushers had grown weary and were now arguing among themselves. Surely to God, at this late hour, with the light failing, the Big Fellow must have gone back to Cork by another road. Most of them gave up and drifted off to Long's for a few pints before heading for home. But six men – Tom Hales, Tom Kelliher, Jim Hurley, Dan Holland, Sonny O'Neill and John O'Callaghan – were determined to stick it out. Hales decided that the mines on the road should be deactivated so that farmers could use the road the following morning. He was carrying one mine and had removed the detonator from the other when Smith the motorcyclist hove into sight from the direction of Bandon. Kelliher and O'Neill, on the hillside, fired shots alerting Hales who just had time to chuck the mine over the fence and vault after it, before the convoy came round the corner. The mines had been rendered harmless, the only tommy gun had been left behind in the pub, and the handful of men flanking the road had only small arms. As the Crossley tenders, Whippet and touring car approached, Tom Hales's chief thought was how to make an escape. They were outnumbered five to one, and facing three machine-guns as well as other automatic weapons.

But the barrier was still in place, and alongside was a donkey cart which had been abandoned by its owner, unable to get past the roadblock. Smith almost collided with the animal peacefully grazing at the roadside, and skidded into the ditch. Dalton, realising that they were approaching an ambush, ordered Corry to 'Drive like hell!'. This was the correct procedure in such a situation; it had saved Johnny French's life in 1919 when Michael tried to ambush the Lord Lieutenant. Ironically, Michael countermanded the order and decided on a showdown. In view of the repeated warnings that day he may have decided to face the enemy; Dalton noted that Michael had picked up his rifle as they approached Beal na mBlath. With the first ragged fusillade from the hillside, Michael put his hand on Corry's shoulder and cried, 'Stop! Jump out and we'll fight them.' While the men jumped out and began returning the enemy's fire, McPeak in the armoured car drove slowly back and forward, raking the hillside with his Vickers machine-gun. Unfortunately, McPeak did not have his gunner's mate with him that fateful day, and it was left to one of the passengers (a staff officer) to feed the belts of ammo into the gun. Inexpert handling of a belt caused the gun to jam at a crucial moment, just when McPeak was about to enfilade the ambushers. The two Lewis guns in the Crossley tender do not appear to have contributed much to the action.

By now the ambushers who had been slaking their thirst at Long's had emerged, suitably refreshed, and began taking pot shots at the convoy from the top of the hill, too far away to have any effect. At this juncture an IRA flying-column retreating at high speed from Kerry came on the scene and joined in the fun. While bullets were flying in all directions Michael had been sheltered by the side of his car, firing back on Kelliher and Hales. When the six men of the ambush party got up and began running off, Michael leaped to his feet, brandishing his rifle and crying, 'Come on, boys! There they are, running up the road!' He ran back down the road about fifty yards to get a better view of the men retreating up the hillside on his left. He was out on the open road now, without cover of any kind, in full view of some of the toughest guerrillas in all Ireland. Most accounts agree that Michael was standing up and coolly aiming back at the enemy. Dalton claimed that 'Mick wouldn't keep his head down. If he'd ever been in a scrap he'd have learned to stay down. For I was flat down and Mick was killed standing up.'

The shooting had tailed off, and the enemy were clearly disengaging, when there was an anguished cry of 'Emmet!'. Dalton and Sean O'Connell darted out from cover behind *Slievenamon* and ran to Michael, now lying on the road, 'a fearful gaping wound at the base of the skull and behind the right ear'. O'Connell said an Act of Contrition and imagined that Michael responded by a slight squeeze of his hand. On the hillside, Sonny O'Neill, an ex-British army marksman, fled in the gloaming. He had paused only long enough to loose off a last long shot at the tall figure in the roadway. He thought he might have hit him, but did not wait around to find out.

The entire engagement had lasted about half an hour. The light was going and life was ebbing out of Michael as Dalton and O'Connell dragged him back into the shelter of the armoured car. Smith, though shot through the neck – he was the only other casualty on either side – helped to bandage the gaping wound in Michael's head and even lent a hand to carry him back to the open tourer. Emmet held Michael in his arms in the back seat as the convoy drove the nineteen miles to Cork. Historians have speculated endlessly ever since as to why they did not head back to Bandon where surgical help might have saved Michael's life. At Long's pub the party spent some time trying first-aid, before setting off for Cork around 9.30 p.m. In the pub were several IRA men, though none of those who had taken part in the ambush. Word was speedily transmitted to Murray's farmhouse where Liam Deasy was holding a council of war. Later he described his reaction to the news that Michael Collins had been killed:

> The meeting was adjourned immediately and many of us left Murray's with heavy hearts. To those of us who had known Collins personally, and there were many, his death was tragic; to Tom Hales, Tadhg O'Sullivan and myself who had known him intimately, our sorrow was deep and lasting. We parted without discussion of any kind . . . each of us all too conscious of the tragedy and the loneliness that only time could heal.[31]

The party paused at Bellmont Mills near Crookstown, seeking directions for Cork and the services of a priest. Ironically, Canon Tracey lived outside the village and had actually heard the gunfire that evening without realising its appalling significance. Rather than lose further precious minutes trying to find the Canon's presbytery the convoy pressed on to the curate's house at Cloughduv which they reached around 11 p.m. Dalton records what happened next:

> On the way back we came upon a church – with a stretch of gravel and railings in front – along the road. One of my men went in asking for a priest. A priest came out as far as the railings, looked in at the dead Collins lying on my shoulder in the back seat of the car then turned on his heel and walked back in. One of my officers raised his rifle to shoot the priest and only that I struck up the barrel the priest would have been shot. The bullet was actually discharged . . . This incident left a grim impression on the minds of the entire party.[32]

The priest, Father Timothy Murphy, told a different story. He said that he actually walked out to the car and noted the soldier lying with his head on the lap of a young officer who was sobbing and crying. Father Murphy said an Act of Contrition and other prayers and made the Sign of the Cross. Then he told an officer to wait while he went back to the house to fetch the holy oils, but when he returned the convoy had driven off. A bystander afterwards told him that he had heard an officer say 'That priest is not coming back' and ordered the convoy to drive off. Needless to say, Father Murphy was oblivious to the fact that he, too, was almost shot dead.

They came to a triple road fork and took the wrong turning. Driving down this strange road in total darkness, the leading car picked out the figure of a man in the headlights, walking towards them. Immediately they suspected a trap. The convoy screeched to a halt and safety catches were eased off. At gunpoint, the stranger told the panicky soldiers, now painfully sober, that they were on the wrong track and, in fact, on the edge of a precipice. To prove his point he led them a few yards on foot to where the road suddenly vanished into the night. The bridge spanning the Cork-Macroom railway line had been blown up, leaving a forty-foot drop to the tracks. The only way out was to reverse a few yards, then head across four fields back to the main Cork road. This short-cut proved to be even more tedious, for the vehicles were soon stuck fast in thick mud. Eventually they managed to extricate one of the Crossley tenders on a raft of blankets and army greatcoats, but *Slievenamon* sank deeper and deeper into the bog and had to be abandoned. Then the open-tourer refused to start and it, too, was left where it stuck. Michael's bloody corpse was manhandled several hundred yards across muddy fields, a nightmare journey for the pall-bearers, drenched in his blood and spattered with his brains. Back on the road again, the body was laid in the tender with a soldier standing guard on either side.

It was around two o'clock in the morning when the sorry cavalcade rolled into Cork after further detours and delays. Two members of the Civic Patrol met them at the corner of Washington Street and Grand Parade and led them to Shanakiel Military Hospital. Some historians have made much of the fact that Michael's body was taken to the British Military Hospital, still staffed by doctors and nurses of the British army, and not to one of the civilian hospitals. Indeed, this fact has been adduced in support of the theory that Emmet Dalton was in the pay of the British Secret Service to have his Commander-in-Chief killed; but it was pure accident that the Civic Guards should have led them to Shanakiel rather than the Bon Secour. Dalton had the presence of mind to send a telegram from the Imperial Hotel (one of the few hotels in Ireland that boasted such facilities) to Valentia Island Cable Station, and thence to Dublin via the transatlantic cable to New York, then back across the ocean to London and across the Irish Sea to Dublin. Not surprisingly, the London *Daily Express* and Dublin's *Freeman's Journal* had the news in their first editions the following morning, before *The Cork Examiner* even had wind of the tragedy on its own doorstep. From New York the news had spread to Randolph Hearst who cabled Dalton immediately, offering him £1,000 for his story. Dalton was enraged on receipt of this wire.

At Portobello Barracks, where the General Staff had their quarters, first to get the news from the duty telegraphist in the middle of the night was the adjutant-general, Gearoid O'Sullivan. He went immediately to the bedroom of Emmet's brother, Charlie, who recorded:

> He did not greet me as customarily, but stood rather bewildered-looking for a second or two and then broke down weeping and spoke in a rather uncertain voice saying, 'Charlie, the Big Fella is dead'.[33]

Joe O'Reilly and Tom Cullen were the next to hear the news. Cullen spoke first: 'Something terrible has happened – I know what you have come to tell me – the Big Fella is dead! I've been dreaming about him.' Dawn was breaking as they dressed hurriedly and went off to tell Batt O'Connor, one of Michael's oldest friends. The strain of the dreadful news they had to impart was too much; when they called round at Cosgrave's house in Lansdowne Road to tell him that he was now head of the Provisional Government, their faces were grey, like death itself. They accompanied him to the Government Buildings ringed with sandbags and festooned with barbed wire, to break the news to the Cabinet. Seeing the frightened faces of the ministers, both O'Reilly and Cullen began weeping uncontrollably. Cosgrave alone kept his head, stepping forward with his finger raised gently, 'This is a nice way for soldiers to behave.' Mulcahy immediately drafted a directive to all military units:

Stand calmly by your posts. Bend bravely and undaunted to your work. Let no cruel act of reprisal blemish your bright honour. Every dark hour that Michael Collins met since 1916 seemed but to steel that bright strength of his and temper his gay bravery. You are left each inheritors of that strength, and of that bravery. To each of you falls his unfinished work. No darkness in the hour – no loss of comrades will daunt you at it. Ireland! The Army serves – strengthened by its sorrow.[34]

Hannie went to work at the Post Office Savings Bank as usual that Wednesday morning, unaware of the tragedy. She was called into her boss's office and he had the unenviable task of breaking the news to her. Hannie went deathly pale, then burst into tears, and two of the girls who worked with her were detailed to accompany her back to her flat. Later that morning, having recovered her composure, Hannie went round to the home of Sir John and Lady Lavery in Cromwell Place where Michael had stayed that June, but found that the Laverys were out of town. In a daze, she wandered back to her flat and began packing a small suitcase. At 8.45 p.m. she boarded the Irish boat train at Euston. Winston Churchill, having been apprised of Hannie's acute distress by the Laverys' butler, had personally reserved a compartment for her and paid her travelling expenses. A newspaper reporter at Euston recorded that Miss Collins, dressed from head to foot in black, was seen off by a lady friend. 'She was a calm but pathetic figure. She travelled alone.'[35]

Epilogue

When we make ourselves fit we shall be free. If we could
accept that truth we would be inspired again with the same
fervour and devotion by our own 'grim resolve' within the
nation to complete the work which is so nearly done.
MICHAEL COLLINS, *The Path to Freedom* (1922)

Well may strong men wring their souls in the depths of
black despair, and doubt if Ireland can emerge bleeding and
torn from the burden and cruel Cross of calamity and red
ruin laid upon her shoulders.
The Midland Reporter, 23 AUGUST 1922

EARLY IN THE MORNING OF THURSDAY, 24 AUGUST, A LITTLE STEAM-
ship, her brand-new tricolour at half mast, nosed her way into the mouth of the
Liffey and slowly approached the North Wall. The *Classic* had put into Cork
from Fishguard early the previous morning, and was diverted from her normal
run to bear a very precious cargo to Dublin. That evening green-coated soldiers
had borne the coffin up the gangplank and reverently laid it on the foredeck,
draped with the tricolour. Many contemporary accounts also mention a blood-
stained general's cap laid on the coffin. Michael's cap, in fact, was found early
on the morning of 23 August at Beal na mBlath by a passing farmer who took
it home, washed it and buried it in a biscuit tin in the farmyard. Not long
afterwards, though, worried that the interment of any human remains, however
microscopic, might bring Michael's ghost to haunt him, the farmer exhumed
the cap and handed it over to a priest who appears to have taken it immediately
to Cork. The blood-spattered uniform which Michael was wearing at the time
of the ambush was purloined by one of the doctors at Shanakiel Hospital and
was taken with him when he emigrated to Argentina.

As the vessel weighed anchor the bell tolled in St Colman's Cathedral and
troops stood to attention with rifles reversed. Along the shore and at the

pierhead in Cobh weeping crowds knelt in prayer.

Only six and a half years previously, a young man had stood in the bows of a similar vessel and expectantly surveyed the scene. Now he lay sightless on the deck of the ship that was bringing him from his home county to the scene of his greatest triumphs. A vast crowd congregated on the Dublin quayside. Many people wept unashamedly and uncontrollably, and as the steamer tied up the wailing and keening rose to a crescendo. No nation ever mourned its fallen so volubly, no people grieved with such total abandon. The body was borne through the once-familiar streets to Vincent's Hospital where Oliver St John Gogarty and Desmond Fitzgerald supervised the embalmer who prepared Michael for his final public appearance in a fresh uniform. Their grisly task completed, Gogarty sent Sean Kavanagh to fetch the sculptor Albert Power to take Michael's death mask. As Gogarty and Fitzgerald made their way back into the city they heard sporadic gunfire from Irregular snipers.

Michael's body remained in the mortuary chapel of St Vincent's Hospital all that day. Only three weeks previously, his close friend Harry Boland had lain on the very same slab. It was here that Sir John Lavery performed a last act for his friend:

> I was allowed to paint him in death. Any grossness in his features, even the peculiar dent near the point of his nose, had disappeared. He might have been Napoleon in marble as he lay in his uniform, covered by the Free State flag, with a crucifix on his breast. Four soldiers stood around the bier. The stillness was broken at long intervals by someone entering the chapel on tiptoe, kissing the brow, and then slipping to the door where I could hear a burst of suppressed grief. One woman kissed the dead lips, making it hard for me to continue my work.[1]

Early on Friday Michael's body was transferred to the City Hall for the public lying-in-state which continued until Sunday evening. Under leaden skies a queue over a mile long waited patiently to file slowly past the bier and pay homage to their dead Chief. No Irishman, before or since, evoked such genuine grief and a devastating sense of loss. Everyone, friend and foe alike, felt Michael's death as keenly as if he had been one of the family. The Dublin Guards, Michael's old Squad and his Intelligence colleagues took turns to provide the guard of honour.

Among the thousands who came to pay their respects was a poor old woman from the slums, black-shawled and down-at-heel. She gazed down at the serene figure and in a high-pitched voice cried out, 'Michael Collins! Michael Collins! Why did you leave us?'

The senseless death of Michael Collins stopped the nation in its tracks.

Public reaction throughout Ireland, throughout the British Isles, throughout the world, was one of immense tragedy and an irreplaceable loss. These feelings transcended the ancient animosities of British and Irish and even the on-going bitterness between pro- and anti-Treaty factions. Commandant-General Tom Barry, then a Republican prisoner in Kilmainham, described the reaction within the prison:

> I was talking with some other prisoners on the night of August 22nd, 1922, when the news came in that Michael Collins had been shot dead in West Cork. There was a heavy silence throughout the jail, and ten minutes later from the corridor outside the top tier of cells I looked down on the extraordinary spectacle of about a thousand kneeling Republican prisoners spontaneously reciting the Rosary aloud for the repose of the soul of the dead Michael Collins . . . I have yet to learn of a better tribute to the part played by any man in the struggle with the English for Irish independence . . .[2]

Lady Gregory's manservant brought her the bad news from the post office at Coole. She noted in her diary that it was 'a bad blow, my hopes had been so much in him. I was stunned. I could not stay in the house but went and sat in the garden for a long time – found at last a little comfort in Mulcahy's fine call to the army.'[3]

It was common knowledge in the upper echelons of society that Hazel Lavery was besotted with Michael – 'his abject admirer' was Lady Gregory's description. Sir John Lavery, then at the height of his fame as a portrait painter, showed remarkable indulgence towards his young and beautiful wife, turning a blind eye to her coquetry and affairs. The Laverys got the news on the morning of 23 August, and Hazel collapsed. Even after she regained consciousness she wept copiously and kept saying to her husband, 'All day I have been seeing them carrying Michael covered with blood. Wherever I go I cannot get rid of the sight,' at which she would lapse into hysterics again. Sir John managed to get her to bed and sat with her until well on into the night, and at last she went to sleep. At seven the following morning her very English maid came in with tea. After she had put down the tray, she said, in a voice showing not the slightest trace of interest, 'They have shot Mr Collins, my Lady.'[4]

The Irish press was fulsome in its eulogies for the dead leader. Even that redoubtable Orange organ, *The Belfast Telegraph*, conceded that 'His removal is a great loss to the Government with which he was so prominently identified.' In England, *The Daily Telegraph*, which had often been his implacable enemy, admitted, 'The dead man, beyond all doubt, was of the stuff of which great men are made,' while *The Daily Chronicle* spoke of the 'young and brilliant leader' and *The Daily Sketch* stated that 'the hand that struck down Michael Collins, guided by a blinded patriotism, has aimed a blow at the unity of Ireland'. In America, Michael's death resulted in a marked swing of Irish-Americans in favour of support for the Free State.

Personal tributes came from all directions. Erskine Childers wrote: 'We pay our tribute to an Irishman who, whatever his errors, worked untiringly according to his own conscience and judgement for the good of Ireland.' Kevin O'Higgins said, 'His death was the quenching of our shining lamp,' and P.S. O'Hegarty stated simply, 'He passed the great test for any adult in that children loved him.' Lord Birkenhead was, predictably, profoundly shocked at Michael's death:

> He was a complex and a very remarkable personality; daring, resourceful, volatile and merry, and differed in almost every conceivable way from the more dour and placid Mr Arthur Griffith . . . I never doubted that both Collins and Griffith, having once given their word, would sacrifice life itself in order to carry out their promise.[5]

Lloyd George was just as generous, in the message of sympathy which he sent to William Cosgrave, the Acting Chairman of the Provisional Government:

> His engaging personality won friendships even amongst those who first met him as foes, and to all who met him the news of his death comes as a personal sorrow.[6]

In a personal letter to Cosgrave, Sir Nevil Macready, Commander-in-Chief of British Forces in Ireland, wrote:

> On the many occasions during the last year when we met on official business I always found him ready and willing to help in all matters that were brought to his notice in connection with the forces under my command. I deeply regret that he should not have been spared to see in a prosperous and peaceful Ireland the accomplishment of his work.[7]

George Bernard Shaw, on his return to London, wrote to Michael's sister Hannie on 25 August:

> My Dear Miss Collins – Don't let them make you miserable about it: how could a born soldier die better than at the victorious end of a good fight, falling to the shot of another Irishman – a damned fool, but all the same an Irishman who thought he was fighting for Ireland – 'A Roman to a Roman'? I met Michael for the first and last time on Saturday last, and am very glad

I did. I rejoice in his memory, and will not be so disloyal to it as to snivel over his valiant death. So treat up your mourning and hang up your brightest colours in his honour; and let us all praise God that he did not die in a snuffy bed of a trumpery cough, weakened by age, and saddened by the disappointments that would have attended his work had he lived.[8]

In Shanakiel Hospital, Cork, the body of Michael Collins had been cleaned, bandaged and laid out, still in his original service dress and hob-nailed boots, with a crucifix between his hands, on a bed in the little chapel, flanked by two tall candlesticks. Shortly after admission, the dead leader was examined by Dr Patrick Cagney who had served with the Royal Army Medical Corps during the First World War and was an authority on gunshot wounds. He had no hesitation in concluding that Michael had died from a wound inflicted by a Lee-Enfield .303 high-velocity rifle. The bullet had made a neat hole on entering the skull at the hairline, but had torn away a substantial part of the bone and brain before exiting behind the ear. The size of the exit wound, to the untrained eye, gave rise to several myths that endure to this day. One is that Sonny O'Neill was using dum-dum (exploding) bullets; another that he was armed with an elephant rifle which, originally part of a consignment of arms sent by Michael to the IRA for their campaign in Northern Ireland, had been held back because O'Neill was partial to it. This reinforced the moral that Michael had unwittingly become a victim of his own Northern policy. A third myth was that the bullet that caused his death was a large-calibre round from a Mauser pistol – and Emmet Dalton was carrying such a side-arm. From this it was but a short step to suggesting that General Dalton was in the pay of the British Secret Service and had received up to £10,000 blood money (various sums were adduced) to slay his own Commander-in-Chief. This was a monstrous lie; Emmet Dalton would cheerfully have given his own life to protect his Chief, but the rumour persisted and all but ruined this fine man. He resigned his commission as a protest over Mulcahy's ruthless treatment of Republican prisoners, then lost his job as Clerk to the Senate (a sinecure found for him by Cosgrave) when he took to the bottle. In the 1930s he drifted from one dead-end job to another before snapping out of it and carving a highly successful niche for himself in the Irish film industry. He turned down an invitation to join an élite SAS-type formation during the Second World War, composed of guerrilla experts from England, Scotland, Ireland and Wales, but is believed, nonetheless, to have engaged in intelligence work for the British.

Emmet Dalton was not the only person to suffer as a result of the ambush at Beal na mBlath. John McPeak, the Scots machine-gunner, never lived down the fact that his gun had jammed, and from this unfortunate technical hitch some of the blame for Michael's death landed on his head. Born in Glasgow in

1894, he was the son of parents from Tyrone. After war service in the Machine Gun Corps, he returned to Glasgow and joined the IRA. Arrested during a police raid on St Joseph's Hall, he was sent to Barlinnie but released soon after the Treaty in December 1921. Later he enlisted in the National Army and was posted to Portobello Barracks where the armoured cars were kept. Far from any act being premeditated, he was only given the order to take out *Slievenamon* the night before Michael's last journey. On the fateful trip to Beal na mBlath, McPeak's assistant gunner was left behind in Cork; in his place were two staff captains who had come inside when the evening got chilly. When the shooting started McPeak asked them to make themselves useful by refilling the belting from a box of loose ammunition, but because this was unevenly done, the gun jammed.

The myth that McPeak was given a hard time by other Free State soldiers after the event was concocted to explain his subsequent desertion to the IRA. In fact, Jock continued to serve as armoured car machine-gunner on escort duty to Generals Dalton and Ennis at Cork and Bandon till late November. During a raid on a farm he was appalled when two IRA prisoners were summarily shot, and after this incident he decided to desert. The Cork IRA agreed to help, provided that he brought the armoured car with him. On the night of 2 December, one of the IRA men, dressed in Free State uniform, actually drove the car out of Bandon Barracks with McPeak in his gun turret. The seizure of *Slievenamon* was a great coup, and it played a major role in the IRA capture of Ballyvourney; but McPeak was never involved. Instead, he was whisked off into the hills of Kerry where he was on the run till June 1923 when he was smuggled aboard a cargo boat bound for Glasgow.

Back in his native city his freedom was short-lived. He was arrested and extradited to Dublin, a matter which caused widespread protests and questions in parliament, but McPeak was duly sentenced to six years' imprisonment. In Portlaoise he joined other Republican prisoners on hunger-strike and for this, and breaches of prison discipline, he was given a very hard time, spending most of his sentence in solitary confinement. When he was released in 1928 a Republican group had a whip-round and gave him £60, but there is no truth in the assertion that de Valera, on coming to power, secured for him a Secret Service pension. Instead, McPeak returned to Scotland, changed his name to Logan (his mother's maiden name), married a Glasgow girl and moved south, latterly living at South Ockenden, Essex, where he died in 1974.

Denis 'Sonny' O'Neill, the man who fired the fatal shot, never got over the fact that his unlucky bullet had killed Michael Collins. The tragedy was underscored by the fact that he, along with other members of the ambush group, were local men who had to go on living and working in the same community as the friends and family of the dead leader. Sonny confided in

Tom Hales that it was he who had shot the Big Fellow, but otherwise he kept it to himself for almost thirty years. In 1950, having discovered that he had only months to live, Sonny, a deeply religious man, determined to visit Johnny Collins and ask for his forgiveness; but sadly he died on 5 June that year, while returning from a pilgrimage to Knock, before he could make his peace with the Collins family.

After he was burned out of Woodfield, Johnny Collins had moved east, married his cousin Nancy O'Brien, and raised a second family at Donnybrook and later Booterstown on the outskirts of Dublin. Jim Hurley, another of the ambush team, paid several visits to Johnny from 1923 onwards. On the first occasion he broke down and sobbed, 'How could we do it? We were too young.' He had only been nineteen years of age at the time of the ambush. Johnny forgave him and subsequently they became good friends. In 1965, when Jim was dying of cancer, he went to Mount Mellaray on retreat and then, knowing that his death was imminent, sent for Johnny's son Michael. It was his dearest wish to be interred in Clonakilty churchyard alongside Johnny Collins. In granting the dying man his wish, young Michael Collins brought the greatest of all Ireland's tragedies to a fitting close.

Hazel, Lady Lavery, flouting convention and ignoring her long-suffering husband's feelings, was determined to show herself at the graveside in widow's weeds. Fortunately, saner counsels prevailed and she was talked out of such a foolish gesture. Premier place at the obsequies was therefore yielded to Kitty Kiernan. When told of Michael's death this highly strung girl, physically ill and hysterical by turns, went to the mortuary chapel at St Vincent's Hospital, where the body of Harry Boland had reposed only three weeks earlier. Now the cruel war had robbed her of both the men she loved. It was she who interrupted Sir John Lavery as he sat at his easel. On another day Kitty, accompanied by Michael's sister Helena (Sister Celestine), went to the lying-in-state at the City Hall, and on the day of the funeral she and Maud were given seats near the catafalque during the Requiem Mass in the Pro-Cathedral. A white Annunciation lily from Kitty was the only flower to be placed on the coffin when it left the Cathedral.

For weeks she grieved bitterly and refused to be comforted by anyone; but in the autumn Maud took her away for a brief holiday in Paris and it was there that she took stock of her future. Had she been married to Michael, she would have received a generous widow's pension from the State; but as a fiancée she was not entitled to anything.

Maud married Gearoid O'Sullivan that October and moved into the Adjutant-General's residence, Dunallen House, and a few months later Larry married and brought his bride to Granard to run the Greville Arms. Kitty, now the only unmarried Kiernan, could not settle to the old life. She went to Dublin and drifted around for a year, even thinking of joining the Abbey Players and going on the stage. Then she met Felix Cronin, recently appointed Quarter-master-General of the Free State Army, and in 1925 she married him. The two sons of this marriage were named Felix Mary Cronin and Michael Collins Cronin. Kitty died on 24 July 1945 of Bright's disease, an ailment that claimed the lives of her brother and three sisters also.[9]

On Sunday evening Michael's body was taken to the Pro-Cathedral whence, after a Requiem Mass the following morning, Ireland accorded her greatest son a stupendous state funeral. Hundreds of thousands flocked into the capital to line the streets from the Pro-Cathedral to Glasnevin, six miles away. Many had stood in those same streets only twelve days earlier to salute Arthur Griffith and pay tribute to the man who had played such a major role in founding the Free State; but on this sombre Monday morning they came in droves out of sheer love for the Big Fellow, the Laughing Boy whose essential humanity had touched them so deeply.

The coffin, draped with the Irish tricolour, was mounted on a gun carriage drawn by a team of six black horses and mounted artillerymen. The coffin was flanked by Richard Mulcahy, now promoted to Commander-in-Chief, and seven other generals of the National Army. Then followed the nineteen members of the Provisional Government, a vast retinue of Irish, British and foreign dignitaries and a convoy of military vehicles laden with wreaths and floral tributes brought up the rear. The cortège was over three miles in length. The guard of honour was commanded by Captain (later Judge) Barra O'Briain, whose unit Michael had inspected at the Curragh only a few days previously. Because this body of troops was virtually the only one which had mastered the ceremonial drill required for such an occasion, it was required to march at the double, along alleys and back streets, from the City Hall to the Pro-Cathedral and thence to Glasnevin, in order to be in the right place at the appropriate part of the ceremony. As the cortège wound its way along O'Connell Street, it halted briefly beside Nelson's Pillar so that the flower-sellers could place their wreath on the coffin. It was just the sort of homely touch which Michael himself would have enjoyed.

At the cemetery the funeral oration was delivered by General Mulcahy. Patrick O'Driscoll, Michael's brother-in-law from Clonakilty who had become a reporter in the Dail, took down this address in shorthand on the fly-leaf of his prayerbook. Mulcahy reviewed the many sterling qualities of the dead leader: his place in the hearts of the people, the fruits that would come in the determination and renewed strength resulting from his death, the light that he was in the darkness of the times. But it was in his closing words that he enunciated what everyone felt in their hearts:

Tom Ashe, Tomas MacCurtain, Traolach MacSuibhne, Dick McKee, Michael O'Coileain, and all of you who lie buried here, disciples of our great Chief, those of us you leave behind are all, too, grain from the same handful, scattered by the hand of the Great Sower over the fruitful soil of Ireland. We, too, will bring forth our own fruit.

Men and women of Ireland, we are all mariners on the deep, bound for a port still seen only through storm and spray, sailing still on a sea 'full of dangers and hardships, and bitter toil'. But the Great Sleeper lies smiling in the stern of the boat, and we shall be filled with that spirit which will walk bravely upon the waters.[10]

Sadly, Michael's death did not have the immediate effect of bringing the warring factions to their senses. An offer of amnesty to Irregulars who gave themselves up produced a pitifully small response. If anything, the war continued more ferociously than ever. Mulcahy, who had been so quick to order 'Let no cruel act or reprisal blemish our bright honour', would be the instigator of the harsh policy of summary executions of Republican prisoners in retaliation for Republican excesses. Liam Lynch, who swiftly emerged as the strong man of the Republican movement, issued a controversial directive to the effect that any Dail deputy who had voted for the Treaty, and every officer of the Free State forces above the rank of lieutenant, was to be shot. As a result, Major-General Sean Hales was later killed and Padraic O'Maille, Deputy-President of the Dail, was wounded. That same night, 8 December 1922, four of the leading Republican prisoners taken at the fall of the Four Courts – Rory O'Connor, Liam Mellowes, Dick Barrett and Joe McKelvey – were executed by Free State firing-squad. Rory O'Connor had actually been best man at the wedding of Kevin O'Higgins, who would later sign the execution order. He himself would fall to an assassin's bullet in July 1927.

Erskine Childers, captured by Free State troops at the home of his cousin Robert Barton, was sentenced to death for carrying a pistol, a small automatic which, ironically, Michael had given him as a present. He, too, would face a firing-squad. The night before he was executed he wrote to his wife: 'I die full of an intense love for Ireland.' His young son, also named Erskine, would eventually become President of the Republic.

Liam Lynch was fatally wounded in a skirmish on the Knockmealdown Mountains in County Tipperary. His death knocked the stuffing out of the Republicans and a month later, on 24 May 1924, his successor, Frank Aiken, gave them the order to dump their weapons and give up the fight.

Seldom in the history of any country has a single unlucky bullet so utterly altered the course of events. Indeed, it would be no exaggeration to say that

Ireland suffers the consequences to this day. Had Michael lived, it is highly probable that he would have brought the civil war to a speedy conclusion and succeeded in healing the breach with the North, leading to the removal of partition which few British politicians, from Lloyd George and Churchill downwards, regarded as anything other than a purely temporary measure in 1922. After Michael's death, however, the South had no one with the breadth of vision and the negotiating skills to tackle Sir James Craig, and as time passed, the breach between North and South widened. Michael would almost certainly have prevented the Ulster boundary crisis of 1925, with its tragic consequences for Anglo-Irish relations over the ensuing seven decades. This arose when the report of the Boundary Commission was published, revealing that not an inch of Northern Ireland was to be ceded to the Free State, despite the wishes of at least a third of the inhabitants of the Six Counties. This bombshell reopened old wounds and almost triggered off a renewal of civil war in southern Ireland.

Had Michael lived, the economic history of Ireland would also have been very different. His organisational and administrative skills, especially in the realm of finance, would surely have steered Ireland through the critical years of the 1920s and 1930s. The army mutiny of 1924 (led by his old subordinates, Generals Cullen and Tobin) would certainly have been averted, and the bitter trade war with Britain in the 1930s would have been avoided.

Michael's death also spelled the death-knell of Sinn Fein. Out of the bitter wreckage of the civil war would emerge Fianna Fail, the Republican party headed by de Valera, and Cumann na nGaedheal led by William Cosgrave, the forerunner of the present-day Fine Gael party. For several years after the civil war the Republicans continued to boycott the Dail, but eventually gave way and took their seats in 1927. De Valera became prime minister in 1932 and from then until the 1970s (latterly as President) dominated Irish politics. Had Michael lived, Dev would have had a worthy adversary and a powerful check on many of the policies that isolated Eire, not only in the context of the British Isles but in the wider sphere. In particular, the matter of Irish neutrality during the Second World War (especially from 1942 onwards, after the United States entered the conflict) might have been handled very differently.

Michael dreamed of a League of Free States replacing the Empire. Such a Commonwealth of Nations, in fact, came into being in 1931. Today the Commonwealth embraces many republics, their interdependence being far stronger than any outmoded concept of allegiance to the Crown. The Republic of Ireland, proclaimed by John Costello in 1949, left the Commonwealth, severing the last constitutional links and making the reunification of the island even more remote.

Today, almost three-quarters of a century after Michael's untimely death, Ireland is a very different place. Despite the supreme tragedy of Northern Ireland since 1969, with a new set of Troubles, even another Bloody Sunday, cross-border co-operation at all levels and in every sphere of life is now well established. Playing a not inconsiderable part in this process is the Michael Collins Memorial Foundation, established in 1966. This arose out of the laudable desire by Joe McGrath, Michael's quondam colleague, later the organiser of the Irish Hospitals' Sweepstake and one of the wealthiest men in Ireland, to secure for his old friend a national memorial that was truly worthy of him. In this he had been thwarted at every turn by de Valera, whose shabby treatment of Johnny Collins over the matter of the cross erected over Michael's grave in 1939 is a saga of pettiness, spite and sheer vindictiveness.[11] It was Johnny who, in the end, persuaded Joe that a more fitting memorial to his brother would be a trust fund to educate some bright boys. McGrath, who was then dying of cancer, set the ball rolling and handed over the administration to Johnny's son Michael, then one of Ireland's foremost accountants, and in due course the Memorial Foundation was instituted, with the aim of 'the educational, cultural and artistic training and development of Irish men and women from any of the four Provinces, without distinction of creed, class or politics'.

De Valera, approached by the dying McGrath to become Patron of the Foundation with the words 'My days are numbered and there's no differences in the grave', mulled over the proposal for several minutes before giving his carefully considered reply: 'I can't see my way to becoming Patron of the Michael Collins Foundation. It's my considered opinion that in the fullness of time history will record the greatness of Collins and it will be recorded at my expense.'

Michael does have his tangible memorials, not only in Glasnevin but at Beal na mBlath. At Sam's Cross, opposite the Four Alls, stands a huge boulder on which is mounted a bronze roundel bearing his profile by Seamus Murphy, erected in 1965. Woodfield itself has been tastefully landscaped as the Michael Collins Memorial Centre, inaugurated by Dr Patrick J. Hillery, President of the Republic, on 14 October 1990, two days before the centenary of Michael's birth. The foundations of the house burned down by Major Percival's men in 1921, set in trim lawns and gravel paths, now have the timeless quality of any archaeological site; but the humble building in which Michael was actually born, later relegated to become a cowshed, survived and has been beautifully restored.

In Glasnevin cemetery Michael is at rest in the plot reserved for the dead of *Oglaigh na hEireann*, the Irish armed forces, from the civil war right down to soldiers killed on active service with the UN peace-keeping forces in many parts of the world.

Somehow it seems fitting that Michael lies here among the warrior dead of Ireland.

Notes

Chapter I. Boyhood, 1890–1906

1. For the history of the Collins family see Tim Pat Coogan, *Michael Collins: A Biography* (1990), Margery Forester, *The Lost Leader* (1971), Rex Taylor, *Michael Collins* (1958) and Hayden Talbot, *Michael Collins' Own Story* (1923)
2. Genealogical details in the parish registers of Rosscarbery and Timoleague, National Library of Ireland
3. Forester, p.6
4. Letter from MC to Kevin O'Brien, 16 October 1916
5. Ibid
6. Lyons papers, quoted by Taylor, p.42
7. Establishment records, Post Office Archives, London
8. Collins papers, quoted by Taylor, p.45
9. Sean Deasey to Rex Taylor, 16 November 1955, quoted by Taylor, p.46
10. Forester, p.16
11. Previous writers, notably Forester, refer to MC's position in the Post Office Savings Bank as Temporary Boy Clerk, but this applied only to his first six months' probationary period

Chapter 2. London, 1906–16

1. Establishment and Pension records, Post Office Archives, London. The relevant entry for MC shows 'Michael J. Collins, 303099, Boy Clerk, SB, July 1906'
2. Albert Lawrence, *West London Observer*, 25 August 1922
3. Kelly's Directory for West Kensington and Fulham, 1906–14 editions; Hammersmith and Shepherds Bush Directory, 1914–17 editions
4. *The Irish Post*, 14 March 1987 and 4 July 1987; *West London Recorder*, 10 July 1987
5. James Mackay, *Official Mail of the British Isles* (1983), p.149
6. P.S. O'Hegarty, *The Victory of Sinn Fein* (1924), p.23
7. Desmond Ryan, *Remembering Sion* (1934), p.235
8. Patrick Hodges to Rex Taylor, 19 March 1955
9. Forester, p.22
10. National Library of Ireland, MS 13329
11. Taylor, p.27
12. Ibid, but not named
13. National Library of Ireland, MS 13329
14. Frank O'Connor, *The Big Fellow* (1937), p.23
15. Taylor, pp.47–48, from a private source
16. Collins papers, Public Record Office, Ireland
17. Forester, p.31
18. Seamus de Burca, *The Soldier's Song* (1957), p.65
19. Coogan, p.30

20. National Library of Ireland, MS 13556
21. Coogan, p.17
22. Robert Mackey, obituary in *Guaranty News*, September 1922
23. O'Connor, p.22
24. Coogan, p.20
25. MC to Susan Killeen, 19 October 1915
26. Piaras Beaslai, *Michael Collins and the Making of a New Ireland* (1926), vol. I, pp.80–81

Chapter 3. The Easter Rising, 1916
1. O'Connor, p.34
2. Beaslai, vol. I, p.80
3. Transcript of Moriarty's evidence in the trial of Sir Roger Casement
4. Post Office Archives, London, Post 30/91, Ire 241/1918
5. For the full text of the Proclamation see Tim Pat Coogan, *Ireland since the Rising* (1966), pp.17–18; a facsimile appears as the frontispiece in Peter de Rosa, *Rebels* (1990)
6. Quoted by Beaslai, vol. I, p.92
7. O'Connor, p.35
8. Ibid, p.37
9. Desmond Fitzgerald, *Memoirs* in the archives of University College, Dublin
10. MC to Sean Deasey, May 1916
11. Desmond Ryan, *Michael Collins and the Invisible Army* (n.d.), p.24
12. MC to Sean Deasey, undated, quoted by Taylor, p.50
13. Post Office Archives, London, Post 31/91, Ire 241/1918, miscellaneous accounts
14. Taylor, p.71
15. *Sinn Fein Rebellion Handbook* (1916), pp.71–81
16. MC to Sean Deasey, May 1916

Chapter 4. Republican University, 1916
1. MC to Hannie Collins, 16 May 1916, quoted by Forester, pp.50–51
2. O'Connor, p.46
3. MC to Susan Killeen, quoted by Coogan, p.49
4. Ibid, p.50
5. MC to Sean Deasey, undated, quoted by Taylor, p.75
6. MC to Sean Deasey, 12 September 1916, quoted by Taylor, p.73
7. MC to Susan Killeen, undated, quoted by Coogan, p.56

8. Roberts' memoir, quoted by Coogan, p.51
9. Ibid
10. MC to Kevin O'Brien, 6 October 1916, quoted by Taylor, pp.7–8
11. Sean O'Mahoney, *Frongoch: University of Revolution* (1987), p.124
12. Ibid, p.125
13. Quoted by Taylor, p.81
14. O'Connor, p.50

Chapter 5. Prelude to War, 1917–18
1. MC to Susan Killeen, 31 December 1916, quoted by Coogan, p.59
2. Timothy O'Grady and Kenneth Griffith, *Curious Journey* (1982), p.108
3. Sean MacEoin to Kevin McClory, MacEoin papers. O'Connor, p.56 hinted at an affair, but the matter only really came out into the open with the publication of the Collins-Kiernan correspondence in 1983, edited by Leon O'Broin under the title *In Great Haste*
4. MC personal papers, quoted by Taylor, p.88
5. Ibid. MC to Sean Deasey. Taylor gives the date of this letter as 6 September 1917, but it was actually written a month later
6. O'Connor, p.18
7. Quoted by Coogan, p.85
8. O'Connor, p.63
9. Sean O'Luing, *Art O Griofa* (biography of Arthur Griffith) (1953)
10. Darrell Figgis, *Recollections of the Irish War* (1927), and Michael Hopkinson, *Green Against Green* (1988), pp.1–6

Chapter 6. The Work of Four Men, 1918–19
1. O'Connor, pp.67–69
2. Ibid, p.70
3. Robert Brennan, *Allegiance* (1950), p.152
4. Numerous despatches of this sort are quoted by Taylor, pp.101–7
5. O'Connor, p.73
6. Verbatim report in *The Southern Star*, Skibbereen, November 1918
7. Arthur Mitchell, *Revolutionary Government in Ireland* (1995), p.9
8. Shortt to Right Hon. Justice O'Connor, January 1919, O'Broin papers, National Library of Ireland
9. Quoted by Beaslai, vol. I, p.271

Chapter 7. The First Dail, 1919

1. Hathaway to US Secretary of State, I February 1919 (US National Archives, DS, 841.d.00/22)
2. Beaslai, vol. I, p.267
3. The Earl of Longford and Thomas P. O'Neill, *Eamon de Valera* (1970), pp.84–86
4. Beaslai, vol. I, p.269
5. Longford and O'Neill, p.90
6. Leon O'Broin, *In Great Haste* (1983), pp.6–7
7. Figgis, p.193
8. Collins papers, MSI 17090, National Library of Ireland
9. Quoted by Beaslai, vol. I, p.284
10. Quoted by Coogan, p.102
11. For a detailed analysis of the socio-economic background of the Sinn Fein leadership see Mitchell, *op. cit*, pp.33–35

Chapter 8. The Intelligence War, 1919

1. David Neligan, *The Spy in the Castle* (1968), pp.71–74
2. Coogan, p.82
3. Report of the meeting of Cork Commissioners, *The Cork Examiner*, 11 October 1966
4. Tim Healy, *Letters and Leaders*, vol. II, pp.611–12
5. *Daily News*, 3 November 1919
6. Frederick Dumont to State Department, 2 and 14 January 1920
7. Figgis, p.262
8. Beaslai, vol. I, p.393
9. Ibid, pp.396–400
10. Collins papers, National Library of Ireland

Chapter 9. The Year of Terror, 1920

1. Collins papers, National Library of Ireland
2. Quoted by O'Connor, p.121
3. Quoted by Coogan, p.131
4. Coogan, p.134
5. Kathleen Napoli MacKenna papers, National Library of Ireland
6. MC to Art O'Brien, 1 May 1920, O'Brien papers MS8426, National Library of Ireland
7. O'Broin, *In Great Haste* (1983), p.9
8. O'Connor, *The Big Fellow* (1937) p.132
9. O'Connor, *My Father's Son* (1966), pp.122–26, describing an interview between O'Connor and Colonel Joe O'Reilly in 1934

when Joe, as if hypnotised, began a terrifyingly accurate imitation of MC in one of his demented bullying moods, a charade that lasted for two hours before Joe collapsed with exhaustion
10. Florrie O'Donoghue papers, MS 31, 192, National Library of Ireland

Chapter 10. The Black and Tans, 1920–21

1. Dorothy Macardle, *The Irish Republic* (1937), p.419
2. Coogan, pp.146–47
3. MC to Donal Hales, 1 August 1921
4. O'Broin, pp.10–11
5. O'Connor, p.142
6. Quoted by O'Connor, p.151
7. Ibid, p.148
8. Ibid, p.150

Chapter 11. Bloody Sunday, 1920

1. Dan Breen, *My Fight for Irish Freedom* (1924), p.225
2. Thornton papers, Bureau of Irish Military History, Dublin
3. Quoted by Taylor, p.132; the present location of this note is not known
4. Coogan (p.159) suggests that he may actually have been Thomas Markham
5. Charles Dalton, *With the Dublin Brigades, 1917–21* (1929), pp.107–8
6. Sir Hamar Greenwood, CAB 27/108, Public Record Office, London
7. Quoted by Taylor, p.133
8. *The Irish Times*, 16 November 1965
9. Taylor, p.134, from a private source
10. Frederick Dumont, Consular weekly report, 23 November 1920, USNA, DS/800
11. *Irish Independent*, 28 August 1963

Chapter 12. Peace Process, 1921

1. O'Connor, p.157
2. Taylor, p.136n, quoting Sean Luing
3. Tim Pat Coogan, *De Valera*, p.197
4. De Valera to James O'Mara, 2 February 1921, quoted by Patricia Lavelle, *James O'Mara: a Staunch Sinn Feiner* (1961), p.236
5. O'Connor, p.192
6. Coogan, p.173
7. Uinseann MacEoin, *Survivors* (1987), p.405
8. Mulcahy papers, University College, Dublin

9. MC to Sister Mary Celestine, 5 March 1921, quoted by Coogan p.177
10. O'Malley notebooks, University College, Dublin
11. *Philadelphia Public Ledger*, 22 April 1921
12. Casement diary, quoted by Coogan, p.213

Chapter 13. Treaty, 1921
1. Wilson Diaries, vol. II, p.305
2. Forester, p.201
3. MC, 13 July 1921, quoted by Taylor, p.140
4. Taylor, p.142
5. Quoted by Mitchell, p.304
6. Sturgis diary, 25 August 1921, MS P7498, National Library of Ireland
7. Dail official reports, 304, 1921
8. Anthony Gaughan, *Austin Stack* (1971), p.172
9. Quoted by Taylor, p.171
10. Frank Pakenham, *Peace by Ordeal* (1935), p.116
11. O'Connor, p.221
12. Lord Birkenhead, *The Last Phase* (1959), pp.158–59
13. Quoted by Taylor, pp.148–49
14. Birkenhead, pp.158–59 and Taylor, pp.163–64
15. MC to O'Kane, 15 November 1921
16. MC to O'Kane, 17 November 1921
17. Quoted by Taylor, p.172, who got it from Sean MacBride
18. Quoted by Beaslai, vol. II, p.225
19. Taylor, p.173, quoting a private source
20. Ibid, p.176
21. Forester, pp.243–57 has an excellent account of the interplay of personalities against the background of the closing stages of the negotiations
22. Winston Churchill, *The World Crisis: The Aftermath* (1920), p.306

Chapter 14. The Split, 1922
1. Kathleen Napoli MacKenna, quoted by Coogan, p.294
2. Beaslai, vol. II, pp.311–12
3. T. Ryle Dwyer, *Michael Collins and the Treaty* (1981), p.106
4. Padraig de Burca and John F. Boyle, *Free State or Republic* (19220, p.3
5. Ibid, pp.13–14
6. Desmond Ryan, *Remembering Sion*, p.273

7. De Valera to J. McGarrity, 27 December 1921
8. Coogan, p.382
9. O'Broin, p.99
10. Ibid, p.22
11. As recently as 14 January 1996 an article by Ciaran Byrne and Olga Craig in *The Sunday Times* repeated the hoary old allegation of bed-hopping
12. *Dail Debates on the Treaty*, p.335
13. Lady Gregory, *Journals, 1916–30*, p.166

Chapter 15. Civil War, 1922
1. De Burca and Boyle, *op. cit.*, p.88
2. O'Broin, p.95
3. Ibid, p.96, MC to Kitty Kiernan, 12 January 1922
4. Quoted by Forester, p.277
5. Sir Henry Robinson, *Memories Wise and Otherwise* (1923), p.325
6. Churchill, *The Aftermath*, pp.316-17
7. For an excellent eye-witness account see Ernie O'Malley, *The Singing Flame* (1978), pp.55–60
8. Taylor, pp.236-7
9. Michael Collins, *The Path to Freedom* (1922), pp.15–17
10. Winston Churchill to MC, 15 May 1922
11. Taylor, p.226
12. State Papers Office, Dublin, S1570
13. Coogan, pp.375–76
14. General Sir Nevil Macready, *Annals of an Active Life* (1924), vol. II, p.65215.
15. Dorothy MacArdle, *The Irish Republic* (1937), p.740
16. Taylor, p.234

Chapter 16. Pass of the Flowers
1. J.M. Curran, *The Birth of the Irish Free State* (1980); R. Fanning, *Independent Ireland* (1983)
2. Winston Churchill to MC, 7 July 1922, CO 739/6
3. *The Sunday Express*, 18 May 1952
4. MC's private notebook, 27 June to 6 August 1922, quoted by Taylor, p.237
5. Quoted by Michael Hopkinson, *Green Against Green* (1988), p.131
6. Quoted by Taylor, p.238, from a private source
7. *Irish Times*, 1 August 1938

8. O'Broin, p.209
9. Ibid, p.210
10. Ibid, p.211
11. Ibid, p.212
12. Ibid, p.213
13. O'Connor, *My Father's Son* (1966), p.180
14. O'Connor, *The Big Fellow* (1937), p.290
15. John Feehan, in *The Irish Press*, 18 October 1982, p.3
16. Ibid
17. John Feehan, *The Shooting of Michael Collins* (1988), p.84
18. Colonel MacDunphy, 2 September 1936, State Papers Office, Dublin
19. For an admirably detailed examination and evaluation of all the evidence, see Coogan, pp.389–92
20. Forester, p.331
21. O'Broin, p.219
22. O'Connor, p.291
23. Uinseann MacEoin, *op. cit.*, p.99
24. O'Connor, p.292
25. Coogan, p.401, quoting General Collins-Powell. Beaslai, vol. II, p.428 and Emmet Dalton's account in *The Freeman's Journal*, however, say that MC arrived at the Imperial Hotel at 8.30pm. Beaslai probably followed Dalton in this respect, but the timing is impossible
26. Flor Begley to Florrie O'Donoghue, quoted by Coogan, p.405
27. Liam Deasey, *Brother Against Brother* (1982), p.78
28. Emmet Dalton, account of the fatal ambush, in *The Freeman's Journal*
29. Ibid
30. Coogan, quoting Liam O'Donnchadcha, p.410
31. Ibid, p.412
32. Emmet Dalton, in *The Sunday Independent*, 23 August 1970
33. Ibid
34. Taylor, p.251
35. *West London Observer*, 25 August 1922

Epilogue
1. Sir John Lavery, *The Life of a Painter*, (1940), p.217
2. Tom Barry, *Guerrilla Days in Ireland*, p.180
3. Lady Gregory, *Journals, 1916-30*, pp.180–81
4. Lavery, p.217
5. *The Daily Sketch*, 24 August 1922
6. Ibid
7. Ibid
8. Lavery, pp.218–19
9. O'Broin, pp.223–24
10. *Forum*, special Treaty commemorative number, December 1946
11. Coogan, in fact, devotes an entire chapter (Honouring the Dead?), pp.416–32, to this rather mean and sordid story

Select Bibliography

Ash, B., *The Lost Dictator* (Cassell, London, 1968)

Barry, Tom, *Guerrilla Days in Ireland* (Anvil, Tralee, 1962)

    The Reality of the Anglo-Irish War (Anvil, Tralee, 1974)

Beaslai, Piaras, *Michael Collins and the Making of a New Ireland*, 2 vols (Phoenix, Dublin, 1926)

Bennett, Richard, *The Black and Tans* (New English Library, London, 1970)

Birkenhead, Earl of, *The Life of F.E. Smith, First Earl of Birkenhead* (Eyre & Spottiswoode, London, 1959)

Boyle, Andrew, *The Riddle of Erskine Childers* (Hutchinson, London, 1977)

Breen, Dan, *My Fight for Irish Freedom* (Talbot Press, Dublin, 1924)

Brennan, Robert, *Allegiance* (Irish Press, Dublin, 1950)

Bromage, Mary C., *De Valera and the March of a Nation* (Hutchinson, London, 1956)

Callwell, C.E., *Field-Marshal Sir Henry Wilson: His Life and Diaries*, 2 vols (Cassell, London, 1927)

Caulfield, Max, *The Easter Rebellion* (Frederick Muller, London, 1964)

Churchill, Winston, *The World Crisis: The Aftermath* (Butterworth, London, 1929)

Collins, Michael, *The Path to Freedom* (Talbot Press, Dublin, 1922)

Colum, Padraig, *Arthur Griffith* (Browne & Nolan, Dublin, 1959)

Connolly, James, *Labour in Ireland* (Maunsel, Dublin, 1922)

Coogan, Tim Pat, *Ireland Since the Rising* (Pall Mall, London, 1966)

    Michael Collins: A Biography (Hutchinson, London, 1990)

    De Valera: Long Fellow, Long Shadow (Hutchinson, London, 1993)

Crozier, Brigadier-General F.P., *Impressions and Recollections* (Laurie, London, 1930)

    Ireland for Ever (Cape, London, 1932)

Curran, Joseph, *The Birth of the Irish Free State, 1921–23* (Alabama University Press, Montgomery, 1988)

Dalton, Charles, *With the Dublin Brigades, 1917–21* (Peter Davies, London, 1929)

De Burca, Padraig, and Boyle, John F., *Free State or Republic?* (Talbot Press, Dublin, 1922)

De Rosa, Peter, *Rebels: The Irish Rising of 1916* (Transworld, London, 1990)

De Vere White, Terence, *Kevin O' Higgins* (Methuen, London, 1948)

Deasey, Liam, *Brother Against Brother* (Mercier Press, Cork, 1982)

Driberg, Tom, *Study in Power and Frustration* (Weidenfeld & Nicolson, London, 1956)

Dudley-Edwards, Ruth, *Padraig Pearse: the Triumph of Failure* (Gill & Macmillan, Dublin, 1981)

Dwyer, T. Ryle, *Michael Collins and the Treaty* (Mercier Press, Cork, 1981)
  Michael Collins: The Man Who Won the War (Mercier Press, Cork, 1990)
Feehan, John, *Michael Collins: Murder or Accident* (Mercier Press, Cork, 1981)
Figgis, Darrell, *Recollections of the Irish War* (Ernest Benn, London, 1937)
Forester, Margery, *Michael Collins: The Lost Leader* (Sidgwick & Jackson, London, 1971)
French, Major the Hon. Gerald, *The Life of Field-Marshal Sir John French, First Earl of Ypres*
  (Cassell, London, 1931)
Gallagher, Frank, *The Anglo-Irish Treaty* (Hutchinson, London, 1965)
Gaughan, Anthony, *Austin Stack* (Kingdom Books, Tralee, 1971)
Gleeson, James, *Bloody Sunday* (Peter Davies, London, 1962)
Gogarty, Oliver St John, *As I Was Going Down Sackville Street* (Hutchinson, London, 1937)
Greaves, Desmond C., *The Life and Times of James Connolly* (Lawrence & Wishart, Dublin,
  1971)
  Liam Mellowes and the Irish Revolution (Lawrence & Wishart, Dublin, 1971)
Gregory, Augusta, Lady, *Journals, 1916–30*, ed. Lennox Robinson (Putnam, London, 1946)
Griffith, Kenneth, and O'Grady, Timothy, *Curious Journey* (Hutchinson, London, 1982)
Gwynne, Stephen, *The Life of John Redmond* (Harrap, London, 1932)
Hodges, Michael, *Ireland: from Easter Rising to Civil War* (Batsford, London, 1987)
Holt, Edgar, *Protest in Arms, 1916–21* (Putnam, London, 1960)
Hopkinson, Michael, *Green Against Green* (Gill & Macmillan, Dublin, 1988)
Jones, Thomas, *Whitehall Diaries*, vol. III: *Ireland, 1918–25*, ed. K. Middleton (Oxford
  University Press, 1971)
Kee, Robert, *The Green Flag* (Weidenfeld & Nicolson, London, 1972)
Kelly, Freida, *A History of Kilmainham Jail* (Mercier Press, Cork, 1988)
Laffan, Michael, *The Partition of Ireland* (Dundalgan Press, Dundalk, 1983)
Lavelle, Patricia, *James O'Mara* (Gill & Macmillan, Dublin, 1961)
Lavery, Sir John, *The Life of a Painter* (Cassell, London, 1940)
LeRoux, Louis N., *Tom Clarke and the Irish Freedom Movement* (Talbot Press, Dublin, 1926)
  Patrick H. Pearse (Phoenix Press, Dublin, 1932)
Litton, Helen, *The Irish Civil War* (Wolfhound, Dublin, 1995)
Lloyd George, David, *War Memoirs*, 2 vols (Odhams, London, 1934)
Longford, Earl of, and O'Neill, Thomas P., *Eamon de Valera* (Hutchinson, London, 1970)
Lynch, Diarmuid, *Florrie O'Donoghue* (Mercier Press, Cork, 1957)
Lyons, F.S.L., *Ireland Since the Famine* (Weidenfeld & Nicolson, London, 1971)
Lyons, J.B., *Oliver St John Gogarty* (Blackwater Press, Dublin, 1980)
Macardle, Dorothy, *The Irish Republic* (Gollancz, London, 1937)
  Tragedies of Kerry, 1922–23 (Maunsel, Dublin, 1924)
MacCartan, Patrick, *With de Valera in America* (Brentano, New York, 1932)
McDonnell, Kathleen Keyes, *There is a Bridge at Bandon* (Mercier Press, Cork, 1972)
MacEoin, Uinseann, *Survivors* (Argenta, Dublin, 1980)
Mackay, James, *The Story of Eire and Her Stamps* (Collecta, London, 1968)
Macready, General Sir Nevil, *Annals of an Active Life*, 2 vols (Hutchinson, London, 1924)
Mansergh, Nicholas, *The Irish Question, 1840–1921* (Allen & Unwin, London, 1965)
Martin, Francis Xavier, *The Irish Volunteers, 1913–15* (Dublin, 1963)
  Howth Gun-Running (Browne & Nolan, Dublin, 1964)
  Leaders and Men of the Easter Rising, Dublin 1916 (Methuen, London, 1965)
Mitchell, Arthur, *Revolutionary Government in Ireland* (Gill & Macmillan, Dublin, 1995)
Neeson, Eoin, *The Civil War in Ireland, 1922–23* (Mercier Press, Cork, 1967)

The Life and Death of Michael Collins (Mercier Press, Cork, 1968)

Neligan, David, *The Spy in the Castle* (McGibbon & Kee, London, 1968)

Ni Dheirg, Isold, *The Story of Michael Collins* (Mercier Press, Cork, 1978)

O'Broin, Leon, *Dublin Castle and the 1916 Rising* (Sidgwick & Jackson, 1966)
>   *Revolutionary Underground, the Story of the IRB, 1858–1924* (Gill & Macmillan, Dublin, 1976)
>   *Michael Collins* (Gill & Macmillan, Dublin, 1980)
>   *In Great Haste* (Gill & Macmillan, Dublin, 1983)

O'Connor, Batt, *With Michael Collins in the Fight for Irish Independence* (Peter Davies, London, 1929)

O'Connor, Frank, *The Big Fellow* (Nelson, London, 1937)
>   *An Only Child* (Macmillan, London, 1958)
>   *My Father's Son* (Clonmore & Reynolds, Dublin, 1966)

O'Connor, Ulick, *Oliver St John Gogarty* (Cape, London, 1964)

O'Donoghue, Florence, *No Other Law* (Irish Press, Dublin, 1954)

O'Farrell, Padraic, *Who's Who in the Irish War of Independence* (Mercier Press, Cork, 1980)

O'Hegarty, P.S., *The Indestructible Nation* (Maunsel, Dublin, 1918)
>   *The Victory of Sinn Fein* (Talbot Press, Dublin, 1924)

O'Luing, Sean, *Art O Griofa* (Sairseal agus Dill, Dublin, 1953)

O'Mahony, Sean, *Frongoch: University of Revolution* (FDR Teoranta, Dublin, 1987)

O'Malley, Ernie, *On Another Man's Wound* (Anvil, Dublin, 1979)
>   *The Singing Flame* (Anvil, Dublin, 1978)

Pakenham, Frank (later Earl of Longford), *Peace by Ordeal* (Cape, London, 1935)

Riddell, Lord George, *Intimate Diary of the Peace Conference* (Gollancz, London, 1933)

Ryan, Desmond, *Michael Collins and the Invisible Army* (Barker, London, 1932)
>   *Remembering Sion* (Barker, London, 1934)
>   *Sean Treacy and the Third Tipperary Brigade, IRA* (Kingdom Books, Tralee, 1945)

Ryan, Meda, *The Day Michael Collins Was Shot* (Poolbeg, Dublin, 1989)

Shakespeare, Sir Geoffrey, *Let Candles Be Brought In* (MacDonald, London, 1949)

Stevenson, Frances, *Lloyd George: A Diary* (Hutchinson, London, 1971)

Street, Major C.J., *Ireland in 1922* (Philip Allen, London, 1922)

Talbot, Hayden, *Michael Collins' Own Story* (Hutchinson, London, 1923)

Taylor, Rex, *Michael Collins* (Hutchinson, London, 1958)
>   *Assassination: The Death of Sir Henry Wilson* (Hutchinson, London, 1961)

Tierney, Michael, *Eoin MacNeill: Scholar and Man of Action, 1867–1945* (Oxford University Press, 1980)

Townshend, Charles, *The British Campaign in Ireland, 1919–21* (Oxford University Press, 1975)
>   *Political Violence in Ireland* (Oxford University Press,1985)

Ward, Margaret, *In Their Own Voice: Women and Irish Nationalism* (Attic Press, Dublin, 1995)

Wells, W.E. and Marlowe, N.A., *History of the Irish Rebellion of 1916* (Maunsel, Dublin, 1917)

Winter, Brigadier-General Sir Ormonde, *A Winter's Tale* (Richard's Press, London, 1955)

Yeats, Padraig, and Wren, Jimmy, *Michael Collins* (Tomar, Dublin, 1989)

Younger, Calton, *Ireland's Civil War* (Frederick Muller, London, 1968)
>   *Arthur Griffith* (Gill & Macmillan, Dublin, 1981)

Index